FITTED IN

THE CARDIFF 3

AND THE LYNETTE WHITE INQUIRY

by

Satish Sekar

co-editors: Andy Soutter and Michele Bailey

First published in 1997

Cover photographs courtesy of Robin Mayes and the *Guardian*

Published by
The Fitted In Project
3 All Saints Road
Notting Hill
London
W11 1HH

ISBN 0 9527325 0 5

British Library Cataloguing in Publication Data.
A catalogue record for this book is available from the British Library.

Printed by
Professional Books
Oxford
England

Typeset by
Advance Design & Print
18 Crown Mead
Wimborne
Dorset
BH21 1HN

For Franca

This book is dedicated to Yusef Abdullahi, John Actie, Ronnie Actie, Steve Miller, Tony Paris, all victims of miscarriages of justice and to the memory of Lynette White.

The Fitted In Project

Satish Sekar is a thirty-four year old freelance journalist specialising in legal issues. He lives in London and his work has been used in national broadsheets, television and radio. He is about to do some short term research for the 1990 Trust on the criminal justice system. In 1998 he will take up a three year research post on racism in the criminal justice system for the 1990 Trust as well as continuing freelance journalism. *Fitted In : The Cardiff 3 and the Lynette White Inquiry* is his first book.

Foreword by Michael Mansfield QC

It is of considerable interest and is a substantial tribute to Satish Sekar that the police announced on 14th January 1996 that the investigation into the murder of Lynette White on Valentine's Day 1988 was to be re-opened. This case, otherwise known as the Cardiff Three, became eclipsed by a large number of other miscarriage of justice cases such as the Guildford Four, the Birmingham Six, the Tottenham Three, Judith Ward and so on. It is likely therefore that the significance of this appeal has been overlooked and is timely that the public and more particularly the authorities should be reminded about what went wrong in this case.

There is a 'new realism' permeating the thinking of official bodies, the higher judiciary, politicians and commentators on the criminal justice system. What this amounts to is a somewhat amorphous gut feeling that the scales of justice have tipped too far in favour of defendants. In a recent analysis David Rose cites the Chief Constable of Kent, David Phillips, with these words, "Our justice system has been Americanised, permeated with concern for criminal civil rights. We have produced a system which is so concerned with protecting criminals it works against the notion of justice. ...The system allows offenders to avoid all responsibility because the trial is a game."

It is this theme which has meant that the opportunity to rectify the real injustices of the system has been hijacked by the law and order brigade who believe that "prison works" and that they have a monopoly on the truth about who is guilty. Besides the push towards building more prisons (privatised) increasing prison sentences, depriving the judiciary of their independence on sentencing, a proposed increase in cases attracting the mandatory life sentence and incarcerating more 12-14 year olds, there has been an unprecedented attack on basic freedoms that for too long have been taken for granted.

These freedoms were mostly eroded by the Criminal Justice and Public Order Act which came into force in 1995 and relate to the ability of ordinary people to gather for the purposes of protest or opposition, particularly where it involves the desecration of the environment.

This same statute also overthrows what has been termed the golden thread of British Justice namely the Right to Silence and another basic and fundamental principle, that of the presumption of innocence. Almost without a second thought Michael Howard's proposals on disclosure which will effectively limit the extent to which the prosecution are duty bound to disclose the result of enquiries but place a greater burden on the defence to disclose in advance details of their case were welcomed by Jack Straw, then Shadow Home Secretary, and have produced little or no public debate. The fact is the majority of miscarriage cases arose through both deliberate and negligent non-disclosure by the Crown.

Somehow or another anyone who supports these principles or freedoms is deemed to be a liberal freethinker of the old order who has not come to terms with the reality of crime in the 1990s. However, what the new realists fail to address is that no one, least of all themselves, is protected by a system that locks up the wrong people.

Both the system and the means of investigation must be based on democratically accountable institutions and on basic principles of human rights that have been enshrined in charters and conventions throughout the world many times over. Apparently we expect adherence to these conventions and charters by Third World countries but seem quite unwilling to appreciate their relevance to our own backyard.

Here it has been said that the shortcomings of the past are behind us and we can now proceed on the basis that there is a new breed of policing and policemen. Whilst recognising that a number of responsible police officers are trying to eradicate the malpractice that Sir John Woodcock described as 'noble cause corruption' there is a long way to go.

The example which shows just how far we have to travel is the Cardiff Three because the main elements of this occurred between 1988 and December 1992. It is clear from this chronology that what went wrong has occurred within a framework broadly supported by the Police and Criminal Evidence Act 1984 (PACE). This Act was a product of a Royal Commission in the early 1980s which itself was born out of the Confait Inquiry examining the risk of wrongful conviction based upon unreliable confession evidence. This vein is richer than almost any other in providing miscarriage cases and one would have thought that by the 1990s the lessons would have been learnt. The recent Royal Commission, however, in line with the thinking described above seemed to concentrate far more on ensuring that the guilty get convicted than the innocent being acquitted. The Cardiff Three case occurred just in time for it to be considered in detail by the Commission. However, neither the Commission's proposals nor any statutory enactments since have reduced the risk of recurrence.

The problems can be simply stated, albeit not simply resolved. They arise primarily from what I have defined in writing and on film as 'targeting.' Put shortly this is where an investigation operates upon preconceived notions of who is believed to be guilty. Such preconceptions may derive from criminal intelligence accumulated over a number of years or from prejudices about the kind of people who commit the kind of crime under investigation or from individual bits of information from local sources. The risk is that a hypothesis or hunch becomes a fact. It leads to the exclusion of material that is seen to be inconsistent or inconvenient and a concentration upon avenues thought to confirm or corroborate the thesis being pursued.

What Sekar has demonstrated is that targeting can percolate through to the management of scientific evidence. In other words, it is not about what the jury did hear, namely that there was no forensic science link between any of the defendants and the scene of the crime, but about material the jury did not hear. It is an irony that this material concerns the very area that Michael Howard has claimed will be in the forefront of the war being waged upon the criminal - DNA.

Whilst one has reservations about elevating science into God-like tablets of stone there is no question that properly conducted scientific investigation is likely to yield far more profitable results than the interview room in a police station. The trouble is that forensic science costs money and despite the serious errors highlighted by the Maguire case, the Judith Ward case, the Kevin Callan case of 1995, the government has not been prepared to establish a nationally resourced forensic science service equally accessible to all. With the usual cutbacks and budgetary constraints that are being witnessed in all areas of social welfare both investigative agencies and independent scientists are strapped for cash and resources. At the end of the day shortcuts will be taken and quality will be affected. What is particularly important in the field of DNA is the provision of experts within the United Kingdom who are able to verify the work of the forensic science laboratories in this field both with regard to the inclusion and exclusion of suspects.

The recent Royal Commission discovered a serious dearth of those available to do this kind of work. Increasingly, over the last two years British lawyers have had recourse to both German and American laboratories which no longer feel able to continue to satisfy the demand in addition to their domestic workload. The real risks of this shortfall were clearly laid out in a television exposure by *Equinox* in 1995. Under no circumstances should DNA be regarded as genetic fingerprinting. But what it clearly can do with considerable confidence is eliminate and this is what was not adequately carried out in the Cardiff case.

I would like to conclude by praising Satish Sekar's determination, persistence and meticulous research against all the odds. In all these cases it is the individual efforts of those who have an undying quest for the truth who are able to touch the consciences of others. It is a refreshing testament to see such a work of principle when many of those who should know better have sacrificed adherence to basic principles in favour of the comfort of compromise and collusion.

Preface by Paul Foot

The spate of wrongful convictions in high-profile murder and terrorism cases which followed the freeing of the Guildford Four in October 1989 wiped the complacent smile off the face of the British judiciary and shook the entire legal system to its foundations. Something very serious must have gone wrong when so many innocent people were convicted in so many cases: the six men convicted of the Birmingham pub bombings in 1975; the three men convicted of the 1985 murder of PC Blakelock in the so-called Broadwater Farm riots; Judy Ward, convicted of the M62 motorway bombing; Eddie Browning, convicted of the 1988 M50 murder; the Darvell brothers, convicted of the murder of a Swansea shop manager; Alban Turner, convicted of the 1987 Notting Hill carnival murder - and many many others - were released after being convicted in full-length murder trials in which the whole expensive array of British justice was on show for all to see.

This great stream of acquittals was not accidental. They arose naturally from a system of justice which preferred to convict the accused rather than examine the truth about the crime. Rotten forensics, enforced confessions, bogus statements from prison grasses: the pattern of incompetent or biased prosecutions established itself again and again.

The world knows about most of these injustices, thanks to a small band of dedicated journalists who refused to be browbeaten by the police and prosecution and eventually bust the cases open. Satish Sekar absorbed himself in one of the most monstrous of these injustices, the case of the Cardiff Three. To all the usual ingredients of injustice, the Cardiff Three case added a new one: racial prejudice. My own interest in the case was provoked when a man rang me at the *Daily Mirror* where I then worked. He had walked straight from the court to the telephone box, indignant. "We have been acquitted," he said, "and the blacks have been convicted.[1] But we are all innocent."

Satish Sekar has devoted much of his life to a full exposé of this shocking case and its outcome. His book is a monument to his endless hard work on and devotion to his case. It should be a permanent feature in any lawyer's office: a grim reminder of what went wrong and a warning that nothing of the kind can be allowed to happen again.

[1] The cousins John and Ronnie Actie who were acquitted were light skinned mixed race, whereas Yusef Abdullahi, Steve Miller and Tony Paris were much darker skinned.

Foreword by Gareth Peirce

It takes a shocking case to alter the public's appreciation and understanding of what happens to defendants every day of the week. There was probably nothing in the case against the original five defendants in Cardiff that does not happen daily. The investigation involved the police having a clear idea and the resources to prove it of the likely murderer of Lynette White. He had all the hallmarks of a single killer affected by deep psychological problems with a battery of distinctive psychiatric features and a history of violence which could not have been contained for his entire life and, in addition, was probably a client of Lynette's.

Instead, however, ignoring strong leads in the logical direction, the police adopted an approach which has repeatedly proved almost certain to provide false and unreliable evidence, namely pressuring potential witnesses until they give an account that helps the police 'towards a solution' of the crime and then, on the basis of an unreliable and deeply flawed series of improbable allegations, detaining persons not fitting the known information, but who then are 'fitted in' to the police's scenario.

It is frighteningly and spectacularly easy to obtain 'evidence' and prosecute a case to a conviction on such a basis. This, after all, was the basis for prosecuting Judith Ward, the Birmingham Six, the Guildford Four and the Tottenham Three. Although tried and tested and found to be disastrous, nevertheless, it continues daily and once again bore tainted fruit in the sad case of what eventually became the Cardiff Three.

Stephen Miller could no doubt have asserted until the end of his days that he had been bullied in the police station and he would not have been believed. It would have been said to him that the police were entitled to question him as they did and he had the full protection of a solicitor present as well as the complete protection of a tape recording being made. This was what was said to him by two High Court judges at two separate trials and by a third High Court judge who turned him down on his application for leave to appeal, after which, without solicitors or barristers who had advised him that he had no further prospect of winning an appeal, he was totally alone.

It does not, therefore, feel like a great triumph of the judicial system for him to have, by a number of accidents, managed to have found allies and renewed his application for leave to appeal and, eventually, not only won it with the ringing endorsement of the then Lord Chief Justice, the late Lord Taylor of Gosforth, that the interviews of him were disgraceful and should never happen again, but with the additional effect of causing his two co-defendants to win their appeals on the basis of his suspect interviews.

The interviews were deeply shocking. The 'bullying' interviews with the police literally shouting him down were, to me, not as appalling as the extended and insidious advocacy conducted by the persuasive officers whom he did not regard as bullies. In the end it was the extended persuasion that overbore Stephen Miller's will.

This happens every day in a police station. Perversely, tape recorded interviews make it easier for police to over-talk witnesses, to go faster, to ask more questions and to be more oppressive than when they took, or were meant to take, detailed notes of interviews by hand. But it is custody itself, to me, that offends every concept of individual liberty. Why not tap on Stephen Miller's door and ask if they could speak to him? They could have achieved the truth that way.

To lock up an individual in a cell can have no other purpose than to coerce him and to make him do what he would not otherwise willingly and voluntarily do. *That is oppression*. Moreover, the cell is a stinking, dark and dirty place, like being in a lavatory. Indeed, it is with a lavatory built into a bench on which there is at best a thin mattress and a dirty blanket. Consequently, when the police refer to 'custody suites' to 'rest periods' and to 'safeguards', these are euphemisms for locking a person up to soften them up, in which the only relief from isolation and total lack of stimulation, indeed, from all sensory deprivation, is to bring them out for interrogation.

We have held on to, with some difficulty, the principle of the right to silence, albeit in an emasculated form. To me, the ability to detain a person for the purpose of questioning is to allow the police to detain a person for the purpose of undermining their fundamental right to silence. If the police can obtain evidence by proper investigative means, then they have the right to prosecute and bring a person to justice.

If they depend entirely upon what they can extract from a suspect, then this violates the basic concept brought about by John Lilburne's resistance to the infamous Star Chamber in 1640, from which we came to believe that no person should be forced to be their own executioner. In other words, people should not be required to provide evidence to convict themselves from their own mouths.

To me, the detention and interrogation of Stephen Miller smacks of the rack and thumbscrew and the decision of the Court of Appeal should not have been to the effect that here were safeguards and the safeguards work, but that the custodial process in itself was unfair and unsafe and a violation of individual rights.

We seldom achieve great advances in acknowledgement of individual rights; nevertheless, putting up individual markers is vital, and for Stephen Miller, Yusef Abdullahi and Tony Paris, I rejoice in their freedom. However, I regret that in some ways their acquittal cheated them of a total explanation and exoneration.

Stephen Miller was fortunate in that his longest standing and most energetic ally, Satish Sekar, saw long before most others that something was terribly wrong with his case and I can personally give testimony that Satish nagged and persisted, often up to midnight, with phone calls, meetings and constant reminders that this was a case that had to be defended and that I should do anything that I could to help Stephen Miller. The oppressive process worked. Any person locked up in the awfulness of imprisonment for a wrongful conviction is lucky to have Satish for an ally. He persists. He is constant and he gets results. I therefore thank him and Stephen Miller for having encouraged me to work on the case.[1]

[1] The views expressed in this book are those of the author. The following appreciations should not be interpreted as implying that the contributors necessarily agree with the views and criticisms expressed in the book by the author: (The Fitted In Project).

Satish Sekar has pored over, combed through, sifted and weighed every molecule of available evidence. His attention to detail is extraordinarily impressive. His book should become a classic, and if it does achieve such status, as it deserves, it will be a powerful deterrent, not only to the kind of malpractice which Sekar analyses so thoroughly, but against attempts by such as Blom-Cooper, to question the acquittals of innocent men and women.

Corin Redgrave (Actor and producer)[1]

I am sure that Satish Sekar's conclusions are important and should be fully investigated, particularly in view of the unsatisfactory nature of scientific investigations at the time.

Alun Michael JP, MP[2]

Satish Sekar contacted me in 1995. I had reservations as to his intentions because he is an investigative journalist. However, since then I grew to admire his never ending persistence and confidence in investigating my daughter's murder as though it had become personal to him and I'm sure at times it had. He never ceased to amaze me with the many discrepancies which had come to light during his investigation.

How can you excuse a police force for overlooking discrepancies at the initial investigation of such a violent and horrific murder? After reading through evidence of DNA testing and results I came to the conclusion that those found guilty were, in fact, innocent. I believe that forensic evidence most certainly pointed to someone else, who had been questioned about my daughter's murder at the time. However, in 1995 the case was re-opened and further DNA testing was carried out by the police which has taken a further two years to complete and has used up most of the DNA. Consequently, it is unlikely that there is enough DNA left to give conclusive evidence or identification to get the real murderer convicted.

Had the police carried out the most sensitive method of amplifying DNA as soon as the inquiry was re-opened, then I feel sure that the person responsible would not be free today. The police could have handled this appalling case and scene of crime samples containing precious DNA with a lot more care and consideration.

Mr Sekar had informed me of a forensic expert, Professor Brinkmann in Germany, who is apparently more advanced in the field of forensic science than our own experts. I asked the police for the samples to be sent to Germany. The

---

[1] This quote was written by Corin Redgrave on December 1st 1997 and refers to Sir Louis Blom-Cooper QC's recently published controversial book, *The Birmingham Six And Other Cases : Victims of Circumstance*, which seems to cast doubt upon the acquittals of the Birmingham Six despite a plethora of evidence of their innocence.

[2] This quote was made by Alun Michael JP, MP, on March 1st 1997. Mr Michael is currently Minister of State for the Home Office.

police were very reluctant to let this happen, even though I offered to pay for such tests. The police suggested that they would consider my concerns after they had finished with their tests and then only if they had no results. They also said, "We will leave no stone unturned."

The police have completed one round of testing which yielded nothing. Can we now assume they will unturn the stone? I have waited patiently for two years for these tests to be completed, subconsciously suspecting that there would be no further results due to the type of tests they were doing. Whilst I respect what our forensic experts have done, the police should now take advantage of Professor Brinkmann's offer to test *what's left* of the DNA samples.

In conclusion, if ever there was a case which demanded a judicial review to resolve the many causes for concern in the whole case, surely this was it. Knowing what I now know I have come to the conclusion that only a fully independent inquiry conducted by an external police force can answer the many questions that remain unanswered. The interests of justice and the memory of my daughter deserve nothing less.

I am very grateful to Mr Sekar for bringing to my attention all the flaws in this case. I thank him for thoroughly investigating the flaws within South Wales Police's investigation. He deserves to be recognised as a very successful investigative journalist and I wish him good luck in his career.

Peggy Pesticcio (Lynette's mother)

There ought to be a better way - but whatever systems are put in place, it is the power of investigative journalism and public opinion which form the court of last resort when all legal avenues have been explored in vain. It can be a lonely and obsessive furrow to plough, but for those who do so it can be rewarding beyond any other form of journalistic endeavour. Satish Sekar has done patient and exhaustive duty to the case of the Cardiff Three - a case which exposes so many of the institutional flaws which contribute to the miscarrying of justice.

David Jessel (Presenter of Channel Four's *Trial And Error*)

One wonders how a case as horrific as the murder of Lynette White could have been mishandled as badly as it was, resulting in a terrible miscarriage of justice being allowed to happen once again. The case of the Cardiff Three is even more scandalous given the fact that the so called safeguards in PACE were in place at the time. It is tragic that yet another easily preventable miscarriage of justice was allowed to happen. Satish Sekar's book illustrates to the fullest what the police are capable of.

Billy Power (One of the Birmingham Six)

The miscarriage of justice which blighted the lives of the Cardiff Three is all the more disturbing because it dates not from the half-forgotten, legally different era of the 1970s, but from the 1990s, when police officers and lawyers tell us wrongful murder convictions are not supposed to happen. Satish Sekar has written a clear and meticulously detailed account which will be read by all serious students of criminal justice.

David Rose (Home Affairs Correspondent of the *Observer*)

Satish Sekar's book on the investigation into the horrifying death of Lynette White and the trial of five men for her murder is a work of painstaking analysis and careful attention to detail. He leaves few stones unturned in his quest to identify the real killer or killers and spares no-one in the questions which he poses in relation to the original enquiry and the trial.

Not all of his conclusions, theoretical analysis or criticism of individuals will find favour with everyone, but few who read this book will leave it without pondering on the many issues it raises.

Sekar is to be congratulated upon producing a book which so thoroughly rehearses the facts of a most puzzling case and which takes the reader in detail through the high and low points of the cases against the five men who originally stood trial.

Gerard Elias QC (Tony Paris' lead barrister)
The Leader of the Wales and Chester Circuit

Until it happened to me I thought that this type of thing only happened in films. I now know that it happens all the time.

Yusef Abdullahi (One of the Cardiff Three)

Satish Sekar is one of those diligent seekers after judicial truth who, not being himself a member of the legal profession, is perhaps better able to discern its shortcomings. He has a longstanding interest in the case of the Cardiff Three, which he rightly perceives as a pivotal one in the recent turbulent history of British justice.

This book is an admirable one, for two reasons: it provides such an exhaustive and highly readable account of this especially vexed case; and Sekar analyses how the defects of this one extraordinary inquiry throw light on the malpractice and incompetence that is all too frequently to be discovered at the heart of the judicial process.

Sekar's own fresh investigation of this case has uncovered valuable information. In the light of his painstaking work, the inquiry ought to be fully re-opened.

Bob Woffinden (Author of *Miscarriages of Justice* and *Hanratty : The Final Verdict*)

This thoroughly researched book reveals a very disturbing account of how a major murder inquiry can go seriously wrong by the failure of those investigating to keep a level head and to remain sceptical of evidence that may be tainted. It also shows the fearsome dangers of over reliance on the old fashioned methods of interrogation.

As one of the lawyers involved in the two trials it was a disturbing experience. This book should be read by all those people involved in the criminal justice system and above all by those who wish to see the restoration of total confidence in that system.

Roger Backhouse QC (Yusef Abdullahi's lead barrister)

The murder of Lynette White and the trial of the Cardiff Five (which came to be known as the case of the Cardiff Three) is one of the most disturbing cases of recent years. Satish Sekar has written a painstaking and conscientious account of this extraordinary story.

Duncan Campbell (Crime Correspondent of the *Guardian*)

There are many occasions where miscarriages of justice have taken place; however, the case of the Cardiff Three as it came to be known represents the glaring inadequacies of the British criminal justice system. That such a heinous crime as the murder of Lynette White should result in the scandalous convictions of three of the five men originally charged serves to further compound what can only be described as a disgraceful travesty of justice. Satish Sekar's book provides a meticulous analysis of events covering the arrest, investigation, trials and the eventual exoneration of the Cardiff Three, culminating in the murder inquiry being re-opened as a direct result of his research.

Indeed, this book exposes major flaws in the legal process and also the application of forensic science examinations of scene of crime evidence crucial to the identification of the real murderer of Lynette White. This book is important not only in terms of a historical record, but as a key text for lawyers, law students, miscarriage of justice campaigners and the public as a whole. It illustrates the dangers of moral panic over-riding the professionalism and integrity of South Wales Police, graphically illustrated by the outrageous interviewing methods that they used on Stephen Miller.

Our involvement in this case was prompted by the father of one of the defendants contacting me. I was immediately disgusted at the obvious injustice relating to this case and was motivated by my belief that had the Cardiff Five been white they would never have been arrested, let alone convicted. Indeed, this case is particularly difficult to understand. The prime suspect was a white sex offender with an appalling record of crimes against children. Yet ignoring a strong circumstantial case against this man and two photofits of white men urgently sought by police who were never traced, the police preferred to bring an absolutely ludicrous case against five innocent black men.

Can anyone really believe that such a case could have been tolerated for a single second if the police had a black child abuser as their prime suspect and ignored a stronger case against him in order to pursue five innocent white men? Change black for white and that is exactly what happened in this case. Such racism has no place in a competent criminal justice system.

As an active member of the Cardiff Three Campaign I was crucially aware of the importance of the investigative work being carried out by Satish Sekar. However, it is only in re-examining the key facts outlined in this book that a full realisation of the value of his work, combined with that of a radical campaign, can be achieved. It is work such as this which bring the full facts of cases such as the Cardiff Three into the public domain.

I recommend it to you and my hope would be that it prompts legislative and policy reform in the vital areas of the criminal justice system and the way that forensic science can be abused in circumstances where the lack of forensic evidence all but proved the innocence of the five men who originally stood trial for the murder of Lynette. The Cardiff Three, their families and friends; indeed, society and the memory of Lynette White deserved far better.

Lee Jasper (National Black Caucus and Director of the 1990 Trust)

[This book] contains all the material for a devastating indictment of the adversarial system of justice as now practised. The facts speak for themselves. The police did behave badly; but ... the human capacity for self deception is so strong that the police can, and do, convince themselves of the truth of what they would like to believe. I am also of the opinion that a judicial element should be introduced into police investigations at an early stage, as in France and to a limited extent in Scotland.

The English legal system is not concerned with the proof of innocence but with proof of guilt. This is why the Court of Appeal did not make any findings as to the innocence of the three appellants.

The Rt Hon Sir Frederick Lawton (former Lord Justice of Appeal)

Miscarriages of justice have left an indelible stain on the reputation of our criminal justice system. False confessions, flawed scientific evidence and non-disclosure by police, scientists and prosecutors of evidence vital to a defendant, have all played a part in keeping too many innocent people behind bars for too many damaging years.

The previous government's response has been not to provide greater safeguards against injustice for defendants - but to erode existing ones. The absolute right to silence has gone; while defendants will have to give a broad outline of their case to the prosecution, police will have to disclose less; the forensic science budgets have been squeezed; and three years after it was first recommended by the Royal Commission on Criminal Justice, the new independent authority for investigating miscarriages of justice has still not been set up.[1]

[1] On April 1st 1997 the long awaited Criminal Cases Review Commission (CCRC) started its work of reviewing alleged miscarriages of justice, although it has already attracted criticism from groups and individuals concerned with the issue of miscarriages of justice.

What Satish Sekar illustrates in this detailed examination of the murder of Lynette White and the miscarriage of justice that befell the Cardiff Three is how important such safeguards are. Even with the full right to silence, police obtained a damning and false confession in the case; the scientific testing of blood samples was neither conclusive nor revealed in its entirety to the defence; and as with most cases of alleged injustice the fight to get their case re-examined by the Court of Appeal has proved an uphill task.

In that struggle the Cardiff Three have been lucky in having Mr Sekar work painstakingly through the evidence, badgering lawyers, scientists, police and politicians with his findings. And even though the three are now freed and the injustice exposed, he fights on. His scrutiny of the DNA testing in the case has recently forced the South Wales Police to re-open the murder investigation.

Now, in *Fitted In*, he sets out the entire unhappy saga so that the public can see how easy it was to lock up the wrong men - and how we must ensure such mistakes are never made again. Mr Sekar says the memory of Lynette White deserves no less. Society and justice deserve no less.

Heather Mills (Social Affairs Correspondent of the *Observer*)

Fitted In describes the story of the Cardiff Three and the Lynette White Inquiry. It tells of injustices surrounding our legal system.

In reading the daily and Sunday newspapers is it any wonder that ordinary people have come to distrust the British criminal justice system? Some go so far as to say that it has been Americanised.

In reading the case studies in this book we are forced to ask ourselves in the words of the prophet Micah:

> 'What does the Lord require of you
> but to do justice and to love kindness
> and walk humbly with your God.'

This is the standard we ought to promote and these words must be applied to all those who govern, including the judiciary as well as those who are being governed in our country.

His Grace Alwyn Cambrensis (Archbishop of Wales)

Contents

[1] The main text of this book was completed on September 4th 1997, although certain events that occurred later, such as the Louise Woodward case, have subsequently been included.

Acknowledgements

My thanks are due to Alex Abdullahi, Malik Abdullahi, Pauline Abdullahi, Yusef Abdullahi, Tony Paris, Rosie Paris, Lloyd Paris, Sharon Paris, Paul Paris, Maria Britto, Nicki Gordon, Madge Miller, Debbie Taylor, Steve Miller, John Actie, Ronnie Actie, Taryn Ali, Steve Peckham, Kervin Julien, David Orton, Susan Burke and all the other members of the Cardiff Three Campaign too numerous to mention by name.

I would like to acknowledge the assistance of Craig Davies, Jackie Harris, Debbie Actie, Courtney Davies, John Eaton, Mike Royle, Rev David Haslam, Brian Moore, Barry Pullin, Richard and Audrey Adams, Duncan Campbell, Paul Foot, David Jessel, Heather Mills, Bob Woffinden, Mike Ormsby, Rachel Borrill, David Rose, Tim Rogers, Tom Mangold, Jennifer Nadel, Greg Swift, Geoff Small and Paul Blake.

I am very grateful to the Rt Hon Sir Frederick Lawton, Alun Michael JP, MP, Corin Redgrave, Peter Herbert, His Grace Alwyn Cambrensis, John Alderson CBE, QPM, Gerard Elias QC, John Charles Rees QC, Gareth Peirce, Michael Mansfield QC, Roger Backhouse QC, Nick Lloyd, Marilyn Bishop, Bernard de Maid, David Webster, Layla Attfield, Stuart Hutton, David Evans, Nicholas Blake QC, Ian Pritchard-Witts, Jocelyn Gibbs, Michael Hall, Michael Reid, Sadiq Khan, Carol Thomas, Martin Parker, Lee Wakeling, Michelle Hughton, Tony Burgess, Karen Jackson and, especially, Sandra Watson for their generous assistance and support in the writing of this book. I would also like to thank Bill Godber of Turnaround Publisher Services and Alan Gill of Advance Design & Print for their invaluable assistance without which this book could not have been produced.

Special thanks are also due to Gerry Conlon (Guildford Four), Billy Power (Birmingham Six), Peggy Pesticcio and to Mark Webster of Forensic Science Consultancy. My thanks are due to Saraswathi Sekar (my mother) and Chandra Sekar (my brother) without whom this book could not have been written.

I would also like to thank Dev Barrah, Surjit Nazran, Anna Vallois and Krishan Bhanot for their invaluable assistance in designing the front cover of this book. My immense gratitude is due to the Churches' Commission for Racial Justice and the Lord Ashdown Charitable Trust for their encouragement and support. I would also like to express my appreciation to Lee Jasper (Director of the 1990 Trust) for his invaluable assistance in making this book a reality and to the workers and volunteers of the 1990 Trust for their generous assistance and support. I would also like to thank Allan Waltham and Ian Gilmore for their assistance in the editorial process. Most of all, my thanks are due to Franca Jade for her invaluable support and suggestions for improvements without which this book could not have been written. Thanks are also due to many others too numerous to mention by name, but whose contributions are, nonetheless, valued very highly. Thanks to one and all who helped make this book a reality.

Part 1

THE INQUIRY

"The truth is that more mischief hath come to good men, by these kinds of approvements by false accusations of desperate villains, than benefit to the public by the discovery and conficting of real offenders."

Chief Justice Hale, 1650

CHAPTER 1

The Crime

Murder

In the early hours of Sunday February 14th 1988, in a run-down flat in the Butetown district of Cardiff, Lynette White was brutally murdered. She was a young white prostitute who worked the beat in the docklands that were once known as Tiger Bay.

Learnne Vilday led police to their discovery of the body. She was one of Lynette's few friends on the beat, and had earlier given her the keys to her flat at 7 James Street, which was used solely to entertain punters.

Two officers returned with Vilday to the flat on that wet winter night. It was on the first floor of the building, above a betting shop. Vilday allowed them to break down the door. They went in ahead of her and asked her to wait on the landing. When they entered the bedsitting room they made a gruesome discovery.

The room was small and was furnished with only a bed base and mattress. An unused condom out of its packet was lying on the bed. Lynette White's body, one shoe off, clothing dishevelled, lay between the foot of the bed and the nearby window. She had sustained at least fifty serious stab wounds and some superficial ones as well. Some of these were inflicted as she was close to dying, or even after death.

She had put up a terrific struggle for her life. There were defensive injuries that would have delayed her death, which was caused by massive haemorrhaging from triangular cuts to her throat. In fact, the killer had used such force that he had cut through to the spine. Lynette's breasts had been attacked. Her wrists had also been cut and it would later be shown that they were slashed long after her throat had been lacerated.

The renowned pathologist, Professor Bernard Knight, was able to establish that Lynette died between midnight and four in the morning. Her watch had stopped at 1.45. Shocks to the wearer can cause watches to stop. Thus, the watch established that the most likely time of the murder was 1.45-1.50 a.m.

The body seemed to have been moved from near the foot of the bed to the nearby window. Both the wall beside the bed and the bottom of the bed base were heavily bloodstained. The wall opposite the bed was also covered in blood near where the walls met and up to the nearby window. And on the chimney breast was a partial handprint without a speck of blood on it, indicating that it had to have been put there during the murder. There was very little blood on the mattress itself. The entire attack took place on, or close to, the floor in that corner of the room.

Fingerprint experts were to find no less than one hundred and fifty sets of finger and palmprints in the flat. Some of them were eliminated as having valid reasons for being there, others were not suitable for identification purposes and the others were to remain unidentified. Of all these prints the most important was clearly the partial handprint on the wall. It could only have belonged to the murderer or someone who witnessed the murder.

The forensic team would discover hairs, saliva, semen, large amounts of Lynette's blood which had spurted on to the walls and carpet, and also samples of a very rare blood group containing the male chromosome, as well as a trainer or shoe print. There was plenty of evidence to work on.

The semen discovered was subsequently found to have been deposited in Lynette and on the crotch of her panties within six hours of her death and was therefore of limited importance as it would not necessarily belong to the killer. It was aspermic. This much is known from the fact that Lynette was trying to become pregnant, so she would not have been using a spermicide. But it may have been deposited in her within an hour of her murder. If, despite reservations, it is taken as read that the aspermic semen was deposited by the killer, it was the sort of thing that would have registered in a psychological profile of Lynette's murderer, possibly in terms of the killer's inability to relate to women and lack of control in his sexual practices. It is also possible to identify that man using the most sophisticated DNA technology now available.

The broad indication was that Lynette was about to entertain a client when for some reason he attacked her in such an atrocious fashion. This was to reinforce the persistent belief in Butetown and elsewhere that Lynette was murdered by one man and that he was a punter.

Meanwhile, Vilday was still on the landing when she heard one of the officers radio for assistance with a suspected homicide. She started to cry. This much is contained in the statement of Sergeant William Bisgood, one of the officers who accompanied Vilday to the flat. She did not see the body. It was 9.17 p.m. The crime had gone undetected for about eighteen hours.

Another Saturday Night

The previous night was a Saturday night and had been a busy one in the pubs and clubs of Butetown. There was a big promotion at the Casablanca, one of Butetown's long-established clubs near the waterside. It was their St Valentine's Night bash. The reggae artiste Sandra Cross played and drew a reasonably big crowd, although it became a gig she would want to forget as she was booed off stage for what was considered a substandard performance.

Among the many local residents, hustlers and punters going about their business from one venue to another in the course of the night and early morning was Steve Miller, a young black man known by some as 'Pineapple-Head' on account of his flamboyant hairstyle. At various times throughout the night and early morning he was at the Casablanca with his friend David Orton.

Steve Miller, originally a Londoner, was Lynette White's boyfriend. Towards the end of her life he was also her pimp. Apart from a few odd jobs, Lynette was Miller's only source of income. She paid for his liking of cocaine. Miller accepted that he paid for it from her earnings, but claims that she gave it to him voluntarily, although there is evidence to suggest that the drugs he bought was for Lynette's use as well as his own.

Lynette was twenty years old when she died. She had left school with no qualifications and drifted into prostitution some time before she met Miller. He portrays his relationship with Lynette in a positive light and there is some evidence to support his views, but there is also plenty of evidence that he treated her like dirt.

It was said by many prostitutes that she would be sent out to work the streets by Miller until she returned with the amount he required to feed his habit and that Miller would get violent to her if she didn't have as much as he wanted. Miller absolutely rejected that. While there was no love lost between the prostitutes and Miller, there were others who helped him in the aftermath of Lynette's murder who backed up the claims of the women on the beat. However, while Miller's accounts of Lynette voluntarily giving him between £60-90 per day for cocaine appears unlikely, the picture that others were to paint of him was just as unlikely.

Miller tries to portray a loving and harmonious relationship and claims to have tried to persuade her to come off the game. When Miller first met Lynette he was no pimp and he was not a regular user of cocaine. At first, he refused to believe that she was a prostitute at all. When he was shown proof that he couldn't ignore he made his objections clear to her.

According to one account, Miller gave Lynette an ultimatum to choose between prostitution or him and Lynette gave up the beat for a couple of months. Miller was no angel and at least some of the way that he treated Lynette was manifestly unacceptable, but he was no monster either; he was somewhere in between. Miller is said to have been gutted when he found out that Lynette had returned to the beat and cried about it. At first he objected to it vociferously, but when his use of cocaine became so frequent that he needed Lynette's earnings to subsidise it his objections ended. This was when their relationship changed from lovers to that of ponce and prostitute.

By the end of Lynette's life Miller was undoubtedly her pimp, but it would be untrue to claim that he put Lynette on the streets and that their relationship was never anything more than pimp and prostitute. Nevertheless, he would drive her to the beat every day and meet her in the North Star every night where he would get money off her. He rationalised this as Lynette lending it to him while he was out of work, yet he didn't even sign on and, apart from Lynette, his only source of income was very occasional odd jobs for their landlord.

Miller was undoubtedly living off Lynette's earnings, although he insists that he was not her pimp. Despite his exploitation of the woman he claimed to love, Steve Miller loved Lynette and she certainly loved him even after she left him.

Lynette had gone missing five days before her murder. She was not seen in her usual haunts, but several people had seen her in Cardiff at various times during the week. She had disappeared from the neighbourhood before, but she usually showed up far sooner. This time was different. Nearly ten years after her murder her precise whereabouts in those five days still remain a complete mystery.

Most of the women working the Butetown beat did not have pimps. They had a long-established tradition of looking after each other's interests. Lynette was an exception. In the last five days of her life she chose to break up with Miller. Consequently, she chose to do without his protection. During those five days she was not seen working the beat.

Her friends and fellow prostitutes, Learnne Vilday and Angela Psaila, saw her early in the week as she spent the night at Psaila's flat. An old school friend, Yasmin Abdullahi, saw her in Cardiff within a couple of days of her death. Around 10.00 p.m. on the night of the murder she shared a minicab with a client who took her to 7 James Street. She was last seen alive shortly before midnight at the Montmerence Club, while Miller was across town.

Miller wanted her back. She was making him look bad in front of his peers and worse still, he was virtually penniless. He spent the night to-ing and fro-ing from the Casablanca; he always had an eye out for her. Since she had disappeared he had searched for her high and low, but to no avail. He needed her: without her he had no income and was totally dependent on the charity of his few friends, especially David Orton. He couldn't even afford to run his car to look for her, or buy food and his credit for drugs was bound to dry up sooner rather than later. She was his meal ticket, the goose that laid the golden egg and he had lost her. He needed her back and soon.

Yusef Abdullahi, a well-known figure on the local scene, was not, as he often was, amongst the throng in Butetown's pubs and clubs that night. He had debts to pay off and the drug dealing he was sometimes involved in wasn't sufficient for this purpose. He was working eight miles away in Barry Dock as a general labourer on board the MV *Coral Sea*, manhandling chunks of scrap metal and tossing them on to the dockside to a team of scrap dealers. In the course of this he sustained a nasty burn to the hand. The work involved cutting and welding, which meant that the scraps were very hot. It was raining hard that night, which made the wax on the gloves soggy, so he wedged the gloves between his hands and the scrap metal. The gloves slipped and he burnt his hand. He dropped the metal, covered his hand in a tatty bandage and carried on working.

In the course of redevelopment Butetown's population had dwindled to a few thousand, but it was still a community of large extended families. The Acties were another well-known example. Debbie Actie had begun work with Robyn and Stephanie Reed the previous evening at the Transport Club. They finished at 1.00

a.m. and after ten minutes cleaning up they got a cab. They dropped Stephanie off in James Street at about 1.35 and two minutes later they were at the Casablanca, where Debbie's cousin, John, was working the door that night. They went to the bar for a drink and began to mingle. Among others, they noticed Steve Miller playing pool in the crowded back room.

Tony Paris, who also worked in the Butetown clubs, was five foot two inches tall, a bit chubby and very short sighted. In addition to this, he had been the victim of domestic violence and had a tendency to faint at the sight of blood. Despite this and somewhat bizarrely, he sometimes worked, as did beefy John Actie, on the door at the Casablanca. That night however he was doing his more usual glass-collecting duties and doing them well by all accounts, because on a busy night such as this the barkeeper's nightmare scenario of a mass of dirty glasses accumulating did not materialise.

Learnne Vilday was also having a busy night. At about 10.00 p.m. she had brought four punters back to Angela Psaila's home, where she was living at the time. It was in a block of flats some seventy feet away from 7 James Street. She entertained two of the clients herself while Psaila sat with Vilday's baby and the other two. Psaila then entertained one of these before Vilday took on the fourth. While she was with him a woman called Maria Britto arrived, having been on her trail.

Britto had just discovered that her partner, Paul Paris, Tony's brother, was the father of Vilday's baby and she wanted to confront Vilday about it. She hit Vilday in the face and then poked her with an umbrella before leaving. Later on, around 3.00 a.m., Vilday met up with Ronnie Actie in the North Star and he immediately noticed her facial injuries. He saw that both of her eyes were swollen and there was dried blood on her nose. She told him that a client had caused them.

Vilday had expressed more concern over Lynette's recent five-day disappearance than anyone else and she told Ronnie of her fears and even said, "She could have been murdered for all we know." Actie told her not to be so stupid and that Lynette could take care of herself.

Although Vilday was a lesbian by preference, Ronnie Actie was a boyfriend of sorts. He had been seeing her off and on for some time. That night Vilday wanted to go nightclubbing, but he refused because it might have looked as though he'd beaten her up. After twenty minutes or so in the North Star he took her to his sister Michelle's home. Vilday accepted his offer and spent the remainder of the night with him.

He temporarily allayed her fears about Lynette, but concern nagged her during the course of the next day. Eventually she took a cab to the James Street flat and looked through the letterbox and saw the kitchen door closed. This was unusual because the door was usually held open with a piece of string. She went back to the cab and told the driver her worries, and, following his advice, got him to take her to Butetown Police Station. Shortly after this the ill-fated Lynette White Inquiry began when this young woman was discovered to have been the victim of a frenzied and bloody killing which drew comparisons with those committed by the Yorkshire Ripper.

South Wales Police immediately set up a full-scale investigation under DCS John Williams and established an incident room at Central Police Station, Cardiff.

Early Days

In the immediate aftermath of the crime there was a cast of thousands of potential suspects. Every family in Butetown seemed as though they were visited at some stage in the inquiry and many were, but the police were in possession of a vital clue. They had no eyewitnesses to the crime then, but they had the next best thing: a definite suspect, although they had no name to the face.

The police assured punters through the *South Wales Echo* that if they came forward voluntarily they would be treated confidentially and their use of prostitutes would not be told to their families or friends. Some took advantage of this, but most preferred to try to forget all about it.

There were a few sightings of a white man in his mid to late thirties. He was 5'8"-5'10" tall with dark greasy hair which had a lightening streak towards the front. He looked dishevelled. His hands were cupped towards his face and he had cut himself. His clothes had blood on them. He was seen crying in the vicinity of the flat, outside the nearby Maritime Museum, by several people on Valentine's Day. The most crucial sighting was by a sixteen year old girl, Melanie Mail.

She not only saw the man but placed him outside the block of flats where the murder took place. She saw him follow her to the museum from 7 James Street. Before her statement, made within days of the crime, the man had been seen in the vicinity of the crime, but she placed him at the scene of the murder between 2.45-3.15 p.m. Once the post mortem report showed clearly that the murder had taken place in the early hours of the morning, this appeared to be strange behaviour for a killer. Where had he been until then? What was he doing and why, if he was Lynette's murderer, did he not make good his escape as quickly as he could?

Despite the reservations, South Wales Police clearly took these sightings very seriously as they rapidly compiled a photofit of this man whom they urgently wanted to question. They had found their chief suspect, or so it seemed. There was a person whose similarity to the photofit was so striking that he was detained in accordance with PACE on February 25th after a woman picked out his photograph. According to Detective Superintendent Ken Davies, Malcolm Morris was regarded as a person who had to be eliminated because of his previous history of violence and the instability of his character. Melanie Mail failed to pick him out although she had reservations about him.

Detective Superintendent Davies went on to say that Morris' home was searched, that he was interviewed in depth and that his clothes and scalpels taken from his home resulted in a negative response after forensic analysis. In addition to this, police obtained an alibi statement from an associate of Morris. On February 26th Morris was released. Davies claimed that Morris was never firmly eliminated from the inquiry; he was merely considered to be a less likely suspect. However, despite Davies' protestations, Morris had effectively been eliminated. Morris was among several suspects to be eliminated in this way, yet five men who were entitled to be eliminated on the same basis would later stand trial for Lynette's murder.

March 17th's *Crimewatch* described the photofit face as that of the person who must be the chief suspect. DCS Williams made it plain that he and the police as a whole believed that the man in the photofit was responsible for Lynette's murder, telling the nation that a white man was seen in the vicinity of the murder in a distressed state, having cut his hand and that he had Lynette's blood on him. There were several sightings of this man. One put him in Cardiff in the week before the murder as having been thrown out of a cafe by the owner. Another placed him in the Casablanca on the night of Sunday February 14th. Yet, despite all this, he could not be traced and would never be eliminated from their inquiries.

In the early days of the inquiry the police were more interested in Francine Cordle than anyone except Steve Miller. And Cordle had a possible motive for wanting Lynette out of the way. Lynette had been due to give evidence against her the week after she died.

Cordle had been the girlfriend of Tony Miller, Steve's elder brother. The brothers were said to be close. But Tony's relationship with Cordle was stormy. They eventually parted on extremely acrimonious terms several months before the murder, but both Tony Miller and Francine Cordle were regarded as potentially important suspects.

Prior to going out with Cordle, Tony Miller had been going out with a prostitute named Maria Jacobsen, although he claims that he didn't know that she was a prostitute until Cordle told him and broke up with her because of it. When Cordle came on the scene, he finished with Jacobsen, or so it seemed. Even while he was going out with Cordle, he allegedly still had a fling with his old flame which enraged Cordle to the point of wanting revenge on Jacobsen.

During the week after her death Lynette had been due to give evidence against Cordle in relation to a serious assault on a prostitute named Tina Garton. Cordle had a temper; she was an extremely jealous and possessive woman according to her old flame. Tony Miller confirmed that Cordle was convinced that Garton had slept with her man. She was not about to tolerate such a diabolical liberty.

Tony Miller claims that when he saw Cordle confronting Garton he tried to intervene and get assistance, but nobody else seemed interested, so he let them get on with it. Garton was severely wounded. Steve Miller claims that he and Tony Brace saw Garton bleeding outside the North Star and brought her inside, laid her on a pool table and used a jacket to try to stem the bleeding. Lynette had seen her bleeding as well, but, according to Miller, neither of them saw the actual attack.

Miller insists that Lynette just didn't want to give evidence against Cordle because she was frightened of Cordle and her mother in particular as both had reputations for taking no nonsense at all. Their reputation and Lynette's knowledge of them may well have caused her to be wary of them. However, the (Garton) case against Cordle fizzled out because the publicity surrounding Lynette's murder made it impossible to guarantee a fair trial. Cordle was to be acquitted of the attempted murder of Garton, but convicted of assaulting her with a shoe at a retrial a few months later.

It is not difficult to see why police interest focused on Cordle and Farrugia. However, there are sound reasons for ruling out both Peggy Farrugia and Francine Cordle. Farrugia's blood group clearly proves her innocence. And, by April 14th, the police knew that the murderer was a man as Dr Peter Gill had discovered the male chromosome on all five areas that he tested on the bottom of Lynette's jeans. Obviously, that ruled out both Farrugia and Cordle and any other female suspects who did not possess the male chromosome for that matter. In addition to that, Cordle's bail conditions meant that she had to stay in Birmingham. There was conflicting evidence about whether she complied with her bail conditions, but the police believed that she was in Birmingham when Lynette was murdered.

Then, there was the other case that Lynette was due to give evidence in. Two unsavoury low-lifes, Robert Gent and Eric Marasco, were also standing trial when Lynette was murdered. These two had procured the services of a thirteen year old girl for prostitution. This was too much for some of the long-established prostitutes to tolerate. Child prostitution was going too far. Both Lynette White and Angela Psaila felt that way. Police were tipped off and Gent and Marasco received four years imprisonment for their crime. Not surprisingly, police were interested in that trial as well. After all, Marasco and Gent certainly had a motive for wanting Lynette out of the way, but police interest in them subsequently waned.

The Great Wall Of Butetown

The police decided to concentrate their search on Butetown. They also decided that the key to the inquiry was the prostitute community, but when they discovered that clients would come from as far as mid Wales to use prostitutes in Cardiff, they were faced with serious problems. If the murderer was a lone punter this information would widen the search to epidemic proportions. Rather than follow up these leads fastidiously, they chose to concentrate their resources on Cardiff and, even more so, on Butetown.

When the police discovered the existence of a prime suspect and issued a photofit of him, they appealed for further witnesses to come forward. They even gave fairly detailed descriptions of two men whom they believed had seen this suspect near 7 James Street in the afternoon of February 14th. The appeals failed to persuade those men to come forward.

Then they appealed to taxi drivers as the key to the inquiry. They thought that

Lynette may have taken a taxi from the Montmerence Club to 7 James Street on the night of the murder. They hoped to piece together the last moments of her life, vital information for any murder inquiry, but they were destined to remain frustrated. If their hunch was correct they were never able to prove it. Consequently, it still remains a complete mystery how Lynette got from the club back to 7 James Street on that tragic night and who she returned with.

The police soon invoked the memory of a previous notorious failure. Nora Wilfred, an Asian prostitute, was stabbed to death in December 1972. That inquiry was complicated by the fact that the murder occurred on the same day as a rugby international at Cardiff Arms Park. It would prove impossible to trace all those who had attended the match. Despite being stabbed more than twenty times, her murderer escaped. The crime remains unsolved to this day. And, despite leaking similarities between the Wilfred killing and that of Lynette to the *South Wales Echo*, the police appear not to have investigated the possibility that both women could have been murdered by the same person. This is puzzling.

In Wilfred's case the police explained their failure by claiming that the prostitute community had erected a wall of silence which protected the murderer. They quickly made it clear that they feared a similar wall of silence over Lynette's murder, but stressed that they would solve it. At first, the police seemed to expect the prostitute community to solve the murder for them, but it soon became obvious that the women didn't know who murdered Lynette. They told the police what they knew, as was seen by the sheer volume of statements that they gave. There would eventually be over twenty-two thousand pages of information from several sources anxious to help to clear up this exceptional crime.

Despite this, the police reinforced their claims that the prostitutes were not co-operating by stressing that they still worked the beat in spite of Lynette's brutal murder. But this was their livelihood. It wasn't that they didn't care about Lynette or their own safety; they simply had no choice and they didn't know who killed her. They helped the police to the best of their abilities.

It was a frustrating time for Lynette White's family and friends and, even more so, for her fellow prostitutes who still had to work the beat, but now knowing that there was a maniac or maniacs on the loose.

DCS Williams claimed that all their inquiries led them back to Butetown. Consequently, the police established a base there and used it as the centre of their inquiry. They claimed that the people of Butetown wanted the murder cleared up and came to trust the police to do that. To some extent this was true, but few were prepared for what followed.

Butetown

> "Butetown is a nocturnal, upside down, topsyturvy world where people carry knives as part of their clothing."
>
> *David Elfer QC*

Butetown, previously known as Tiger Bay, is one of Britain's oldest black communities. It is also one of the most firmly entrenched. For almost two centuries it has been perceived as a threat by the establishment which, even now, is still unable to understand its traditions, culture, and, even more crucially, its aspirations. (Hence, as in the above quote, the clichéd adjectives 'nocturnal' and 'topsyturvy' and the sensationalist idea that everyone walks around with knives.)

But Butetown was even more of a threat to the status quo than most of Britain's black communities because it was not a black separatist community that could be easily isolated. Realising that black residents in Butetown had much in common with white residents it soon became well integrated, but not one that sacrificed its unique identity in the process.

However, the rest of Cardiff was of a completely different cultural make-up. This made the docks community an even bigger threat to the powers that be and brought it to the attention of the authorities' law enforcers. Their reaction betrayed the classic symptoms of fear, suspicion and lack of understanding.

They wanted to control it by driving a wedge between its black and white residents, as was seen in 1919 when the first Race Riot in British history took place. It could have divided Butetown irreconcilably, but it failed to do so. Butetown eventually emerged from the spectre of the Race Riot a stronger and even more firmly integrated community. The powers that be had played the race card and it had failed. Consequently, different tactics were called for. Butetown's capacity to fight back had to be diminished. Brute force had failed, but money talks.

From 1919 to the present day developers had steadily chipped away at Butetown. A thriving community of several thousands had diminished to a couple of thousand at the time of the murder and the developers had their eye on yet more. The present-day economic conquest of Butetown was continuing and it was succeeding where the Race Riot had failed. Butetown had once been a thriving community, but as the shipping industry fell into decline so did Butetown's fortunes. As with many of Britain's declining docklands, some redevelopment was begun at the turn of the 80s. Warehouses became offices, other sites were demolished, some of the grand buildings were lovingly restored, media businesses and the odd upmarket restaurant appeared and a faint whiff of the heritage industry came to the old seaport.

This significantly reduced the size of the indigenous community without significantly improving the fortunes and conditions of those who remained. Consequently, this proud community's ability to resist the march of time had been drastically reduced. Butetown, a once vibrant community had been sentenced to a slow and painful death in the name of progress. But further development was felt to be threatened by this murder: it was bad publicity for an area which had aspirations to new businesses and leisure industries and badly needed investment. For eight weeks the redevelopment of Butetown was stopped in its tracks. The crime had to be cleared up quickly.

Steve Miller

Steve Miller was picked up for questioning within hours of the discovery of his girlfriend's body, early in the morning of February 15th. When he was taken in for questioning the police joked with him, telling him to sit in the other corner of the interview room because of the smell of his clothes. He voluntarily helped the police with their inquiries and gave them as detailed an explanation of his movements as he could. While there Miller was allowed to see post mortem photographs of Lynette's butchered body, which for some inexplicable reason were left in the interview room during a period when Miller was alone there. This distressed him greatly. DI Richard Powell would later give evidence that the photographs had not been left there to distress Miller.

Miller made a long statement to DI Powell on February 16th. Part of that statement dealt with his movements on the night of the murder. He claimed that he went to Eugene Savage's house about quarter past eight. He accompanied Savage to the Bosun and then visited Orton. At about 11.15 he went to the Casablanca with Savage and Orton. After that they went to the Big Windsor, staying there for about half an hour before returning to the Casablanca with Orton. At about 2.15 he went to the North Star and went home at about 3.00 a.m.

When he was released without charge in the early hours of February 16th, South Wales Police made it clear that they had ruled Miller out from their inquiries. He was the first suspect to be eliminated. However, South Wales Police would later backtrack on this firm elimination of Steve Miller when they arrested him nearly ten months later, claiming that they never eliminated him unequivocally; they just thought of him as a less likely suspect.

David Orton had just made a statement saying that he had spent every night with Miller from January 31st to February 14th. He told the police that Miller had been with him for most of the night of the murder. Miller returned to Orton's house between 9.00 and 9.30 that night. After half an hour they went to the Casablanca and stayed there until about 3.00 a.m. They left separately. This amounted to a complete alibi at the most likely time of the murder. But Orton later added to his original statement by saying that there had been a couple of occasions during the night that Miller was out of his sight, but it was established that Miller had gone to the North Star in search of Lynette.

In the month following her death Steve Miller made eight statements to the police. He attended Butetown Police Station voluntarily. When he was first brought in he was wearing the same clothes he wore on the night of the murder. There was plenty of dirt on them but no blood. These clothes and others belonging to Miller were forensically tested. The results were negative. A sample of his blood was taken to be tested against blood found in the flat. The results were negative. His car was taken to the police pound and virtually torn apart. After several months it would be returned to him minus a seat. The police had run it through forensic tests. The results were negative. There was to be no forensic evidence against him. In fact, Miller and the four men who would stand trial with him were the only people against whom there was no forensic evidence who were not eliminated on that basis. South Wales Police's failure to eliminate them due to negative forensic evidence is baffling.

Meanwhile, there were conflicting reports on Miller's reaction to Lynette's death. According to some, Lynette was barely cold when Miller found himself a new woman to walk the streets for him. Unlike many, these reports were credible. They came from Yusef's sister, Yasmin, and her friend Debbie Pennington. They put a roof over Miller's head after Lynette's murder, yet both were to claim that Miller had struck a prostitute named Tracey Puttick for not giving money to him.

Business as usual? But this was only one side of his reaction to Lynette's death. While Miller seemed to have belatedly found another goose to lay the golden egg for him, Lynette's fate played on his mind. He knew people still looked at him with suspicion even though he had been all but ruled out by police. A few days after the murder he confronted Vilday in the presence of David Orton. Tony Paris overheard the confrontation as he was in the shop next door. Miller told her in no uncertain terms that since Lynette was murdered in her flat he expected her to find out who did it and tell him. Orton and others spoke of Miller crying about Lynette's murder, being very upset about it and swearing to kill whoever had killed her.

In addition to this, Miller's long-standing dislike of police officers was put on hold. He pumped friends, acquaintances, even perfect strangers for information. He begged, pleaded, cajoled and pestered the living daylights out of anyone he came across for information and what he got he passed on to police entirely voluntarily. DI Powell claimed to be sick of the sight of him in Butetown Police Station.

Apart from his behaviour towards Puttick, his reaction at the time was perfectly normal in every way for such extraordinary circumstances. Miller's friend, Jackie Harris, was Yusef Abdullahi's common-law wife, but the two men did not like each other. In fact, Abdullahi was known to dislike West Indians. Harris was a sometime barmaid at the Custom House, a venue much frequented by prostitutes and Vice Squad officers. She was a person who would come to play a key role in the murder inquiry. She felt that Miller could not bring himself to go to Lynette's funeral because he was still in a state of denial. He hoped that if he didn't see her laid to rest there was still a chance that one day she would return to him alive and well. Even Miller's girlfriend, Debbie Taylor, spoke of him still loving Lynette.

Yusef Abdullahi

Like many in Butetown Abdullahi is of mixed race (his father was a Somali). He is also renowned as a ladies' man. The police believed that Abdullahi was a drug dealer, but their attempts to convict him failed miserably every time. It galled them. Abdullahi also suspected that Harris' brother-in-law, Ronnie Williams, was a police informer. And he had often told anyone who would listen that the police were following him, but most people thought that he was paranoid. South Wales Police wanted him off the streets and every failed attempt to get him jailed intensified their desire to convict him.

Abdullahi did not like Lynette. He regarded her as two faced. He suspected that she had told police that Tony Miller and Francine Cordle had been hiding at his place after the assault on Tina Garton. However, despite the fact that he disliked Lynette, he found her murder appalling. He was prepared to call a truce in his long standing battle of wills with South Wales Police. He hated police informers, but this was different. All the normal rules on helping the police went out of the window for this inquiry. Even Abdullahi's suspicions that the police were after him for something had to be put on hold. Hostilities could resume after the killer had been brought to justice.

In the new-found era of glasnost between Abdullahi and South Wales Police, Abdullahi set about trying to help police with their enquiries. He insists that he had heard from a certain Jennifer Parkin (later to become a crucial witness against Steve Miller) that she knew who the murderer was, although he had no idea who Parkin was talking about at the time. He encouraged her to tell the police what she knew and overruled her reluctance by telling the police about her.

Abdullahi insists that because he knew the Butetown scene so well, he was asked at one point by police to look out of a window in Butetown Police Station to observe several white men that they had brought in for questioning and say if he had seen any of them in Butetown before. He freely obliged.

However, if Abdullahi had been aware at the time of certain goings-on, he might well have thought twice about assisting police about anything.

Before Lynette's murder his tempestuous relationship with Jackie Harris hit yet another rocky patch. But this time there was an added complication. Harris thought that she had found her knight in shining armour. Geoff Smith seemed like a nice guy. He provided a sympathetic ear and a shoulder for her to cry on, but Smith was no ordinary saviour for Harris; he was also a policeman attached to Vice Squad. Abdullahi had his suspicions that Smith was something more than just a good friend to Harris. He would eventually be proved right.

The affair had begun six months before the murder at a time when Abdullahi was knocking her about at home. Smith cultivated Harris' friendship gradually. At first, he made her the centre of attention. He advised her on how to get injunctions against Abdullahi in response to his violence against her. She thought that he was a nice guy whose concern about her was genuine. Later she would come to believe that Smith was merely cultivating a useful source for later use.

Tony Paris

Paris knew most of the prostitutes and people in the docks and seemed to get on with most people. He phoned the police anonymously to tell the Incident Room that he had a conversation with Angela Psaila who told him she knew a ginger haired girl, who turned out to be called Sandra, who claimed to know who the murderer was. When Paris told South Wales Police about his conversation with them, he couldn't have known that they had already received similar information. It suggests that he was passing on the word from the street to the best of his abilities.

Because he knew the local prostitutes he was sometimes accused of pimping, but Paris got his money from elsewhere. He signed on and did the occasional stint in the Casablanca. But he received the bulk of his income from shoplifting, which was his only serious form.

Tony Paris was perhaps the hardest of any to find a convincing reason to fit into the inquiry. He only had convictions for petty matters such as cannabis offences and shoplifting. He was not a villain and he had a solid alibi which was backed up by numerous witnesses in the Casablanca.

John Actie

John Actie is a huge man. He stood over six foot tall and was well built. He had a reputation for taking no nonsense at all. In fact, he was well known for throwing his weight around. Nobody could push past him without having the requisite injuries to complement the tale, a fact that would later assume great significance.

On March 1st Actie and his common-law wife, Taryn Ali, were visited at their home by the police. They were asked to fill in a questionnaire by PC Osborne. Both were fully co-operative. Osborne was not aware of any inconsistencies in what they said. Actie's account was that he had stayed at home until about midnight and then went to the Casablanca. He stayed there until about 3.30 a.m. He did not associate with prostitutes at all and this was well known.

John Actie couldn't help South Wales Police. He didn't get on with them and he intimidated them, but this was different. It was the type of crime where even the most hardened villain freely helps the police to the best of their abilities. Actie had no information to give as he didn't associate with any of the major players in the inquiry. Although he couldn't provide them with any leads, it was not for lack of will on his part.

But he did have previous convictions which included violent offences, although there was nothing approaching the scale of Lynette's murder or any killing for that matter. John Actie was no angel. And there was no love lost between the police and Actie. They wanted him off the streets.

Ronnie Actie And Learnne Vilday

Ronnie Actie made his first statement to the police in March. He certainly did mix with the oldest profession and he was Vilday's boyfriend. Among his convictions was one for robbing a prostitute at knifepoint. He served time for this. Suffice to say, Ronnie Actie was no saint and the police wanted him off the streets.

Despite this, it ought not to have been hard to eliminate him as a suspect.

Among others, his friends Johnny Crook and Michael Taylor as well as Vilday herself confirmed his movements on that Saturday night. The clothes he wore on the murder night were forensically tested and the results were negative. And Ronnie Actie also helped the police as best he could.

He confirmed that Vilday had spent the night with him and said that she had left his house at 6.30 in the morning. This time was to be a matter of contention.

By her own admission, Vilday spent the night of the murder with Ronnie Actie at his sister's house. At first, she claimed that she left there at 7.30 in the morning. She asked Ronnie to back her up. He didn't know why she wanted him to lie for her, but he refused to and told the police that she left an hour earlier. After his statement to that effect Vilday changed her own account accordingly.

What were her reasons for wanting people to believe that she left an hour later than she did? What happened in that hour? In other versions of her story she claims that she went to buy a newspaper, but the shop in question didn't open until much later on Sundays.

There was a substantial gap in her accounts. She could have visited the scene of the crime during this time, but it is clear that no attempt was made to interfere with the forensic evidence. If she found the body in the morning, what were her reasons for not going to the police then? There were so many holes in her accounts that it must have caused the police and her fellow prostitutes to suspect that she knew more than she was letting on.

From the moment that she discovered Lynette's mutilated body, it became clear that everyone expected her to provide that crucial piece of information that could lead to the apprehension of the murderer. The women who worked the streets were anxious for it to be cleared up quickly as they did not want to work with a murderous lunatic on the loose. After all, any one of them could have been next.

They pressurised Vilday for information, as did the police. Even Ronnie Actie sometimes tried to pump her for information. She was getting pressure from all sides and could not get a moment's peace.

And Vilday herself could not explain why she went to 7 James Street on the Sunday night. It seemed very strange that she took a taxi to the flat. It was almost as if she expected to find something horrible there and wanted a witness. Did she already know that Lynette was dead? Was she just using the cab driver, Eddie Dimond, as verification of her suspicions and, more importantly, as an independent witness that it was her suspicions that led to the discovery of Lynette's body when it was found?

It was not difficult to see why police became obsessed with Learnne Vilday. They were absolutely convinced that she held the solution to the Lynette White Inquiry. There were ample grounds for doubting her accounts, but there was just as much evidence to suggest that she knew nothing of interest about Lynette's murder. If she discovered Lynette's body in the morning of February 14th there was no reason not to report her concerns immediately. After all, if there was one inquiry where she would have known that she would get police protection if she required it, this was it.

And if she had discovered the body earlier than she would admit to, realised that it would bring her all the hassle that it eventually did and tried to get Lynette's body out of her flat, it is absolutely amazing that there is not so much as a solitary fibre tying her to such an attempt, especially in a case where there would have been a plethora of forensic evidence to betray such an attempt. There was none.

CHAPTER 2

The Switch

Rumours

Yusef Abdullahi, like everyone else on the street, talked and heard talk. There were theories, stories, hunches and Chinese whispers. And as the inquiry continued and March gave way to April, Abdullahi wasn't happy with what he heard. For one thing he was now strongly suspicious that Jackie Harris was carrying on with the Vice Squad man Smith. He felt like people were laughing at him behind his back for having a cop put the horns on him. And he suspected he was being set up for a drug bust. But there was more to it than narcotics.

From March his common-law brother-in-law, Ronnie Williams, had been providing the Lynette White Inquiry with specific information. Williams fancied himself as a private eye and was posing as one in the immediate aftermath of the murder. He wrote to DI Thomas Page to tell him that his inquiries had revealed that Lynette went to the Casablanca to confront Miller about his relationship with another woman. They had a heated argument and Lynette threatened to tell the police of either his involvement with drugs, or another case that was pending.

Williams went on to claim that Lynette was stabbed at the club, but it was not fatal. She was then taken to the flat. He said that there were a couple of witnesses to this who saw the body and were subjected to a strict code of silence. Suffice to say, Williams' claims were distinctly unreliable.

On other occasions he claimed to be working for the police in connection with the murder inquiry. While this was untrue he was liaising with the police. Williams was a police informer and if there was a reward going anywhere, he wanted it. Williams put Abdullahi in the frame, not as a suspect at first, but by June he would be making Abdullahi's behaviour look suspicious.

For example, he would claim that Abdullahi may have been able to leave the *Coral Sea* unnoticed; and that he had information about the murder, such as that Lynette's last meal had been chicken and chips. This implied that Abdullahi had either been with Lynette just before her death, or knew who was with her, or had observed her close to her death.

As a matter of fact this dietary information had already appeared in the pages of the *South Wales Echo*, but Williams was far from finished. He would insist that Abdullahi told him that he knew who murdered Lynette and that the photofit was a load of rubbish. He would even claim that Abdullahi pointed out one of Lynette's murderers to him in the North Star and then went and socialised with him – Steve Miller. This is unlikely, since Abdullahi didn't like Miller.

Williams would also claim that Abdullahi approached him to act as an intermediary with the police, claiming that he wanted to do a deal when the price was right. Williams was a strange choice as intermediary as it was common knowledge that Abdullahi and Williams detested each other. However, Williams' claims were similar to those to be made by DC Mike Cullen a few days later. Suffice to say, many Butetowners thought that Williams was motivated by his personal dislike of Abdullahi and his desire for a reward.

Then, on April 15th, Jane Sandrone gave a remarkable statement to South Wales Police. Sandrone, along with Noreen Amiel and her partner, was a co-licensee of the Dowlais pub on Bute Street. Like many others Sandrone had already helped complete a police house-to-house enquiry form. The completed form referred to a conversation she had overheard between Abdullahi and Noreen Amiel. It read, "[Mrs Sandrone] overheard conversation in Dowlais pub...stating that police were after him. He also showed scar on hand." It went on, "Mrs Sandrone *did not* hear conversation. Just third hand from Amiel." [my emphasis]

But the statement that South Wales Police took from her on April 15th was very different to her recollections in the house-to-house enquiry form. Now she was claiming that she had definitely overheard the conversation Abdullahi had with Noreen Amiel and, during this, he had confessed to the murder.

This was extraordinary. Mrs Sandrone was not the unreliable source that Ronnie Williams was. But publicans, like informants, also have obligations to the police.

Whatever the reason Jane Sandrone changed her statement, it didn't look good for Abdullahi. Nevertheless, he wasn't pulled in.

Enter Mr X

On April 14th, the day before Sandrone's new statement, the sex of the person who had left blood on Lynette's jeans had been determined as male. This strengthened the possibility, evident from the start, that the murderer was a punter. Police had already been taking statements from any who could be traced and these included a person who can only be named as Mr X.

He occurred as a major suspect to South Wales Police on April 20th, some two months into the inquiry, when DC Geoff Thomas of South Wales Criminal Investigation Bureau compiled a list of twelve suspects whom he considered to be worthy of serious investigation. And amongst the information Thomas had access to was Professor Bernard Knight's post mortem on Lynette which stated that the attack had sexual overtones to it. After all, she was a prostitute; it appeared as if she was about to do business; the killer may have left his semen in her; and her breasts had been mutilated.

Mr X was fifty years old at the time of Lynette's murder and had a long history of criminal activity. He was a convicted sex offender whose crimes included the rape of a six year-old girl as well as other offences of gross indecency. He had been sentenced to a total of ten years imprisonment for indecency offences and his way of relating to women and children was characterised by a lack of control. He lived with his mother, some twenty minute's drive from Butetown. He frequently visited Cardiff, had no alibi for the night in question and used prostitutes.

X had once worked at the Night Shelter in Crichton Street, Butetown, and was familiar with the area. He had only worked at the Shelter early in 1987 for about ten days and left when it was suggested that he wasn't cut out for the job. This wasn't unusual for X. He had left school at fifteen years old, was deemed to be of below average intelligence and was considered unsuitable for short term employment several times.

Mr X was described as a psychopath by his own doctor and he had spent time in mental institutions. His doctor felt that X ought to be locked up permanently and also observed that following a violent attack on him by a woman with a meat cleaver, he seemed to have withdrawn into his shell more. Nevertheless, he was still believed to be very dangerous and capable of snapping at any time.

The nature of that assault on X was very interesting. It had happened in May 1985 and was at the hands of Margaret Liptovari, who lived in the same block of flats as X. Some weeks previously Liptovari had made a complaint of indecent exposure against X. She alleged that X was completely naked in the common hallway between their flats and exposed himself to her before retreating into his flat, but she was more concerned for a group of seven girls aged between four and seven years old who were playing nearby. She said that the very large clear window on the landing meant that the children could easily have seen X as he stood close to it.

Liptovari claimed to be very shocked and upset by the incident. Originally she had intended to have a word with X's mother and not report it to the police, but after further consideration she felt that she ought to report it because young children tended to play nearby.

X said he had not meant to expose himself to her and was on the landing for only a few seconds, although he could not explain how he came to be there in that state in the first place.

But it was a case that would never come to court. In spite of X's previous history of sex offences and the possibility that he was up to his old tricks again, the police had no success with witnesses and appear not to have interviewed any of the group of younger girls. They told Liptovari that there was no evidence to support an allegation of indecent exposure. Consequently, that was the end of the matter.

This experience may well have prompted her to take the law into her own hands. A few weeks later, at a street party, she went for him in a sustained and violent attack.

She shouted out, "You fucking pervert!" and belaboured him about the head with a meat cleaver as he vainly tried to protect himself. X ended up with extensive injuries to his head and face and needed surgery to his hands because the tendons and sinews had been severed. He also had injuries to his back and buttocks. Several of these injuries, especially those to the face and hands, were strikingly similar to those that were to be inflicted on Lynette White.

Liptovari pleaded guilty to wounding with intent. But the court was told just how big a danger X was to children. In 1972 he had been sentenced to six years imprisonment for rape, buggery and indecent assault. In 1977 he drew one year for indecent assault and in 1981 he received three years for another indecent assault. It was adjudged that she had tried to kill him while temporarily homicidal. The judge told her that if it hadn't been for X's deviant activities she would have got four years imprisonment. Instead she was put on probation.

Now, the police investigating the Liptovari attack had collected several exhibits of objects allegedly stained with X's blood. The bloodstained exhibits were tested, but, in order to establish that it was X's blood, they needed a control sample. So they took a blood sample from X and gave it to officers from South Wales Police who conveyed it to the Home Office Forensic Science Laboratory in Chepstow. This is where most of the samples in the Lynette White Inquiry were set to be sent for grouping tests. A little detective work could now reveal what X's blood group was.

Given all this, it would appear quite natural for Mr X to appear on DC Thomas' suspect list on April 20th. One might even say that his was the kind of form which would stand out like a sore thumb. Yet, strangely, X was not immediately interviewed.

Atkins and Grommek

X was also linked to two other key protagonists whose names were Paul Atkins and Mark Grommek. Now X had homosexual tendencies, but the last homosexual affair he would admit to was while in prison in 1981. He may have tried to repress these tendencies, but he still associated with gay men. He had known Atkins for a good while and he knew Grommek by sight. Atkins was known to frequent 7 James Street. Mark Grommek occupied the flat above the one where Lynette was murdered. Like Atkins, he was gay and susceptible to police pressure: both were petty criminals who had been to prison before.

Days after X appeared on Thomas' suspect list, Paul Atkins was making claims which were incriminating Grommek. Atkins' prints had been found in the murder flat, but he had been eliminated as a suspect because there is no way of accurately dating fingerprints and he had visited the previous tenants, Clare and Julia Thomas, there before the murder, i.e. before Vilday acquired the tenancy.

He claimed to have learned of the murder on the morning of February 15th. He said that the night before he had been away babysitting for the Thomases at their new home. His story was corroborated by the two women. Clare Thomas, an occasional prostitute, had featured in the inquiry at an early stage. Along with her lover, Julia Thomas, she had lived in the murder flat, moving out in November 1987. She provided early verification that Paul Atkins claimed to have learned of the murder after the fact.

As the inquiry dragged on she began to make statements that helped the police more and more. She had told the police that Atkins was babysitting for Julia and her on the night of the murder. If true, this meant that Atkins couldn't have been at Grommek's flat. Eventually she was persuaded to say that she found out that while babysitting for them Atkins used to go out. This left Atkins vulnerable.

And on April 26th Atkins signed a statement, first claiming that Grommek was Lynette's murderer and then breaking down tearfully and confessing that he had done it himself. In fact, his statement contained four completely different accounts in the one document.

A second photofit was compiled in April resulting from statements given to police by a taxi driver, Glyn Sterling, who had taken a punter accompanying Lynette White back to 7 James Street on the night of the murder. There was no evidence to confirm when this man might have left the flat, or whether he could gain access later. This photofit was more significant than the one previously released, but unaccountably, the police chose not to release it to the media and the man was never traced.

Coincidences

The months were passing by and the inquiry was dragging on. Within the prostitute community, the longer the case plodded on, the greater the pressure on them became. This was especially true of Learnne Vilday. She was a streetwalker, a single parent and a lesbian who used addictive and/or illicit drugs. She was vulnerable to pressure. And she had been the one to discover an exceptionally nasty murder in circumstances which were not all explicable.

Until the murder Vilday had lived with Angela Psaila. They were supposed to be good friends, although they parted company because of it. Within a week of Lynette's death Vilday had moved out. Psaila was fed up of the ceaseless police presence and threw Vilday and her baby, Craig, out, hoping to get some peace.

Through her lover, Debbie Paul, Vilday and her child found accommodation with a couple named Brian Spriggs and Maria Kehone. This transferred the police presence to their home instead of Psaila's. According to them, it was rare for a day to pass without some police officer coming round looking for Vilday. Spriggs and Kehone felt that they were being treated like scum in their own home and that the police felt that they could do as they pleased there.

On one occasion police ignored the privacy of the couple's bedroom and entered it demanding to know where Vilday was, because they didn't like being told that she wasn't in and wanted to see for themselves. Spriggs and Kehone threw them out. This gives some indication of the kind of attention that Vilday was getting from the police.

Her fellow prostitutes also believed that Vilday knew more than she was prepared to admit to. It left her very isolated, but did she know any more than she let on? Why had she taken a cab there? Why had she earlier told Ronnie Actie in the North Star that Lynette could have been murdered? Her movements and behaviour on the night of the crime may well have been innocent, but they were vague.

Apart from Vilday's laudable concern for her friend, the only other person to be so concerned by Lynette's disappearance was Steve Miller. He had tried very hard to find her and even harder to find her killer. But Miller was growing tired of it all and moved back to London. Vilday resented this. He had given her some hassle over the murder. She felt that he should have stayed around and had some of the hassle that the police were giving her.

After a few months of this sort of pressure, on May 19th, in the presence of a number of fellow prostitutes, she blurted out the names of the alleged killers in a drunken stupor. She claimed that "Dullah" and "Pineapple-Head" had done it. Some of the girls she was with agreed that it made sense. Now Vilday disliked Miller. But there was no obvious reason why she should also name Abdullahi.

The purpose of the house-to-house enquiry form that so many locals helped police complete in the murder's immediate aftermath was simply to establish if the person could assist police in their enquiries. It had been clear from Abdullahi's replies, limited though they might have been, that he was working away from Cardiff on the night of the murder. All he could do was assist the police in eliminating anyone whom he knew was on the *Coral Sea* that night. He had also helped them by viewing for identification purposes possible white suspects being brought into Butetown Police Station.

However, on May 19th, DI Powell questioned him again and took a statement from him. In this Abdullahi firmed up and elaborated on his house-to-house account and said that he had started working on the *Coral Sea* on February 9th and continued until February 15th.

Oddly, it was on this same day in May that Learnne Vilday made her vociferous accusation against Abdullahi. Sergeant David Hathaway interviewed Vilday late that same evening. He said that she readily admitted naming Abdullahi and Miller as Lynette's murderers while drunk. But Vilday told Hathaway that her allegations had not been true and that it was just drunken rambling and that she was upset that her lover had just left her to live with one of her former lovers. Vilday told Hathaway that she had been speaking to DI Powell earlier in the day and he had mentioned Abdullahi and Miller. In the evening she then drank herself into a state and just spouted off false accusations.

DI Powell's next step was to encourage her to be hypnotised. He told her he thought she may have the key to the murder locked away in her unconscious.

Vilday said why not, she had nothing to hide and it would get the police off her back at last. A session with a hypnotherapist was arranged for June 15th.

Professor Cracker

On May 26th South Wales Police received the report they had commissioned early on in the inquiry from Professor David Canter, who was the pioneer of psychological profiling in Britain, a technique shortly to be made famous by the TV series *Cracker*. Canter's work had, for example, enabled the police to focus their attention on investigating John Duffy in the inquiry into the Railway rapes and murders. Duffy was subsequently convicted of those crimes, but prior to Canter's intervention the police were unable to bring a case to court. Canter's work has been used in several cases. He is the leading authority in the field and several police forces have used his skills.

His technique of psychological profiling was in its infancy and was never capable of amounting to direct evidence against anyone. The purpose of the profile was to enable the police to concentrate their resources in investigating particular suspects. The technique would identify likely character traits of Lynette White's killer. Professor Canter's psychological profile of the likely characteristics of Lynette's murderer was most illuminating.

He analyzed the scene of crime reports in order to develop a hypothesis of what happened and to try to develop ideas relating to the likely motive for the murder and the characteristics of the murderer. He also hoped to identify any possible relationship between Lynette and her killer. He also intended to suggest other lines of inquiry.

Canter had looked for material relating to behavioural and psychological characteristics. He recognised the importance of both the forensic evidence and the pathologist's report, similar crimes, details of the scene of the crime, the context of the crime and a psychological post mortem of Lynette.

Professor Canter suggested that it would be worth trying to establish the frequency of the use of the flat for prostitution, or other purposes, as it would help to establish the likelihood of anyone witnessing the murder. He also mentioned the possibility of hearing screams, or a struggle in progress. He suggested that if the probability was high that someone would have witnessed the attack, then the police ought to consider whether information was being withheld. He felt that if the probability was low, it would be worth considering if Lynette was trying to avoid someone.

Canter felt that the use of the premises for prostitution and the unused condom being on the bed suggested an encounter with a client. But he thought that the curtains being open and the fact that she was still fully clothed apart from a shoe and her jacket being only half on pointed away from a punter. He concluded that Vilday may have been able to shed further light on the questions of the condom and the curtains. Vilday later acknowledged that the curtains being open or closed was a signal for whether Lynette was entertaining a customer.

Canter felt that the clothes didn't suggest that Lynette had been interfered with sexually. He felt that a right handed person may have tried to put the jacket on to Lynette and after getting the left sleeve on her, tried to roll her over in order to get the right sleeve on, but abandoned the attempt. It was also consistent with the jacket being partially on her and rolled in it to give access to her head and hands. He suggested that forensic evidence could resolve that question.

The report then turned to the nature of the relationship between Lynette and her killer. Canter felt that it was probable that Lynette went to the flat with a client. He believed that the attacker was a person who was quick to sudden violent attacks and that he was likely to be a person who would be known to the police, either because of his sudden violence, or lack of control. He also felt that the person was familiar with the area, either from using prostitutes, or because he knew Lynette's habits.

Professor Canter thought that the aspermic semen was important. Even though it may not have belonged to the killer it would eventually be possible to obtain a good quality DNA profile using the state of the art technique of Short Tandem Repeats (STR) if the original samples have been stored adequately. This could resolve the issue once and for all.

Canter pointed out that John Duffy had a low sperm count and felt that it contributed to Duffy's motivation to commit such crimes to defend his masculinity. He also felt that people like that tend to do a lot of fitness training, or some kind of martial arts to compensate for feelings of inadequacy. He also suggested some aspects of the crime pointed to the killer being on drugs.

Professor Canter believed that the position of the body and the position of blood in the room suggested that Lynette was attacked while beginning to undress. This indicated that her murderer was a punter. He considered that the wounds, especially to her face, suggested a very sudden attack. He thought that attacking the face and breasts suggested that the attack was not planned. He emphasised that the attack was consistent with an angry attack on an individual who is known to arouse feelings of anger in the assailant, or represents something that angers him and makes him lose control.

Canter's opinion was that Lynette's murder was consistent with a disorganised and unplanned attack. He felt that it was the type of attack most likely to have been committed by someone of little mental ability with a history of impulsive behaviour and inability to cope with social relationships. He thought that the attacker was likely to have an unskilled and intermittent job history. He also felt that the attack was consistent with an alcohol or drug induced state.

The report pointed out that the killer's attempt to remove Lynette's head and hands suggested an attempt to prevent her being identified. Canter thought that this attempt was bizarre given the circumstances of the crime and the fact that the killer abandoned the attempt. He felt that it suggested a killer who was mentally disturbed and bursts out into uncontrollable rages.

The fact that the killer had a knife available and attempted to hide Lynette's identity suggested a person with a criminal history of violent attacks. However, it was also pointed out that the failure to complete the attempt was consistent with remorse. It was likely that Lynette White's attacker was known to her and that they had a particular relationship with each other.

Canter proposed a possible scenario. He suggested that her attacker had been one of Lynette's clients in the past who was angry at her earlier absence and, on reaching the flat, was overcome by a violent rage and attacked her as she began to undress. She tried to fight back and some blood went on to her attacker. He tried to obliterate her identity, thereby hiding his connection with her, but aborted the attempt in remorse and ran away.

Canter felt that such a person was likely to have had a severe mental disturbance that would have resulted in hospitalisation or imprisonment. He thought that the person was likely not to be socially trusted and probably came from a broken home with a history of violence in it. Canter thought that the attacker was likely to have been in his early twenties, but he accepted that the age was the thing he was most likely to be wrong about. He felt that the attacker was likely to have had a base near the scene of the crime.

He also suspected that the attacker was of the type likely to confess to the murder if asked about it firmly. He suggested that the killer may have already confessed to somebody, but he also acknowledged that due to the unsocial character of the attacker, it was possible that he didn't have enough contact with others to confess to anyone.

Professor Canter acknowledged that his profile could be affected if Lynette's murder was linked to any other similar crimes. And he stated that the existence of any highly controlling client who displayed aggressive tendencies could affect the results. He also suggested that Lynette's scheduled court appearances could put the murder in a completely different light.

The report identified several lines of inquiry. Some of them were very interesting to South Wales Police. His comments about possible screams and witnesses withholding information appealed to them immensely. His identification of Vilday's importance and the need to establish Lynette's usual routine concerning the flat were all very interesting. Some of his report justified their own beliefs about Vilday. And the report's relevance to Mr X was only too clear.

The day after Canter's report was received two more strange things happened. First, Jane Sandrone's co-licensee, Noreen Amiel, made a statement to DC Jock Mitchell referring to that conversation with Abdullahi in February when he had come into the Dowlais with a bandage on his hand. This was perfectly true, but there was evidence that the bandage was due to a burn and not any kind of cut. Amiel's statement appeared to back up what Sandrone had said in April, i.e. that Abdullahi had indeed confessed the murder to her. But there was one significant difference: once she had made her statement, Amiel did not sign it.

That same day there was a police Management Meeting to consider the progress of the Lynette White Inquiry. At this meeting South Wales Police took the decision to regard Yusef Abdullahi and Steve Miller as possibly having been involved in the murder.

Long Hot Summer

The following month saw a hive of activity as this line of enquiry decided upon at the Management Meeting was pursued. However, at each step it was confounded.

On June 3rd Vilday gave police another statement. She said she was getting nervous about her forthcoming hypnotherapy session. And she retracted her claims of a fortnight before and specifically exonerated Abdullahi and Miller, saying that she had damned Miller out of resentment that he'd gone back to London and escaped the hassle that she was getting.

The police talked to Abdullahi again on the 7th. Again he insisted he was definitely working on the *Coral Sea* on the night of the crime and had returned to Cardiff the following day.

The next day they talked to Debbie Actie about her movements on the murder night. She told them she'd seen Steve Miller playing pool in the Casablanca around 2.00 a.m. on the night of the murder. Robyn Reed was later to support this: around the same time, Debbie Actie had pointed Miller out to her as he carried drinks to the pool room at the back of the club. These women had just arrived and would naturally be checking the place out, seeing who was around and who wasn't.

Miller had sold the remains of his car to Jackie Harris and left Cardiff permanently. Shortly after his departure, unbeknown to him, South Wales Police had decided to view him as possibly involved in the murder. Before leaving Cardiff, he called in at the police station and gave them a forwarding address and a phone number. Until his return to London Miller had kept in constant contact with South Wales Police. He had pumped everyone he knew for information, even telling some of them that he had to find something to take to the police.

The police appeared to be flogging a dead horse at this point. Against Abdullahi and Miller there was no strong witness evidence and no forensic evidence. And the more they pursued the pair, the stronger their alibis seemed to grow. However, DC Cullen referred to a conversation that he had with Abdullahi back in February. Cullen claimed that Abdullahi had told him that the photofit was leading the police in the wrong direction and had responded to Cullen's appeal for information by demanding payment for it. Cullen had made no contemporaneous note of this the "It'll cost you!" conversation. It wasn't convincing.

Two days after this, Vilday, accompanied by Debbie Paul and DI Powell, went to see Dr Una Maguire, a hypnotherapist of over thirty years experience and an expert who had worked in a similar capacity for another police force for several years. The purpose of the hypnosis was simple. It was to aid Vilday's memory and to dredge up the events in question from whatever recesses they might be lost in. Vilday would be questioned whilst in a trance.

Maguire soon established that Vilday was a suitable subject and at first induced a light state of hypnosis. It got deeper as the interview progressed. She was taken back through the week of the murder, right up to the murder night itself.

The last time that she remembered actually seeing Lynette was early in the week of her disappearance. She allowed Lynette to use her flat for entertaining customers. If the curtains were drawn, it meant that Lynette was with a client, but, if they were open, then Lynette wasn't in. During the last five days of Lynette's life, Vilday had never seen the curtains drawn. In fact, she remembered nothing about the murder at all.

There was no denying it: from South Wales Police's point of view the experiment was a failure.

Maguire was convinced that Vilday had told her the whole truth during the hypnosis interview. She told Powell, "She hasn't given you any more information because she hasn't got any more."

The videotape of the hypnosis interview also shows Ms Paul, DI Powell, Dr Maguire and Vilday all agreeing that they didn't think that 'the pimp' (i.e. Steve Miller) had committed the crime.

The line of inquiry suggested at the May 27th meeting appeared to be leading nowhere. But it was not abandoned. Spring turned to summer. As well as seeking further information as to the whereabouts on the murder night of Miller and Abdullahi, police were now showing an interest in Ronnie Actie and were gathering statements about his movements.

At this time there was, however, another white man who one would imagine to be of interest to them. Suffice to say, this man, who shall be referred to as Mr Y, had a blood group which established him as a man who had to be eliminated. It was effectively a perfect match to the blood factors discovered on Lynette's sock.[1] That blood group occurs in approximately one in three thousand eight hundred people. That means that there are about sixteen thousand people in Britain who had the blood group that they were looking for. Obviously not all of them murdered Lynette, but any person having that group had to be eliminated by police. This was why Mr Y's blood sample was taken to the Home Office Forensic Science Laboratory in Birmingham for DNA testing. Police now knew that they had a man who had to be looked into because of his blood group. They would later insist that Y was never a suspect and that he was not a villain.

Nevertheless, his blood group established him as a man who had to be safely eliminated. The significance of his blood group could not have been missed. On August 5th 1988 Dr John Whiteside, the Chief Scientific Officer at the Home

[1] Throughout the book I have termed what are actually blood groups as blood factors for convenience. This has enabled me to refer to a combination of blood factors as a blood group rather than use the more cumbersome combination of blood groups every time: the author.

Office Forensic Science Laboratory in Chepstow where the blood grouping tests had been carried out, conveyed Y's sample together with other important samples to Birmingham for DNA testing.

Forensics

The DNA – Deoxyribonucleic Acid – Double Helix was discovered in 1953 by the Cambridge based scientists James Watson and Francis Crick. It was undoubtedly one of the most important scientific discoveries of the century. But its potential for identifying criminals was not developed to the point where it could be used as evidence until the early 1980s. The pioneer of DNA in the fight against crime was the Leicester based scientist Professor Alec Jeffreys who developed the testing system using multi-locus probes and was later knighted. DNA carries the genetic code that determines an individual's characteristics. In order to fully understand the limitations of DNA testing, a brief explanation of the procedures may prove useful.[1]

All human cells, including those in blood and in semen, contain DNA and in any one individual the DNA code is identical for every cell. The process of DNA profiling starts with DNA being extracted from the crime stain and also from a sample taken from the suspect. In each case the DNA is cut into smaller lengths by specific enzymes. The fragments produced are sorted according to size by a process of electrophoresis. This involves placing the fragments in a gel and drawing them electromagnetically along a track through the gel. The fragments with smaller molecular weight travel further than the heavier ones. The pattern thus created is transferred from the gel on to a membrane. Radioactive DNA probes, taken from elsewhere, which bind with the sequences of most interest in the sample DNA are then applied. After the excess of the DNA probe is washed off, an X-ray film is placed over the membrane to record the band pattern. This produces an autoradiograph which can be photographed. When the crime stain DNA and DNA from the suspect have been run in separate tracks through the gel, the resultant autoradiographs can be compared. The two DNA profiles can then be said either to match or not.

Even if a number of bands correspond exactly, any discrepancy between the profiles, unless satisfactorily explained, will show a mismatch and will exclude the suspect from complicity. Thus, the first stage in seeking to prove identity by DNA profiling is to achieve a match.

However, unlike fingerprinting, a DNA profiling match is not unique. The second stage is therefore the statistical evaluation of the match. This depends upon the number of bands which match and the frequency in the relevant population of such band matching.

Scientists rely not just on visual comparison but also on measurements. The

---

[1] The following is extracted from a judgement delivered by the Lord Chief Justice, Lord Taylor of Gosforth who would retire due to ill health in 1996.

measurements are assisted by using blobs of DNA of known length as markers. They are placed in tracks at both edges of the gel and in its centre. Control tracks are also run to ensure that the gel's consistency is uniform throughout it. The control tracks will use the DNA from a known profile, usually an officer of the laboratory. These procedures were devised to minimise the possibility of a handling error.

Because any scientific analysis or measurement will produce some variation even between samples from an identical source, allowance has to be made for some acceptable range of deviation in assessing whether there is a match. In one case the variation accepted by the Crown's expert was plus or minus one millimetre. The allowance of error such as this can lead to a match being declared when the suspect may be entitled to expect to be eliminated, especially in borderline cases.

DNA profiling can be carried out on a variety of body fluids and tissues including blood, semen and hair roots. Profiles can be obtained from samples left at the scene of a crime and also from persons associated with the crime. If a suspect's profile is *different* from that of the crime sample, then that suspect *cannot* be the source of the crime sample. If a suspect's profile is the same as that of the crime sample, then the crime sample was left by *either* the suspect *or* another unknown person, who, by chance, has the same profile as the suspect. To assess the evidential value of a match it is usual practice to estimate the probability that an unknown person, unrelated to the suspect, would share the same profile. This figure will be of the order of one in several thousands, but may vary considerably from case to case and is given for each specific case when reported in the case statement. The point is that DNA profiling can only hope to *eliminate* a suspect with any degree of certainty; in the case of a match it can only deal in probability.

This degree of certainty is crucial. In February 1988 DNA testing was in its infancy, as it was through much of 1988. Multi-locus probes were commonly used rather than the single-locus probes which would later be favoured for greater sensitivity. Neither was PCR based STR analysis in use - this technique can be more successful in dealing with small samples or degraded material.

Forensic analysis takes time. Police had to decide which was of more immediate use to them, fingerprints or DNA profiles. They decided that fingerprints should take priority. The forensic scientists had to wait until the fingerprint tests were done before they could obtain the samples for further tests. Nevertheless, there was to be cause for concern over the quality of the material belatedly submitted for forensic analysis. There would also be serious concerns about what happened to the samples in between testing for fingerprints and DNA profiling. These concerns would come to be of the utmost significance in the case of Lynette White and the Cardiff Three.

Although several blood samples from the scene of the crime at 7 James Street were subjected to a variety of tests, only nine of these were crucial to the Lynette White Inquiry. They were given reference numbers after whoever found them. The crucial samples were SS2, SS5, SS6, SS12, RH26, RH27, JAW12, JAW14 and JAW27. SS2 was a wallpaper sample which was removed from the chimney breast in the living room on February 18th. It was taken to the Fingerprint Department at the Western Criminal Records Office in Cardiff. Five days later wallpaper sample SS12 was removed from beneath the window near where the body was found and also taken to the WCRO.

RH26 was discovered on March 10th. It was a wallpaper sample that was taken from behind two curtains on the left hand window, which had been drawn. It was very near to SS12. On March 16th a bloodstain was obtained from it. The bloodstain was RH27. During his evidence at the first trial Dr Whiteside would reveal that SS5 and SS6 which were retrieved from the hall outside the murder room were grouped as AK1 which were present in 93% of the population, but could not have belonged to Lynette. Police officers discovered these six samples.

The other relevant samples were discovered by Dr Whiteside. He visited the scene of the crime on February 14th and 15th. This was when he took possession of JAW12, which was a bloodstain from the sock that Lynette wore on her right foot. JAW14 came from the bottom of Lynette's jeans. JAW27 was a blood sample taken from the skirting board under the window where SS12 came from. It was taken by Whiteside on February 24th.

SS2, SS5, SS6, SS12 and RH26 were examined for fingerprints first. They were treated with the chemical Ninhydrin in order to bring out latent prints. JAW27 was grouped as PGM 1+1-; AK 1. This group occurs in about 17% of the population. Significantly, these blood factors were different from the victim's. According to Whiteside, RH27 was submitted for analysis on March 27th. It was grouped as PGM 1+1-, which occurs in about 18% of the population. Again, it could not have come from Lynette White. Her blood group was O; PGM 1+; EAP BA/CA; Hp 2-1; Gc 2-1s; AK 2-1.

The most important samples grouped were JAW12 and JAW14. They were the samples from the sock and the jeans respectively. JAW12 was grouped as AB; PGM 1+1-; EAP B/CB; HP 2; Gc 2-1s; AK 1. It only occurred in about one in three thousand eight hundred people. Needless to say, it was substantially different from Lynette's blood group. The JAW14 sample was grouped as AB; PGM 1+1-; EAP B/CB; Gc 2-1s; AK 1. JAW12, like JAW14, was substantially different from Lynette's blood group. It was so small that almost the entire sample was used up in trying to establish its group, which was even rarer than the sample from the jeans. Consequently, JAW12 contained insufficient DNA for DNA profiling to be carried out. This also meant that the gender of the donor could not be determined.

JAW27 was not subjected to a DNA test. And neither – yet – was JAW14, the sample from the jeans. However, on April 14th Dr Peter Gill reported to Whiteside that all five areas of JAW14 that he had tested reacted to the presence of the male Y-chromosome. "All stains typed were demonstrated to be male in origin," wrote Gill. He was satisfied that the person who shed the blood on the jeans was a man. So conventional blood grouping tests had revealed that the killer possessed a very rare blood group which was found on the bottom of Lynette's jeans and in a tiny drop of blood on the sock she wore on her right foot. It cannot be said with certainty that the blood on the sock came from the same source as the blood on the jeans, although it is most likely. Which brings us back to August 5th and Mr Y.

Although he was not considered to be as important a suspect as Mr X, Mr Y's blood group was even more astonishing than that of X. It was AB; Le a-b+; PGM 1+1-; EAP B/CB; Hp 2; Gc 2-1s; AK 1. Y possessed all six factors that were found on the sock, but he also had a seventh, although that factor would not have been detected in bloodstaining in any case.

Mr Y was twenty-four years old and lived in Maerdy in the Rhondda Valley, a fair distance from Butetown, at the time of the murder. Y made his only statement to the police on July 29th. DC Allan Barker took that statement. He gave a sample of his blood for elimination purposes. Police would later say that he had not occurred to them at all until the Chepstow laboratory brought him to their attention on account of his blood group which established him as a man to be traced, interviewed and eliminated.

But the police were not the only people aware of Mr Y's blood group. Dr Whiteside personally conveyed Y's blood sample to Birmingham for DNA testing on August 5th. He was unlikely to have done this unless he had been aware of Y's blood group and realised its significance.

After all, conveying samples from one laboratory to another was a mundane task, usually conducted by the police. It was not a task that would normally be conducted by the Chief Scientific Officer at the Chepstow laboratory. And then there was Mr X.

Back to Mr X

August passed. Life on the streets of Butetown was made no less anxious by the fact that a psychotic killer was still on the loose. Jackie Harris had just given birth to her third child and Abdullahi grew more convinced that it was by Geoff Smith. The pair split up acrimoniously and Harris went to live in a women's refuge at Pontypridd on the outskirts of Cardiff. The police waited for the results of DNA testing on Y's blood sample.

Meanwhile, on September 14th, they finally went back to Mr X. On that day X voluntarily attended Whitchurch Police Station, where he was interviewed by DCs Graham Toogood and Paul Fish.

He told them that he had been unemployed for at least twenty years. He had sought help from the Samaritans over a number of problems including his employment prospects. He had been a voluntary worker at the Night Shelter in Crichton Street, which was close to the beat worked by several prostitutes. He claimed that he used one of them soon afterwards. He admitted that the first one he used was Lynette White.

He claimed that he paid for full sex with the next one, but was only masturbated. In other words, he was admitting to having been, as he saw it, ripped off by a whore. He claimed that this second girl was the last one he used. He had a gripe against prostitutes. He was then asked to account for his movements on the weekend of the murder. He said he could not remember and offered no alibi.

Toogood and Fish had deliberately adopted a softly-softly approach to their suspect. They felt that they didn't have enough evidence to charge X. They didn't want to upset him. They wanted his prints and his blood.

Both officers thought that X was ready to confess to the murder if asked forcefully enough, but that this was not the time to pressurise him. So, the way they treated X was a model of restraint and although the statement they finally took produced no confession - indeed he wasn't asked directly if he was the murderer, the interview did reap a certain reward. X looked more than ever like their man - even his solicitor believed he was on the verge of confessing - and what's more X had now consented to provide the police with a sample of his blood and fingerprints for elimination purposes.

And so the Lynette White Inquiry was now waiting on forensic results from two people, one of whom was undoubtedly a prime suspect. It is nevertheless unfortunate that samples and details of Mr X's blood - those taken during the Liptovari case - were already on file and had been for three years, still unbeknown, it seems, to those investigating the murder at 7 James Street. So too of course, since he had criminal convictions, were X's fingerprints.

The forensic investigations were also slowed down on another front by the fact that it was only now in early September, some six months since they had been first obtained and sent for fingerprinting, that four wallpaper samples taken by DS Stephen Steele and DI Reginald Hearse (SS2, SS6, SS12 and RH26) were sent to Birmingham to be DNA tested by Dr Nicholas Prance. This was an inexplicable delay.

Prance had made the first statement in reference to his work on September 27th, when he noted that attempts to prepare DNA profiles from the jeans had been unsuccessful. Prance thought that this failure was presumably due to insufficient DNA, or that the DNA had degraded over time. Dr Prance used multi-locus probes (MLP) DNA profiling, then widely used, rather than the far more sensitive single-locus probes (SLP) which have now come into favour.

On October 18th he made his second statement. He had not been able to obtain a profile from RH26. It had not been grouped. This ended RH26's relevance. But RH27 was obtained from it and had been grouped. He also failed to obtain a DNA profile from SS6 which blood grouping tests established could not have originated from Lynette. The failure to obtain a DNA profile ended the relevance of SS6 to this inquiry - at least for the moment. And as for SS5, it did not arrive at the Birmingham laboratory until December 1st and no profile could be obtained from it. As with SS6, a blood grouping test proved that it could not have been deposited in the flat by Lynette. So the failure to obtain a DNA profile from SS5 ended its relevance to this inquiry for the time being.

Dr Prance obtained limited profiles from SS2 and SS12. There were just four bands on each profile. They were fuzzy, but they would eventually prove to be the most important samples in the Lynette White Inquiry. Prance believed that the Ninhydrin used to treat the samples for fingerprinting may have interfered with the results. He stated, "The limited nature of the DNA profiles obtained from the bloodstain on the wallpaper will limit the ability of the technique to identify uniquely the individuals from whom they originated." Prance also thought that the samples where no results were obtained could have been due to insufficient or degraded DNA.

However, Prance was confident enough to state that because Mr Y's DNA profile did not match the limited profiles obtained from wallpaper samples SS2 and SS12, Mr Y must therefore be eliminated from the inquiry. And so he was.

Again, there was a sudden flurry of significant moves. The very next day, as part of a trawl of the docks organized by DC Mitchell, police lighted on Violet Perriam, who worked as a receptionist at Butetown Health Centre. She also worked nights as a stewardess at a Cardiff yacht club.

Now, this search for people who may have been driving past 7 James Street at the time of the murder was belated to say the least and it was surprising that Perriam was not approached by the police far earlier, as it was known that she drove through the area around the relevant time. Perriam was also known to DI Page, who frequented the yacht club where she worked. Page was one of the senior officers involved in the case and had been handling the informant and private-eye fantasist Ronnie Williams, Abdullahi's inimical acquaintance.

On October 19th Perriam talked to DC Jock Mitchell. She made no formal statement, but she said that as she had driven slowly along James Street that night – she had to stop at traffic lights and her daughters were asleep in the car – she had seen four black people congregating outside number 7. But for the moment she wouldn't name them. DC Mitchell completed an action sheet the following day and forwarded it to the Incident Room. He reminded them that Detective Superintendent Davies felt that the message that Perriam thought one of the men she saw was an associate of John Actie and another was an associate of Peggy Farrugia was very important. Remember that Farrugia was Francine Cordle's mother and Lynette had been due to give evidence against Cordle regarding the assault on Tina Garton.

And it was also on the 19th that DI Graham Mouncher organised an 'elementary surveillance probe' on Mr X. This was designed to identify X's associates, the places he went and what he did. X was kept under observation for three days.

Mouncher felt sure that if X was to realise that he was under surveillance he would commit himself to a mental hospital to evade capture. He felt it important to try to establish X's habits on weekends and to try to link him to Atkins and Grommek, or their associates. On October 25th he wrote to Detective Superintendent Davies, pointing out the many ways in which X matched the Canter psychological profile; emphasising that X's rare blood group was strikingly similar to that of Lynette White's murderer; and requesting permission to mount further surveillance. He wanted ten men on the job. Mouncher was all but convinced that they had got their man.

His request was immediately granted and X was watched from October 27-30th. DCI Adrian Morgan wrote to DCS Williams on November 7th. He told Williams that X had emerged as the prime suspect and gave details of the interviews, the surveillance, the forensic evidence and the close match to the Canter psychological profile. It seemed now that X was all but under arrest. Then, two days later, came a bombshell from Birmingham. Dr Prance reported that X's DNA profile did not match the various profiles obtained from the murder room samples. X, like Y, was eliminated on the wallpaper samples alone. This, despite the similarity of their blood groups to the jeans and sock samples, neither of which were able to yield DNA profiles. So, despite a meagre supply of sampling material, the possibility of its degradation and other inexactitudes of the DNA profiling technique, as well as strong circumstantial evidence against X, the police now felt obliged, as they had done with Y, to eliminate Mr X as a suspect. They were quite right to do so.

The Switch

This was clearly a frustrating turn of events. But the inquiry was by no means stalled. If anything, it stepped up a gear. The next day, November 10th, police talked to Violet Perriam again and this time she made a statement to DC John Seaford.

It seemed that she was the answer to their prayers. She had already claimed to have seen four black people congregating outside 7 James Street on the night of the murder. Now she claimed that she could identify two of them, but refused to because she was frightened. DC Seaford had more work to do.

It was now that Yusef Abdullahi began to see a lot more of Learnne Vilday, especially in the North Star. She didn't seem to be spending any time on the streets these days. She never seemed to be short of money and always had new crispy ten pound notes. Others too noticed that Vilday had begun to hang around Abdullahi and some suspected the two were having an affair. But Abdullahi wasn't paying much attention to any of this. Nevertheless, Vilday was saying that she had been told to stick to him.

On November 16th, a month after her original interview with DC Mitchell, Violet Perriam now felt confident enough to name two of those she claimed to have seen outside 7 James Street on the night of the murder. They were John

Actie and Rashid Omar, a mixed race local man. She made a statement to this effect to DC Seaford.

Events now began to pile up on each other. Angela Psaila lived in a block of flats, 19 St Clare's Court, which is down a side road that leads off James Street opposite number 7. Her flat was some seventy feet down this lane. 7 James Street can be seen from her flat at St Clare's Court.

Police had been regularly interviewing Psaila since the beginning of the inquiry. She originally claimed to have stayed at home looking after Vilday's baby on the night of the murder. As late as May she was insisting that she first learned of the crime from Vilday when the body was discovered. But neither she nor Vilday had ever been able to account for their movements on that night in a convincing fashion. This may have made them more vulnerable to pressure.

Without Perriam's statements South Wales Police could not have applied the pressure that they were able to on Psaila on November 17th, the day after Perriam named two of the four men she claimed to have seen on the night of the murder. Perriam's claims led to Psaila being visited by police again. They insisted that Psaila must be connected with the crime. Psaila put herself first when it became obvious that police refused to accept her claims that she knew nothing of the murder. Now the police's persistence was beginning to bear fruit.

Psaila was interviewed twice that day. These interviews were conducted by DC Mike Daniels and DC John Gillard and were recorded by contemporaneous note. She was asked about John Actie and Steve Miller. She said that at about 1.00 a.m. on the night of the murder Miller had come to her home and threatened her because he thought Lynette was there. At first, she denied suggestions that she may have seen John Actie or Ronnie Actie outside 7 James Street and said nothing seriously incriminating.

But the timings of the interviews appear wildly wrong. The first interview is recorded as lasting almost three hours. It can be read in ten minutes. Even allowing for time to think and the speed that her answers were written down, the interview seems to have lasted far longer than appears necessary from the transcript of that interview. If this is true, what was actually happening during this time? After a delay of two and a half hours, the second interview began. It lasted an hour and three quarters. For the same reasons as the earlier interview it seems too long.

This second interview begins with the police mentioning that a detective inspector has reassured her of something during the interval. And it is now that Psaila makes incriminating claims. She says she saw John Actie and Steve Miller outside the flats before they walked off to James Street. She saw Steve Miller, John and Ronnie Actie, Abdullahi and Tony Brace, a bouncer at the North Star, outside 7 James Street around midnight. Psaila said she knew Lynette was there and Lynette had told her she was hiding out from Miller. She claimed she heard screams from the James Street flat and saw just John Actie and Steve Miller at the street door. Later, after John Actie and Miller had left by cab around 3.00 or 4.00 a.m., Psaila said she saw Ronnie Actie return, shout up to Grommek's flat and be let in by a man. The next morning, she said, Miller had threatened her with a knife. When asked if she had seen anyone else with Steve Miller and the Acties, she claimed Tony Paris was there too, milling around selling cannabis.

Psaila was to amplify all these claims on November 22nd and December 6th. At this stage her evidence was of limited value. It was circumstantial at best. Yet DC John Gillard had behaved in a most unusual fashion in relation to her. He had used money from police funds to pay an outstanding fine for soliciting for Psaila. Gillard would later claim that he only lent her the money, although it is unclear if she ever repaid it. But it ought to be remembered that if Gillard had not paid it Psaila would have been imprisoned for non-payment.

Mark Grommek had become resident disc jockey at the North Star that October. Grommek's initial response had been to deny that he was at home on the night in question, but he was later placed by an eyewitness at the front door of 7 James Street in the early hours of Valentine's Day, about four hours after the most likely time of the murder. Initially, Grommek had tried to put himself as far from James Street as possible. There is nothing too surprising in that, but it does raise the question of why he lied. He tried to explain away his inability to remember that he was at home by pointing to the effects of medication he had been taking for depression.

Psaila was now saying she heard screams from her distant flat, but nobody in the actual building where Lynette died claimed to have heard any screams until November 22nd, when Mark Grommek and Paul Atkins said that they had heard them. Grommek had previously repeatedly insisted that he had heard no screams on the night of the murder. He changed his mind after sound tests were carried out in his flat which showed that any screams could have been heard.

Grommek and Atkins claimed to have seen four men outside 7 James Street on the night of the murder. Grommek said that he eventually went down and opened the door to Ronnie Actie. He quickly returned to his flat, fearing that they would beat him up because of his sexuality.

He placed Yusef Abdullahi, Ronnie Actie, Martin Tucker, (a local white man and heroin user), and an unnamed black man with shoulder length dreadlocks at the scene of the crime. He was more or less supported by Atkins. Three of the four crucial witnesses were now making broadly similar statements, give or take a name or two. And on November 22nd these three key witnesses had all been apparently overcome by their consciences at different times on the same day.

The inquiry had changed gear effortlessly. It had switched from a search for a single white man who fitted the psychological profile and some of the forensic evidence and who had relevant form to a group of black people, most with alibis, none with any forensic evidence or similar convictions against them and none coming anywhere near fitting Canter's profile. The police made this switch from one white man to a few black men literally overnight, from X's elimination on November 9th to DC Seaford taking a statement from Violet Perriam the very next day. And the inquiry was continuing apace.

CHAPTER 3

The Arrests

Countdown To A Travesty

On December 2nd Angela Psaila had the misfortune to be raped by a punter. Four days later she was persuaded to give a blood sample to try to establish forensic evidence against the rapist. Following this, she joined Vilday at Spriggs and Kehone's home.

The day she gave her blood sample she also gave a crucial statement to the Lynette White Inquiry. Now Psaila was saying that Learnne Vilday was involved: Vilday had been with her at St Clare's Court, her story went, and when the two women heard screams from 7 James Street, Vilday had gone there to investigate. Psaila's contradictory accounts had reached double figures by now.

Learnne Vilday too went to Butetown Police Station and made a statement on December 6th. Paul Atkins also made a statement that day and, not to be outdone, so did Mark Grommek. The fact that four vital witnesses should have independently chosen the same day, nearly ten months after the crime, to tell South Wales Police what had happened makes it a most remarkable coincidence.

Before being held at the police station, Vilday had always insisted that she knew nothing at all about the murder. Now she put herself in the murder room. She had heard screams, run up the lane to 7 James Street, but had only arrived after Lynette was dead. By this account, she did not see who had stabbed Lynette. All she could say was that one of them had said that they had all had a go. In the room she put Miller, Abdullahi, Ronnie Actie, Tony Miller, an unnamed mixed race man and Martin Tucker. Vilday didn't name John Actie or Tony Paris – yet.

She was the first to claim that she had witnessed the murder, although she said that she ran out without being forced to take part in it herself. She claimed that she chanced upon it after hearing the screams, confronted the murderers and then left. Psaila, Grommek and Atkins all made statements which were more or less similar to hers.

Grommek and Atkins repeated their earlier claims to have seen four men outside 7 James Street on the night of the murder and Grommek was to make a further statement two days later against these four. After making their statements of December 6th Psaila and Vilday went into protective custody.

Steve Miller Is Interviewed

On December 7th a surprised and shocked Steve Miller was arrested with his brother, Tony, at Camberwell Magistrate's Court. Both were appearing there on unrelated charges which were overtaken by the Lynette White case, although the charge of assaulting a taxi driver would be picked up against Tony Miller three years later and would result in his conviction. He consulted his lawyer and was assured that they had arranged legal representation for him in Cardiff during his interviews.

Miller was refused access to a solicitor for the first two interviews. A magistrate had approved the police's application to refuse access to a solicitor in accordance with the procedures laid down in PACE. South Wales Police justified his detention and that of the others on the grounds that it was a very serious offence and that, if left at liberty, they might attempt to interfere with the witnesses. After nearly ten months the latter point was implausible to put it mildly. Had they wanted to interfere with the witnesses, they had ample opportunity to do so in the months prior to their arrests. They made no attempt to do so.

After the first two interviews, Geraint Richards sat in on the rest of Miller's interviews. But Richards' performance would be lacklustre to say the least.

Miller endured nineteen gruelling interviews (nearly thirteen hours worth) in four calendar days. The first seven interviews consisted of the police rubbishing Miller's alibi and accusing him of the murder. Miller denied involvement over three hundred times and expressed anger that Vilday had implicated him in a crime he insisted he did not commit, but his denials were not believed by police. They stated Vilday's account as if it was fact and told him that they had witnesses; why should they lie? Miller did not know why they were lying but insisted that they were lying. Once again police did not believe him.

Of these interviews the seventh was the crucial one and would return to haunt the criminal justice system. Miller was subjected to a torrent of abuse about his perceptions of his relationship with Lynette. Reading the transcripts and listening to the tapes of Miller's interviews, especially tape seven, it soon becomes clear that from the start Miller was being bullied by the police into admitting some involvement in the crime. The distress in his voice is clear. He repeatedly insists that he was not there and after each denial an officer says, "You were there!" It leaves Miller in little doubt of what was expected from him.

And in tape seven he is told by DC Greenwood:

> "How you could sit there and say that after being in that room, seeing that girl there in the state that she was in, and you're supposed to have all this wonderful care for her, seen her damn head hang off and her arms cut and stabbed to death and you sit there and tell us you know nothing at all about it; nothing at all about it..."

At this point Miller interrupted the torrent of abuse and again denied being in the room. Greenwood ignored him and continued the barrage. Miller kept repeating, "I wasn't there." Greenwood kept on at him. It was a war of relentless attrition. Tape seven showed that Miller's interlocutors were prepared to use any methods at their disposal short of physical violence to get him to say what they wanted to hear. The seventh interview conducted by DCs Peter Greenwood and John Seaford was oppressive. Miller had tried to fend off the abuse as best he could, but he was incapable of protecting his own interests and his solicitor, Geraint Richards, should have intervened, a fact he would later accept. Although there were no admissions in this interview it marked the end of Miller's resistance. And it was the last interview conducted by the 'nasty' officers. During the interviews with the 'nasty' officers, Miller was softened up for the 'nice' officers, DCs Simon Evans and John Murray.

Their methods were different from those of Greenwood and Seaford. Miller came to trust them and viewed them as his protectors from Greenwood and Seaford. In the eighth interview Miller adopted the police's suggestion that he might have been "blocked up" on cocaine, ganga and brandy and, that while under the influence of the cocktail of alcohol and drugs, he might have been in the room and just not remembered it, a suggestion that he had rejected in his fifth interview with the same officers. But after he had been softened up in the seventh interview he was more amenable to their suggestion. But having accepted their suggestion he is then told that he has to remember the details that they had just accepted he couldn't remember because of the effects of drugs on his memory. From then on, only the precise detail that his confession would contain was still in dispute.

At first he insisted that he had stumbled in on the crime and had tried to prevent it. Then he provides more details, but most of his admissions had been suggested to him by police first. And the details he provides off his own back contradict proven facts or are absurd for other reasons such as the skin colour of a man allegedly on the stairs changes and he is never asked to name this man or about the disposal of the murder weapon, which was never found, in any of his interviews - an astonishing oversight in what was held up as an extremely thorough investigation, especially as police claim that Miller was freely confessing. Michael Mansfield QC would later point out that Miller supplied no indisputable fact which has not been supplied to him first by police. But this confession would come to dominate the whole case, especially the first six minutes of the eighteenth interview which is full of his descriptions of Tony Paris kneeling over Lynette stabbing her repeatedly as if in a frenzy. It is also the last of Miller's interviews where both of the Acties were not in the room when Lynette was murdered.

In his nineteenth interview, he says, for the first time, that there was a code of silence - but only after DC Evans had suggested it first. This consisted of everyone stabbing Lynette at least once, so all were part of the crime. Now he accepted that he stabbed Lynette at least once, but only because the others forced him to do so.

However, he retracted immediately and insisted that while all the others stabbed Lynette, he only punched her. It was a nonsensical claim, especially as he was clearly tied to Lynette and came from outside Cardiff. If the others were guilty, they would have made sure that he stabbed her as well. But he stuck to it rigidly.

This was also the first time that he noticed Psaila's presence in the room. He is reminded that he has put all the blame on Tony Paris before then claiming that everyone stabbed her. In the previous tapes there are significant discrepancies between his account and Vilday's. Yet, by the nineteenth interview, he accepts virtually everything that the police put to him.

But the 'confession' had all the hallmarks of a man who had been bullied so much that he sacrificed his long term interests for a brief respite from the questioning. Miller's confession contradicted virtually all of the undisputed facts relating to Lynette's murder. For example, he thought that the first wound was in the belly, but according to Professor Knight's early accounts the throat wounds were first. Had Miller really been in 7 James Street when Lynette died, he would have known that.

The nineteenth interview was the first tape where Miller accepts that either of the Acties were in the room and stabbed Lynette at all. Prior to that, they hadn't so much as touched her and Ronnie was never inside the room, although he was supposed to have been in the flat. The significance of this will become apparent below.

In other interviews, his accounts contradict Vilday's in several ways, such as his position in the room, Lynette's position and whether he had stabbed her at all. By the nineteenth interview, he accepted all of Vilday's claims apart from how many times he stabbed Lynette and why. His story, or rather his stories, were so inconsistent as to be ridiculous.

The one common feature about his interviews is that at no point in any of them is his involvement anything more than minimal and that of the others, especially Tony Paris, is substantial. He seemed to be throwing out a signal that he would do what Vilday and Psaila did and turn prosecution witness in return for his freedom, but he was to be disappointed.

They were not interested in Miller as another witness. Miller was a chief suspect. Unlike those of Vilday and Psaila, Miller's admissions were taken as evidence of his guilt. His hopes of regaining his liberty that day were not only dashed then, but dashed indefinitely.

Given his confused and browbeaten state, it was easy for Miller's interrogators to convince him that they had cracked his alibi. He was told that witnesses had named him as one of Lynette's killers. In actual fact, only Vilday had named him at the time and despite the police placing so much reliance on her, it should have been obvious to them that she was a thoroughly unreliable source.

However, Miller knew that the police believed that he was in that room. He knew that he was going nowhere until he gave them what they wanted, but thought that if he obliged them, he would be allowed out on bail and then he could retract. He wasn't to go home for four years because of it.

Clearly, the police deceived Miller about the strength of the evidence that they had against him. All of the Cardiff Five endured gruelling interrogations, yet with the exception of Miller none of them cracked in any way. But they were better equipped to deal with South Wales Police's interviewing methods. Miller's character flaws and vulnerabilities made him easier game.

The police may not have known it, but Miller's compliance was significantly promoted by something that made him even more vulnerable to pressure, even though his vulnerabilities should perhaps have been apparent to any reasonably sensitive officer. He had an IQ of just 75. This was well below the average; it was the equivalent of an eleven year-old child. In fact, it was on the verge of subnormality. He also had the reading age of an eight year-old. And he was highly suggestible. Forensic psychologists and other experts who would study Miller's taped interviews would be united in their opinion that Miller's low IQ and high level of suggestibility cast strong doubt upon the reliability of his interviews, especially the crucial seventh interview. Such methods were borderline when dealing with a suspect of normal or even above average intelligence, but with a suspect suffering Miller's vulnerabilities they were wholly inappropriate.

Furthermore, their sole basis for interviewing Miller was wholly suspect, it being the umpteenth account of Learnne Vilday, a woman whose unreliability was absolutely beyond question. However, whatever the police's true beliefs were about Miller's guilt or innocence, there can be little doubt that the bullying that he suffered during the recording of tape seven ought to have rendered his subsequent admissions distinctly unreliable, especially with a suspect of Miller's vulnerabilities.

The methods used in the Miller interviews were wholly inappropriate. Rightly or wrongly the police convinced themselves that Miller was involved in Lynette's murder. Despite numerous denials the police persisted to the point that it became obvious even to Miller that he had to give them what they wanted if he wanted the questioning to stop. For example, in his fifth interview Miller is asked if he was "blocked up" on the night of the murder. He denied it, but by the eighth interview he accepted the police's scenario that he could have been so blocked up that he went there, but was unable to remember. The fifth interview suggested the scenario that Miller eventually adopted; the one the police believed to be the case even before the arrest of the Cardiff Five. It planted the seed in Miller's mind that put him in the flat and led to further admissions.

It was absolutely crucial to extract a confession from him. The bullying and undermining of his confidence in his innocence was the first phase. Getting him to accept the drugs scenario and, consequently, his presence in the room was the second phase. The third was to persuade him to adopt their chosen scenario and prevent him relapsing back into protestations of innocence. However, despite his vulnerabilities, Miller tried to retract, but it was already too late.

In the twelfth interview he tried to fight back. Miller said, "I don't know why I've been bullshitting you. I wasn't there." He was then reminded by an officer whose annoyance was obvious from the tone of his voice that he faced life imprisonment. This from one of the 'nice' officers. It suggests again that the police had no interest in hearing anything that contradicted what they wanted to hear.

Miller caved in and agreed that he was there. The so called 'nice' officers went on to get him to confirm details that they wanted to hear about the others, offering him a minor role in the crime. He seized the chance, unaware that he was tightening the noose around his neck. This ended the third phase of his interviews. The fourth and last phase consisted of tightening the noose further.

Having got Miller to give them what they wanted, they decided that they wanted even more. Miller's account had to be made to tally with Vilday's as much as possible and he had to introduce Psaila into an eyewitness role. In addition to that, he had to be induced to accept a more substantial role for himself.

The fourth phase was not fully achieved as Miller never unequivocally accepted the role that the police devised for him about the extent of his involvement in Lynette White's murder. But Miller's low IQ and high suggestibility made him as vulnerable to false confessions and police bullying as a suspect could be. And the police had dealt with Miller before. They felt that he was not as sympathetic as he tried to portray himself. They also knew that he was no genius. While some claim that Miller's low mental age may not have been apparent to police officers, anyone who had dealings with him at this time could see that something was wrong. Miller may have been streetwise and he had learned to cope despite his low mental age, but the signs were there from an early age.

Neither was Geraint Richards up to the task. In fact, his presence in the interviews was a positive disservice to Miller. He let his client down appallingly. The police and later the prosecution would interpret Richards' inactivity as proof that there was nothing wrong with the way that Miller was interviewed. They were wholly wrong. It was proof of Richards' failings and nothing more.

All five officers involved in the Miller interviews (DC Graham Toogood replaced DC Evans in interviews sixteen and seventeen) would claim that they believed that he held the key to the inquiry. By the nineteenth interview, they told Miller that the rest has got to come because they needed it. They were still playing Mr Nice and Mr Nasty and Miller was still doing his best to please the officers he regarded as his protectors from Greenwood and Seaford, quite unaware that he was actually helping them bang nail after nail into his coffin.

Miller had reached breaking point and DC Evans and DC Murray were very reluctant to stop the interview when Richards requested it. Miller was ready to give them everything that they wanted, but if he was allowed a consultation, he might have gathered his wits and stopped his confession. They promised to record Richards' objections after the interview ended. Despite this promise, no record was made of these objections.

This was an abuse of PACE that should have caused the officers concerned to be reprimanded at least, but they were not. In order to secure that prized confession the police manipulated or ignored sections of PACE that could have helped Miller protect his interests.

When Miller first accepted that he might have been in the room but couldn't remember because of the drugs he had allegedly taken, Richards should have stopped the interview and insisted that he be allowed to consult his client and explain the implications of what he had just said. He didn't. It was one of many areas of concern that Richards failed to pick up on during the interviews.

Richards would come to accept that he failed to protect Miller's interests. He only interrupted the interviews successfully twice and had other objections ignored completely. He remained silent when Miller was subjected to a torrent of abuse about his relationship with Lynette. He allowed the police to ride roughshod over a confused and frightened Miller's emotions.

On one occasion Miller requested a break from the questioning to gather his wits. He was given just five minutes while they changed tapes. Richards failed to insist that Miller be given sufficient time to compose himself.

Richards raised no objections when the police overtly put their interests first and told Miller that he had to give it all to them as it must have been eating him up. More significantly, he was told that he had to give it all to them, especially getting him to elaborate on his alleged role because they (the police) needed it. It does not appear from the tapes that they were remotely interested in what Miller knew, or didn't know, about the murder. They merely required him to confirm what they wanted to hear.

Evans and Murray portrayed themselves as the nice officers whom Miller could trust. At one point Miller pleaded with them not to leave him alone with Greenwood and Seaford. Evans and Murray exploited his trust in them to secure the admissions they needed from him. Richards did nothing to prevent it.

With Miller safely in their clutches, they switched tactics. It was the last of his nineteen interviews. Evans and Murray needed to establish Miller's exact role in the murder and tie up the numerous loose ends. The 'nice' officers suddenly confronted Miller with full details of the case that South Wales Police wanted to bring. Miller was so tired and emotionally drained by his ordeal that he would probably have confessed to being Jack The Ripper if necessary. Without a responsible and assertive solicitor he was putty in the hands of experienced interrogators.

After the interviews were over and the damage was well and truly done, Richards wrote to Miller's solicitor in London, Graham Dobson, expressing his concerns that Miller exhibited signs of abnormal suggestibility. This was the one area of Miller's case that was pursued with anything like the necessary vigour. They contacted one of Britain's leading experts on forensic psychology, Dr Gisli Gudjonsson, who would later highlight the problems of interviewing suspects such as Miller, but his views would be subject to the decisions of both trial judges.

Not So Vulnerable

Arrested along with Steve Miller on December 7th were Tony Miller, Yusef Abdullahi, Ronnie Actie, Rashid Omar and Martin Tucker. Tony Paris and John Actie were arrested two days later. They were all as stunned as Steve Miller, but they were by no means as vulnerable and could not be induced to admit any kind of involvement in the crime.

Ronnie Actie was told by DC Gillard that half of the docks said that he was involved. This had no basis in fact whatsoever. At the time, they had Vilday, Atkins and Grommek. They tried to bully Ronnie Actie into confessing. Vilday was supposed to be his girlfriend, but she had named him. They stressed this repeatedly. He wasn't having it and shouted back at them. They told him that he had no alibi, which was not quite true at the time, but almost. The interviewing officers knew that his credibility was very low and continued trying to badger Actie into admitting his guilt, but to no avail.

John Actie was a different matter as he did not associate with any of the main witnesses. Police stressed that his appearance was distinctive and that he had been put at the scene by witnesses they believed. Actie was having none of it. He insisted that he had never been inside the murder flat, that there were other people who resembled him and that he was wholly innocent. However, when Actie was arrested the evidence against him was somewhat flimsy. Psaila had put him outside the flat, Vilday had not implicated him and nor had Atkins or Grommek. And Violet Perriam was uncertain if she had seen him outside the flat or not. The justification for his arrest appeared wafer thin at best. They tried to exploit some confusion between him and Taryn Ali, about his movements on the night of the murder. He was wrong about his movements, but this didn't prove him guilty. The police tried to obtain a confession from him and got nowhere.

DC Seaford and DC Greenwood, Messrs Nasty from the Miller interrogation, interviewed Tony Paris also. He had never been to prison before and he had never been interviewed over anything remotely serious, but he didn't let them get into his head. Paris was told by his interrogators that the others were putting him at the scene doing the business and his only protection was to stick them in before they put everything on him. But Paris wasn't having it. Like all the others bar Miller, he rejected their advice with contempt. They even tried suggesting that he had stumbled in on the murder and tried to stop it. They cast him in the role of hero, but he rejected their offers. He maintained his innocence throughout his interviews and insisted that he knew nothing about the murder.

Yusef Abdullahi kept his composure throughout his twenty interviews. He answered their questions freely. For the first two interviews, he simply demanded his solicitor. After that, he answered virtually every question by saying that he was on the *Coral Sea* working. He had been told that they had smashed his alibi to ribbons and that they had witnesses putting him at the scene of the crime. He maintained his innocence and insisted that he had been on the *Coral Sea*.

One officer told him that he could not hide for ever. He was also told, "For God's sake, help yourself!" This meant agree with the police, but Abdullahi was no Steve Miller. He was on the *Coral Sea* that night and nothing was going to make him say that he wasn't. One officer counted up that Abdullahi had mentioned the *Coral Sea* an incredible five hundred and forty-five times. Abdullahi stuck to his guns and was only allowed to develop on his work on the *Coral Sea* in his last two interviews. The attempts to crack his alibi and the abuse did not stop here. But, as their attempts to drag a confession out of him failed, they got riled by him. He kept incredibly calm throughout the interviews. It all got too much for DI Mouncher. In tape twenty Mouncher launches into a vitriolic attack upon Abdullahi:

> Mouncher: You hated Lynette White.
> Abdullahi: Not at all.
> Mouncher: You had good reason to see her dead.
> Abdullahi: Not at all.
> Mouncher: You more than anybody.
> Abdullahi: Not at all.
> Mouncher: You thought that she'd grassed you out didn't you?
> Abdullahi: Not at all.
> Mouncher: You are a vicious, evil, wicked man.
> Abdullahi: So you're telling me.
> Mouncher: I am telling you.
> Abdullahi: Well I don't think I am...
> Mouncher: Well I think you are...
> Abdullahi: I am an innocent man who you persecuted...
> Mouncher: I think you are...
> Abdullahi: An innocent man...
> Mouncher: You're a disgrace to the human race!

The tone of Mouncher's language is worse than that used in the Miller interviews. Yet Mouncher's onslaught on Abdullahi is even more inexcusable when it is borne in mind that one month earlier he seemed absolutely convinced that Mr X was their man. Abdullahi had not given police what they wanted. They would have to rely on what they could gather against him.

The police's approach to Tony Miller was completely different to the way they dealt with his brother. Tony Miller had made a statement back in March, when he told the police that he used to go out with Francine Cordle. He gave an account of a fight that Francine had with Tina Garton around March 1987, which resulted in Cordle being charged with attempted murder, a charge she would later be acquitted of.

Lynette had been due to be a witness in the case against Cordle, so it is easy to see why the police would be interested in Cordle: she had a strong motive for wanting Lynette out of the way. Their interest in Tony Miller stemmed from the fact that when Garton was assaulted he was still going out with Cordle.

Cordle had been bailed to live at the Millers' family home in London. She did so for a month, but after a court appearance she never returned. However, by the time of Lynette White's murder, Tony's relationship with Cordle was long dead. It had broken up acrimoniously and there was now no love lost between the two. In fact, in September 1987 Tony Miller had married Karen Austin. He claimed that he had been in London with his wife on the weekend of the murder.

That was the extent of police knowledge of Tony Miller's movements before the arrests. The day following his arrest he was interviewed by DC Paul Philips and DC A. Evans. The written record of this interview suggests that the manner of his interviewing was vastly different from the way that his brother was questioned. The officers seemed genuinely interested in establishing what he knew, although it should be pointed out that the written record does not and cannot convey the tone of voice that the officers used. Tony Miller insists that he was interviewed in a hostile manner and that the police kept insisting that his alibi wasn't good enough. There are three interviews that were recorded by contemporaneous note and not by tape. The records of those interviews suggest that his recollections are mistaken.

Tony Miller claimed that he certainly hadn't been to Cardiff since his marriage. The officers were not afraid to tell him what he had said in the statement he made in March, although police would not allow Steve Miller access to his. For example, they told Tony that he said that he had been at home in London with his wife on February 13th, 14th and 15th. He still had no firm recollection, but remembered that he had bought her a rose. Tony was given every opportunity to expand on his alibi. He named people who had seen him in London during that weekend, told police how to contact them and outlined his normal Saturday routine.

There was even a break in the interview for him to consult his solicitor. Compare this with the repeated fobbing off of Steve Miller's solicitor when he wanted to take instructions from his client.

The officers gave Tony Miller yet another chance to name anyone else who could verify his movements that weekend. He was then asked what he knew about Lynette's murder. He said that all he knew was that Lynette had been stabbed about fifty times and that Steve probably told him this. He claimed to be really close to Steve. The officers then asked him what Steve had said about the murder on his return to London.

He claimed that Steve told them that he didn't know why Lynette had been murdered and that the police had tried to suggest that he (Steve) had done it. The officers tried again to get Tony to say that Steve knew why Lynette was murdered, but Tony was having none of it. He insisted that Steve wanted to know who did it as well. They then told Tony that they had three witnesses who placed Steve alongside Lynette's body. This was not true. All they had was one, namely Learnne Vilday. It was designed to suggest that there was no point in Tony persisting with his claim that Steve did not know anything of interest. But Tony Miller stuck to his guns.

Then they came to the crux of the matter. They told him that if Steve had not committed the crime himself, he must have known who had. This was similar to the tactics that the 'nice' officers used on Steve Miller, but the results were different. His interviewers tried to get him to tell them that Steve knew who the killer was, but Tony was having none of it. He insisted that Steve had never told him who the killer was and that he didn't know.

There was no attempt to browbeat Tony Miller into saying what they wanted to hear. He was allowed to answer their questions and was given every opportunity to expand on his explanations. His interviewers knew what they wanted to hear and they tried a number of routes to get what they wanted, but they never resorted to underhand methods apart from misrepresenting the number of witnesses who had put Steve Miller in the room.

The police seemed to be far more interested in what Tony knew about Steve's knowledge of Lynette's murder than his own alleged involvement. They left Tony in little doubt that they believed Steve was either involved in the murder itself, or he knew who was. It seemed that the point of dragging Tony Miller in for questioning was to get a little more ammunition on Steve, rather than a serious attempt to link him to the murder.

On December 9th he was interviewed again. This was at his request and he freely agreed to be interviewed without his solicitor present. The officers involved in this interview were DC Lucas and DC Toogood. This interview established that Tony Miller had thought about his movements further during the night. Now he claimed that he had been to a party on the weekend of the murder. He told them how to contact his friend, Ian, who had held the party. The police said they would get their colleagues in the Metropolitan Police to check the information that he provided as soon as the interview ended.

They still seemed more interested in Steve than in Tony. He insisted that Steve had never talked about the murder in any depth and he was sure that Steve knew nothing of interest. He claimed that Steve was obviously upset about it and that he left Steve to talk about it in his own time. He repeated that he was very close to his brother.

He described a conversation with his brother in the cells the night before. Tony had said that the police suspected him of involvement and Steve replied that he knew it was ridiculous. They had both laughed at the absurdity of being arrested for something that they hadn't done. After this, the police dropped their bombshell.

They told Tony Miller that in his last interview the previous day, his brother had admitted being in the James Street flat when Lynette was killed and that he had named others. They gave him a condensed version of Steve's admissions from his eighth interview and asked Tony if he could tell them who the others were. Tony Miller stuck to his story and insisted that Steve had told him nothing about that at all.

Then they suggested that he could assist both Steve and them if he knew anything about it, but Tony insisted that he could not help. He repeated that he was in London on the weekend of the murder and said that he and a friend had met two girls at the party and gone to their house. He only knew their first names and that they were white.

As in his previous interview, Tony Miller seems to have been given a relatively easy ride. As before, he was given opportunities to expand on his movements for the day of the murder. However, as with the previous interview, the police seemed far more interested in establishing that Steve had told him something of interest than they were in his own movements. And as before, Tony Miller was having none of it.

On December 10th he was interviewed by DC Toogood and DC Lucas again. They told him that police had interviewed his friend in London and he had denied having a party on the weekend of the murder. Miller stubbornly insisted that there had been a party and that Ian just didn't like the police. Toogood and Lucas promised to make further enquiries and interview him again. It is unclear if they ever did.

The way that Tony Miller appears to have been interviewed by South Wales Police was a marked contrast to the treatment his brother, in particular, received. They wanted specific information from Tony, but they were prepared to allow him to answer their questions and they did not shout him down, or make thinly disguised threats of prosecution if he did not give them exactly what they wanted to hear.

Tony Miller would still maintain that the police gave him a really rough time. He claims that they kept insisting that his alibi was no good and that he must know something about the murder. But these interviews establish that Tony Miller was undoubtedly given far more opportunity to provide an alibi than any of the others and that the police seemed more interested in what Tony knew about Steve Miller than in Tony Miller himself.

Ending With A Whimper

On December 10th the discovery of Psaila's blood group was a dream come true for the inquiry. Psaila's blood grouping tests revealed that her blood group was the same as the rare blood group found on Lynette's sock and contained all the factors referred to on Lynette's jeans. Police told Psaila that it proved that she had been in the room when Lynette died. Psaila was eventually persuaded that she must have been there, so much so that she would insist she was there because forensics had proved that her blood was there. It had not. It showed only that somebody of her blood group had been there and that applied to about sixteen thousand people in Britain. Moreover, the donor of that sample in the flat was almost certainly one man.

On December 11th Psaila now claimed that she was an eyewitness: that she had been forced to take part in the murder as well and that Vilday had noticed her presence. She named Tony Paris, Steve Miller, Tony Miller, Yusef Abdullahi, John Actie and Ronnie Actie. Tony Brace and Jack Ellis disappeared from her accounts altogether.

On the same day Vilday made a statement naming five of the eight arrested as Lynette White's killers: Steve Miller, Tony Paris, Yusef Abdullahi, and John and Ronnie Actie. Her previous statement of December 6th had not included John Actie or Tony Paris. And there were several other discrepancies between her statements of December 6th and December 11th.

For example, in her first account both Martin Tucker and an unnamed mixed race man are allegedly present. Now they were effectively removed. Vilday gave no explanation for the 'disappearance' of the mixed race man. However, she admitted that she only named Tucker because she disliked him. She seemed to be making a habit of rashly making serious accusations out of mere spite – remember her drunken outburst against Miller and Abdullahi in May and her retraction shortly afterwards.

However garbled Vilday's latter accounts appeared to be, she was careful in what she said. She insisted that she had been forced to cut one of Lynette's wrists and Psaila had to cut the other, but she would insist that she did not cut the throat as Psaila had claimed in her statement of December 11th and would later claim in her evidence. The reason for this was that it had been the throat wounds which killed Lynette and if Vilday had inflicted the fatal wounds, even if forced to do so, she would have been in great difficulties as duress is a very problematic defence to any charge and is no defence to a charge of murder.

When she claimed to have been in the room for the first time on December 11th, Psaila named six people as responsible. Vilday only named five that same day and Atkins stuck to four. Three days earlier Grommek had maintained his account that the four men described by Atkins were responsible, although they could only provide names for three of them. Unlike Vilday, Psaila named Tony Miller as well. On December 11th the discrepancies between Grommek's account and that of Vilday and Psaila became a yawning chasm. What were previously broadly similar accounts became difficult to reconcile, especially regarding exactly who was in the room at the time of the killing. John Actie and Tony Paris, for example, do not feature in Grommek's accounts at all.

But the biggest mystery about his evidence is why Steve Miller didn't feature in Grommek's stories. South Wales Police have never provided a satisfactory explanation for this and nor has Grommek. It seems that he just settled on the names of those arrested in the first batch who frequented the North Star. As he had been the resident disc jockey there, he had the opportunity to observe them to such a degree that he could be sure that he could have picked them out at an identification parade. This could also explain the absence of Steve Miller from his accounts. By the time Grommek became the North Star's disc jockey, Miller no longer frequented it as he had returned to London several months earlier.

Thus, while Grommek appears to have no axe to grind, his account was so dubious that it was unlikely that it could have withstood thorough investigation. Grommek was an extremely unreliable witness, a fact that was well known to South Wales Police.

On this day Tucker, Tony Miller and Rashid Omar were released. They were charged with lesser offences which would shortly be dropped with no explanation. Tony Miller had an alibi of sorts and he gave the police absolutely nothing approaching an admission of any kind. After five days in custody he was released and returned to London. He sent Steve a Christmas card and would not contact him again for three years.

The three men released had been named by Vilday, or Psaila, or both, except for Rashid Omar, whose arrest was absolutely mystifying. Not one of the alleged eyewitnesses ever implicated him. The sole basis for his arrest was the claims of Violet Perriam. And the evidence was hardly much stronger against the other seven as Vilday and Psaila couldn't agree which of them were there. Vilday named Martin Tucker while Psaila didn't and Psaila named Tony Miller while Vilday didn't - at least for now.

Vilday didn't name John Actie or Tony Paris until December 11th. This suggests reluctance, especially in Paris' case, as he was the uncle of her baby. However, with Psaila's latest claims police had an insurance policy.

Now the five – Steve Miller, Yusef Abdullahi, John Actie, Ronnie Actie and Tony Paris – were charged with the murder of Lynette White. They were remanded into custody at Cardiff Prison the next day, December 12th 1988.

Three days later Mr X, already eliminated on November 9th, was interviewed again. X now admitted knowing Atkins and recognizing Grommek. X's mother was also interviewed. She couldn't alibi X but did not incriminate him. She said that she did his washing for him and that she had never seen any bloodstains on his clothes.

A week before Christmas, Miller was still sticking to his story, even to friends. He was visited in prison by his girlfriend, Debbie Taylor, and Peggy Farrugia's sister, Tessa Sidoric, and what he repeated to them was a more or less garbled version of what he had told police in his "confession".

The year ended with a whimper which would later become more of a bang. On Boxing Day Learnne Vilday sat down and wrote to Nicola Heysham, a woman whom she referred to as her best friend. This letter would later assume great importance in the trial of the Cardiff Five.[1]

> "Three weeks ago the police arrested me for her [Lynette's] murder. Well Nick I know you knows me and if I would have done something like that I wouldn't be able to keep something like that to myself. Well anyway Nicola, after being locked up for a couple of days the police said they had 3 witnesses to say that the 5 boys locked up now for it, was there and they said I must either go on the police's side or on the boys' side. That meant I either say, 'Yes I was there and saw the 5 boys and get out of the police station that day and then be a main witness to this fucking murder case, or the other option I had was to say the same as I've said from the day I found the girl, which is the fucking truth Nicky'. I hope you believe me anyway! If I would have said what I've been saying for 10 months which, honest to God is the truth I would have been in the dock with them for murder Nicky. So I've lied to the police, just so I could have got out of that fucking police station. Nicola I was scared. And I don't, not that I don't want to believe it. I just can't believe that the boys in prison are the right ones. I suppose you've heard who they are. 1) is Dulla, I can believe it was him. 2) is Pineapple, I can believe it was him as well. 3) is Tony Paris, Craig's uncle, I can't believe it was him. 4) is Ronny Actey (sic), no way can I believe it was him. 5) is John Actey (sic), he may have had reason to because Lynette and Pineapple owed him a couple of hundred for cocaine, but I don't know Nicola. All I know is Carl and Steven Actey (sic) are looking to put me in the same place as Lynette White. That's why I can't go to Cardiff at all and no-one must know my address. Nicola, that's why I trust you to have it, because I know you won't tell anyone. Nicola this is fucking serious. I'm getting threats to my life and I'm scared stiff, especially for Craig's..."

---

[1] This letter was an exhibit at both trials. Vilday would deny the allegations of police pressure in both trials, claiming that she just made them up because she was ashamed of having been part of the murder of Lynette White. She would be cross-examined long and hard about it, but the police appear not to have been asked about these allegations. However, it should be noted that between this time and the first trial Vilday would deny being present at the murder to several other people. She would say that it was easier to say that than to say that she was involved.

CHAPTER 4

Independent Eyes

No Turning Back: The CPS Fails Its Test

After the well publicised arresting and charging of the Cardiff Five, the Crown Prosecution Service might have been expected to quickly discontinue the prosecution before it could begin to haunt all concerned. But the wheels of justice had begun to turn in the wrong direction.

The first tier of the criminal justice system had failed the Cardiff Five and the public. The police had arrested and charged them despite the lack of credible evidence against them. The CPS were in the best position to either correct that failing within days, or compound the initial error by failing to exert its independence.

The CPS was established by the Prosecution of Offenders Act of 1985 and became operational in October 1986. The CPS often insists that it is completely independent from the police. In fact, it was established because of the real problems associated with the police prosecuting people they had arrested. Decisions on whether to prosecute or not needed to be seen to be separate from the police. The CPS had the powers to prove its independence in practice; the question was whether it would use them?

Among other things, it was empowered to discontinue prosecutions, or require the police to conduct further research. The CPS often cites the fact that it discontinues about 10% of cases the police refer to it as proof of its independence. Its reasons for doing so are either that the police cannot fulfil their evidential criteria, or that prosecuting would not be in the public interest.

Thus, a case brought against the Cardiff Five had to meet both of those criteria. According to the CPS there must be a realistic chance of conviction before a prosecution can proceed. There could be no doubt that prosecuting men accused of such a brutal murder was in the public interest if there was evidence of a case against them. Consequently, the CPS had satisfied the public interest criterion, but by far the most important considerations for the CPS was sufficiency of evidence.

The CPS' Code for Crown Prosecutors was designed to be a declaration of principles governing the decision making process of the CPS. The purpose of the Code was to encourage public confidence and consistency in prosecuting decisions. The principles enshrined in the Code were endorsed by the Attorney

General's Guidelines, which have been the basis for deciding whether to prosecute and that those entrusted with prosecuting on the basis of the Code must be an independent body.

It also stressed that Crown Prosecutors would be allowed a great deal of discretion at every level of the decision making process, but the use of such discretion would be the responsibility of the prosecutor and must be based on sound legal principles. However, it does warn about the dangers of misuse of discretion on public confidence in the reputation of justice and for the CPS itself.

According to the Code for Crown Prosecutors, the first question to be asked is whether there is enough evidence to proceed. The Crown Prosecutor must be satisfied that there is substantial, reliable and admissible evidence that a crime has been committed by an identifiable person. The Cardiff Five had been identified, but the evidence against them was hardly substantial or reliable.

The CPS' standards lay a heavy burden on its prosecutors. It is not satisfied with establishing that there is a prima facie case against any suspect. It insists that there must be a realistic chance of securing a conviction.

The first test is that a prosecutor should not risk a prosecution if there is a realistic chance of an acquittal being ordered by the judge, or of a magistrate or judge accepting a submission of no case to answer. It is already clear that the reliability of the evidence gathered left more than a little to be desired and that in the hands of a prosecutor who was more interested in discovering the truth, there was a real chance that the case would have been discontinued within days of the defendants being charged.

Prosecutors should also be aware of lines of inquiry open to the defence which could undermine the Crown's case before they decide whether to proceed or not. Yusef Abdullahi's strong alibi could present an obstacle to securing his conviction and the lack of forensic evidence against any of the defendants would clearly present an equally serious obstacle to the Crown.

The Rules Of The Game

The CPS recommends that Crown Prosecutors should pay particular attention to thirteen criteria when they evaluate evidence. The CPS stresses that this is not an exhaustive list of criteria, but should be applied to individual cases, especially if they are borderline.

The Code warns prosecutors that they must be sensitive to the requirements of PACE and whether there have been breaches of it which could be serious enough to get the case thrown out of court. It reminds prosecutors to be sensitive to the issue of suspects being properly treated in police custody in terms of the effects of improper treatment on the reliability of evidence obtained, particularly confessions, and even statements.

It states that Crown Prosecutors would want to satisfy themselves that confessions were properly obtained and that there was no suggestion of oppressive behaviour. That criterion was an extremely important factor in this case. Steve Miller's confession was extracted under duress.

If Miller was not bullied, the Crown's interpretation of oppression is a standard that can never be attained. Consequently, the very first evidential criterion of the CPS meant that Miller's confession should have been thrown out by the Crown before the case even came to court.

However, they had further evidential criteria to fulfil. Crown Prosecutors are advised to consider whether other evidence had been obtained improperly and whether such circumstances might result in a court feeling that such evidence could not be admitted in evidence without prejudicing the fairness of the proceedings. Prosecutors were advised to be mindful of what effect the exclusion of such evidence would have on the sufficiency of evidence criteria and if such admissions were crucial to the Crown's case.

If so, they are advised that it should substantially affect the decision on whether to proceed at all. In the case against the Cardiff Five, the Miller confession was the most crucial piece of evidence of the entire case. It would account for the bizarre verdicts. If there was a likelihood that it had been obtained improperly, the case against the Cardiff Five was palpably in tatters.

The next criterion that the CPS recommends Crown Prosecutors to be aware of relates to the admissibility of confessions. It recommends that Crown Prosecutors should consider what to do in cases where the case depends on admissions in circumstances where the reliability of the confession could be challenged due to the mental age, intelligence and level of understanding that the accused possesses.

The defence would later show that Stephen Miller had the IQ of an eleven year-old child and was highly suggestible to boot. So, there were clear reasons for questioning the reliability of Miller's confession.

Things were to go from bad to worse. There were other criteria affecting the sufficiency of evidence. Crown Prosecutors are advised to be aware of the possibility that a witness may be exaggerating, have a faulty memory, be hostile or friendly to the accused, or may be unreliable in other ways. The last part in particular applies to all of the Crown's key witnesses.

Neither Vilday, Psaila, Atkins or Grommek had told the story, or stories, that they eventually told South Wales Police in December 1988 in any of their previous statements. Surely, that affected their potential reliability. In addition to that, their evidence was clearly untrue on several points, but that was not all.

The next criterion for prosecutors is whether a witness has a motive for telling less than the whole truth. Both Vilday and Psaila's evidence made them self confessed accomplices. They strongly feared that they would have been charged themselves if they did not help the police clear up the murder. If they had maintained their original story that they didn't know who killed Lynette White, they could have been in the dock along with the Cardiff Five. Clearly, they had a very strong motive for telling less than the whole truth.

The uncritical reliance of South Wales Police on two such unreliable witnesses was extraordinary. The CPS should have pointed this out to the police and at the very least required some proof that the women's final accounts could be relied on. It did not.

Crown Prosecutors are advised to be aware of the possibility that there could be matters which could be put to a witness to attack his or her credibility. And they must consider what impression a witness is likely to make and think about how he or she would stand up to cross-examination.

Both Vilday and Psaila would be torn apart in cross-examination, as were Grommek and Atkins and other witnesses. Even the most cursory glance at their claims would have revealed that they could not give a good impression to a jury. The next criterion was, if there is a conflict between eyewitnesses, does it go beyond what one would reasonably expect and hence materially weaken the case? All four of the alleged eyewitnesses clearly contradicted themselves, each other and indisputable evidence irreconcilably. For example, Paul Atkins never noticed the presence of Angela Psaila at any time, although he was supposed to have gone into the room shortly after the murder. The contradictions between them all, the conflicting permutations of who exactly was in the murder room and under what circumstances, were legion and destroyed whatever credibility their claims may have had.

Crown Prosecutors are advised to be mindful to the possibility that in the event of witnesses' stories concurring, there may be suspicion that a false story had been concocted. There is evidence that this happened in the case of the Cardiff Five. The timings of the crucial statements leading up to the arrests suggest that the witnesses must have known what was happening.

On November 16th 1988 Violet Perriam had named two of the black men she claimed to have seen outside 7 James Street on the night of the murder. The following day Angela Psaila's resistance showed the first substantial chink as she began to name names. On November 22nd Grommek and Atkins' resistance cracked. On the same day, Psaila's claims became even more detailed, but, on December 6th, Vilday claimed to have been in the murder room on her own. The other three all made statements which were broadly similar to hers.

On December 11th Psaila claimed that she was in the room as well and Vilday noticed her presence. The two women told very similar lies and Grommek and Atkins stuck to their original claims. Perhaps it was coincidence that the four crucial eyewitnesses all seemed to be making statements at the same time and their claims seemed to follow a pattern.

The next two criteria to be mindful of, namely that all the witnesses are available and competent to give evidence and to ask in cases where child witnesses are involved whether they are likely to be able to give sworn evidence, did not apply in this case.

The next criterion affects the cogency and reliability of identification evidence. Grommek and Atkins' identification evidence left a lot to be desired. And as with

Grommek and Atkins, both Vilday and Psaila had implicated innocent men who had not been charged with Lynette's murder. The identification evidence was a mess, but this somehow failed to register with the Crown Prosecutor.

The next criterion that Crown Prosecutors should be aware of is whether the facts of the case are such that the public would consider it oppressive to proceed against the accused. This criterion was designed mainly for dealing with offences committed by juveniles and did not apply in this case.

The final criterion affects cases where there is more than one defendant. A Crown Prosecutor is advised to be aware of the possibility that the trials could be severed. Furthermore, it is suggested he or she be mindful about the need to have sufficient evidence to prove the case against each of the defendants individually. Clearly, severance was an important issue in the case against the Cardiff Five.

Miller had confessed in a manner which greatly prejudiced the cases of the other defendants. His confession went on to become the case's most crucial piece of evidence. Had the trials been severed, to avoid the risk of Miller's tapes prejudicing the other defendants' right to a fair trial, the Crown's case would have been in ruins.

So, of the thirteen criteria listed by the CPS for Crown Prosecutors to consider when deciding whether to prosecute or not, three did not apply to this case, but ten suggest that the Crown should not have proceeded against the Cardiff Five. All of this raises the question of whether the CPS was failing to apply its own criteria with adequate rigour by allowing this prosecution to be brought.

The Crown Prosecutor has the right to use the discretion to terminate a prosecution under Section 23 of the Prosecution of Offenders Act of 1985, but this is not exhaustive. A Crown Prosecutor also has the continuing power to withdraw evidence or offer no evidence. It stresses that Crown Prosecutors should review the case constantly as the discretion to discontinue is a continuing one. Crown Prosecutors were advised to be mindful of their discretion as new evidence could come to light affecting the original decision to proceed. They were also advised to be resolute in such circumstances and should not hesitate to discontinue if the need arises.

A comparison of its criteria against the evidence at its disposal suggests that the proper course of action for the Crown Prosecution Service in this case was to discontinue it immediately. Had that been done soon after the charges were brought then five innocent men would have been spared a total of sixteen years wrongful imprisonment.

The Committal Hearing (Part One)

On February 6th 1989 Angela Psaila became the first person to accuse the Cardiff Five of the murder of Lynette White from the witness box. She was unable to take the oath in the morning due to loud barracking from the dock and the public gallery. In the afternoon, she was able to give evidence.

She insisted that she had not been threatened with prosecution by the police if she didn't name names. Then she contradicted herself and claimed that she had been threatened with a conspiracy to murder charge months before she made her crucial statements in December 1988, but she felt that it was the only way to encourage her to tell the truth even though, by her evidence, she didn't do so for several months.

She claimed that she had seen Miller stab Lynette in the chest first. At first, she claimed that Vilday had cut Lynette's throat because she was forced to; then, she only thought that Vilday had done so and, in the end, she just couldn't remember at all.

She would not be drawn further on whether Vilday had killed Lynette when she cut her throat. However, Psaila also gave evidence concerning an outburst she had made just outside of court, but within earshot of court officials. She was heard to say to a police officer, "How many fucking times do I have to tell you, I wasn't there!" When challenged by a defence barrister that this was an admission that she wasn't at 7 James Street, Psaila insisted that she had been there and explained that her outburst was due to her having had stomach pains and was fed up of being asked by the officer if she had seen the doctor.

Compounding The Error (Part One)

If there was any doubt about the quality that her evidence would attain at trial her performance at the committal hearing dispelled it. She had contradicted her statements left, right and centre and came over as thoroughly obnoxious. She had admitted to naming people who had not been at 7 James Street at the time of the murder, when asked why she had named Tony Miller. She said it was because the barrister was confusing her. But she had made the same claims to South Wales Police long before the barrister could have confused her. She had been abusive to any lawyer who had the temerity to question her veracity and put her contradictions down to fear of the defendants, yet she had associated with some of them freely at a time when if she was to be believed she knew them to be brutal murderers.

But the most obvious discrepancy with her evidence is that the throat wounds obviously occurred early in the attack, yet Psaila's account implied that it was towards the end of it. If she had given a truthful account surely she would not have made such a crucial error. And, regardless of whether she wanted to do it or not, if Vilday cut Lynette's throat then, she murdered her, as duress is only a partial and extremely problematic defence to a murder charge, which succeeds very rarely.

And then there was the question of her outburst in the lobby of the court which was heard in the courtroom itself. Her subsequent explanation that she had had stomach pains and she was fed up of the officer asking her if she had seen the doctor was hardly credible. But if Psaila was an incredible witness, perhaps Vilday could repair the damage.

Committal Hearing (Part Two)

Vilday repeated her claims that the five men in the dock were responsible for Lynette's murder. She claimed that she was curious when she heard the screams from 7 James Street, but, despite not being a courageous person, she decided to go to her flat. She claimed that when she went into the room Lynette was already dead. She was cross-examined vigorously as to her veracity by defence lawyers who exposed numerous lies in her statements and her failure to act consistently. Like Psaila, she explained her inconsistency and previous lies in her statements from fear of the defendants. She was also cross-examined long and hard over naming Martin Tucker, a man she now acknowledged was innocent. She claimed that she hated him but would not have let an innocent man go to prison.

She denied the suggestion that she knew that Psaila, Grommek and Atkins were at Butetown Police Station on December 6th 1988, the day all four prosecution witnesses were supposed to have independently decided to go there and name those subsequently arrested and she insisted she had not been pressurised by the police into naming names. She claimed that the police had consistently pestered her for the truth, so she volunteered the information as it convinced her that there was no point in lying any more.

Vilday was questioned on events leading up to her statement of December 11th in which she had implicated John Actie and Tony Paris for the first time. She claimed that she had been suffering from withdrawal from amphetamines when the police came to get her in the night of December 10th. She told the court that she had no choice but to go with them. She said that she had been questioned all night even though she had head and stomach pains and was not allowed to sleep. Nevertheless, she insisted that the police did not tell her what evidence they had; they just told her they had something.

Then she went on to contradict Psaila and Atkins on several points. She admitted to only knowing John Actie by his reputation and that he had never done anything to her prior to the murder. She insisted that on December 10-11th the police did not pressurise her to say that John Actie had been there. While she was giving her evidence, John Actie had had enough and left the dock. The magistrates decided to continue without him.

Vilday admitted that when she had made her drunken outburst of the previous May, she had subsequently made a statement in which she said, "I was so pissed I don't really know why I said it; just, I suppose to get at [Steve] Miller because he is away and not getting any hassle and I hate him anyway." Earlier in her evidence she had admitted to making false claims about Martin Tucker because she hated him.

Compounding The Error (Part Two)

The magistrates had now heard from both of the Crown's eyewitnesses to the murder. Psaila's had been a brash performance that did not sit well with her insistence that she was terrified of the defendants. Vilday had also claimed to be frightened of them yet she too associated with some of them after she knew them to be brutal murderers if her evidence was to be believed. The Crown's case had deteriorated further as a result of Vilday's evidence.

She had vehemently insisted that she did not cut Lynette's throat. The significance of the throat wounds was that whoever inflicted them for whatever reason was responsible for Lynette's death. But there had been numerous inconsistencies between her statements and those of other key prosecution witnesses. Although their accounts were broadly similar there were serious discrepancies between her account and that of Psaila.

She had also given evidence which strongly suggested that her crucial statement of December 11th had been obtained at a time when she appeared not to have been medically fit to be interviewed due to the effects of withdrawal from amphetamines. It strongly suggests that it was not appropriate to interview her at such a time especially as she also claimed to have been deprived of sleep. This could render the information obtained under such circumstances unreliable. Her evidence also suggested that she had not seen who had actually killed Lynette. By her account Lynette was already dead when she arrived at the scene. This was of crucial importance because it meant that she could not have seen who stabbed Lynette. She claimed that she knew it was all five of the defendants because one of them had shouted out that they had all had a go. This was not evidence; it was hearsay.

Her evidence had been studded with inconsistencies and lies on crucial points. At the end of it there could be little doubt that she was a self confessed liar, who claims that this time, unlike all the others, she was telling the complete truth. The two women who were supposed to be the star witnesses were completely unreliable. There could be little doubt that they would not make convincing witnesses at trial, but before the Crown could even think of the impression they would make at trial, the magistrates had to be convinced that the Cardiff Five had a case to answer. There were two more witnesses for them to hear. Perhaps they could tie up the loose ends enough to convince them to commit the defendants for trial.

Committal Hearing (Part Three)

Mark Grommek was next into the witness box. He contradicted Vilday and Psaila by claiming that Lynette's murderers were Martin Tucker, Ronnie Actie, Yusef Abdullahi and a black man with shoulder-length dreadlocks whose name he did not know. During cross-examination he said that the names of John Actie, Stephen Miller and Tony Paris meant nothing to him.

When questioned about his statements Grommek said that he had been interviewed several times by police, but some of these had been informal interviews and admitted that he told lies previously. Referring to his previous denials of having been home at the time of the murder Grommek claimed that it was due to the effects of medication that he was taking at the time.

Grommek detailed the events leading up to his statements which implicated some of the defendants. He insisted that he had not been threatened with being charged with conspiracy to murder if he did not name names. He also told the magistrates that the police had never suggested the names that they wanted to hear to him.

Grommek insisted that the men that he had implicated were responsible for Lynette's murder. Then he accepted that he had not known any of them prior to the murder. He admitted that after the murder he had discussed it with Paul Atkins and both had decided not to tell the truth about it. Grommek claimed that he had been interviewed several times in the lead up to the arrests of the Cardiff Five and that some of these interviews were informal.

He claimed that he had been asked about John Actie, Stephen Miller and Tony Paris between November 22nd and December 8th by Detective Chief Inspector Morgan, who didn't take a statement. He claimed that Morgan just asked a couple of questions and then agreed that he might have been told what others had said. Then he claimed that he decided to tell the truth on November 22nd and was unaware that Atkins had decided to do the same thing on the same day.

Compounding The Error (Part Three)

The Crown's case was now in serious difficulties. Like Vilday and Psaila, Grommek had proved himself vulnerable to cross-examination. If his latter statements were true, he was a proven liar in his earlier ones. His explanation for his previous denials of being at home on the murder night were hardly credible and had only become necessary when Frederick Calliste's unorthodox identification of him placed him in 7 James Street at about 6.00 a.m. on the murder night.

Even more significantly, the discrepancies between his testimony and that of Vilday and Psaila were serious ones. He had exonerated three of the Cardiff Five in the witness box and had implicated two others whom Vilday and Psaila had not implicated from the witness box. Even the number of murderers was different. And Grommek could not be shaken from his firm belief that Tucker was one of Lynette's murderers even though independent evidence exonerated him. There were also serious difficulties over the quality of his identification of Lynette's murderers. By his own account he had never seen them before the night of the murder and even then it was a very brief sighting. Such a vivid recollection of perfect strangers seen for a few seconds several months earlier seemed unlikely. The case appeared to be in serious danger of unravelling. Now there were more loose ends than ever and the chinks in the Crown's case were becoming yawning chasms. But there was still one more witness to hear before the magistrates would have to decide if the defendants had a case to answer.

Committal Hearing (Part Four)

Paul Atkins was the last witness to give evidence in the committal hearing. He began by repeating the claims he made in his statements. He claimed that he had visited Grommek on the murder night and heard an argument in the flat below about sex. Prior to that he had heard shouting outside the flat. He told the magistrates that neither he nor Grommek had left Grommek's flat at that stage. He claimed that shortly after hearing the screams, he saw Vilday coming up the stairs and claimed that she had kicked the door in as it was locked.

Atkins claimed that he went to investigate and saw the body and blood everywhere. Then he saw three men on the stairs and they warned him not to say anything. He described them, but later contradicted himself about how they looked. Initially he claimed that 'Dullah' (Abdullahi) was a white man he used to drink with who was interested in the gay scene. During cross-examination his description of Dullah changed skin colour from white to mixed race and finally he was coloured.

Atkins told the magistrates that he was seen by the police repeatedly throughout 1988 and had it made clear to him that he had no choice but to accompany them to the police station. He claimed that they told him what they suspected had happened and who they suspected, especially Ronnie Actie. He also claimed that they threatened him with being charged with conspiracy to murder unless he named names, but he couldn't remember who had threatened him. He claimed that he wasn't offered money to name names; he just wanted it off his conscience. He was unaware that Grommek had had an attack of conscience the same day.

He claimed that he didn't discuss the murder with Grommek at first, but did so after it became obvious that the police were pressurising them. Towards the end of 1988, they agreed to give the police what they wanted and were told what the police wanted to hear again. He then claimed that he broke down and gave them what they wanted because they were bullying and threatening him with a conspiracy charge and they held him in the police station for hours. The magistrates, led by Kenneth Spurlock, had now heard all the evidence that they would hear. They found that there was a case to answer and committed the Cardiff Five for trial in Cardiff.

Compounding The Error (Part Four)

The Cardiff Five had now been committed for trial, but the discrepancies between the evidence of Vilday, Psaila and Grommek had been legion, but after Atkins had finished his testimony there were yawning chasms between them. For example, Atkins' claims regarding Vilday kicking in the door to the flat flatly contradicted the claims of Vilday and Psaila who had given evidence that it was open with John Actie standing by it, but they had simply pushed past him, an unlikely story at best.

Atkins had been a witness of appalling quality. He had contradicted his previous statements and many of his claims from the witness box. He seemed to be trying to please everybody. He made contradictory claims to the point where he must have been one of the worst witnesses ever heard by a Crown Prosecutor.

However, unknown to the Crown Prosecutor, the police were fully aware of Atkins' unreliability as DCI Adrian Morgan had mentioned it in his letter to DCS Williams on November 7th 1988. Consequently, the police knew that Atkins was an unreliable witness long before he gave evidence and before the Cardiff Five were arrested.

From three witnesses who contradicted themselves, each other and indisputable evidence irreconcilably, the Crown Prosecutor now had four witnesses who were at loggerheads on absolutely vital points. But Atkins made things even worse. His evidence brought the question of police oppression and impropriety into the equation.

One would not have expected the CPS to prosecute even a parking offence with witnesses of such calibre as these, but no evidence was withdrawn and the prosecution was not discontinued. The Cardiff Five had been committed for trial, but South Wales Police knew that they still had work to do in order to secure the result that they wanted.

A Crucial Change Of Venue

The case of the Cardiff Five was clearly a very important one and it was one that ought to have been heard in one of the major courts. It was set to take place in Cardiff, but it was moved to Swansea. The official reason concerned another murder trial where a witness was not mobile and the Cardiff court had better facilities, therefore it had precedence. In order to avoid unnecessary delays in bringing the case of the Cardiff Five to court, their case was moved from Cardiff to Swansea.

It seems a very strange reason to move a trial. There were other courts in Cardiff. However, if it was essential to move the trial, why take it to Swansea? Bristol had an environment more in tune with Cardiff and could have provided a much more reliable jury pool for reasons which will become apparent below. And moving the trial to Swansea made it impossible for the defendants' family and friends to observe the trial as it was not feasible to commute to Swansea every day of what would become the longest murder trial in British legal history. It was even more difficult for Miller's family as they lived nearly two hundred miles away in London.

Swansea was completely different to Cardiff. It had only a very small black community of about 1%. It was similar to Simi Valley, the overwhelmingly pro-police, white, middle class area in California where four white police officers were acquitted of the brutal beating of black motorist Rodney King despite a videotape of the beating being seen on television sets all over the world.

A jury of one's peers means a jury of people who come from a similar walk of life to the defendant. Thus, there was an obvious problem in guaranteeing that the defendants would be tried by a jury of their peers. Two probation officers who prefer not to be named would claim that the Cardiff Five received neither a fair trial, nor a jury of their peers, the right to which is one of the fundamental tenets of British law.

Over the years a plethora of black defendants have been convicted by all white, or overwhelmingly white, juries who came from an alien environment to that of the defendants. The absence of jurors from the same racial background as the defendant, especially in racially sensitive cases, has contributed to the denial of natural justice.

Numerous black defendants have attested to the fact that they feel more confident presenting their defence to a jury that has at least one black face in it. So far as black defendants are concerned, a jury of one's peers means a racially balanced jury. The Society of Black Lawyers has demanded that the criminal justice system guarantee black defendants at least four black jurors in racially sensitive cases.

If the trial had been allowed to take place in Cardiff, which had the largest black community in Wales, there was a danger that these people would not like what they saw. Worse still, they might see the case as an attack on their community. Had the trial been allowed to take place in a place more in tune with Butetown the prosecution's tactics would not only be likely to backfire, they could be seen as a liability. But the police knew that they could not rest on their laurels. There was still work to do before they would present their case to a jury.

CHAPTER 5

The Trawl Widens

The Review That Never Was

It was February 1989. The Cardiff Five had been committed for trial. Both the police and the CPS had the chance to appraise the state of the evidence. They had now seen how their star witnesses coped with cross-examination. Yet there was no dispassionate review of the weight of the evidence at their disposal. There were more inquiries to be made. The case against Tony Paris was particularly weak. Abdullahi's alibi presented a real obstacle to securing his conviction. There were inquiries into forensic issues which needed investigating. And there was the matter of gathering evidence of the police's view of the conduct of the Cardiff Five during the committal hearing.

The police attributed the poor performance of their witnesses at the committal hearing down to the antics of the defendants and their supporters. Officers now gave statements that the defendants bar Miller turned the committal hearing into a circus. They said that the public gallery and four of the Cardiff Five hurled abuse, threats and made threatening gestures at the women to intimidate them. And there were struggles with the police.

But there was still much work to do. The case against Paris needed serious police time and effort.

Showing Him The Ropes

Tony Paris had never been in prison before and had no idea of how things worked on the inside. He needed someone to show him. Ian Massey, a convicted armed robber, knew the prison system inside out. He was on the same wing that Paris and Ronnie Actie had been put on. And within days of his return to Cardiff Prison in November 1988 from one of many visits to Strangeways he was given his old cleaning job back. That gave him greater access on his landing than other prisoners. In the meantime he also ran his little earners. He seemed to have a charmed life. Massey was serving a fourteen year sentence and seemed the ideal person to show Paris the ropes.

Paris had been warned not to confide in anyone, since this could make fabricating evidence against him simplicity itself. But Paris was naive as well as innocent and told anyone who would listen anything they wanted to know. He thought he had nothing to hide and broadcast his innocence widely.

Massey quickly got pally with Paris, who thought that Massey would be able to explain to him the meaning, in legal terms, of his statements and depositions. So Paris showed Massey everything he had, including the crucial statements of Vilday and Psaila. This enabled Massey to acquaint himself with the case South Wales Police wanted to bring.

In fact, Massey cultivated Paris' friendship almost from the moment Paris arrived in Cardiff Prison in December 1988. But there were things that Paris did not know about Massey.

Massey seemed to be looking for a bargaining chip to bolster his appeal against his armed robbery conviction which was due to be heard soon. Shortly before Paris was remanded into custody Massey intimated to a police contact in the Greater Manchester force that he had information regarding a double murder in Milford Haven or Haverfordwest. Dyfed-Powys Police evaluated his information, but concluded that there was nothing concrete in it. Massey needed another bargaining chip.

This was not Massey's first attempt to cut himself a deal. In 1988 he had accused a policeman, Thomas "Ged" Corley of supplying him with weapons. Massey was one of several Mancunian armed robbers to accuse Corley of conspiracy to rob and supplying criminals with weapons. By June 1988 Massey had given evidence at the committal hearing against Corley. His performance was not up to the mark and his claims were to be allowed to lie on the file. Corley would subsequently be convicted of conspiracy to rob and supplying weapons to other armed robbers. However, Corley would eventually be exonerated on appeal with the ringing endorsement of the Court of Appeal, headed by the Lord Chief Justice. But Massey had gained a taste for the incentives on offer which included lighter sentences, private visits from girlfriends and the like. However, as Massey's appeal approached, his police contacts seemed to cool off.

Massey had been promised high level police assistance for his appeal. He was getting nervous. Dyfed-Powys Police were not interested in him. That left the Cardiff Five and Tony Paris in particular. Paris thought that Massey was helping him to understand his depositions. What he didn't know was that Massey had already been in touch with his contacts in Greater Manchester Police about him before the committal hearing had even ended.

On February 9th 1989 DI Mouncher received a call from his colleagues in Manchester. He was told that they had an informer in Cardiff Prison with information on the Lynette White Inquiry. According to Mouncher he was not given the informer's name. A little detection could easily resolve that issue as Massey was the only Manchester based villain in Cardiff Prison at the time. Mouncher would claim that it took them at least five months to deduce Massey's identity.

Meanwhile, Massey was now up on appeal before Lord Lane, the Lord Chief Justice. He expected to be freed. Chief Superintendent Arthur Roberts and Inspector Peter Jackson of Greater Manchester Police told the appeal judges that Massey had been very helpful in the Ged Corley Inquiry. When Lane heard that

Massey had not volunteered his information against Corley until after he had been arrested, he was distinctly unimpressed.

Massey's appeal was dismissed. He returned to Cardiff Prison furious, vowing to have no further dealings with the police. But police had already developed an interest in him. DI Mouncher received another call from his colleagues in Manchester. And in March Detective Superintendent Davies made fresh inquiries about Massey. Now police had established Massey as a useful source. But they had to wait until his anger at losing his appeal passed and he regained his taste for the inducements on offer for co-operating with police would come to get the better of him before long. In April Massey was taken back to Manchester where he had private visits with one of his girlfriends in a police station every day for five days. It was a timely reminder of what was on offer if Massey chose to assist the police. And, by now, Tony Paris represented his best hope of cutting a deal for early release from his fourteen year sentence.

Forensic Mess

Meanwhile, forensic issues had to be resolved. Dr John Whiteside had made two statements relating to the work that he had done to date. Other forensic scientists did the same. Whiteside identified the scene of crime samples which could not have come from Lynette, but there was no mention of SS5 and SS6 in either statement even though he would acknowledge in his evidence that they could not have come from Lynette either. And he made a vital assumption concerning the origin of SS12, the wallpaper sample that would later assume the greatest significance of all the samples in this inquiry. He concluded that it was reasonable to assume that SS12 had the same donor as nearby samples JAW27 and RH27 which conventional blood grouping tests had proved could not have come from Lynette. However, it would later emerge that one bloodstain in this inquiry was likely to have had two separate donors as after further work on stain four of the jeans Dr Whiteside concluded that it was likely that two haptoglobin results had been present. Belated attempts to conduct sex determination and conventional blood grouping tests on SS12 had failed by now.

Meanwhile, Dr Peter Gill had reported that it was possible that the blood on the jeans could have been a mixture of male and female blood. Dr Whiteside explained that of the major players in this inquiry, which did not include X and Y as despite their blood groups they had been eliminated on DNA before the Cardiff Five were arrested, only a mixture of Psaila's blood with Abdullahi could provide that result. However, it should be pointed out that the blood in the flat was just as likely to have been a cocktail of any people with compatible blood groups. While it applied to Abdullahi and Psaila it also applied to millions of other people in Britain. Clearly it did not apply exclusively to Abdullahi and Psaila, but this fact is not clearly stated in either of Dr Whiteside's statements. And the possibility that the blood in the flat was deposited by an unidentified man was never eliminated. It is unclear from Whiteside's statements if he considered this possibility even though this was a far more likely explanation than any cocktail theory involving Psaila.

Now, on April 25th, came the bombshell which altered the course of the Lynette White Inquiry. Dr Nicholas Prance excluded John Actie, Ronnie Actie, Tony Paris, Steve Miller, Angela Psaila and others as the source of the blood on SS12 by DNA profiling. Abdullahi's bloodstain had deteriorated to the point that no DNA profile could be obtained from it. This was a serious blow for the police. DNA was no longer any use to them. It indicated that at least four of the Cardiff Five were innocent. Many others including Mr X had been eliminated from the inquiry on that basis.

But there was an escape clause. Dr Prance felt that he could not eliminate the possibility that Lynette was the source of the blood on SS12. If that was true, all the DNA eliminations had to be discarded. But the police applied it selectively. They would come to use Dr Prance's theories to rubbish the DNA eliminations of the Cardiff Five (a separate DNA test would exclude Abdullahi later), but not apply its consequences to any of the other DNA eliminations.

Although nobody knew it now, this was a significant point in the inquiry. It offered a chance to put the inquiry back on track. Had the police not convinced themselves of the guilt of the Cardiff Five, they would have realised that Dr Prance's opinion meant that DNA was useless as a means of eliminating anyone. While this meant that the Cardiff Five could not be eliminated on DNA as well, it meant that the reason for eliminating Mr X and others was equally flawed.

And it meant that the blood groups of X and Y in particular became increasingly important. Unfortunately, the blood groups of these suspects were not disclosed to the defence even though Dr Whiteside's cocktail theory was just as consistent with a mixture of their blood with that of Psaila as a cocktail of Abdullahi and Psaila's blood. In fairness to both Dr Whiteside and the police it ought to be pointed out that both X and Y had been eliminated months earlier so they may have thought that there was no need to disclose their blood groups or the importance of X as a suspect. Unfortunately, the failure to disclose the blood groups of these men prevented the defence from conducting their own investigations into them and from challenging the cocktail theory as effectively as it could have been if they had this information at their disposal for the trial. Suffice to say, while there may have been no firm obligation on either the police or Dr Whiteside to disclose this information the better course of action would have been to disclose it as the non-disclosure resulted in Abdullahi having to counter the cocktail theory with one hand tied behind his back.

Meanwhile, Massey was indulging his taste for private visits from a girlfriend. And police had to deal with the somewhat thorny issue of Abdullahi's alibi.

A Thorn In Their Side

Police knew that Yusef Abdullahi's alibi posed many problems for them. The police traced thirty-five witnesses to the *Coral Sea*. They began their investigation of Abdullahi's alibi by trying to prove that Abdullahi was not on the *Coral Sea* at all. But several of Abdullahi's co-workers on the ship verified that he had indeed worked on it.

This forced South Wales Police to move the goalposts. The evidence clearly showed that Abdullahi had worked on the ship. Consequently, the crucial issues were when he did the work, what work he did, whether he left the ship on the night of the murder and, if so, who he left with and for how long.

Over the period of days that he was working at Barry Dock Abdullahi initially said that he returned to Cardiff a couple of times, but was adamant that it was not on the night of the murder. Police inquiries now unearthed no less than three people who claimed that they had given Abdullahi lifts back to Cardiff, but were unsure which night. There were several discrepancies with all of these accounts. For example, police suggested that Abdullahi could have used a quayside phone to call Ronnie Actie to come and pick him up. Actie could have come and driven Abdullahi back to Cardiff on the murder night. However, a little detection would reveal that Abdullahi could not have called Actie as there was no quayside phone. Police chose to rely on Les McCarthy, Danny Wilson and Dennis Hippolyte even though their accounts lacked certainty about which night Les McCarthy had given Abdullahi a lift back to Cardiff in his van.

Now police faced a stark choice. They had difficulty establishing how Abdullahi had got back to Cardiff, but Ronnie Williams and Peter Brooks had already told them that they had seen Abdullahi in the North Star club at about 1.30 a.m. on the murder night. Williams had been wrong about Lawrence Mann being with him, but Brooks filled the void. But police took statements from several users of the club. Not one of them had seen Williams or Abdullahi in the club that night. And the manageress, Cheryl Rogan, had been by the door. She knew both men, but told police that neither man had been in the club that night.

Police preferred to believe the accounts of Williams and Brooks. But there were several problems. Police had interviewed a *Coral Sea* worker named Brynley Samuel long before Abdullahi had been arrested. Samuel had told them that he had seen Abdullahi with Peter McCarthy, Les' brother, about midnight on the murder night and shared a half hour break with them. After twenty minutes or so Samuel and one of the Merseyside team of workers needed help. Samuel's colleague, John Hulse, went for assistance. He returned with Abdullahi and McCarthy. They worked together for a further forty minutes. According to Samuel's timings it was then about 1.30 a.m. Samuel also said that he saw Abdullahi again at about 6.00 a.m.

Samuel later shifted his account. The work done remained more or less the same, but the timings had changed. Samuel had told them that he definitely didn't see Abdullahi between 10.00 p.m. and 4.00 a.m. on the murder night. But he also told police that he had a conversation with Abdullahi in the mess room and that he did not notice any change in Abdullahi's demeanour or clothing. But the jury were not to hear from Brynley Samuel.

Now police interviewed Samuel again, but he just couldn't remember. But both Peter McCarthy and John Hulse had given broadly similar accounts of the work they did on the murder night, although it is right to point out that Hulse made no mention of his going to get assistance in his statements. This was supported by other members of the Merseyside group of workers.

Police knew that when they had allowed Abdullahi to detail the work that he did on the murder night in his interviews, it was strikingly similar to the type of work that Samuel, McCarthy, Hulse and the Merseyside workers described doing that night. Now police faced a major problem: how could Abdullahi have known what work had been done that night in such detail unless he had been there doing it? They could not find any witness to tell them that Abdullahi had been told what to say.

And then there was Lawrence Mann. He was a good friend of Ronnie Williams. But they disagreed about Abdullahi's whereabouts on the night of the murder and about the weather that night. Mann insisted that it had rained heavily and that he left the ship between 1.15 and 1.30 a.m. Just before he left he had seen Abdullahi, whom he did not like, and they had a minor disagreement. This was not what the police wanted to hear, but Mann remained certain that he had seen Abdullahi that night. He had even checked with the local weather centre to check that it had rained on the murder night.

Now that police had investigated Abdullahi's alibi it was time to take stock. The evidence seemed to support Abdullahi's claims that he had indeed been working on the *Coral Sea* throughout the murder night. This was an impressive alibi. If true, it proved Abdullahi innocent. But there was no review of the evidence. And Abdullahi was not aware that Brynley Samuel effectively supported his alibi. His statements were not to be disclosed until 1991.

But police knew that they were on far safer ground with the alibis of the other defendants. Ronnie Actie had claimed to be club hopping. His friends Michael Taylor and Johnny Crook had told police that they were out with him on the murder night. But police knew that Taylor had completely backtracked on an alibi for Actie by now. And Crook was at best unsure if he had been out with Actie that night. And there was the matter of Crook providing a false alibi for a friend before.

Police enquiries established that Tony Paris claimed to have worked as a glass collector on the murder night. Paris had claimed that he was wearing a black jacket, white shirt, Dickie-bow tie and smart trousers. Police now knew that Paris had support for his alibi. Witnesses had told them what Paris had been wearing, that he had been seen by different people throughout the night, that there was no build-up of dirty glasses and that Paris was one of a few people to stay behind for a drink after the club closed. Witnesses had told police that Paris' demeanour was affable as usual.

Police enquiries regarding John Actie delivered them an unexpected bonus. Actie had forgotten his alibi. In his interviews Actie had denied having been to the Casablanca on the murder night. He had made a mistake. Police had already been told as much by people close to Actie. Now the police were satisfied. They could prove that Actie was lying. In fact, Actie had just made a mistake over dates. But as far as the police were concerned they had caught him out in a deliberate lie.

Police felt that they were on even firmer ground with Miller's alibi. After all, they had convinced him that they had cracked his alibi. David Orton had alibied him initially. But even he had backtracked. And they had been told that Miller was not as sympathetic as he liked to portray himself by people whose accounts helped Miller in other ways.

Debbie Pennington, Yasmin Abdullahi, Derek Ferron, Eugene Savage and David Orton had all said that they had seen Miller in either the North Star or the Casablanca. But all had also contradicted Miller's opinion of himself. Police were now convinced that Miller's alibi posed no threat to them. They could look forward to the trial. But Miller's alibi had never been destroyed in the way South Wales Police convinced him it had. Yet there was still work to do before the case could be presented to a jury.

Emotional Verbals

Abdullahi's relationship with Jackie Harris broke down in August 1988. She went to live in the Women's Refuge in Pontypridd. Police had spoken to Harris before the arrests. She hadn't said anything of interest to them. Harris resented Abdullahi. She wanted revenge on him for the way he had treated her.

Now she told police that Abdullahi's violence to her got worse after the murder. Lynette's keys had gone missing. Harris told police that she found keys under a mattress, but got rid of them on Abdullahi's orders. Harris went on, telling police that Abdullahi had told her that he was glad Lynette was dead because she had grassed him up when Francine Cordle and Tony Miller were found at his place.

This was better for police, but it was not enough. Police had no admissions from Abdullahi himself. So Harris now provided the next best thing, a confession to her. She told police that Abdullahi had sworn on his children's lives that he had killed Lynette while he was high on drugs.

However, the police knew that Harris had her doubts. She had asked if she could see Vilday. Harris claims that she was told that she had no chance, but Vilday was subsequently brought to see her. There were at least four meetings between the two women who were to be vital witnesses against Abdullahi a few months later. They took place between March and May 1989. But Harris had no desire to help Abdullahi.

Now she told police that Abdullahi had asked her not to give evidence and had tried to get her to marry him so she wouldn't give evidence. Police could see their efforts bearing fruit. Harris had now given them admissions to the murder from Abdullahi, something they could not obtain from his mouth in twenty tape recorded interviews. And they had Sandrone, Amiel, Ronnie Williams and Peter Brooks to add to Vilday, Psaila, Grommek and Atkins. And they knew that while DNA had eliminated the remaining four suspects as the source of the blood on SS12, or ought to have done, Abdullahi's bloodstain had deteriorated to such an extent that no DNA profile could be obtained. They did not have a positive match, but Abdullahi had not been eliminated on DNA either. It was time to concentrate on Paris again.

Paris And The Supergrass

Police were having difficulties gathering evidence against Tony Paris. They had Miller's admissions which were inadmissible against Paris. And they had Vilday and Psaila, but Grommek and Atkins could not be used against Paris. They also had Helen Prance, but they had no admissions from Paris during his interviews. And they had 'anonymous' information from Massey which had been passed on to Mouncher by Greater Manchester Police in February.

Police knew that Massey had claimed that Paris was very worried about his leather jacket as it was heavily bloodstained. But Massey's claims were far from credible. There was no evidence that Paris was wearing his leather jacket on the night of the murder and forensic analysis would prove that it was not heavily bloodstained. A pinhead of dried blood would be discovered in a pocket. It would be so small that it could not even be grouped. And Massey had claimed that Paris was scared of two homosexuals (clearly Grommek and Atkins) even though Paris already knew that neither of them had incriminated him at all. Clearly police would or should have been aware that Massey was an unreliable source at best. But they persevered.

Meanwhile, in May, Ged Corley had been sentenced to seventeen years. Corley was going to appeal, but Massey expressed his delight at Corley's fate to a fellow armed robber, Courtney Davies.

Now, on June 29th, Massey left Cardiff Prison for Long Lartin. He fought the transfer tooth and nail, but was dispatched to the more secure jail. Now, police could make their move.

They began visiting Massey regularly beginning on August 10th. Massey told other prisoners that these visits were due to the Corley case. But these visits had nothing to do with that. South Wales Police, led by DI Mouncher, were visiting him. He would later agree while under oath that he took no notes of these interviews with Massey despite being obliged by the law to do so.

Meanwhile, Massey and Davies met up again in Long Lartin. Davies did not trust him and voiced his concerns that Massey was setting somebody up as Massey was now receiving several visits from police. And there was evidence that Massey had told Davies that he had some business going on with Mouncher which would do him (Massey) a favour. This is prisoners' terminology for setting someone up. Massey offered Davies the chance to jump on board and do himself a favour. Davies was disgusted. He was becoming more and more convinced that Massey was up to no good.

But Massey was a reasonably popular prisoner. He helped out other prisoners and listened to their problems. Could this man who regularly shouted at and cursed prison officers really be hand in glove with police? Corley was a police officer. Setting up a police officer was not only fair enough, it established him as a hero in the prison system. So Massey told the others that the police visits were due to the Corley case. Davies was not convinced, but he had no proof.

The Police Get Their Man

Mouncher cultivated Massey throughout August and September. Now he wanted a statement. The case against Paris still looked fragile. Massey could bolster it. Now police made the right noises. DS Duxbury had told him that if he helped South Wales Police that would be a feather in his cap for parole. Those words echoed in Massey's ears. This was his last chance of early release, but there were problems. Other prisoners despise grasses, especially prison informers who fabricate evidence for their own ends.

For Massey to throw in his lot with the police now meant that he would have to sweat it out and pray that nobody discovered his shenanigans. This was extremely dangerous. Courtney Davies already suspected him. Despite having no proof Davies was already voicing his suspicions to other prisoners. And there were several Welsh prisoners in Long Lartin Prison, any one of whom could have been friends of one or other of the Cardiff Five.

Massey had an important decision to make. He could help the police and get out early with all the hazards to his health that entailed or he could refuse to give them a statement and lose both early release and all the other inducements he had come to savour. Massey was missing his daughter. He wanted out. But time was running out for the police. It was the last week in September. The trial was due to begin the following week. They needed a statement now.

On September 25th Mouncher was booked in to see Massey. His cultivation of Massey was about to bear fruit. Massey was ready to make a statement. Massey told Mouncher that he was shocked at the violence of the murder and had decided to tell all. He repeated most of the things that he had told police in February. He claimed that Paris had admitted that all five defendants were guilty but that he had not meant to kill Lynette.

Now police had admissible evidence against Paris even though Massey was hardly a credible witness. After all, Massey had previously told police that Paris was scared of his leather jacket because it was heavily bloodstained. It wasn't. Now Massey claimed that Paris had expressed delight that forensics had messed up. But there was a problem. June 29th was the last date that Paris could have spoken to Massey. The forensic analysis of Paris' jacket had not been completed then. Massey had put information into Paris' mouth which he could not have known at the time. Yet rather than review the quality of Massey's evidence, the Crown Prosecutor prepared for the imminent trial.

Massey Unmasked

Now Massey had to sweat it out. Davies was convinced that Massey was cutting himself a deal at Paris' expense. He telephoned his solicitor and asked to be put in touch with Paris' solicitor. He is convinced that he ended up in the pound (a punishment cell separated from mainstream prison life) for his pains. Now he shouted up his accusations at Massey from the pound. Massey shouted back his denials that he was helping to frame the Cardiff Five.

But Davies was not alone in suspecting that Massey was up to no good. Among the many Welshmen in Long Lartin was John Eaton, who was serving eleven years for armed robbery. He was a friend of John Actie, but he didn't know Tony Paris. Eaton had met Massey before and didn't trust him. He seemed to have too many perks. Eaton received a copy of Massey's statement against Paris. This was incontrovertible proof that Massey was up to his old tricks again. Now that prisoners knew what Massey had been up to they wanted his hide. But Massey was in no mood for a fight. He was taken down to segregation and put on Rule 43 for his own protection.

It was now September 30th. The trial was due to begin in a few days time. Police knew that they would not be able to spring Massey on an unprepared defence. Paris' lawyers would be able to research Massey's criminal career. They would discover powerful evidence of Massey's duplicitous behaviour.

But while South Wales Police may have blinded themselves to the flaws in Massey's claims the CPS and Crown Prosecutor were there to provide an independent eye. Sadly, they now failed to do that and would rely uncritically on Massey. It would be up to a jury to deliver justice.

Part 2

THE TRIALS

"I hear much of people's calling out to punish the guilty, but very few are concerned to clear the innocent."

Daniel Defoe 1661-1731

CHAPTER 6 [1]

The Dress Rehearsal

The Trial Within A Trial

After nearly ten months in custody the waiting was almost over. The first trial began at Swansea Crown Court in the first week of October 1989; Mr Justice McNeill presiding. The CPS brought in David Elfer QC from the western circuit to take over as lead counsel for the Crown. A jury was about to hear the evidence. But first the judge would hear submissions regarding the admissibility of Miller's confessions and other legal arguments.

Miller's interviews would inevitably be an issue in the trial. They were the basis of the Voire Dire, or 'trial within a trial'. In the absence of the jury, McNeill heard defence submissions that Miller's interviews were conducted oppressively, that his IQ was abnormally low and as a result the confession should be inadmissible as evidence. Even though Crown Prosecutors are advised to be aware of these issues before deciding to pursue a case, Elfer vigorously contested the submissions made on Miller's behalf by Anthony Evans QC. Elfer submitted that Miller had not been bullied at all and the conduct of the interviewing officers was exemplary.

During these submissions Mr Justice McNeill heard all of tape seven, the one in which, according to defence submissions, the most outrageous bullying could be heard. He also listened to each taped interview after the seventh and heard defence expert Dr Gisli Gudjonsson's views that Miller was highly suggestible and had the mental age of a child. However, McNeill concluded that the interviews were admissible but not the testimony of Dr Gudjonsson.

The Trial

The Crown had won the first round. Now Elfer could begin his opening address. Elfer told the jury that he would prove each of the Cardiff Five guilty. In a memorable opening he told the jury that Butetowners were not like ordinary

[1] The accounts of both trials are based on handwritten notes made by one of the legal representatives rather than on actual transcripts which could not be obtained. These notes are not a verbatim account of everything that was said and done in the two trials. And it should be remembered that the account of the second trial (chapter 7) should be seen as incorporating their evidence given in the first trial. This has been done in order to avoid repetition of evidence given at the first trial wherever possible, although some repetition is unavoidable: the author.

people. Just as ordinary people like them (the jury) were getting up to go to work Butetowners were just coming home. They wore tracksuits and they carried knives as part of their clothing. And Elfer continued in the same vein when he outlined the evidence that he would present to the jury and painted a less than flattering picture of the character of the defendants. None of the defence lawyers got the chance to refute Elfer's claims now. Their chance would come at the close of the prosecution case.

Professor Bernard Knight was one of the first witnesses in the case. He gave the jury an account of the horrendous injuries that Lynette suffered and how she died. Gary George, a second cousin of John Actie, told them that he had seen a half caste man about thirty years old shouting abuse at the flat with a group which included John Actie laughing at him. The Crown submitted that the man doing the shouting was Steve Miller even though his QC, Anthony Evans, highlighted the serious discrepancies between the description given by George and Miller. He would assure the jury that the man George saw could not have been Miller.

The first of the major witnesses whom Elfer called was Learnne Vilday. She told the jury that the five men in the dock were responsible for Lynette's murder and that she had been forced to take part in it. Elfer would later submit that she was a courageous woman who had held the truth in for ten months before finally revealing it. She was cross-examined for several days. Defence lawyers highlighted several contradictions in her accounts. When the letter she wrote to Nicola Heysham was put to her she denied that its contents were true and insisted that she had not been subjected to pressure from the police. She claimed that she was ashamed of her part in Lynette's murder and did not want Heysham to know the truth. Evans would submit that the jury could not possibly conclude that it was safe to rely on her.

Angela Psaila was next into the witness box. She claimed that she had been forced to cut both of Lynette's wrists and Vilday had been forced to cut Lynette's throat even though Vilday had insisted that she had been forced to cut one of Lynette's wrists and had denied cutting Lynette's throat. Psaila claimed that Lynette was dead when she cut her wrists. Defence lawyers would submit that this meant that Vilday had killed Lynette. And Psaila told the jury that Mark Grommek had come into the murder room for a few minutes. During cross-examination Psaila told Anthony Evans that she was sick of answering his stupid questions. She insisted that she had been scared for her life and that this accounted for some of her errors.

She took exception to Evans' suggestion that she had not been in the room, telling him in no uncertain terms that her blood had been found in the flat and that proved that she was there. She said that one of the defendants had punched her causing her lower lip to bleed, but she could not account for how her blood came to be on Lynette's jeans. She told the jury that she had made a statement to DC Evans on February 16th 1988 and that the mark was still there when she was interviewed, but nobody commented on it. She also took umbrage at Anthony

Evans' suggestion that her brash style of giving evidence did not sit well with her claim to be frightened of the defendants. Evans would later submit that the jury could not rely on her evidence either.

Mark Grommek told the jury that he had been at home on the murder night with Paul Atkins and had opened the door after the bell had been ringing for ten minutes or so. Facing him when he opened the door were Ronnie Actie, Yusef Abdullahi, Martin Tucker and an unnamed black man with dreadlocks. He said that Ronnie Actie bought him drinks at the North Star and that Abdullahi had asked him if his name had come up when he was interviewed by police in November 1988. He went on to deny Psaila's claim that he had gone into the murder room for a few minutes or that he had made a mistake over Martin Tucker's presence.

Elfer would later submit that Tucker could have been one of the white men Miller mentioned as having been on the stairs during his interviews. And Elfer would suggest that the description of the black man fitted Miller's brother Tony, but as he had been in London on the murder night they may conclude that it was Steve Miller. But Grommek told the jury that he could not say Steve Miller, Tony Paris or John Actie were there on the murder night. He told the jury that he only saw Abdullahi for a few seconds and that he could not remember any distinguishing features. He insisted that he had not been offered indemnity from prosecution and like Vilday and Psaila he had not been aware that they were making statements at the same time. Grommek also assured the jury that he had not been subjected to police pressure.

During cross-examination Grommek's credibility was attacked by defence lawyers. Evans would later submit that the whole case was founded on the basis of the evidence of Vilday, Psaila and Grommek and that the police could not accept the possibility that they might not have been telling the truth. This completed the eyewitness testimony.

Vilday, Psaila and Grommek had contradicted themselves, each other and other indisputable evidence irreconcilably, but Elfer would submit that these witnesses, despite the contradictions, had told the truth, that their evidence could be safely relied on and the jury should remember the ordeal that they had been through. He would back up these submissions by referring to portions of Miller's confession which supported the claims made by Vilday and Psaila in particular.

Elfer had witnesses to support the testimony of his main witnesses. Gary George had already given evidence. Tessa Sidoric told the jury that she had intended to visit Tony Miller in prison, but had seen Steve instead as Tony had been released by then. She said that Miller denied killing Lynette, but had walked in on it. He had told her that he was told something like "If you can't control your woman I'll show you how." Sidoric claimed that Miller had told her that he didn't stop the murder because he and his family would have been killed. Miller had described the others as crazy animals claimed Sidoric who denied the suggestion that she could have been wrong about the content of that conversation.

Jackie Harris was next into the witness box. She told the jury a slightly different account to the ones she had told the police a few months earlier. She backtracked on some of her allegations of violence by Abdullahi, but confirmed that he had confessed to her while he was high on drugs. Abdullahi would later deny this confession and many of Harris' allegations against him. Harris went on to say that Abdullahi had said that he hated Lynette and that she deserved it. Again Abdullahi would later deny this.

Harris also let slip that she and Vilday had been allowed to meet at her request. But she insisted that they did not discuss the case. She told the jury that she discussed the case with DC Rachel O'Brien who said that Abdullahi was guilty, but she still couldn't believe it, even though she had previously told the jury she believed him guilty. She said that she still loved Abdullahi despite the fact that he had hurt her many times before. She claimed that she was told that she could be locked up in a cell and treated as a hostile witness or she could go into protective custody. She then denied that Abdullahi had said that he killed Lynette White. And she received a warning from the judge on the risks of perjury.

Elfer then moved on to evidence relating to the committal hearing. Once again he submitted that the contradictions between his main witnesses could be put down to fear of the defendants. Several officers from South Wales Police had made claims about the conduct of the public and four of the defendants during the committal hearing and now they were called to give evidence.

At least seven officers detailed the alleged conduct of the public gallery and all the defendants bar Miller. These officers told the jury that the other four, led by John Actie, had tried to intimidate the witnesses. Psaila had been too scared to take the oath. The defendants had hurled abuse and threats at the witnesses and Actie had made cut-throat gestures at both witnesses and a police officer.

Some said that with the exception of Miller all the defendants refused to leave the dock after a scuffle in the public gallery concerning one of John Actie's brothers. According to police, order was restored only when more officers arrived on the scene. They claimed that their greater presence restored order and kept the lid on a volatile situation following these occurrences of the morning of February 6th.

All of the defendants bar Miller would freely admit that they had barracked the witnesses. They would claim that they had shouted at the witnesses to tell the truth and some would admit swearing at them. They would insist that they had only done so to encourage them to tell the truth, not to intimidate them. They would vociferously deny the veracity of police evidence concerning their behaviour at that hearing. John Actie would also make the extraordinary claim that Psaila was obviously reluctant to give evidence and had to be carried in by police. Both Abdullahi and Actie would confirm that they had heard a police officer saying that Psaila was on speed.

John Actie would deny in full the prosecution's allegations about the committal hearing. He would reject their claim that he was the ringleader of a deliberate plan to turn the committal hearing into a circus. He would insist that he had never threatened the witnesses at all and had made no gestures at them other than banging his fist on the dock once and repeatedly barracking them.

The defence would call further evidence about the committal hearing. Bernard de Maid had been there representing Abdullahi. He would tell the jury that he had seen no threatening gestures although he would accept that the atmosphere had been electric. He would confirm that his client had told him about hearing that Psaila was on speed and that he had tried to confirm it, but the officer would not repeat it.

John Actie would call Marilyn Bishop who had represented Tony Paris. She would confirm that there had been an incident in the public gallery after Carl Actie had shouted something like, "It's always the Acties." A scuffle developed and John Actie refused to leave the dock because he was concerned about his brother. Bishop would say that she thought the police could have handled the incident better. By then John Actie had said Psaila was reluctant to give evidence on the first day of the committal hearing. Bishop would contradict him on the day, but would confirm that she was told that the late start the following day was due to Psaila being reluctant to give evidence. Bishop would claim that Psaila had been ill but was dragged into court by Ken Davies and a woman officer kicking and screaming. She would also say that she had not seen any cut-throat gestures.

One of the magistrates, the Chairman of the Bench, Kenneth Spurlock, would also be called to give evidence on John Actie's behalf. It was highly unusual for a magistrate to give evidence at a criminal trial, but for one to be a defence witness was virtually unheard of.

Spurlock would tell the jury that the only gesture he had seen in the whole of the committal hearing was Ronnie Actie point at a witness, although he would admit that he wasn't in court all the time. Spurlock would confirm that he had fifteen years experience as a magistrate. He would claim that it was a gross exaggeration to describe the committal hearing as a circus, as the prosecution had put it. He would describe the scenes that had occurred on the morning of February 6th. He would claim that when the defendants had entered the dock there had been a disturbance in the public gallery which had threatened to get completely out of hand, so he had immediately adjourned the proceedings. When the proceedings reconvened in the afternoon, he had complimented the defendants and the public on their improved conduct.

He would confirm that John Actie had not made any threatening gestures. He had heard Actie shout, "Tell the fucking truth!" at Psaila and would confirm that John Actie had left the dock during Vilday's evidence saying that he didn't want to hear any more of that shit. He would say that he didn't think that there was any point summoning Actie back to order him to leave the dock, but sent Actie a message that he would not be allowed back until he apologised. Actie had done so the following day.

Spurlock would insist that the committal hearing had not been a frightening occasion. There were occasions when he had felt it necessary to reprimand the defendants over their behaviour, but this was regarding their barracking of witnesses to the point where the magistrates could not hear what the witnesses were saying. Spurlock would say that he could not remember telling defence lawyers to warn their clients to improve their behaviour. He would tell the jury that threats had been shouted from the public gallery but not from the dock. Apart from seeing Ronnie Actie point at a witness he had seen no gestures from the defendants. Spurlock would claim that he had seen no aggression between John Actie, who had been listening to the evidence intently, and the officer handcuffed to him. He would deny Elfer's suggestion that he had only allowed the proceedings to continue to get them over as quickly as he could. Elfer would later suggest that it was amazing that such an honourable man seemed to have forgotten so much.

After the evidence about the committal hearing Elfer called Miller's girlfriend, Debbie Taylor. She told the jury that together with Miller's sister Nicki Gordon, she and Tessa Sidoric had visited Miller in Cardiff Prison. Miller had told them that he was innocent and had stumbled in on the murder. Miller had pointed out Tony Paris on the visit. On other visits Miller had told her that he had nothing to do with it and didn't know why he was in prison. He said that he had seen into the room but never been in it even though the two women had put him inside it. He told her that he saw Tony Paris stabbing Lynette. Then he said that he hadn't been in the flat but had seen it from the stairs. Taylor told Elfer in no uncertain terms that Miller had not asked her to become a prostitute.

After this witness all of Miller's taped interviews were played to the jury. Both David Elfer and Anthony Evans questioned the officers on the basis of these tapes. Elfer would later use this evidence to show that Miller's confession had been true and Miller had given it voluntarily. He would use examples of Miller not agreeing with the officers to show that he was not suggestible and that the jury should accept the confession as a genuine admission of guilt.

Next Elfer called the officers who had interviewed Miller. DC Greenwood told the jury that no stone had been left unturned. He knew that Psaila's statements had varied, but believed her. He believed that Miller was involved and held the key to the inquiry. He denied that the denial of a solicitor was to try to get a confession before he could get legal advice. He told the jury that he believed that the December 6th statements of Vilday, Psaila and Grommek was the truth. He said that he interviewed Miller on the basis that these statements were true and that Miller held the truth to the enquiry. He claimed that he believed that Vilday, Psaila and Grommek were independent of each other and none of the three disliked Miller.

Greenwood denied that Miller had been pressurised at all by police. He thought that Miller might have pressurised himself. He admitted that voices had been raised, but insisted that the interviews were firm but fair. He said that the interviews would have gone on until he got the truth not until Miller admitted presence at the scene of the crime. He told the jury that his approach was to keep an open mind. He believed Miller held the truth about Lynette's death.

Greenwood's partner John Seaford was next to give evidence. He also told the jury that he believed the statements of Vilday, Psaila and Grommek. He said that he would not have believed that Miller was not there when Lynette was murdered and that the truth had to include an admission from Miller that he had been there. He said that he would have gone on putting things to him until he agreed that he was there. He denied that there was any mention of Miller as the weak link. He denied that it was a case of getting Miller to fit the case they were interested in. They wanted the truth and believed they got it. He denied that there was a hard/soft tactic. He said that after interview seven he believed that Miller was ready to tell the truth. He stressed that there had been no complaint by either Miller or his solicitor. He believed that they had been fair.

DC John Murray told the jury that there had been no tactic of Greenwood and Seaford being the hard men softening Miller up for Evans and himself. He knew that Miller had denied involvement in Lynette's murder in all interviews with Seaford and Greenwood. He insisted that when he said, "There are times we can help you," to Miller that didn't mean they couldn't help him until he admitted his presence in the murder room. He denied making promises to Miller that they would help him if he admitted that he was there. He rejected the suggestion that he had changed his mild manner in the last interview. He said that he warned the custody officer that the solicitor might make a complaint, but admitted that he did not record the complaint that Richards had made during that interview. He believed that Vilday and Psaila were asked to attend the police station late at night because of the discovery of Psaila's blood group. He also confirmed that there were times that he thought that Miller was just saying things to try to please them.

DC Simon Evans said that the truth as he saw it was that Miller was there. He said that there was no question in his mind that the witnesses were telling the truth and that Miller was there. He told the jury that he would have gone on until they got the truth. He said that it could not be seen as pressurising the accused as they gave him a half hour break. Evans claimed that he didn't think that Miller was suggestible and just going along with him. He gave examples where Miller didn't agree with him as proof that Miller wasn't suggestible. He accepted that the code of silence expression had come from him and not from Miller. He rejected the suggestion that the interviews were conducted on the basis of the police couldn't help him until he admitted that he was there. He insisted that it was not his intention to give Miller the impression that he should stick the others in before they did it to him.

When it was his turn to give evidence Miller would claim that Greenwood and Seaford had bullied and pressurised him to the extent that he regarded the other two officers as his protectors. He would claim that the details in his confession had either been suggested to him in the interviews, made up by him to please them or details that he had picked up in previous interviews. Elfer would suggest that he had supplied true details of the crime voluntarily. Miller would respond that he only said what he said and that he was happy to continue the interviews because he wanted to get them over with as soon as possible. Miller would say that he felt that he had been blackmailed into saying that he was in the flat. He would deny that the confession was true and accuse the police of obtaining it improperly. Miller would insist that he had tried to tell the truth, but had not been believed. He would accuse the officers of only being interested in hearing lies. He would tell the jury that he interpreted the phrase that there could be a nice way round this as meaning that he could say what they wanted and still go home.

The last witness Elfer called against Miller was Jennifer Parkin. She told the jury that she had been a prostitute, but wasn't any more. She claimed that Miller had threatened to put her in the same place as Lynette White if she talked to the police, but said it with a smile on his face. She denied Anthony Evans' suggestion that she did not have that conversation with Miller. She admitted that she had had a nervous breakdown eleven years ago and denied taking drink or drugs before coming to court. This ended the Crown's case against Miller who would deny the veracity of Parkin's evidence and insist that he never had that conversation with her.

Now Elfer moved on to Tony Paris. He called Helen Prance, but she did not stick to the letter of her statements. She told the jury that Miller and Paris were not close friends. She said that she had been hassled by police, locked up for five hours and had lost her job because of police pressure. She claimed that she just signed her statements to end the harassment and that what she had told the police was totally different to what was in her statements.

She told the jury that she was upset when Paris got married as they had been seeing each other. She claimed that the police just pressurised her into saying things against Paris and she told them that some of her statements read stronger against Paris than she had actually put it to police. However, she did confirm that Miller had asked her to go to London with him and that Miller had treated Lynette like shit. Miller would deny her allegations and the officers who dealt with Prance insisted that they did not pressurise her or put words in her mouth.

Prance had not supported the case against Paris, but the Crown still had Ian Massey who told the jury that he had helped Paris with his case and had read whatever papers Paris showed him. He claimed that at first he thought that Paris wasn't involved, but came to believe that he was guilty. Massey denied that he was giving evidence now in expectation of personal gain. He insisted that Paris had confessed to him, but denied that there had been any discussions with police on privileges he would get. He denied reading the information in those statements to turn it to his own advantage. He told the jury that he knew that the police could not help him as it was the Home Office's decision regarding parole. Massey insisted that he was not giving evidence to feather his own nest, but because Paris had told him that the girls, then in protective custody, were going to be sorted out.

However, the armed robber Courtney Davies would tell a different story. He would admit that he didn't like grasses and would tell the jury that Massey had told him that he was setting them up. Massey was cross-examined regarding the Corley case and claimed that it was thanks to him that Corley got bail.

Paris would later tell the jury that he talked to Massey, but would vehemently deny confessing to him or anyone else. He would also deny telling Massey that Vilday and Psaila were going to be sorted out. Elfer exhibited a camping knife belonging to Paris, but it was accepted that this was not the murder weapon. However, Elfer would later suggest that Paris had another knife which the police did not find and that the jury may conclude that it was used by Paris to kill Lynette. Paris would deny that he had murdered Lynette or even been to the flat. He would claim that Massey was lying to try to get parole and that he had been working in the Casablanca on the murder night. He would call evidence to support his alibi.

Elfer moved on to Ronnie Actie. He called police evidence regarding the interviews and Rockman Ali who had stolen the green Cortina that police claimed Actie drove at the time of the murder. Ali's evidence suggested that Actie had the car around the time of the murder. But this evidence would be contradicted by Ronnie's sister Michelle and by Actie's good friend Johnny Crook who would claim that Actie drove a red Triumph at the time. Andrew Steadman would claim that he drove the Cortina at the time, but Elfer would be able to highlight inconsistencies in their evidence.

Now Elfer moved on to Yusef Abdullahi. The jury had already heard from Jackie Harris. Jane Sandrone confirmed her statements, although she did not say that what Abdullahi said amounted to a confession. Ronnie Williams was called and repeated his claims about his conversations with Abdullahi and seeing Abdullahi in the North Star on the murder night. Abdullahi would vociferously deny Williams' claims and would insist that he would never choose Williams as an intermediary with the police as he regarded Williams as a police informer and he would insist that he was working on the *Coral Sea* on the murder night.

Williams told the jury that he was a good friend of Lawrence Mann which was why he thought that he was with him that night. He said that he had made a mistake and that all mention of Mann should have been Peter Brooks. Williams rejected the suggestion that he was a police informer, especially for Tommy Page as he had arrested him before over a case Williams claimed he was not guilty and couldn't pursue because of the cost. But Page suggested that Williams used to come in quite often and was a source of information. Page could not explain how officers knew on December 10th information that Williams would put in his statement on December 11th to him.

Peter Brooks assured the jury that he had been with Williams in the North Star when they saw Abdullahi. He denied discussing a reward with Williams and despite previous convictions he described himself as an honest person.

Elfer called Danny Wilson and Dennis Hippolyte to refute Abdullahi's alibi. Both claimed that they had been given a lift in Les McCarthy's van along with Abdullahi either on the Saturday or Sunday night. They could not remember which, but thought from other events that it was the Saturday night. Abdullahi would insist that he worked on the ship throughout that night and would call witnesses to prove it.

After this Elfer moved on to the scientific evidence. DS Stephen Steele told the jury that of 150 fingerprints left at the scene of the crime, none of them, including marks without the required sixteen characteristics, could tie any of the defendants to the murder flat. Steele also said that Angela Psaila's fingerprints had not been found in the flat. DS Steele revealed that there were eleven unidentified marks which were of good quality. Elfer would later submit that as it was possible that the crime could have been committed without leaving marks behind, the failure to discover fingerprints linking the defendants to the flat did not undermine the Crown's case.

Dr Whiteside was next into the witness box. Earlier Psaila had told the jury that her blood had been found in the flat and that proved that she had been there. She had doled out an earbashing to any lawyer who had the temerity to suggest otherwise. Now Whiteside would give the jury an inkling into the scientific basis for Psaila's claim.

Whiteside told the jury that smeared traces of blood which did not originate from Lynette had been discovered on the bottom of her jeans. He said that this blood group occurred in approximately 1:3800 people and that a drop of similar blood had been discovered on her right sock where it met the jeans. The results of testing on the jeans revealed that it contained male material. Whiteside informed the jury that five areas were tested in order to cover as wide an area as possible.

Dr Whiteside told the jury that he had discovered Psaila's blood group as a result of an unconnected case. He thought it significant and told the police. He said that the discovery of Psaila's blood group made him question the result indicating that the blood on the jeans was male. He explained to the jury that it was possible that the blood on the jeans was a mixture of male and female blood, and that if the blood was from Psaila it had to have mixed with that of a man. Whiteside also revealed that traces of smeared blood on the wallpaper in the landing, SS5 and SS6, did not come from Lynette. He said that he believed that all the blood which was not deposited by Lynette came from the same source.

However, in cross-examination Whiteside told the jury that anyone who had been near Lynette when she was killed would have had extensive bloodstaining on their clothes and he had found no blood evidence linking any of the defendants to the room bar Abdullahi as blood grouping tests could not eliminate him as a possible source for bloodstains on the walls. Whiteside revealed that with the spread of blood on both legs of the jeans it was difficult to see how it could have mixed, but that it was possible for it to have mixed in the hand and then been smeared on the jeans, but that this was unlikely. He also revealed that if there was a large amount of female blood in the mixture then the male blood could belong to any man. Whiteside accepted that there was nothing in the tests on the jeans to indicate that it had been a mixture of male and female blood.

Dr Peter Gill followed Whiteside into the witness box. He told the jury that his test only determined whether male material was present in the blood not whether it could have been a mixture. Some of the results were weaker than others. Gill said that he hadn't considered the possibility of a mixture until he was told that it was female blood. He told the jury that 1:10,000 women possess the male chromosome but that Psaila was not one of them. Dr Nicholas Prance then told the jury that all of the defendants could be eliminated as the source of the blood on SS12, but that he could not exclude Lynette as the source of the blood on SS12. This ended the scientific evidence called by the Crown.

Detective Superintendent Davies outlined the scope of the inquiry for the jury. He told them that the decision to refuse access to solicitors had been taken by DCS Williams after the CPS had been consulted. He told the jury that despite thirty-five witnesses being traced to the *Coral Sea* statements were only obtained from nine of them. With reference to DC Cullen's alleged conversation with Yusef Abdullahi, Davies claimed that it was not unusual to have a delay of two months before a request for a statement was made. He agreed that he would have expected the officer to make a note of that conversation and could not answer for there being no entry to that effect.

DC Mike Daniels told the jury that he had taken the contemporaneous notes of the interviews with Psaila on November 17th 1988 and that DI Mouncher had reassured her about her safety for a couple of minutes. He also said that he had taken her statement of December 11th and insisted that he had not told her about her blood being found in the murder room. He claimed that he was certain that he never put it to her that she was suspected of the crime, but he had always thought that she knew more than she was saying.

Daniels also told the jury that he initially thought that the time sheets proved that Abdullahi had never been on the ship until Mouncher told him that the records were inaccurate. He had interviewed several people who had initially said they had not given lifts to Abdullahi and it was not until Abdullahi's ninth interview that he accepted Abdullahi had been on the ship at all. DC Tooby and DC Fish had also given evidence pertaining to the investigation of Abdullahi's alibi.

DC Cullen detailed the conversation he claimed to have had with Abdullahi for the jury. He accepted that despite being an officer for nine years he made no note about it. He claimed that he passed the information on to the Incident Room and was able to remember the conversation enough to make a statement four months later because it was a short conversation. Cullen denied the suggestion that the conversation was to the effect that Abdullahi had said that it must have been a punter who just freaked out.

Now Elfer moved on to John Actie. He detailed the content of Actie's interviews and asked the jury to interpret Actie's insistence that he had not been in the Casablanca on the murder night as a deliberate attempt to deceive them rather than the honest mistake that Actie would insist it was. The jury had already heard the evidence of Gary George which Actie would vehemently deny and they had heard from the police about his alleged antics during the committal hearing.

Violet Perriam told the jury that she was driving home from work on the murder night about 1.30 a.m. when she saw a group of four excited coloured men outside 7 James Street. She claimed to be sure that one of them was John Actie even though he had his back towards her. She claimed that his head was three quarters towards her so she could see who it was. She also claimed to have seen a brown Cortina at the scene. She told the jury that she couldn't be sure that one of the group was Steve Miller but accepted that she had made a previous statement saying that Miller definitely wasn't one of them. On January 15th 1990 Elfer closed the Crown's case against the Cardiff Five.

Now the defence would have their say, beginning with Miller who told the jury that he did not kill Lynette and had never been to the murder flat. He detailed his movements from Lynette's disappearance up to the murder night. He described his relationship with Lynette and denied that he put her on the street or was her pimp. He accepted that she paid for his drugs and outlined his use of drugs for the jury. He vehemently denied the accusations of Vilday and Psaila and denied that he had ever threatened Jennifer Parkin.

Miller told the jury that he was shocked when he was arrested and had tried to tell the police the truth, but they weren't interested in hearing it. He said that he had hoped to be treated as a witness and felt the police had blackmailed him into making a false confession. As for Sidoric and Taylor, he had denied taking part in the murder, but had repeated some of his confession. He said that he had seen the *Crimewatch* video and had told Jackie Harris that he would kill whoever murdered Lynette. He also told the jury how he regularly visited the police and tried to find out what had happened before returning to London in April 1988.

During cross-examination by Elfer, Miller denied that he treated Lynette like dirt and said that he was happy to continue with the interviews to bring them to an end as soon as he could. He told Elfer that if he knew that his co-defendants had done anything he would say so now and if he had done anything he would take whatever came, but he wasn't there. He said that he didn't know why he didn't agree with everything, but he was confused. He denied Elfer's suggestion that he didn't have much money at the time of the murder. Miller insisted that if Vilday had told him where Lynette was earlier in the week he would have gone to see her immediately, but he had not been told then and didn't know Lynette had been there until her body was discovered. He agreed that David Orton could help him but didn't know if Orton was going to be called.

Tony Paris was the next person to give evidence. He denied murdering

Lynette and insisted that he had never gone into 7 James Street. He outlined his movements on the murder night for the jury. He admitted talking to Massey but vehemently denied Massey's version of their conversations. He insisted that he had been collecting glasses at the Casablanca and had stayed behind for a drink after the revellers had gone home. He too denied Vilday and Psaila's evidence and insisted that he did not put Helen Prance on the streets. He denied ever having a conversation with Miller about showing him how to control his woman even though Miller had said that they did have such a conversation although it had happened months before the murder.

Paris' QC, Gerard Elias, called Carol Blades and Peter Scott as alibi witnesses. Blades told the jury that she had seen Paris at work throughout the night and that there was nothing unusual about him. Scott said that he had never seen Paris involved in violence and that he had paid him for collecting glasses which he would not have done if Paris had not been working. He denied Elfer's suggestion that John Actie used to drift around while working on the door. Scott told Elfer that he had torn out a page from the ledger of the Casablanca for a phone number and had done so in front of a police officer. Scott admitted that he had a previous conviction for conspiracy to pervert the course of justice, but insisted that he had not come to court to lie. He denied Elfer's suggestion that he had doctored the book and re-iterated that he had only torn out that page in front of the police.

Paris' case ended with Courtney Davies who told the jury of his conversations with Massey. Davies said that Massey had told him that he was trying to do a deal and had met with DI Mouncher while in Cardiff Prison, which both Massey and Mouncher had denied. Davies claimed that Massey was a creep whom he tolerated. He admitted being a ruthless man and thought it unfortunate that grasses weren't beaten up any more. Nevertheless, Davies insisted that Massey had hinted that he was looking for ways to improve his lot by doing a deal with the police. Davies told the jury that he didn't want to be in court and thought that he wouldn't have to give evidence as he didn't think that Massey would have been called. Elfer highlighted some of the discrepancies between his evidence and what he had previously said in his statement, but Davies remained adamant that he had told the truth and had not come to court to lie and had nothing to gain by giving evidence.

Now it was Ronnie Actie's turn to present his case. On legal advice he chose not to give evidence. However, he called witnesses. His sister Michelle told the jury that he drove a red Triumph at the time of the murder, not a green Cortina and that he and Vilday had come to her home about 3.00 a.m. on the murder night. She immediately noticed that Vilday's face was bruised and that Vilday was not her usual talkative self. She told the jury that Vilday had been a fun loving girl, but was different that night. She described the clothes that Ronnie had worn that night and insisted that he had returned in the same clothes that he was wearing when he left her place earlier that night. His clothes were not bloodstained. She explained the discrepancies between her evidence and her statement to the police by pointing out that she had only answered the police's questions and that the other matters had been raised by questions asked by Actie's solicitor when she made a statement to them in 1989.

Actie also called his friend Johnny Crook who told the jury that he couldn't remember the murder night but their usual practice at the time was to go out clubbing. He claimed that he couldn't remember missing a Saturday night out with Actie in six months and that the police must have confused him. He insisted that although he had told police that Actie drove a green Cortina at the time he later remembered that Actie used a red Triumph at the time of the murder. He told the jury that he did not discuss Actie's cars when he visited him in prison. During cross-examination Elfer undermined Crook's veracity by showing that he had deceived the jury by telling them that he had never lied in court when he had a conviction twelve years earlier for aiding and abetting perjury.

Crook was followed into the witness box by Andrew Steadman who told the jury that he had bought the green Cortina from Ronnie's brother Robert. He said that he owned it when he received a parking ticket dated February 16th 1988, but that ticket was the only record that he had ever owned it and he had just left the ticket in the car. He admitted that he had convictions for dishonesty offences, but vehemently denied coming to court to lie for Actie. Elfer would later invite the jury not to believe him.

Brian Spriggs and his niece Cherie were Actie's next witnesses. Cherie told the jury that Vilday had asked her to deliver messages to Ronnie Actie asking him to meet her after the murder. She denied Vilday's earlier claim that she had gone to see Actie on her own volition. Her uncle claimed that after Vilday moved in they got several visits from the police who even searched the house because they didn't believe that Vilday wasn't in on one occasion. Spriggs told the jury that in early December 1988, after being raped by a punter, Psaila was brought to them by police and he let her stay for a couple of days, sharing Vilday's room. Spriggs claimed that after Christmas 1988 Vilday called saying that only Tucker and Miller should have been arrested. He claimed that she also told him who she could believe had done it and who she couldn't believe were responsible. Spriggs admitted that he had his share of trouble with the police in the past, but insisted that he had put all that behind him and was adamant that he had not come to court to lie.

Vilday's friend from Barry, Sarah Whitcombe, told the jury that while she was staying at Psaila's flat Lynette came round on the Sunday or Monday before the murder and said that she was frightened of going to court, although this was not in her statement to police. She confirmed that Vilday had received threats to herself and Craig and although Vilday had told her who made them she could not now remember. She told the jury that she knew that Steve Miller had a cocaine habit which Lynette's earnings financed, but she denied that Miller and Debbie Haggett knew that Lynette could be found at 7 James Street.[1] Whitcombe said that Vilday had changed since the murder from being a fun loving girl to rather a sad

[1] Debbie Haggett is also known as Debbie Paul.

girl. Whitcombe told the jury that she had been staying in Psaila's flat the night when Lynette's body was discovered by Vilday. She claimed that Vilday had returned from the police station about 4.00 a.m. and told Psaila that Lynette was dead. Whitcombe also told the jury that she accompanied Psaila to court on February 15th 1988 and did not notice any injuries to Psaila's face.

Ronnie Actie's last witness was Nicola Heysham, the recipient of the Boxing Day letter from Vilday and a person Vilday had described as her best friend. Heysham told the jury that Vilday, whom she had known for years, started drinking heavily after the murder. Heysham claimed that Vilday had told her that the police threatened to take her baby from her if she didn't give them what they wanted. Vilday, she claimed, came round unexpectedly after Christmas and gave her a letter to read later. She didn't want to keep it, but her boyfriend was a friend of Ronnie Actie and persuaded her to give it to his solicitor. This ended the case for Ronnie Actie. Now it was Yusef Abdullahi's turn to give evidence.

Abdullahi told the jury that he had convictions for robbery and detailed his relationship with Jackie Harris which he admitted included domestic rows and that he had knocked her about. He explained his violence by referring to domestic situations and his belief that she had been having an affair with a policeman, something Harris had denied during her evidence, but would eventually admit to in 1992.

Abdullahi denied that he had ever confessed to Harris or Jane Sandrone. He admitted that he had a conversation with Noreen Amiel but they had not talked about the murder. He claimed that he had told her that he wanted to sail with the ship but could not find his passport. He denied that he had ever stabbed a woman or told Miller that he had as Miller had told police during his interviews. Yet Miller had denied that Abdullahi had told him this when he gave evidence. Abdullahi denied Harris' claims that he had been a drug dealer and began injecting drugs as a result of the murder.

Abdullahi insisted that he did not hate Lynette or say that she deserved to die for grassing him out over Francine Cordle and Tony Miller staying at his place. He admitted disliking her and that her grassing on him didn't help. He told the jury about DI Powell's inquiry into his injured hand. He assured the jury that he had suffered a burn while working on the *Coral Sea* and he put a bandage on it and carried on working. It had eventually blistered. He would shortly be backed up by his mother Pauline, who would tell the jury that when Abdullahi returned she washed and treated his hand and saw it blister. She would insist that she did not come to court to lie for her son.

Abdullahi insisted that he did not like Ronnie Williams because he was always talking to the police and talking to prostitutes with his notebook in hand and used to describe himself as a private investigator. He claimed that he had talked about the murder with Williams but had not said what Williams claimed. Abdullahi told the jury that if he knew anything about the murder he would not have wanted money for it. Abdullahi also claimed that Williams approached him and said something to the effect that we are now in a position to pay a reward, but as Williams was drunk he did not take him seriously.

Abdullahi then told the jury that he did not possess a red tracksuit and had only told the police that because he suspected that they were fitting him up and he knew that he didn't have one and although Harris did, it didn't fit him. Harris had previously confirmed this and Abdullahi's mother would also confirm it.

Abdullahi detailed his movements on the murder night which included the work that he claimed to have done that night and was taken through his police interviews. He admitted that in a previous case which resulted in him getting convicted of malicious wounding he had denied involvement at first, despite being involved in it. He insisted that he was entirely innocent of involvement in the murder of Lynette White and had been on the *Coral Sea* working throughout the murder night. He accepted that in his previous accounts to the police he had been wrong about the date that he started working on the ship, but corrected this during his interviews with police. He remained adamant that he did not leave the ship on the murder night.

Abdullahi vehemently denied the claims of Williams and Brooks that he had been in the North Star on the murder night. He would soon be backed up by Cheryl Rogan who worked in the North Star on the murder night. She would say that while she saw Miller there that night she did not see Williams, Brooks or Abdullahi there and she knew each of them well. She would deny agreeing to lie for Abdullahi and would insist that if Williams had been there that night he would have talked to her.

Abdullahi denied Vilday's claim that he had given her free drugs and rejected the claims of Vilday and Psaila entirely. He told the jury that it was impossible for Grommek to have seen him there as he was on the ship. He insisted that he had never confessed to Lynette's murder or indicated that he had information for sale to anybody. With reference to DC Cullen's evidence, Abdullahi told the jury that if he had said what Cullen claimed he did he would have been taken down the police station and been in a cell before his feet touched the ground. Moreover, he denied having any conversation with Cullen.

Abdullahi told the jury that he kept telling the police to check the times he worked with the time sheets but the police did not want to prove that he had been on the ship. He claimed that he didn't know they were inaccurate at the time, but the jury would now hear from witnesses who supported Abdullahi's persistent claims that he had been working on the ship on the murder night.

Jackie Harris' stepfather Peter McCarthy was the first of the *Coral Sea* witnesses to give evidence. He detailed his movements that night for the jury. He told them that he gave Abdullahi and Brynley Samuel a lift to the ship and tried but failed to drive the crane on the ship. He also told the jury that during that night a fat man from Liverpool came into the mess room and asked for assistance. McCarthy claimed that Abdullahi went with them while he went to sleep. According to McCarthy, Abdullahi was working between 1.30-2.00 a.m. McCarthy also told the jury that he saw Abdullahi drop a hot metal plate, rub his hand and wrap a tatty bandage round it. He admitted that he didn't see the injury and told the jury that he did not see Abdullahi leave the ship. McCarthy vehemently denied Elfer's suggestion that he was lying or that he had invented the incident of the Liverpool worker asking for assistance.

John Hulse was Abdullahi's next alibi witness. He told the jury that he worked until between 2.00-3.00 a.m. on the murder night. He assured the jury that to the best of his knowledge Abdullahi did not leave the ship that night. He confirmed that he had gone to the mess room and asked for assistance. He accepted that this incident was not in his statements and he had only remembered it because he had been reminded of it by Peter McCarthy even though the judge had told McCarthy not to talk to anyone about the case. Hulse indignantly denied Elfer's suggestion that he got together with McCarthy to collude with him. Hulse assured the jury that it was just a quick chat about the job and that talking to McCarthy jogged his memory. He insisted that he had forgotten about it when he spoke to police in January 1989 when he claimed that Mouncher just wanted him to say that Abdullahi had not been on the ship at all. Hulse insisted that he had not come to court to lie for anybody.

Fellow *Coral Sea* worker Sidney Arthur Harrop told the jury that he could not recognise a black and white photo of Abdullahi but did recognise a colour photo of him. James Edmond told the jury that he left the ship about 8.00 p.m. on the murder night returning about twelve hours later. He said that he had seen Abdullahi when he left and when he returned Abdullahi was still working. He told the jury that Abdullahi looked very tired and he had told him that he looked as if he had been there all night and Abdullahi had replied that he had been. Ian Moore confirmed Harrop's account that the oxygen had run out on the Sunday rather than the Saturday night. He told the jury that he had been shown a photo of Abdullahi and told the police that he couldn't say if he had seen him before even though his statements said that he had definitely never seen Abdullahi before. Moore claimed that he did not say what appeared in his statement.

The last of Abdullahi's alibi witnesses was Ronnie Williams' friend Lawrence Mann who told the jury that he worked on the ship until he left at about 1.30 a.m. on the murder night. Mann said that he had a misunderstanding with Williams about whether it had rained that night and had checked at the local meteorological office to make sure before he fixed the night he exchanged terse words with Abdullahi before going home as the murder night. Mann denied Elfer's suggestion that he was lying. However, Elfer would later submit that Mann, McCarthy and Hulse had perjured themselves about the events of that night.

Abdullahi called Noreen Amiel to tell the jury about the conversation he had with her shortly after the murder. Amiel told the jury that she had never been in fear about giving evidence and had not been afraid of the defendants. She said that she just did not want to get involved and that was the only reason she didn't sign her statement until February 1989. With reference to the conversation she had with Abdullahi shortly after the murder she told the jury that he said the police were after him but that he had been on the ship. Amiel claimed that Abdullahi never said that he was involved in the murder and that Sandrone had been nearby but that she and not Sandrone had had the conversation with Abdullahi.

Amiel claimed that the police told her in February that she had a moral duty to sign her statement, so she did so even though she did not want to get involved or go to court. She denied saying that the police didn't understand how evil the five and their families were or that she was afraid of them. Amiel then told the jury that Abdullahi said that the police believed that he was involved in the murder not that Abdullahi had said he was involved in it. She confirmed that he had said he was looking for a ship and insisted that she was not in terror of any of the five defendants.

After Cheryl Rogan gave evidence the case for Abdullahi closed and in the absence of the jury John Actie's QC, John Rogers, submitted that Mr Justice McNeill ought to discharge the jury because of the way he had conducted the trial. McNeill declined and John Actie took his turn in the witness box.

John Actie assured the jury that he did not murder Lynette White and had never been to 7 James Street. Unlike the other defendants, he assured the court that he did not know Vilday, Psaila or Grommek and, like the other defendants, he claimed that he was not good friends with any of the other defendants with whom he would just exchange hellos. Actie vehemently denied Elfer's suggestion that he was the ringleader of a plan to turn the committal hearing into a circus and vigorously protested his innocence.

Actie claimed that he had been working on the door of the Casablanca on the murder night. He said that he had told police that in his questionnaire, but had forgotten it when he was arrested and had wrongly insisted that he was at home alone on the murder night despite statements from Taryn Ali, Janet McHue and David Orton suggesting that he was mistaken. He told the jury that he suspected that the police were trying to put him in the Casablanca as an attempt to fit him up although he could not explain how he was being fitted up.

Actie rejected Elfer's suggestion that he had deliberately lied about being in the Casablanca because he knew that the murder was planned in the club and did not want to be within a million yards of it. Actie told the jury that he had simply made an honest mistake and that he now accepted that he had been at the Casablanca. He also told the jury that he had asked the police to check at the Casablanca which night a particular sound system had played there as that was how he fixed the events of that night without knowing that the entry for it was no longer in the book. However John Rogers would eventually exhibit an entry for Sandra Cross playing the Casablanca which showed that the sound system Actie had mentioned had not played the club on the murder night. During re-examination Actie agreed with Rogers' suggestion that had police made the check as he had requested they would have discovered Actie's mistake and the interviews could have progressed differently.

With reference to Gary George's evidence, Actie would not accept that George was a relative at first, but eventually agreed that he was a cousin. He vehemently rejected George's claims and specifically called his cousin a liar rather than simply being mistaken. He denied the veracity of Violet Perriam's claims and insisted that she was lying about him because she didn't like him. Actie vigorously protested his innocence and told Elfer that his usual practice was to take an odd route home from the Casablanca on Saturday nights, one that took him away from James Street, in order to go and buy a paper from a warehouse.

Actie called John Dodd to verify this. Dodd told the jury that Actie was a customer in 1988 and would come in almost every Sunday morning between 2.00-3.00 a.m. for his paper. Dodd said that he didn't know Actie's name at the time, but that he was a customer as they only had a few, but he could not put a figure on how many Sunday mornings Actie had missed. After Kenneth Spurlock gave evidence John Actie's case closed.

It was now up to the lawyers to present their closing arguments to the jury, after which McNeill would sum up and invite them to consider their verdicts.

Elfer was the first to address the jury. He told them that the defendants had a lifestyle that both he and they were unfamiliar with. Elfer claimed that when he and they retired for the night the defendants were only just beginning their day. Their lives were on the borders of legal protection. He asked them if they had any doubts that the defendants carried knives as part of their clothing. Then Elfer rehearsed the evidence which he claimed proved the guilt of each of the Cardiff Five. He asked the jury to believe Mark Grommek, pointing out that his insistence on Tucker being there could be reconciled by Miller's confession referring to two white men being on the stairs. He invited the jury to conclude that one of them was Tucker. And Elfer claimed that the dreadlocked man Grommek referred to fitted Tony Miller's description, but he was in London, so Elfer asked the jury to conclude that it could have been the defendant.

Then Elfer reprised the scientific evidence. He suggested that the results from the jeans indicated that it was not a true mixture. He claimed that the experts agreed that the male chromosome had been added. Elfer also submitted that this blood all came from one source and that was Psaila. He reminded the jury that the crucial breakthrough came from Dr Whiteside who made the connection, therefore this evidence could not be part of a police conspiracy. So Elfer suggested that it was safe for the jury to conclude from the blood evidence that Psaila had been in the murder room when Lynette was murdered. He reminded them of Psaila's claim that she had tried to help Lynette and had been thumped by one of the defendants and asked them to consider whether the blood mixed on the jeans was a result of that punch. Elfer also claimed that the murderers would not necessarily have left fingerprints behind.

Elfer suggested that the defence had tried to discredit Vilday who was a very courageous woman and outlined the portions of Miller's confession which supported her evidence. Elfer pointed out that Miller had repeated his confession to Sidoric and Taylor after the interviews were over and he kept saying that he was happy to continue the interviews at the time. Elfer asked the jury to consider what they made of Miller's account of his movements and reminded them that even though Miller had said that he thought that Orton could help him he did not call him to give evidence.

He suggested that Tony Paris was in the same line of business as Steve Miller and was running Helen Prance. He invited the jury to believe Massey who Elfer submitted had nothing to gain from coming forward and was reluctant to get involved. Elfer also asked the jury to reject the evidence of Courtney Davies who thought it unfortunate that grasses weren't beaten up any more. Elfer suggested that Davies revelled in the limelight and was happy to come forward.

Elfer also reminded the jury of the evidence relating to Ronnie Actie's car. He invited the jury to reject Actie's witnesses' claims that he was driving a red Triumph at the time of the murder and rely on the witnesses who claimed that he was driving a green Cortina. Then Elfer reminded the jury of Violet Perriam's evidence about a brown Cortina. He asked them to consider whether it was a green car which appeared brown due to streetlighting.

He invited the jury to reject the alibis of all the defendants and suggested that Mann, Hulse and McCarthy had perjured themselves for Abdullahi. Elfer invited the jury to conclude that Abdullahi's alibi had been lies and that he had simply waited to see what others were saying before he chose which line to adopt and pointed out that Abdullahi's claim to have returned on the Sunday night was not credible because of his claim that there were no police outside the murder flat that night when it was clear that there was from the time the murder was discovered.

That said, Elfer reminded the jury that apart from the alleged confession, Sandrone's version of the conversation in the Dowlais was very similar to that of Noreen Amiel. Then Elfer referred to the conversations that Abdullahi allegedly had with Sandrone, Harris, Williams and DC Cullen and invited the jury to reject Abdullahi's persistent denials of the veracity of these witnesses' versions of their conversations.

Now Elfer moved on to John Actie. He invited the jury to conclude that Actie had deliberately lied to them about being in the Casablanca because he did not want to put himself anywhere near there as he knew the murder hatched from the club. Elfer reminded the jury of the evidence of Perriam and Gary George. That said, Elfer invited them to rely on the evidence of Vilday, Psaila and Grommek and submitted that the Crown had proved its case that the Cardiff Five were there and had murdered Lynette.

Now the defence lawyers would have their say beginning with Anthony Evans, who began by reminding the jury that the issue was who really killed Lynette and that although it was a horrific crime which demanded that those responsible are caught it wouldn't help anyone if the wrong people were convicted. Evans then set about debunking the Crown's case against Miller. He told the jury that Miller's lifestyle was irrelevant. That said, he accepted that Miller was close to a pimp but that there was no evidence that Miller put Lynette on the street. It was a strange relationship, but they seemed happy together and he suggested that the jury ask themselves if all Miller wanted from Lynette was for her to be his workhorse would he kill her?

Evans accepted that Miller's lifestyle was unattractive, but he pointed out that many of the Crown's witnesses led equally unattractive lives and that in many cases they had been proven to be liars. Evans reminded the jury that the whole case rested on the credibility of Vilday and Psaila and asked if they could rely on them. That said, he pointed out that Miller's interviews were based on their claims and those of Grommek. Evans told the jury that the police got nowhere for ten months. Then they got the statements of Vilday, Psaila and Grommek and the investigation proceeded on the basis that they couldn't be wrong, yet things put to Miller in his interviews were proved wrong by December 11th 1988. This, Evans argued, showed that police displayed a lack of foresight. Evans suggested that this was not an investigation of who was responsible for the murder, but an attempt to fit the evidence into what Vilday and Psaila had said.

Evans reminded the jury that it had been put to Miller, as a fact, that he had visited Psaila's flat on the murder night; Miller had denied it and in her evidence Psaila had agreed with Miller. Then Evans reminded the jury that the Crown claimed that the half caste man described by Gary George was Miller. Evans submitted that there was no way that George's description fitted Miller.

As to the question of alibi, Evans argued that Miller's wasn't strictly an alibi case as nobody could give him an alibi for the whole night. He stressed that Miller did not have to prove anything. He had accounted for his movements in his statements, yet despite his requests to see them police never allowed him to refresh his memory during those interviews. Evans then moved on to deal with David Orton. He reminded the jury that Elfer had asked why Miller had not called Orton. Evans told them that he and not Miller had taken the decision not to call Orton. Then he reminded the jury that during Miller's interviews police had portrayed Orton's statements as blowing Miller's alibi apart. If that was the case, Evans asked, why didn't the Crown call Orton themselves?

Evans told the jury that there could be no doubt that anyone involved in the murder would have blood on their clothes. He reminded them that Miller's clothes had been taken by the police for forensic examination within days of the murder and the results were negative. Evans also pointed out that there were no fingerprints linking any of the defendants to the crime either. He suggested that although the Crown suggested that they could have been there without leaving fingerprints the jury should ask themselves if it was likely that the five defendants could have gone into the building, up the stairs, into the flat and committed the murder without leaving any fingerprints there at all. Evans invited the jury to reject Elfer's argument.

Evans would never get the chance to complete his closing argument. On February 26th 1990, after nearly five months, this trial was abruptly halted when the judge suffered a fatal heart attack. By this time, defence lawyers had found around forty grounds of appeal, most of them due to McNeill's conduct. McNeill had prepared a draft summing up, which according to some, read like a direction to convict. He did not get the chance to deliver it. Now the Crown had an unexpected opportunity to review the evidence and could assess the credibility of their witnesses with reference to the way they had given evidence in this trial.

CHAPTER 7

Retrial

The Lessons Of The First Trial

A jury had heard the evidence against the Cardiff Five. The contradictions in the claims of the Crown's main witnesses had been ably exposed during cross-examination. Angela Psaila in particular had been brash and obnoxious in giving her evidence. She had claimed that she was frightened yet she had been rude, aggressive and offensive to any lawyer who had the temerity to question her veracity.

Psaila had claimed that her blood had been found in the room and that proved that she had been there. But it didn't. Forensic analysis had shown that a person with Psaila's blood group had been there when Lynette was murdered. There had never been any proof that it had been deposited by Psaila. The male chromosome had been discovered on the jeans. This meant that if Psaila had been there her blood had to have mixed intimately from a split second contact with the blood on the killer's hand before being smeared on to the jeans.

Dr Whiteside had told the jury that he believed the discovery of Psaila's blood group was significant and that it made him question Dr Gill's results indicating the presence of the male chromosome. Why? There were approximately sixteen thousand people who possessed that blood group. It could just as easily have belonged to any one of them and surely the discovery that Psaila did not possess the Y-chromosome meant that she should have been excluded as a possible source for the blood on the jeans, especially as there was not and could not have been any proof that the blood on the jeans was a mixture of male and female blood at the time because there was no test able to determine the exact ratio of X-chromosomes to Y-chromosomes present in the blood on the jeans. And it ought to be remembered that X-chromosomes are possessed by both males and females anyway. It is also amazing that nobody seems to have considered the possibility that if there was a mixture of male and female blood that it was more likely to have been a mixture between the victim and her killer rather than a witness and the killer. Suffice to say, the cocktail theory seemed to be a classic case of making the scientific evidence prove what the Crown wanted to prove rather than allow it to speak for itself.

However, it should also be pointed out that Whiteside told the jury that the mixture theory was unlikely. That alone undermines Psaila's credibility entirely. And Vilday's evidence wasn't much better. Yet it was not just the claims of the witnesses that left something to be desired. Elfer seemed to go further than the evidence proved more than once. Violet Perriam had claimed to have seen a brown Cortina at the murder scene, yet Elfer suggested that due to streetlighting it might have been Ronnie Actie's green one. There was no evidence to support Elfer's contention. And if brown was really green, why not another colour or another make of car altogether? The dangers of such an approach are legion. Had Perriam said that it was a green Cortina Elfer would have been remiss not to remind the jury of it, but he had no right to try to square the circle. Elfer ought to have confined himself to what the witnesses had actually said and let the facts speak for themselves.

Elfer also seemed to suggest that it was significant that the defence did not want to call David Orton. This reverses the burden of proof. Miller did not have to prove anything. Certainly, there were aspects of Orton's statements which contradicted Miller's portrayal of himself and Orton may have been vulnerable to cross-examination, but the decision was taken by Miller's lawyers and, as Anthony Evans pointed out, if the police's suggestion that Orton had destroyed Miller's alibi was true then why didn't Elfer call him as a witness to refute Miller's account of his movements? After all, Elfer had called evidence to refute Abdullahi's alibi.

And there was the question of the absence of Paul Atkins. He had made damning statements in the run up to the arrest of the Cardiff Five and had given evidence at the committal hearing. Surely he would have been an important Crown witness, yet he was not called to give evidence. Given the fact that Elfer seemed to imply that it was significant that the defence did not call David Orton in particular, it is astonishing that he saw no reason to explain the non-appearance of such a potentially important witness as Atkins to the jury.

There was also a disturbing account of Elfer's cross-examination of Miller which was reported in the *South Wales Echo*. Elfer suggested that certain witnesses referred to in Miller's alibi notice were not to be called because, they would talk about the bullying that Miller meted out to Lynette. According to the *Echo*, Elfer went on to say, "They would talk about the other girls you beat up and in the end they would only drag you further down for the murderer that you undoubtedly are." If Elfer's words were accurately reported this is very worrying. Given the fact that certain witnesses such as Helen Prance had not stuck to the letter of their statements when they gave evidence, the judge should not have allowed Elfer to put words into the mouths of putative witnesses. And he should not have been allowed to speculate on the reasons for the defence's decision not to call them. After all, Elfer knew what was in their statements and if they were as damning to Miller's cause as Elfer made out, it is baffling that he did not choose to call them as prosecution witnesses.

The Final Curtain Call?

The death of Mr Justice McNeill caused several problems for the criminal justice system. The Crown now knew how their witnesses would perform and what impression a jury would have of them. The contradictions had been legion. And now the Crown had to decide whether there was still a realistic prospect of securing convictions.

Elfer knew that he would have no credible forensic evidence against any of the defendants. And by March 1990 he saw things get even worse. His key witness against Paris, Ian Massey, had been a dreadful witness and his credibility rating was about to deteriorate further. The Court of Appeal, headed by Lord Lane, quashed Ged Corley's convictions. And West Yorkshire Police were still investigating a complaint about the way that Corley had been convicted. This posed severe problems for Elfer. Massey's motives in coming forward were suspect to put it mildly. His criminal record was appalling and he had been caught out lying about Paris. Also there was the evidence of Davies and possibly that of John Eaton as well to add to the Corley Affair, even though Eaton had not been called at the first trial.

Elfer had a difficult decision to make: should he persevere with Massey, warts and all, or abandon his evidence? The case against Paris was weak with Massey. There was precious little left of it without him. So Elfer chose to try to limit the damage that the Corley case would do to Massey. There was an investigation into the Corley Affair which would later result in criminal convictions against several supergrasses. Two officers would admit to lesser charges, one of whom would be acquitted of conspiring to pervert the course of justice. Another would be charged but would be deemed unfit to stand trial for medical reasons. And Corley was suing over his ordeal. This meant that the potential damage to Massey's reputation could be limited by sub judice regulations. If the criminal justice system had a more inquisitorial bent to it than the current adversarial model unreliable witnesses like Massey could have been rooted out far earlier.

However, Elfer was to get an unexpected bonus. His cross-examinations of Courtney Davies had been aggressive. Davies had held his ground, but ironically, his honesty weighed against him. He freely admitted that he didn't like grasses and viewed Massey as one. So Elfer pressed him hard. Unknown to Elfer he had scored points with Gerard Elias, who felt that Elfer had ruffled Davies' feathers. Elias was concerned about the impression that Davies had given to the jury. And now he had the windfall of the Corley Affair. Paris' defence decided to throw all their eggs in the one basket and not call Davies or Eaton for the retrial.

Elfer reviewed the quality of evidence regarding the committal hearing and sifted out the evidence that he could do without. He decided that the new jury would not hear police claims about the defendants' alleged behaviour at the committal hearing. And most importantly of all, the new jury would not get the highly unusual privilege of hearing a magistrate give evidence for the defence.

Having seen the impression that his witnesses had had upon a jury and the fact that his case was significantly weaker now than it had been when he first came on board, Elfer and the CPS should now have decided that it was inappropriate to continue the prosecution of the Cardiff Five. But they would have to go through the lengthy trial process all over again. And most of the witnesses had learned from their experiences of the first trial and would give far more plausible performances at the new trial. The new jury would know little or nothing of their previous antics. In that sense the first trial was little more than a dress rehearsal.

Meanwhile, Ronnie Actie was not satisfied with the way his defence had been presented. He sacked his entire legal team and instructed a new solicitor in Michael Reid and a new lead barrister in David Farrington. John Actie, too, wanted a change of lawyer. He wanted his junior barrister, John Charles Rees, to take over as his lead counsel for the new trial.

But the most significant change occurred in Miller's defence team. Anthony Evans was not available for the new trial. So Roger Frisby took over as his QC. As will be seen from his lacklustre submission on oppression in the new trial this would prove to be a disaster for Miller as Frisby's advocacy would not reach the standard that Miller depended on and had a right to expect.

However, there were other problems concerning the right to a fair trial for the criminal justice system to cope with following the sudden death of Mr Justice McNeill. Albeit, through nobody's fault, the entire case was already in the public domain and had been extensively reported in the local media. Consequently, press coverage of the first trial would assume great importance in the new trial, since it would be allowed to take place in the same Swansea courts.

The new trial was set to begin just over two months after the abrupt end of the first one. If any of the new jury had read press coverage of the first trial, this could already have prejudiced their impartiality. For justice to be seen to be done, the jury should not have had prior knowledge of any of the facts from the first trial that might not be presented to them in evidence. Because the second trial would also take place in Swansea, despite defence objections, the jury could have been prejudiced before they had even taken the oath by media coverage of the first trial. For justice to be seen to be done a fair trial was now impossible either here, in Cardiff or anywhere else in South Wales. This was a compelling reason not to hold the retrial anywhere in the local media's catchment area. But Swansea it would be.

It was now May 2nd 1990. The new trial would begin today before Mr Justice Leonard, the judge who sentenced Paul and Wayne Darvell to life imprisonment for the murder of Swansea sex shop manageress, Sandra Phillips. He had also been the judge who imposed a harsher sentence for aggravated burglary than he did for the brutal rape of Jill Saward in the infamous Ealing Vicarage rape case.

In 1988-89 Mr Justice Leonard had also been one of the judges who had heard the longest criminal appeal in the notorious case of the men convicted of the 1978 murder of teenage newspaperboy Carl Bridgewater, a case which would be acknowledged as a disgraceful miscarriage of justice in February 1997 after Jimmy Robinson and the cousins, Vincent and Michael Hickey, had served eighteen years imprisonment, but Pat Molloy who was convicted of manslaughter along with them never lived to see his name cleared as he died in prison in 1981 protesting his innocence.

Legal Arguments

The first phase of this trial followed the pattern set in the original trial. The jury were empanelled and immediately sent out while the judge heard legal submissions. Miller's new QC, Roger Frisby, went first. He chose not to play the whole of Miller's seventh interview to support his submission that Miller had been the victim of oppressive interviewing. Frisby objected to all of Miller's interviews, arguing that Miller had been humiliated and degraded, especially in the interviews conducted by DCs Greenwood and Seaford. Although there was no suggestion that Miller had been subjected to physical violence and tapes one to seven contained no admissions, Frisby objected to the admissibility of these interviews as well as the others on the grounds of their unreliability.

Frisby submitted that inducements had been offered and that during tape seven Miller had been subjected to what he called, "A shameful piece of bullying." But Frisby only had the first sixteen minutes of that interview played to the judge. He submitted that the cumulative effect of the bullying must have been enormous. He submitted that every time Miller told police what he said was the truth he was "jumped on" by the officers. Frisby also complained that the admissions in tape eight were the product of leading questions. This time Miller was not called to give evidence before the judge ruled on the admissibility of his confession.

However, Dr Gisli Gudjonsson was called. He told the judge that Miller had a low IQ and was abnormally suggestible. He outlined his tests and conclusions for the judge. He made it clear that Miller had been stressed during the interviews from listening to the tapes. Gudjonsson said that he could not say that Miller had not been pushed. He told Leonard that Miller was not a bright person but was bright enough to realise the position that he was in although a brighter person would have been able to cope better. Gudjonsson also told the judge that people are less likely to accept suggestions when they are angry.

DI Powell was called to state the police's case on Miller's interviews. He insisted that he did not show Miller post mortem photographs of Lynette and he didn't see how Miller could have seen them. Powell stated that Miller had never told him that he knew how Lynette died or what injuries she had suffered when he interviewed Miller in February. It was also pointed out that Geraint Richards had intervened three times during the interviews.

Frisby summed up his objections to Miller's confession. He submitted that Miller had not been given any chance to answer questions, had been offered inducements to incriminate himself and others and had been subjected to appalling bullying. He submitted that it would be difficult enough for any prisoner to cope, but it was far worse when the person had a low IQ and was very suggestible. Frisby also argued that the confession should be inadmissible as it was obtained through oppression contrary to Section 76 of PACE and that Miller's vulnerabilities and the police's interviewing methods rendered the confession unreliable. He asked the judge to use his discretion to refuse to admit it as it would have an adverse effect on the proceedings contrary to Section 78 of PACE.

Elfer submitted that the confession had not been obtained improperly and that the reliability of it was a matter for the jury to decide. Mr Justice Leonard stated that Frisby had accepted the skill and integrity of the interrogation and did not impugn the good faith of the officers. He also said that Miller did not say that he was bullied until after the interviews, that his solicitor had not played a passive role, and had the opportunity to consult his client privately. With regards to suggestibility, Leonard commented that Miller had accepted some things but not others. He said that he did not find Dr Gudjonsson persuasive and concluded that Miller had the safeguard of the presence of an experienced solicitor and had said that he was happy with the interviews at the time. Consequently, Mr Justice Leonard rejected Frisby's arguments and ruled that the jury would be allowed to hear Miller's confession. It would be for them to decide if it was credible or not. And Frisby also unsuccessfully applied for evidence relating to Miller's character to be ruled inadmissible on the grounds of it not being relevant.

The other defence barristers were concerned that Miller's confession could prejudice their clients' right to a fair trial. They wanted Miller's trial to be severed from that of the others. They submitted that this was the only way to ensure that Miller's confession, which was not admissible against the others by law, would not prejudice the jury. But Leonard told them that the inconvenience to witnesses of having to repeat their evidence at two trials, problems over reporting both trials and the cost of two trials would be such that severance would not be appropriate. He also opined that the jury were capable of understanding the admissibility of evidence against each defendant. However, he assured them that he would give the jury strong directions that they could not use Miller's confession against the other defendants.

And Gerard Elias submitted that Massey's evidence ought to be ruled inadmissible because it may have been obtained through inducements, but judgement was deferred until later in the trial.

Expert Evidence

Elfer outlined the case that he would present to the jury and reminded them that they were only allowed to use Miller's confession against him and him alone. Professor Bernard Knight was the first expert witness to give evidence. He told the jury that there had been a mixture of stab and slashing wounds. Lynette had put up a struggle which resulted in defensive injuries. Knight maintained that the wrist injuries had been inflicted after Lynette died. The cause of death was the cut throat and multiple stab wounds. He told the jury that the throat wounds were likely to have been the first offensive wounds, but there was no scientific evidence to prove this. Knight also maintained that there was no doubt that Lynette was alive when these wounds were inflicted, but would not have been able to stand up after her throat was slashed. He then stated that Lynette would have lost consciousness before she died and that there were sexual overtones to the attack. Knight also told the jury that there was nothing inconsistent with there being only one killer and one knife being used although there was no evidence one way or the other. Cross-examination would expose the contradictions between Knight's evidence and the claims of Angela Psaila in particular.

Dr John Whiteside was the next expert witness to be called to the witness box. He detailed the scientific work that he had conducted in this inquiry and told the jury that as a result of his discovery of Angela Psaila's blood group he subsequently doubted that they were looking for a man. He claimed that it could have been a mixture of male and female blood but there was a possibility that it was male blood. Whiteside told the jury that there was nothing to connect any of the defendants with the room and that the mixture theory only applied to the jeans. However, he also said, "Psaila's blood group is one hell of a coincidence."

Dr Peter Gill told the jury that he detected the male chromosome on all five areas of the jeans that he tested. He explained that it was either male blood or a mixture of male and female blood. His test, he told the jury, only detected the male Y-chromosome, so he could not say that female blood was there at all, but he could not exclude the possibility of a mixture of male and female blood. He explained that one in ten thousand women possess the Y-chromosome, but that Psaila did not. He told the jury that the results he obtained from the jeans were of varying strength and that if it had been deposited by a man on his own the results would have been more likely to have been uniform, but he also told them that it was difficult to draw any firm conclusions.

Dr Nicholas Prance told the jury that limited DNA profiles did not originate from any of the defendants or from Vilday, Psaila, Grommek or Atkins, but he could not eliminate the possibility that the source of those bloodstains was Lynette, herself, or Rashid Omar. And DS Stephen Steele told the jury that none of the fingerprints discovered in the flat originated from any of the defendants or Angela Psaila. He also explained that eleven marks containing the required sixteen characteristics remained unidentified even though they were of good quality. This concluded the scientific evidence.

The Main Witnesses

Mark Grommek was the first of the alleged eyewitnesses to give evidence. He told the jury that after persistent ringing of his front door-bell he eventually opened the door to Lynette's killers, whom he identified as Abdullahi, Ronnie Actie, a black man with shoulder length dreadlocks and Martin Tucker. He then quickly returned to his flat. He insisted that he was not wrong about Tucker and that the only car at the scene was a black taxi. Grommek claimed that he heard voices to the effect that Lynette had an argument with her killers over money which she claimed she didn't have. The argument, Grommek claimed, had been followed by a loud scream which seemed to last for ever before it all went quiet. Grommek said that he heard footsteps on the stairs and poked his head out of his door and saw Vilday, who seemed edgy and distressed, on the landing below. Grommek claimed that Paul Atkins had gone into the murder flat and been violently sick when he returned.

Grommek vehemently denied that he and Paul Atkins were involved in the murder and claimed that he decided not to name names because he was too scared to tell the police the truth and didn't think of giving them an anonymous tip off. He explained to the jury that his first eight statements were not a pack of lies; he just didn't tell the police everything and denied that this was an attempt to give himself an alibi.

Grommek admitted that he had never seen Actie or Abdullahi before the murder and only saw Actie again eight months later. He claimed that he had also recognised Abdullahi from that night in November 1988 after he had been questioned by police when Abdullahi asked him if his name had been mentioned. Grommek claimed that although he only saw them for a few seconds several months earlier he had a vivid recollection of a very clear sighting.

Grommek insisted that he never went into the murder flat and that he did not deliberately leave out seeing Vilday on the landing from his statements. He also denied colluding with Vilday in any way. Grommek then claimed that he was never told that he could be prosecuted for wasting police time and couldn't remember when he was threatened with a possible charge of perjury. He told the jury that the police had mentioned Ronnie Actie first and he just decided to tell the truth. He denied that there had been a conspiracy of silence with Vilday and Atkins.

Grommek told the jury that Tony Paris definitely wasn't one of the men he saw that night and nor was John Actie. After all, he said, he could hardly have missed John Actie if he had been there. Grommek accepted that he could not explain how he put names to the voices. He also accepted that Vilday was relaxed in Ronnie Actie's company. Grommek claimed that Ronnie Actie proved quite friendly to him by buying him drinks and told the jury that Actie had never threatened him. He insisted that the black man he had seen that night had the dreadlocks piled on top of his head, although he accepted that he had never said this before.

Grommek admitted taking anti depressants at the time of the murder, but remained adamant that he was not lying about what he claimed that he saw and heard. He emphatically denied having any part in the murder or conspiring with Vilday and Atkins to cover it up.

Learnne Vilday was the next of the Crown's main witnesses to give evidence. She told the jury that she had heard horrible screams from the murder flat while she was by the rubbish chute for Psaila's flat and had gone over to 7 James Street with Psaila. She claimed that Lynette was dead when she entered the room and she had seen Tony Paris stabbing Lynette at the time. She claimed that she had shouted at Miller because he was not stopping Paris and was supposed to protect Lynette. Vilday said that she had been forced to cut one of Lynette's wrists. She claimed that John Actie had dragged her hand across Lynette's wrist. She insisted that even though she was told to cut Lynette's throat she had refused.

She told the jury that she had seen a man on the stairs who could have been Grommek, Atkins or Martin Tucker. She said that she had only seen Paris stab Lynette but John Actie had said that they had all had a go. Psaila, she claimed, had been hit by one of the five because she was swearing at them. Vilday told the jury that she had not seen Psaila get hit, but saw blood on her when they were in the street and realised that she had been punched.

She repeated that she had only cut one of Lynette's wrists and again denied cutting Lynette's throat. She also denied suggesting that the man on the stairs could have been Tucker to fit in with Grommek's evidence. And she contradicted her earlier testimony by saying that she had seen all five defendants stab Lynette.

Vilday told the jury that although Lynette loved Miller she was also frightened of him. She explained her ten month silence by saying that she had lied to the police because she was scared for her baby and had gone to the North Star at about 3.00 a.m. on the murder night because she felt that Ronnie Actie would go to Psaila's flat looking for Craig.

Vilday insisted that she was not normally a liar, but that when you are scared you have no option but to lie. She said that she only lied to cover up for the five defendants because she was very frightened of them. She explained her letter to Nicola Heysham by saying that she was ashamed and did not want Heysham to know that she had been there. She denied that the letter contained the truth. She said that she had agreed to be hypnotised without expecting the police to take her up on her offer. She admitted becoming increasingly nervous as the time to be hypnotised approached. She claimed that she did not go under and had told lies during the session. She insisted that she had witnessed the murder and denied conspiring with Psaila to tell lies. She explained the contradictions between her evidence now and what she had said at the committal hearing by saying that she was scared at the committal hearing and had only answered the questions put to her.

She claimed that Tony Paris was the only one of his family to acknowledge Craig and bought sweets for him both before and after the murder. She insisted that the police had not told her who to name. She accepted that she had previously lied about her relationship with Ronnie Actie and claimed that he used amphetamines himself although he objected to her use of it by injection. She denied being relaxed in Actie's company after the murder, but agreed that it appeared to others that she was happy in his company. And she told the jury that she had been taken to see Jackie Harris on only one occasion and had been accompanied by DI Joy Lott all the time.

She explained that on the night of Sunday February 14th 1988 she had told the taxi driver, Eddie Dimond, that she was worried about Lynette, although Dimond contradicted her by telling the jury that Vilday didn't seem worried or upset when he gave her a lift. Dimond said that she seemed more concerned about her keys, which she wanted back from Lynette, than she was about Lynette herself. Dimond claimed that it was his idea to go to the police. But PC Prosser told the jury that Vilday's demeanour showed that she was a bit upset and concerned for Lynette, but had said nothing on the way back to the flat and had declined his offer to go into the flat with them. Sergeant Bisgood told the jury that he heard Vilday sob but she did not go into the room or ask what he saw in the room. Bisgood said that Vilday gave him no indication that she knew how Lynette's body came to be in the room.

And after Vilday had finished giving evidence Angela Psaila entered the witness box. Psaila contradicted Vilday by telling the jury that she thought that she had cut both of Lynette's wrists herself because she had no choice and that the severe cuts to Lynette's throat had been inflicted by Vilday because she had been forced to do so. She told the jury that she had cut Lynette's wrists before Vilday cut her throat. Psaila also claimed that they had been in the flat for two hours from about 1.45 a.m. She claimed that Paris had been slapping Lynette about and that Lynette was probably unconscious from the beating she received. She contradicted Vilday by saying that she saw all five defendants stab Lynette.

Psaila went on to say that one of the defendants punched her in the mouth causing her to bleed but she couldn't remember which one had hit her. She thought that the blood on her clothes probably came from Lynette. She stated that when she was hit her blood went on to Lynette's jeans, her sock and elsewhere in the flat. Psaila told the jury that her mouth did not bleed much and left no external mark or swelling. She claimed that she could not remember which officer had told her about her blood being found in the flat.

She then told the jury that Atkins did not come into the room, even though cross-examination established that her evidence at the first trial had put Atkins in the murder room. Psaila also claimed that Mark Grommek entered the room for about five minutes, had the opportunity to see what was happening, but was not forced to take part in the murder.

Psaila accepted that even though Miller was Lynette's pimp they loved each other. Then she claimed that Miller was the only pimp she knew of. During cross-examination she was reminded that she had given evidence at the trial of Eric Marasco and Robert Gent who were convicted of procuring a thirteen year old girl for the purposes of prostitution. Psaila also insisted that there was no way that Martin Tucker had been there and was adamant that she had just confused Tony Miller with Abdullahi even though defence barristers pointed out that she had put both of them at the scene of the crime at that time. She later said that she named Tony Miller because she hated Steve. She claimed that Miller had put his hand through her letterbox around 3.00 a.m. on the murder night. During cross-examination it was pointed out that according to her testimony they were all still in the murder flat at the time. She changed her account to not remembering which night Miller had come round.

She vehemently denied making it all up and insisted that she was there and that the five defendants were responsible for Lynette's murder. She claimed that Lynette was dead when she cut her wrists. Psaila would not accept that her version of events would be blown out of the water even if Professor Knight's evidence had shown that the throat wounds were among the first offensive wounds inflicted. She insisted that even though she had told lie after lie to the police she was telling the truth now. Psaila admitted that she had accepted lifts from Ronnie Actie and socialised with him even after the murder, but claimed to be very frightened of him.

Psaila claimed that she had lied to police because she was scared that she would be prosecuted for conspiracy to murder. She had sought reassurances between her interviews by contemporaneous note of November 17th that this would not happen. One of the officers involved in those interviews, DC Daniels, told the court that he had been instructed by DI Mouncher to record those interviews contemporaneously. He claimed that Psaila had been scared during the interval and asked what assurances he could give her. He told the court that he told her that it was up to senior officers to give assurances so she spoke to Mouncher for a couple of minutes but no note was made of their conversation and he made no statement referring to Psaila's request for assurances. Daniels told the court that he didn't think that Psaila was seeking assurance that she would not be prosecuted for conspiracy to murder. He also told the court that he was told about Psaila's blood group around the time of his interview with her of December 11th 1988, but was careful not to tell her.

DC Gillard was Daniels' partner in the contemporaneously recorded interviews with Psaila. He told the court that no contemporaneous note had been made during the December 6th interview with Psaila and that she had been in the station about twelve hours that day. Gillard denied feeling any pressure to clear up Lynette's murder. He then told the jury that after receiving authorisation from a superior officer he had paid a prostitution fine for Psaila. Gillard accepted that a bench warrant had been issued and that Psaila would have been imprisoned if it had not been paid that day. The money, he informed the jury, had been termed an advance on an informant's fee. He denied telling Psaila about the discovery of her blood group as he had been instructed not to. DI Mouncher also gave evidence regarding the payment of Psaila's fine. He confirmed that after he had consulted the CPS, it was paid.

During this trial it emerged that Vilday had been paid £10.00 for information she supplied to police. Detective Superintendent Davies would later tell the jury that he kept in daily touch with colleagues in relation to the enquiries being made. He assured the jury that the police had given everything to the CPS and that if the defence had asked for information about payments to Vilday and Psaila it would have been disclosed to them and that despite a room full of undisclosed material they had always disclosed anything that the defence had asked for.

The Case Against Steve Miller

The cornerstone of Elfer's case against Miller was his confession. Elfer called the officers who had obtained it from him to show that it had not been obtained improperly. Greenwood told the jury much the same as he had told the jury at the previous trial, namely that he believed that Miller was there when Lynette was murdered and that Psaila's statement of December 6th was the truth. Greenwood accepted that he was not going to believe Miller until he admitted that he was there. He did not agree that tape seven was oppressive. Greenwood claimed that he raised his voice because Miller had raised his and the solicitor had made no complaint. DC Seaford told much the same story as Greenwood regarding the interviews they had conducted with Miller.

DC Evans' account was also much the same as the evidence he had given at the first trial, as was that of his partner, John Murray. DC Murray denied prompting Miller and stressed that if Miller had an innocent explanation then he should give it to them. He told the jury that he felt that Miller had been given every opportunity to state his case and didn't find that Miller adopted suggestions readily. He had no idea that Miller was backward. Murray claimed that he felt that it was unfair to suggest that DC Evans had deliberately misled Miller by not telling him that Psaila agreed with him at that stage that John Actie was not in the room. However, he agreed that when he told Miller, "There might be a nice way round this..." it was an unfortunate choice of phrase.

This concluded the evidence regarding Miller's interviews. Elfer would submit that this testimony showed that the confession had not been obtained improperly and he backed up his submissions with examples of Miller holding his own to refute the defence submission that Miller was suggestible and he would point out that Miller repeated details of his confession to Debbie Taylor and Tessa Sidoric without being prompted by them and without the police being there, let alone pressurising him.

Taylor gave much the same account as she had given at the first trial in relation to her visits to Miller shortly after he was remanded into custody. Sidoric also gave much the same account as before. She denied that the "If you can't control your woman, I'll show you how," conversation had actually been referring to an incident in 1987 rather than the murder night and she denied that she kept on interrupting while he was trying to talk to his girlfriend.

Elfer called Diane Seeley and her boyfriend Richard Stephens. They told the jury that a couple of weeks before the murder they had heard a black man arguing with Lynette. They could not hear the content of the argument and noticed nothing out of the ordinary in the black man's hairstyle. Elfer would submit that the black man was Miller and that he was ordering Lynette back out on to the street, although Frisby would point out that there was no evidence to this effect and that it had come from Elfer's imagination rather than the evidence. Furthermore, Frisby would argue that there was reason to doubt that the man was even Miller.

Elfer also called John Actie's second cousin, Gary George, as a witness against Miller. George told the jury that he saw a thirty year-old half caste man with a brillo pad hairstyle shouting up to the flat a couple of days before the murder.

Elfer would submit that the man George was describing was Miller. Frisby would submit that there was no way that George's description could be reconciled with Miller's appearance.

DI Powell told the jury that he saw Miller many times in the immediate aftermath of the murder and Miller sometimes came in of his own accord. Powell claimed that he felt sorry for Miller who was not regarded as a suspect at that time. He claimed that when he told Miller of Lynette's death Miller did not say much and did not appear to be shocked. Powell told the jury that Miller said that he wanted to help and didn't know that Lynette had been staying at 7 James Street at the time. Powell confirmed that forensic analysis of Miller's clothes had proved negative. He also told the jury that he may have accidentally left post mortem photos in his office while Miller was there after all, but that he had not intended Miller to see them as they were not for civilians to see.

The Case Against Tony Paris

Before Elfer could move on to Tony Paris' case he had to deal with a submission by Gerard Elias QC asking the judge to rule the evidence of Ian Massey inadmissible because his evidence may have been procured through inducements and also because he could not fully probe Massey's involvement in the Corley case as he could not call all of the relevant witnesses due to the ongoing investigation by West Yorkshire Police which would result in criminal proceedings being brought against some of the people involved in the conspiracy against Corley. Elias also pointed out that West Yorkshire Police had said that there was no public interest immunity attached to any of the documents they had allowed him to see. Elfer responded by submitting that Massey's credibility was a matter for the jury to decide and that the jury could get the flavour of the Corley case from the evidence currently available. Mr Justice Leonard agreed with Elfer's submissions and ruled that Massey could give evidence.

Massey's testimony regarding his conversations with Tony Paris followed much the same pattern as it had at the first trial. He admitted that he had told some lies at the previous trial to help himself, but that nothing could help him now and that this time he was telling them the complete truth. Massey claimed that he had made statements about Corley before he was told that the police would put a good word in for him at his appeal. He insisted that he had not done deals with them in return.

He accepted that he had received private visits from a girlfriend while he was at Stretford Police Station. Massey rejected the claims of Courtney Davies which Elias put to him. Massey told the jury that he had only come forward to save the lives of Vilday and Psaila. He denied being a violent man despite his record, but said that he could fight.

Massey insisted that he did not tell DS Duxbury that he had spoken to Miller as he had never met Miller. He claimed that he had seen the pathologist's report, but could not recall seeing any other statements. He accepted that Mouncher had visited him five times and that no notes had been taken. He insisted that this was not at his request.

DI Mouncher told the jury that he visited Massey six times in Long Lartin Prison but had not offered him any inducements. He accepted that he brought up Massey's earliest release date, but denied saying that it would be a feather in his cap for parole if he helped them.

Mouncher informed the jury that when Duxbury phoned him and passed on information provided by Massey, Duxbury did not reveal Massey's identity to him. Mouncher insisted that Detective Superintendent Davies eventually established Massey's identity by a process of elimination and Duxbury had confirmed it, but they had never received anything in writing from him. Mouncher told the jury that when he saw Massey he did not know that Massey had been asked to become a supergrass.

The only other corroborative witness that Elfer called against Paris was Helen Prance. But Prance told a somewhat different story to the one that Elfer expected to hear. Prance claimed that she had never lived with Paris, but that they had been friends and that he did not give her a knife; she had taken it from him. Prance told the jury that Miller and Paris knew each other to say hello to, but were not friends and didn't socialise with each other.

Once again Prance claimed that she had not said some of the things that appeared in her statements. She told the jury that she had told the police that Paris had never beaten her up and that she had never drank with any of the defendants bar Tony Paris. Prance insisted that she did not know who had murdered Lynette, but she did repeat her claim that Miller had asked her to go to London with him. She told the jury that she had answered questions and the police had written the statement for her which she signed, but had not read it first as she had difficulty reading. She claimed that statements had been taken from her over the phone, had lost her job through police harassment and had been locked up for five hours in Central Police Station in Cardiff before making a statement. However, it ought to be pointed out that police officers told the jury that there was no truth in Helen Prance's accusations of police malpractice.

Elfer had made a few submissions to treat Prance as a hostile witness which were initially refused. However, the judge eventually relented and Elfer was allowed to cross-examine her. He highlighted the contradictions between the account she had just given the jury and the accounts she had given previously. Mr Justice Leonard would later tell the jury that whatever they made of her evidence they could not use her as corroboration of the case against Paris. That would leave Massey as the sole corroboration of the case against Paris.

The Case Against Ronie Actie

Now Elfer moved on to the case of Ronnie Actie which was based on the testimony of Vilday and Psaila, with Grommek as the sole corroboration. It depended on their evidence and Elfer's suggestion, drawn from the testimony of other witnesses, that Ronnie Actie had been driving a green Cortina rather than a red Triumph at the time of the murder. He also hoped to score points during cross-examination of Actie's witnesses.

The Case Against Yusef Abdullahi

Elfer went through Abdullahi's interviews with the police, highlighting an answer where he appeared to suggest that he had returned to Cardiff on the murder night until he was corrected by his solicitor. Elfer also highlighted Abdullahi's claim to have returned on the Sunday night without seeing a police presence outside 7 James Street. Elfer suggested that this could not be right and indicated that it must have been the night before.

Elfer called Danny Wilson and Dennis Hippolyte who claimed that they thought that they had returned to Cardiff on the murder night in Les McCarthy's van. Wilson thought that they had left the ship about 2.00 in the morning, but neither of them were certain that it was the Saturday night rather than the following night. Ronnie Williams and Peter Brooks gave much the same account as they had given at the first trial. DI Mouncher told the jury that he was unaware that Williams was a police informer, although DI Page told the jury Williams was not strictly an informer, he just gave information sometimes, but was never paid for it.

And Elfer used Jane Sandrone to verify the conversation she had overheard Abdullahi have with Noreen Amiel, but she could not remember the details now. She said that she signed her statement, but that she didn't write it. She told the jury that Abdullahi had been drunk and she didn't believe he had murdered Lynette. DC Cullen also gave evidence about the conversation he claimed that he had with Abdullahi in the aftermath of the murder. His evidence was much the same as he had given at the first trial. DS Love told the jury that he had examined Abdullahi's hand which had numerous scars on it.

The jury were almost deprived of the chance to hear Jackie Harris give evidence as she refused to attend and consulted a solicitor. She eventually gave evidence and told the jury much the same as she had told the first jury. She explained her reluctance to give evidence by saying that she didn't want to take the father of her children away from them. She told the jury that she was allowed to meet Vilday a few times and had pressed her for details. Vilday had named the defendants but got distressed so the police stopped her from asking further questions. Harris claimed that the police heard all of the conversation but no notes were taken. Harris also told the jury that Abdullahi and Miller were not friends or associates, but Miller was her friend and visited her not Abdullahi.

The Case Against John Actie

The main corroboration witness against John Actie was Violet Perriam. She told more or less the same story that she had at the first trial. She confirmed that she did not see a black man with a pineapple-head hairstyle. She accepted that she had been mistaken over Rashid Omar and told the jury that her only conversation with Jock Mitchell had been about a burglary at her place of work. And Mitchell told the jury that Perriam had been very frightened and he had let her say her piece.

DI Page told the jury that he knew Perriam from the yacht club and Butetown Health Centre. Page said that there had been a break in at the yacht club and insisted that he did not drink there.

DC Greenwood claimed that although he had made no note that Perriam had named the people she claimed she saw outside 7 James Street when he first saw her on November 10th she had in fact named them. He also said that he was unaware that officers socialised at the yacht club where Perriam worked.

When Seaford was called, he also told the jury that he believed Perriam had named John Actie in the interview of November 10th. But during cross-examination he accepted that there was no note of it in his diary and that he therefore thought it unlikely that she had actually named Actie as he would have made a note that she had named him, but didn't want it in her statement if she had said that.

Gary George claimed that John Actie was in a small group laughing at the half caste man, a claim Actie would vociferously deny. During cross-examination George would admit that he was wrong to say that the man had approached the group, but denied making the whole of his story up. George told the jury that he didn't like Perriam and regarded her as a busybody. He claimed that he had never talked to DI Page, but had seen him talking to Perriam in the yacht club.

Elfer went through John Actie's interviews with the police. He submitted that Actie had advanced a false alibi deliberately intending to deceive them because he knew that the murder had been hatched from the Casablanca and wanted to put himself as far from the club as he could. This ended the Crown's case against the Cardiff Five.

Soon the defence would have their say. But first Elfer would have to deal with a submission from Gerard Elias QC that Elfer's case against Tony Paris did not reach the necessary standard and that Paris ought to be discharged. Mr Justice Leonard, mindful of the constraints of the Galbraith judgement, preferred to leave it to the jury to decide the credibility of the Crown's case against Paris.

The Defence Have Their Say

Miller was the first of the defendants to deny murdering Lynette. He told the jury that he did not know about 7 James Street and vociferously denied Vilday's claim that she had told him about it. He detailed his use of drugs and life with Lynette to the jury. He also went through his movements on the murder night for them. Miller denied being a pimp and insisted that he did not put Lynette on the streets or use violence to force her to work. He admitted that he lived off Lynette's earnings and claimed that he had told her that she could do better, but she carried on working anyway.

Miller denied admitting that he was involved in the murder to Debbie Taylor and

Tessa Sidoric. And he denied threatening Jennifer Parkin. He said that his co-defendants were just associates not close friends. Miller told the jury that he had seen the post mortem photographs while at the police station, but that DI Powell had not seen him look at them. Miller insisted that he loved Lynette and had no reason to kill her. He was shocked by his arrest and just wanted to get out of the police station as fast as possible. Miller told the jury that he had hoped to be treated as a witness and would have retracted in court if he had been given the chance.

He claimed that he had just told the police what they wanted to hear because they were not interested in hearing the truth. He insisted that he was not describing what had actually happened in his interviews. Miller said that he had agreed with some of what was put to him and made other things up according to what he thought they wanted. He claimed that he knew some of the details from his previous contact with the police. He even told the jury that he would have said that Elfer was there if he had been asked to. Miller insisted that he had not cried from remorse as he had not done anything. He continued to insist that what he said in his interviews was untrue and he had just said what the police wanted because he wanted to get out of the police station. And Miller denied that he was making things up as he went along.

The only witness Frisby called on Miller's behalf was Dr Gisli Gudjonsson who outlined his methodology and findings for the jury. He said that it was evident that Miller was abnormally suggestible. He was, said Gudjonsson, three times more suggestible than normal and had an IQ equivalent to an eleven year-old. He described Miller's memory as idiosyncratic and that his intelligence bordered on subnormality.

Miller, Gudjonsson told the jury, viewed Greenwood and Seaford as nasty and Evans and Murray as nice. Gudjonsson explained that even though Miller was abnormally suggestible he would not expect him to agree with everything. Gudjonsson told the jury that Miller could resist suggestions if he was suspicious or angry and that Miller's low level of intelligence would not prevent him using his imagination. This ended the case for Miller.

Tony Paris was the next of the Cardiff Five to give evidence. Paris detailed his movements on the murder night. He told them that he had been collecting glasses in the Casablanca that night. His account of his movements was much the same as in the first trial. He denied ever having been to 7 James Street and insisted that Miller was not a friend of his, they just played pool occasionally and would say hello to each other. He denied Miller's claim that he had ever had a conversation with him about controlling his woman, a conversation Miller had previously said did take place, but months before the murder and which Miller had treated as a joke. Paris also told the jury that he did not know the results of forensic analysis of his jacket until after Massey had left Cardiff Prison. It would later be confirmed that Paris' solicitor did not receive the forensic report until after June 29th 1989, the day Massey was transferred to Long Lartin Prison.

Gerard Elias called Carol Blades to support Paris' alibi. She told much the same story as she had told at the first trial. Elias would later submit that the jury could conclude from her evidence that it was most unlikely that Paris could have been involved in the murder.

After legal argument Mr Justice Leonard agreed to call Paul Atkins as a judge's witness as none of the lawyers actually wanted to call him themselves.

Atkins told the jury that he did not go round to Grommek's flat on the murder night and had not seen Grommek at all that day. He said that his evidence at the committal hearing had been lies because he was scared of the police and they had put words in his mouth. He denied being involved in the murder. He told the jury that he couldn't explain his fingerprints being in the flat, but he had been there before, but not on the night in question. He claimed that the police had put words into his mouth in his statements.

He was taken through his statement of April 26th 1988 in which he had implicated others before confessing himself. Atkins re-iterated that words had been put into his mouth by the police and he had made other things up because he was scared and the police did not believe him. Atkins told the jury that he was a bit scared of Grommek as well and that in the run up to the arrest of the Cardiff Five he had been threatened with a murder charge.

Atkins claimed that Grommek had told him what to say and had given him some details. He denied knowing a man called Dullah and insisted that he hadn't discussed the matter with Vilday at all. He insisted that the police had told him what to say and had promised to look after him. During cross-examination Elfer had scored points by highlighting the inconsistencies in the various accounts Atkins had given.

As with the first trial Ronnie Actie acquiesced with legal advice not to give evidence. David Farrington called Brian Spriggs to tell the jury of Vilday's stay in his house before she was taken into protective custody. His account and that of his niece, Cherie, were much the same as the ones they had given at the first trial. In addition to that Brian Spriggs told the jury that Vilday had told him tearfully that the police had threatened to charge her with conspiracy to murder and had threatened to put her baby son Craig in custody. Spriggs also claimed that Vilday had once told him that she wanted to see a solicitor to retract her evidence. Elfer impugned Spriggs' honesty by referring to his previous convictions and suggested that he was making up his account. Spriggs accepted that he had had problems with the police before, but he had put that behind him and insisted that he had told the jury the truth.

Farrington also called evidence to show that Ronnie Actie was driving a red Triumph and not a green Cortina at the time of the murder. These included his sister Michelle and his friend Johnny Crook, who confirmed that Actie had driven the Triumph at the time of the murder and that he thought that he might have been out clubbing with Actie on the murder night. Crook did not repeat his mistake of the first trial of denying an abetting perjury conviction. Nevertheless, Elfer scored some points in cross-examination by referring to his record of dishonesty. Farrington would later submit that the jury could rely on Crook as a witness of truth as he had not tried to lie to them by giving Actie a firm alibi.

Farrington also called Joanne Smith, the tenant of the third floor flat in 7 James Street at the time of the murder. She told the jury that she had been in her flat on the murder night, but didn't hear any screams. She claimed that the police did not believe her when she told them this in interviews which were recorded by contemporaneous note on November 22nd 1988. She also told the jury that she had thrown her keys down to Vilday on the Sunday night and that Vilday had seemed her usual self.

Abdullahi was the next of the Cardiff Five to give evidence. He told the jury much the same story as he had told at the first trial. He denied involvement in Lynette's murder and detailed his movements on the murder night. He accepted that he had his share of trouble with the police and vehemently denied making any kind of confession to Jane Sandrone, Noreen Amiel, Jackie Harris or to DC Mike Cullen. Abdullahi assured the jury that he had been working on the *Coral Sea* on the murder night.

Roger Backhouse called Peter McCarthy, John Hulse, Sidney Arthur Harrop, Lawrence Mann and Ian Moore to support Abdullahi's alibi. Their evidence established that Abdullahi had worked on the *Coral Sea*, that he had helped Hulse and Brynley Samuel around the most likely time of the murder and that Lawrence Mann had exchanged terse words with him at around 1.15-1.30 a.m. that night. Mann's evidence also contradicted that of his friend Ronnie Williams.

Cheryl Rogan told the jury the same account as she had given in the first trial that neither Ronnie Williams, Peter Brooks, nor Yusef Abdullahi had been in the North Star on the murder night. And Noreen Amiel re-iterated her account of the first trial that Abdullahi had not confessed to killing Lynette and that she had not been afraid of the defendants. She claimed that she just didn't want to get involved. Backhouse also called Mrs Williams who told the jury that she had seen Psaila shortly after the murder. She accepted that Psaila looked frightened, but there was no blood on her face.

John Actie was the last of the defendants to give evidence. He told the jury a similar tale to the one he had told at the first trial. Actie detailed his movements on the murder night and explained that he had been mistaken in his insistence during his interviews with police that he had not been in the Casablanca on the murder night. He re-iterated that he did not associate with his co-defendants and did not know Vilday or Psaila at the time of the murder.

Actie told the jury that he viewed Abdullahi as a police informer and once again explained that he had just got his days wrong over his alibi. He told them that as soon as he saw his questionnaire of March 1988 he realised his error. It was not, he assured the jury, an attempt to deceive them because he knew the murder hatched in the Casablanca and that he was anxious to put himself as far from the club as he could. That said, he detailed his usual route home after a Saturday night out at the Casablanca, a route which did not take him near James Street.

John Charles Rees called evidence to support Actie's claim that he used to go to a nearby warehouse to pick up his Sunday paper after a Saturday night out at the Casablanca. John Actie also denied knowing Mark Grommek or Paul Atkins. And as in the first trial he denied the claims of Violet Perriam and Gary George. Now all the evidence had been heard.

CHAPTER 8

Errors of Judgement

A Misguided Prosecution

The marathon trial was almost over. The jury had heard all the evidence that would be presented to them. But it should be remembered that the Crown Prosecutors had the discretion to end this prosecution at any time. They chose not to do so despite serious doubts about the credibility of the evidence at their disposal. And as the two trials progressed the cracks in the credibility of the Crown's case became yawning chasms.

There was clear evidence that Steve Miller was as vulnerable a suspect as one could find. He was of borderline intelligence and was abnormally suggestible. He needed a solicitor who recognised his disadvantages and was able to protect his interests fearlessly. Yet even Geraint Richards recognised that he had failed to do so at the first trial. When he heard interview seven he concluded that he should have intervened. Miller had the right to expect Richards to defend his interests fearlessly, but contrary to Leonard's conclusions that Richards was an experienced solicitor and had not played a passive role, Richards' presence was a positive disservice to Miller. Suffice to say, Leonard's ruling regarding Richards' performance seems to contradict Richards' frank admission that he had failed Miller by not intervening. And the conclusion that three interventions, one of which was fobbed off, proves that the suggestion that Richards' presence was not passive is absurd.

But it ought to be pointed out that Leonard arrived at these conclusions without having had the benefit of hearing Richards explain his inaction as Frisby had chosen not to call him for the Voire Dire. This was not the only example of poor presentation of evidence regarding Miller's confession. Roger Frisby described Miller's seventh interview as a shameful piece of bullying yet failed to ensure that the judge heard all of that interview. Suffice to say, Frisby's submission on the oppressive nature of the interviews was lacklustre. Unfortunately, Miller himself was not capable of ensuring that his case was presented to the judge and jury as well as it could and should have been. However, the adversarial model of justice holds that the client is responsible for the conduct of her/his case. It is difficult enough for bright and competent clients to defy legal opinion and insist that their defence is presented according to their wishes, but in the case of a person like Miller it is absurd to expect him to be capable of exercising his legal rights, yet as far as the criminal justice system is concerned the buck stops with him.

Yet there is evidence to suggest that the entire criminal justice system failed to understand the level of Miller's vulnerabilities and the level of support and assistance that he needed if his legal rights were to have any meaning at all. Leonard stressed that he did not find Dr Gudjonsson persuasive. But Gudjonsson was the only witness to put Miller's vulnerabilities in their proper context. He stressed that suggestibility does not mean that a suggestible man, as Miller undoubtedly was, would agree with absolutely everything that is put to him as suspicion and anger affect suggestibility. He also explained that even though Miller was not particularly bright he could still use his imagination.

At the very least, Gudjonsson's testimony suggested that Miller's account that he had adopted what the police told him and filled in the gaps by making things up was not inconceivable. Yet both Elfer and Mr Justice Leonard seemed to expect Miller to agree with absolutely everything that was put to him in order to qualify as suggestible. Such a standard is unattainable, reverses the burden of proof and inevitably leads to false confessions. In short, Miller was exactly the type of person most at risk from confrontational interviewing. Indeed, it was difficult to imagine a suspect more in need of the protections that the law had to offer than Steve Miller as he was precisely the sort of person PACE was designed to protect.

There is also the question of the credibility of the confession itself. It clearly contradicted known facts established by expert witnesses such as Professor Knight. And there were other causes for concern such as why, with a suspect supposedly giving a true confession voluntarily, Miller was never asked about who had the knife, how many there were and who had disposed of it/them? In nearly thirteen hours of interrogation the police seem not to have attempted to solve the mystery of the whereabouts of the murder weapon - a weapon they never found. For what was supposed to be an extremely thorough inquiry this was a glaring omission. Suffice to say, Miller's confession was riddled with inconsistencies and should not have been used against him.

Nevertheless, Miller had made the confession. If the jury were to be allowed to hear it warts and all, his co-defendants had the inalienable legal right not to have it weigh against them. In practice the only way to ensure that the jury kept the evidence which was admissible against each defendant in separate compartments was to sever Miller's trial from that of the others. Miller's confession is the most obvious example of this. A few choice words from judge to jury was a poor substitute for the certainty that Miller's confession could not be used against the other defendants if their trial had been severed from his. The judge's exercise of his discretion to admit Miller's confession and not sever the trial would prove to have disastrous consequences as it would later emerge that the jury based their verdicts on Miller's confession despite the law dictating otherwise.

But this was only one of many failings in this case. The crux of the case rested on the credibility of Vilday, Psaila and Grommek in particular, each of whom were at best self confessed liars who claimed that this time, unlike all the other times, they were telling the truth. Their explanation that their previous lies could all be explained by fear of the defendants was taken at face value by the prosecuting authorities. This was grossly unfair as it had not been proved. There was evidence that Vilday's demeanour had changed after the murder, but how could her claim of fear be reconciled with her behaviour? If she was so scared of them, why did she freely associate with men she knew to be the brutal murderers of her best friend? The same applies to Psaila.

And there is the question of Vilday's drunken outburst. According to the Crown's case Vilday and Psaila had been forced to cut Lynette to ensure their silence. Vilday's drunken accusation of Abdullahi and Miller of May 1988 showed that her silence could not be relied on. Why, if they were guilty, did they not ensure her silence at this point? And even more importantly, why would Vilday freely associate with Abdullahi in November 1988?

And Psaila was no better. She claimed to have been confused between Tony Miller and Yusef Abdullahi even though they bore no similarity to each other whatsoever. But even more importantly, she had named both of them as having been present in her statements. It therefore stands to reason that whatever her reason for naming Tony Miller it could not have been confusion with Abdullahi. Clearly, fear of the defendants alone, if there was any, cannot explain the numerous contradictions in their evidence.

Grommek had also told numerous lies. He claimed to have seen four men outside 7 James Street by stepping out on to his window ledge and looking down. He then saw them again when he let them in. Even by his account, he had only seen them for a very short time. But several months later, for no apparent reason, he could remember vividly the faces of men who were perfect strangers to him at the time of the murder. Such claims are fanciful at best. And there was the question of him fitting his evidence into what the Crown wanted to hear at least in Miller's case. In his crucial statements, evidence at the committal hearing and evidence at the first trial Grommek had stressed that one of the four men he saw that night was a black man with shoulder length dreadlocks - a hairstyle which none of the defendants had.

In the first trial Elfer had suggested that the description fitted Miller's brother Tony, but as Tony was in London the jury should infer that it was Steve Miller. This had no basis in evidence as the description Grommek had given did not fit Steve Miller whose locks were bunched up on top of his head. But at the retrial Grommek said that the man had his locks on top of his head, as Miller had, and he had forgotten to mention this earlier. This was ridiculous as Miller's flamboyant hairstyle was the most distinctive thing about his appearance at the time of the murder. It is beyond belief that Grommek, whose memory is supposed to be so good that he can remember perfect strangers he had only seen for a few seconds several months earlier, had forgotten about such a flamboyant hairstyle. This suggests that Grommek was telling the jury what he thought the prosecution wanted him to say.

And then there was Paul Atkins. His credibility left much to be desired as well, but it should be remembered that his evidence, warts and all, affected Grommek's credibility as well. Grommek had insisted that Atkins had been in his flat that night, yet Atkins insisted that he had not been there and had been forced to lie through police pressure.

Suffice to say, Vilday, Psaila and Grommek were witnesses of the lowest possible credibility and their evidence should not have been the basis of this prosecution or any other for that matter, especially as they contradicted themselves, each other and irrefutable evidence irreconcilably several times. And the corroboration was not much better. It is difficult to see why the evidence of Diane Seeley and Richard Stephens was called at all as they did not say that the black man they saw quarrelling with Lynette was Miller, especially as they made no reference to the man having a flamboyant hairstyle and they did not hear the content of the argument. In his closing address to the jury Roger Frisby would accuse Elfer of drawing conclusions from their testimony which had no basis in fact because Elfer had suggested that the argument was Miller telling Lynette to go back to work despite there being no evidence to support his interpretation of the content of the argument. And, at the very least, there was reason to doubt that the man in question was Miller at all.

The evidence of Debbie Taylor and Tessa Sidoric ought to be seen in the context of the interviews themselves. If the confession itself was unreliable then so was the evidence of these two women albeit through no fault of their own. And then there was the evidence of Jennifer Parkin that Miller threatened her shortly after the murder. One glaring question remains unanswered. Why would Miller tell her not to talk to the police when there was no reason to assume that she had anything incriminating to tell them anyway? And Elfer's claim that the man Gary George had seen shouting up at the flat a couple of days before the murder was Miller, despite the description bearing no resemblance to him at all, was frankly ludicrous.

Nevertheless, the case against Miller stood or fell on the credibility of his confession which Frisby had not opposed as effectively as it could have been. Had he played the whole of tape seven to the judge there was, at the very least, a realistic possibility that Mr Justice Leonard would have thrown the entire confession out on the grounds of oppression. The officers who obtained the confession had given evidence that they believed the crucial statements of Vilday, Psaila and Grommek. Indeed, the interrogation of Miller had been shaped by information obtained from these discredited sources. At the very least, these officers exercised very poor judgement in relying on these witnesses uncritically. They denied Miller access to his statements and soon convinced him that they had destroyed his alibi when in truth they had not. They put him in the room by getting him to accept that he could have been there and not remembered it due to the effect of drugs. And having got him to accept this suggestion they demanded details that they had just accepted he could not remember. On any view, the confession contained more holes than a sieve as did the information that it was based on.

Prejudicing The Trial That Never Was

Another major flaw in the adversarial system of justice was the way that it allowed the testimony of a witness of such appalling quality as Ian Massey to be the sole legal basis for convicting Tony Paris. The evidence established that Massey had the opportunity and motive to fit his evidence in with what the police wanted to hear. And there was evidence that Massey was involved in the Corley Affair in some form. Massey had insisted that his allegations against Corley were true and even had the audacity to claim that it was as a result of his concerns that Corley was released.

But Massey had admitted on oath that he had told lies in the first trial to help himself. Consequently, Massey was yet another self confessed liar who claimed that this time, unlike all the others, he had told the complete truth. And he vociferously denied that he had anything to gain from giving evidence. Yet during the Corley Affair he had received some of the inducements on offer such as private visits from a girlfriend at Stretford Police Station. It would later emerge that while waiting to give evidence at the second trial he received similar treatment at another police station.

Gerard Elias felt that the jury ought to be allowed to hear the whole story of Massey's involvement in the Corley Affair because Paris' case was that Massey had received inducements as a result of his involvement in the Corley case and now he was trying to frame him in expectation of parole. West Yorkshire Police had not finished its inquiries and there was a possibility that Massey would face charges over it and such proceedings, if they were ever to take place, should not be prejudiced. Elias wanted the jury to have all the facts relating to Massey's involvement in the Corley Affair available to them, or failing that, Massey's evidence should be deemed inadmissible, because his motivation for giving evidence could not be probed in full due to sub judice regulations.

But Mr Justice Leonard decided that there was enough evidence that could be presented to the jury that would give them the flavour of the conspiracy against Corley. In effect Massey's right to have a fair trial was scrupulously observed in a case that would never come to trial at the expense of Tony Paris who was already on trial and was facing a life sentence on Massey's evidence. But it need not have been like this. Massey's right to a fair trial could have been observed with the minimum of fuss without depriving Paris of his right to present his case as fully as possible. All it required was to place reporting restrictions on that portion of the trial. Surely it was better that this evidence was heard by the jury with reporting restrictions rather than prevent them from hearing evidence which may have undermined Massey's credibility beyond redemption in their eyes. There can be no doubt that in order to reach true and just verdicts the jury ought to have heard all relevant evidence. Suffice to say, Leonard's decision to admit Massey's evidence without allowing Elias to probe his involvement in the Corley Affair fully was unfair to Paris.

And no notes were taken of DI Mouncher's conversations with Massey. At the very least, the better practice would have been to record all contact that police have with witnesses, especially witnesses like Massey, as there are countless examples of prison informers making implausible claims that other prisoners had confessed to them with no safeguards about how such confessions were obtained or even if they were accurate.

It beggars belief that the system takes the implausible allegations of people like Massey at face value and continues to allow such unreliable and unscrupulous people to use and abuse the criminal justice system by giving false evidence, especially in circumstances where there was irrefutable proof that Massey had lied about Paris by putting words into his mouth that he couldn't possibly have known at the time. Suffice to say, like Vilday, Psaila, Grommek et al the criminal justice system was gravely at fault in relying on a witness of such woeful quality as Ian Massey. And it would later emerge that there was even more evidence affecting Massey's credibility which the jury did not know about as it was not disclosed to Paris' defence.

Disclosure

The quality of the evidence against Yusef Abdullahi was equally unimpressive. Jackie Harris was a case in point. Her accounts of Abdullahi's confession while on drugs was refuted by Abdullahi. Once again there were no safeguards over how it was obtained and whether it was reliable. It came down to her word against his. Yet even Harris would come to doubt that Abdullahi had confessed to her. And there was the question of her meetings with Vilday. Harris had claimed that at one of those meetings she had asked Vilday for details, but was stopped from questioning her further when Vilday became distressed. Police evidence had established that both women were told not to discuss the case, yet this was the point of Harris' request to see Vilday. It should also be pointed out that no notes of those meetings were taken. At best the police betrayed a lack of foresight in allowing them to meet and discuss the case in any form as the opportunity for them to collude with each other had been established.

And then there was the question of the unsatisfactory way that news of these meetings emerged. The better practice would have been for the police to disclose the fact that meetings had taken place and record the content of these conversations in full. Unfortunately, that did not happen. But these meetings were not the only things that should, in the interests of fairness, have been disclosed to the defence as a matter of course. Detective Superintendent Davies had assured the jury that the police had given all their information to the prosecution. If that is true it means that the Crown knew about these meetings but did not tell the defence about them. And it would later emerge that one of Davies' own statements had not been disclosed to the defence along with much more besides.

During the trial it emerged that Psaila had one of her prostitution fines paid from police funds to prevent her being imprisoned for non-payment. This fact alone compromises the integrity of the investigation and Psaila in particular. And Vilday too had been paid for information. Davies' bland assurance that such information would have been given to the defence if they asked for it is not good enough. Payments of any description could compromise the credibility of the witness and possibly even that of the investigation as a whole. But wherever they occur they ought to be disclosed to the defence without delay as failure to disclose such pertinent evidence can give the impression of a conspiracy whether one exists or not.

Cocktail Blunder

The same applies to the forensic evidence. At the first trial Dr Whiteside seemed to suggest that on balance the cocktail theory was unlikely. He had also suggested that the discovery of Psaila's blood group was significant, yet while both juries heard evidence that the discovery of Psaila's blood group was an important breakthrough neither jury was told that earlier in the inquiry police had investigated a person whose blood group was effectively a perfect match to the blood in the flat and that their prime suspect had a remarkably similar blood group as well. In short, there is evidence to suggest that the discovery of Psaila's blood group was not as significant as had been suggested. Then there is the question of why Dr Whiteside thought her blood group important. The discovery of the male chromosome in five areas of the jeans which were tested meant that the killer was almost certainly a man. Further testing established that Psaila was not one of the 1:10,000 women who possess the male chromosome. This suggests that Psaila ought to have been eliminated as the source of the blood on the jeans, there being absolutely no evidence proving that it was her blood.

Nevertheless, it was possible that Psaila's blood had mixed with that of a man. During the first trial Dr Whiteside established that if the blood on the jeans was a mixture of a large amount of female blood and a small amount of male material, any male could have deposited the male chromosome. This meant that even if the cocktail theory is taken as fact it did not and could not come close to proving that Psaila's blood had mixed in with that of one of the defendants. Not only could the cocktail theory not conclusively tie one or more of the defendants to the murder, it could not exclude every single male on the face of the earth. And it should also be remembered that there was no evidence that it had been Psaila's blood rather than that of any other woman who possessed that blood group, because, if it could be applied to Psaila, then surely it could also be applied to any woman who possessed that blood group. As such the cocktail theory should not have been allowed as evidence until and unless it could exclude everyone bar Psaila and one or more of the defendants. And then there is the point that a single male donor with the rare blood group had never been conclusively eliminated.

And there was another very serious problem with the cocktail theory. The officer who took the first statement from Psaila a couple of days after the murder did not notice any injury or mark on her face. In her accounts at the time of the murder Psaila did not mention such an injury even though she had no reason to cover it up. Sarah Whitcombe accompanied Psaila to court on the Monday after the murder and testified that she did not notice any mark on her face. Mrs Williams saw Psaila soon after the murder and also saw no blood on her face. This evidence suggests that Psaila's face was not cut at all. If that is true the cocktail theory does not hold water as Psaila's blood could not have been shed in the flat.

To counter this at the retrial Psaila claimed that she was cut on the inside of her mouth and it had not bled profusely, but if that was true then the proportion of male to female blood in the cocktail would be affected and there would come a point when all of the Cardiff Five would have had to be eliminated because their blood factors which differed from that of Psaila would have been detected. At the very least, there is absolutely no evidence that Psaila's blood had been found in the flat and this is supported by the fact that not one of her fingerprints was discovered there. Consequently, there was no evidence that the discovery of Psaila's blood group was significant at all and there is no credible evidence that proves that she had ever been into that flat let alone witnessed the murder there.

Suffice to say, there was not a shred of forensic evidence which tied any of the Cardiff Five to the flat or to Lynette. And Elfer's claim that even though fingerprint evidence could not tie any of the defendants to the scene of the crime, it was still possible that they were guilty, was scraping the bottom of the proverbial barrel when it is borne in mind that there was an unidentified palmprint which in all probability was deposited there by the murderer or someone who was in the flat at the time. The fact that such negative forensic evidence was enough to eliminate many others suggests that the Cardiff Five were entitled to be eliminated on the same basis and that there was one standard for the Cardiff Five and an altogether fairer one for everyone else. The way the forensic evidence, in particular, was interpreted in this case is a compelling argument for a more inquisitorial system that is aimed solely at establishing the truth. Unfortunately, the full truth about who deposited the blood on the jeans was never established.

The Integrity Of The Investigation

The presentation of the forensic evidence had left something to be desired as the jury did not receive the full extent of the scientific evidence that was available. However, from the evidence given at the two trials there was also a question over the integrity of the investigation itself. The most obvious example of this was the inappropriate interviewing methods that were employed on Steve Miller. His confession was clearly based on an invalid knowledge base and there was evidence that police seemed to overstate the evidence at their disposal during interviews with other defendants such as DC Gillard's colourful suggestion that half the docks had put Ronnie Actie at the scene of the crime when they only had Vilday, Psaila, Grommek and Atkins. And DI Mouncher admitted that he had told Abdullahi that Ronnie Actie had put him in the flat when he knew that Actie had said nothing of the sort to try to put Abdullahi off his guard.

Although the police held the Lynette White Inquiry up as a model investigation, the court had heard complaints from certain witnesses that they had been the victims of police pressure, especially Helen Prance and Paul Atkins. They had made strong allegations of police malpractice - allegations which had been strongly denied - which, through no fault of their own, were unprovable as it came down to whether the jury believed the police or the witnesses. But it need not have been like this. If the same consideration that is afforded to suspects, namely tape recording interviews, was accorded to witnesses as well there would be evidence to resolve these complaints of alleged police malpractice one way or the other. Then, there is the issue of the use of contemporaneous notes to record some interviews with certain witnesses, but not others. There are even examples of some interviews with the same witness being recorded by contemporaneous note while others were not as occurred with Angela Psaila, among others.

The November 17th interviews with Psaila were recorded contemporaneously, yet the equally contentious ones of December 11th were not. Had they been recorded in this fashion the issue of whether she was actually told about her blood group during that interview could have been resolved. And if the taking of statements, especially from obviously important witnesses like Psaila were tape recorded or even videotaped there could be no dispute about what was said during any of those interviews. But even this is not enough. The jury had heard that in the gap between her contemporaneously recorded interviews Psaila was given certain assurances by DI Mouncher. She said that she wanted reassurance that she would not be charged with conspiracy to murder, yet police evidence regarding these assurances stressed that Mouncher did not reassure her over that. If all contact with witnesses was tape recorded or videotaped there would be no dispute over the content of Mouncher's brief conversation with Psaila.

Having taken the decision to record Psaila's interviews of November 17th by contemporaneous note, it seems bizarre that further interviews with her were not subject to the same consideration. The same applies to Grommek and Atkins as their interviews of November 22nd were recorded by contemporaneous note, but the crucial statements they made in December 1988 were not. And none of Vilday's statements were recorded by contemporaneous note. And furthermore, there is the worry that none of the interviews with Massey were recorded by contemporaneous note. Indeed, by Mouncher's own admission, no notes of at least some of these interviews were made by police. There was also the failure of DC Cullen to make any note of his alleged incriminating conversation with Abdullahi.

But perhaps the worst example of police conduct compromising the integrity of the investigation was that of DC Gillard. Evidence had established that a bench warrant had been issued against Angela Psaila for non-payment of fines for soliciting. It is beyond dispute that on the day she appeared before magistrates she would have been imprisoned if the outstanding fines were not paid. Yet Psaila's fines were paid from police funds by DC Gillard. DI Mouncher had told the jury that he had checked with the CPS before it was paid. Under no circumstances should this have happened as it could, at the very least, constitute a powerful inducement to Psaila. But, if it was essential to do this, the defence should have been told about it without delay as it goes to the credibility of the witness. And it would later emerge that there was even more pertinent evidence which affected the credibility of prosecution witnesses and the integrity of the investigation as a whole which was not presented to the jury. This is a grave flaw in the adversarial model of justice as juries can only decide cases on the information they have at their disposal. A truly inquisitorial system could ensure that all pertinent evidence is made available to the jury. Sadly this did not occur in the case of the Cardiff Five.

The Evidence The Jury Did Not Hear

On any view, the state of knowledge of the investigating officers was of paramount importance. As we have seen, at the very least, there are pertinent questions which require answers concerning the conduct of the inquiry. Detective Superintendent Davies had outlined the scope of the inquiry. The jury had been given the impression that this was an extremely thorough inquiry which eventually resulted in the Cardiff Five being arrested and charged. But the picture that Davies had painted for the jury was woefully incomplete. For example, the only reference to Mr X in his statement which outlined the scope of the investigation was to the effect that he had been considered, but eliminated. An unused statement from Dr Prance established that X had been eliminated by DNA profiling as the source of the blood on SS12 a month before the arrests of the Cardiff Five and a few months before all the eliminations on DNA were shown to be useless. The defence were supplied with no information about how seriously he had been viewed as a suspect and that he had been the prime suspect, a fact Davies was fully aware of. Without full disclosure of his importance as a suspect the defence could not cross-examine police witnesses about their investigation of him and the jury were left completely in the dark about his importance in this inquiry. The disclosure of information about X was clearly not sufficient.

Although it has subsequently emerged that Mr X was innocent, this was not known at the time. Had the defence been given full disclosure of police interest in him as an alternative suspect, the jury would have heard that police had considered him not as a person to be traced, interviewed and eliminated, but as the prime suspect. They would have heard that there was a powerful circumstantial case against him, that he fitted Professor Canter's psychological profile while the Cardiff Five did not, that he had a gripe against women and prostitutes in general, that he could be linked to Lynette, was familiar with the area and much more besides.

For example, DI Mouncher initiated renewed police interest in X and referred the matter to Davies. DC Greenwood and DC Seaford took information from X's doctor that he was a psychopath and took part in surveillance on X. In short, police seemed convinced that they had found their man. Time would tell that they hadn't, but what would the jury have made of this information? While it may not have proved X guilty, the quality of the evidence against him was of a far higher standard than the case against the Cardiff Five. DC Greenwood knew about X yet he chose to believe Psaila's statement of December 6th. The material about X should have given him even more reason to reject the wretchedly inconsistent accounts of Vilday, Psaila and Grommek. At the very least, the X material would almost certainly have created a reasonable doubt and could have raised the question of the reasonableness of the police's conduct in the minds of the jury.

Although disclosure was somewhat of a grey area at the time and thus although it could possibly be argued that the police or prosecution were not obliged to disclose the information, the better practice would have been to disclose the full extent of police interest in X and others. This was pertinent information which may have affected the course of the trial. The jury had a right to hear it. A more inquisitorial system could have ensured that important evidence such as the X material was made available to the jury in order to reach true verdicts. This should never be allowed to happen again.

Alibi

There was also the question of the alibis of the defendants and how they were investigated. While the defendants were not obliged to prove anything each of them provided alibis of varying strength. Given the fact that nearly ten months had elapsed before any of them knew that they would need alibis of any description it was a remarkable achievement that they were able to provide alibis at all.

Ronnie Actie's was far from impressive. The closest he came to a supporting witness was Johnny Crook, hardly the most trustworthy of witnesses and one who never offered Actie a firm alibi in any case. Thus, Actie's account of his movements that night of club-hopping only had Crook say that he thought that he was out with Actie that night. There was the evidence of his sister regarding his clothes, but the most convincing part of his claims concerned Vilday's behaviour of meeting him in the North Star and going back to his sister's home shortly after the murder had been committed.

Nor was his cousin's alibi much better. The law says that if the jury believe that a defendant has put forward a false alibi, but had done so deliberately intending to deceive them rather than from panic or stupidity they were entitled to use that as corroboration of the case against that defendant. Elfer would ask the jury to view John Actie's alibi in that light. But the evidence suggests that this was no calculated lie. It is, of course, beyond dispute that Actie was wrong about his movements on the murder night during his interviews with police. He would not accept that he was in the Casablanca that night because he wrongly believed that a particular sound system had played there that night. But the tapes of his interviews showed that he was not totally inflexible about it and grew frustrated that police would not take the trouble to check if the system had played there that night. Evidence showed that limited records from the club could still have proved that the particular system did not play the club on the murder night. Had this check been completed when Actie requested it, it would have established Actie's mistake and the interviews would have been completely different. If anyone is to blame for the pattern that those interviews took it is the police. They could and should have made that check when it was requested. Contrary to DI Powell's bizarre belief that it was not his job to do so, it was.

In fact, there was now very little dispute between the Crown and the defence. The only difference between them was the reason for Actie giving a false alibi and whether he had remained on the door throughout the night. None of the witnesses who were traced to the Casablanca could state this with any certainty.

In other words, the Crown case was that he left work briefly, committed the murder and then returned to work as if nothing had happened. Then, realising that the murder had been hatched from the Casablanca, he put forward a false alibi intending to deceive the jury because he didn't want to be anywhere near the Casablanca on the night of the murder.

The type of work that Actie had been doing that night was such that trouble could have flared up at any moment. If he was out committing a murder while supposedly working, he ran the risk of his absence being noticed. If that happened his alibi was useless. In other words, he could not have planned that murder as meticulously as would have been necessary to be sure of avoiding detection. Secondly, if he had committed the murder and he knew that it had stemmed from the Casablanca, he would want to put himself far away from it. The alibi that he presented during his interviews – that he was home alone with nobody to prove his whereabouts – would be utterly useless.

If Actie had presented a false alibi intending it to deceive, it was one of the most pathetic alibis ever devised for such a purpose. It seems obvious that Actie had made an honest mistake because of the timespan between the murder and his arrest. But Elfer would have none of it. His case remained that he had caught Actie out in a lie and wanted to use it against him if at all possible. Elfer would tell the jury that it was a deliberate lie and ask them to treat it as corroboration against Actie. It seems unlikely that Actie, who is no fool, would invent such a useless alibi. It had all the hallmarks of an honest mistake.

Then, there is the question of Steve Miller's alibi. Like that of Ronnie Actie it was never compelling, yet limited as it was, it still presented an obstacle to the police. Before Miller could be induced to confess he had to be convinced that his alibi had been disproved. David Orton had backtracked on the firm alibi he had previously given Miller, but this in no way blew Miller's alibi out of the water. There were two missing periods in Orton's account, but unknown to Miller there were witnesses who could account for both these periods. One of them was when he went to the North Star and the other was accounted for by two women whose accounts languished in the unused material. Their claims amounted to a complete alibi for the most likely time of the murder, especially in terms of what he would have had to have done in a very short period of time.

If they were telling the truth it meant that Miller, a man with the intelligence of a child, was either a criminal genius who had persuaded highly qualified experts that he was backward, or he was entirely innocent. But Miller did not even know that this alibi for the most likely time of the murder was available to him and, crucially, nor did the jury. Suffice to say, not only was Miller's alibi never blown out of the water, in actual fact, it could be described as compelling after all. Had it been investigated thoroughly and more objectively there is reason to believe that not only would his wretched confession never have been obtained, but that he would not even have been charged. Quite simply this is not good enough.

Tony Paris' alibi posed different problems. The jury had heard from Carol Blades that she had seen him off and on throughout the murder night. While she had not offered him a complete alibi Elias would ask the jury to conclude that her evidence established that it was most unlikely that Paris could have committed the murder. Elias would also refer to the statements of several other witnesses whose claims supported Paris' claims that he was collecting glasses in the Casablanca throughout the murder night. Elias would tell the jury that Elfer must have accepted these claims as he did not call those witnesses to refute them. Although there were sound legal reasons for not calling some, or even all, of these witnesses the jury must have wondered why Elias did not call them if they assisted Paris as much as Elias seemed to indicate.

To be fair to Elias, it ought to be pointed out that part of the reason he decided not to call these witnesses is that disclosure rules allow the Crown to withhold the statements of alibi witnesses in order to test their credibility. But this can work an unfairness to defendants as defence lawyers cannot know what these witnesses have told the police in the undisclosed statements. Lawyers tend to avoid the risk of any unwanted surprises and therefore choose not to call such witnesses. Unfortunately, this can lead to juries receiving a jaundiced view of the strength of a defendant's alibi. This should not be tolerated. The disclosure of the names and addresses of potential alibi witnesses is a very poor substitute for full disclosure of all alibi statements. After all, full disclosure would significantly improve the chance of establishing the truth of a defendant's alibi.

But it was the investigation of Abdullahi's alibi which illustrates these points to the fullest. Take, for example, the evidence of DC Daniels. By his own admission it was not until Abdullahi's ninth interview that he even accepted that Abdullahi had worked on the ship at all let alone on the murder night. But Daniels' approach seemed not to be isolated to him as could be seen by the taking of statements from *Coral Sea* workers that they did not recognise photographs of Abdullahi. When it became clear that Abdullahi had worked on the ship, the goalposts were moved to suggest that he went home early on the murder night. There was considerable confusion and no clear cut evidence as to how Abdullahi had got back to Cardiff that night. Both Wilson and Hippolyte were never unequivocal in their belief that they had been taken back to Cardiff with Abdullahi in Les McCarthy's van.

Nevertheless, the investigation seemed to proceed on the basis that they had explained how Abdullahi got back. Then he was placed in the North Star by Ronnie Williams. Once again the investigation proceeded on the basis that Williams could not be mistaken even though it was eventually accepted by everyone that he was completely wrong about Lawrence Mann being in the North Star with him on the murder night. This serious discrepancy which ought to have affected Williams' credibility was simply brushed aside by the claim that Williams had mistaken Mann for Peter Brooks. There seems to have been no attempt to test the credibility of Williams' claims by checking with North Star customers and staff about whether he had even been there that night let alone seen Abdullahi there. And there was the remarkable admission by Detective Superintendent Davies that even though thirty-five witnesses had been traced to the *Coral Sea* by police, statements had only been taken from nine of them.

And this was without mentioning the firm alibi evidence putting Abdullahi on the ship at the relevant time. Admittedly, Peter McCarthy had damaged his credibility somewhat by ignoring Mr Justice McNeill's instruction not to talk to anyone about the case during the first trial. But this conversation jogged the memory of John Hulse. Elfer had suggested that these witnesses had concocted this incident. Yet these claims closely resembled work that Abdullahi had claimed he did during his police interviews before he could have known that McCarthy and Hulse would give evidence to that effect. And unknown to either Abdullahi, Hulse or McCarthy and, even more importantly, the jury, these claims bore a strong resemblance to ones Brynley Samuel had put in his statements to police. Samuel made these claims long before Hulse, McCarthy or Abdullahi had made them. They couldn't possibly have known this and nor did Abdullahi's defence because the prosecution had decided not to disclose Samuel's statements to them.

Presumably, statements which the Crown decide not to disclose are read first. How else could a decision be reasonably made on whether it is appropriate to disclose them or not? But Elfer had suggested that the evidence of Hulse and McCarthy was perjured. Clearly, the evidence of Brynley Samuel would have exposed that claim as it would have provided credible evidence that the incident had indeed occurred just as Hulse and McCarthy had insisted.

And the treatment Lawrence Mann received was even worse. Mann disliked Abdullahi, had stuck to his guns that he did not go to the North Star with Williams on the murder night which was belatedly accepted and he even went to the level of checking with the local meterological office that it had rained that night before he came forward with his claims of having exchanged terse words with Abdullahi between 1.15-1.30 a.m. that night. At the very least, Mann's claims were never disproved. To suggest that he had perjured himself despite having absolutely no reason to do so while uncritically accepting the claims of Ronnie Williams which were, at best, unreliable is frankly unacceptable. The evidence strongly suggests that Abdullahi was working on the *Coral Sea* throughout the murder night. At the very least, the Crown did not unequivocally prove that he was not.

And there was further evidence that supported his alibi which the jury did not hear due to the rules of disclosure. If Abdullahi's alibi was truthful it means that he was innocent and entitled to be eliminated on that basis alone. After all, many others whom police had referred to in evidence did not have alibis as credible as that of Abdullahi.

The issue of Abdullahi's alibi, in particular, illustrates grave flaws in the system. The way that disclosure rules were utilised in this case deprived the jury of the evidence of a man who, on any view, should have been a pertinent witness - Samuel. The non-disclosure of his statements prevented the jury from hearing evidence which would undoubtedly have affected their perception of Elfer's opinion of the evidence of Hulse and McCarthy. This is not good enough. Juries can only decide cases based on the evidence presented to them. The criminal justice system placed them in an invidious position by putting the defence lawyers in a position where they had to advise their client not to call a potentially vital witness because they could not afford any unpleasant surprises. At the very least, Samuel's evidence was capable of assisting them to conclude that Abdullahi's alibi witnesses had not perjured themselves. Consequently, if they had access to the evidence of such an important witness as Samuel, Abdullahi's alibi would have been strengthened to the point that the jury may well have had great difficulty rejecting it.

Suffice to say, there are grounds for concern over the way that the alibis of the defendants, especially that of Abdullahi, were investigated and presented to the jury. The criminal justice system ought to be concerned with establishing the truth about offences, yet the evidence suggests that the alibis were treated as inconveniences to the police to be disproved rather than possible indicators of innocence which deserve to be investigated thoroughly and impartially to see where the truth lies. Such an approach will inevitably lead to miscarriages of justice.

It is a sad indictment of the criminal justice system that near the end of the exceptionally long trial we are still no nearer to finding out the full truth about the murder of Lynette White and far from being an advert for the adversarial system this case proves that the sooner a more inquisitorial bent is introduced to the criminal justice system the better.

Nevertheless, the jury had yet to deliver their verdicts. And even on the basis of the evidence that they had heard the Crown's case was far from compelling.

The marathon trial was nearing its end. It had lasted more than six months. Combined with the aborted trial this was already the longest murder trial in British history. The jury had heard all the evidence that they would be allowed to hear. Soon it would be left to them to determine their verdicts. But first the lawyers would make their closing speeches to the jury. And the judge would take six days delivering his summing up.

CHAPTER 9

The Verdicts and Their Aftermath

A Mammoth Undertaking

It was now November 19th 1990. The jury had just retired to begin their deliberations. Still ringing in their ears were the closing arguments of the lead barristers and the judge's summing up. David Elfer had highlighted the Crown's case to them forcefully. He had assured them that there was sufficient evidence to convict all of the defendants. He had told the jury that Miller's defence of suggestibility did not wash because he had not agreed with everything that had been put to him. He had put the Crown's case powerfully and told the jury that the evidence demanded convictions.

Roger Frisby had responded by inviting the jury not to believe Miller's confession. He had highlighted the inconsistencies in the confession. Frisby had accepted that the officers had been genuinely searching for the truth and did not impugn their good faith. Nevertheless, he argued that the officers had caused Miller's breakdown and resulted in an unreliable confession.

Gerard Elias had assured the jury that there was not sufficient evidence for them to convict Tony Paris. He had reminded them forcefully of Ian Massey's unreliability. And he had asked them to consider Miller's case last to ensure that his confession did not weigh against the other defendants. He had told the jury that Carol Blades' evidence meant that the jury should conclude that it was most unlikely that Paris was guilty. And he had hammered home the unreliability of Elfer's case.

David Farrington had put Ronnie Actie's case to them very forcefully. He had suggested that the case was upside down as there had been more evidence against Vilday, Psaila and Grommek than there had ever been against any of the defendants. He had pointed out that Johnny Crook was a witness of truth as he had resisted the temptation to give Actie a firm alibi when he could have lied. And there had been more of the same regarding the unreliability of Elfer's case.

Roger Backhouse and John Charles Rees had also scored strong points for their clients. The lawyers had had their say. For the next six days Mr Justice Leonard had delivered his mammoth summing up.

He had told the jury that Vilday and Psaila were self confessed accomplices whose testimony had to be corroborated by law. He had left it to the jury to decide if Grommek was an accomplice or not, but told them that if they believed him to be an accomplice, then his testimony would need corroboration as well.

He had instructed the jury that they could not use Steve Miller's confession against any of his co-defendants. He had reminded them of Elias' suggestion that they should consider Miller's case last to prevent the confession being used against the others. The law did not allow Leonard to do any more than advise the jury to consider Miller's case last. It would soon emerge that his advice had fallen on deaf ears.

Leonard had carefully summarised the cases of each defendant and he had advised the jury what evidence they were entitled to use as corroboration against each defendant. And he had advised them on the law regarding false alibis. They were only entitled to use a false alibi against a defendant if they believed that it had been put forward intending to deceive them and not through panic or stupidity. Elfer had asked them to view Abdullahi and John Actie's alibis in that light. Backhouse had insisted that Abdullahi's alibi had been the truth and Rees had argued that Actie had simply made an honest mistake which he had corrected as soon as he had realised his error.

Leonard had been dismissive of several witnesses. For example, it had seemed clear that he did not believe the testimony of Vilday and Psaila. And as for Massey; well, Massey was the self confessed perjurer and armed robber who claimed that this time he had told the truth. This was particularly important as without Massey there was no case against Paris.

And he had highlighted the complete lack of forensic evidence against any of the defendants, even telling the jury that there had to have been a sixth man in the room if the defendants were guilty - a man none of the alleged eyewitnesses had named, or even acknowledged the existence of. The summing up had been a mammoth undertaking which Mr Justice Leonard had delivered ably and fairly. He had summarised the merits and flaws of both the prosecution and defence cases adequately. And he had told the jury the laws that they would have to observe. It was now up to the jury to decide the fate of the Cardiff Five.

Unlawful Verdicts

The function of the jury in any trial is to bring their common sense to the judicial process. The law was the domain of the judge, but the facts were for the jury to decide. Now the jury began their deliberations.

After more than five hours they made the first of their strange requests from the judge. They asked to hear the first six minutes of Miller's eighteenth interview. Their request was granted. It was now obvious that they had decided to consider Miller's case first, in which case his confession would loom larger than the rest of the evidence.

The following day the jury returned with two verdicts. Some of the jurors were in tears as their foreman told the court that they had unanimously found Stephen Miller and Tony Paris guilty. Paris insisted that he was innocent as he was taken down. The jury had asked to hear an extract of Miller's interview which would have a profound effect upon the rest of their deliberations.

The extract was full of Miller's descriptions of Tony Paris stabbing Lynette whilst he and Abdullahi watched in horror. Paris would always maintain that he was convicted because of that tape. Significantly, the Actie cousins took no part in the murder by this account and were supposed not to have been in the room. But there would be even clearer evidence that Miller's interview was the basis of the verdicts.

On November 21st the jury returned to court to ask two questions. They wanted to know if they could convict a defendant of murder if they believed that he was present when Lynette was killed, but had only gone there believing that Lynette would be slapped about. They also wanted to know if they could convict him if someone else produced a knife, but he himself took no part in the stabbing. The answer was no to both questions, but it raised a very important problem.

In the absence of the jury, Mr Justice Leonard made a very significant remark. He said, "I am conscious of the fact that it is mysterious in that I do not see where the evidence is to justify that conclusion." The jury returned and he told them that they could not convict on that basis.

Later in the afternoon, Ronnie Actie was acquitted, probably by majority verdict. But the evidence suggests that Leonard need not have been so puzzled by the jury's questions. They clearly did not believe Actie's denials of presence at the scene of the crime, but neither did they believe that he had stabbed Lynette White.

In the afternoon of November 22nd 1990, the very day that the Prime Minister, Margaret Thatcher, announced her intention to resign, the longest murder trial in British history came to an end with the unanimous conviction of Yusef Abdullahi and the acquittal of John Actie. As the verdict was announced against Abdullahi, he said, "I wasn't even in Cardiff. You took my life away from me. You took my life away from me. I am innocent. You took my life away from me." That said, he was taken down to begin a life sentence. Some jurors burst into tears.

Meanwhile, an emotional John Actie was escorted out of the dock by friends and family so quickly that he had to return to the dock to be discharged by Mr Justice Leonard. He thanked the jury on his return. Outside the court he was greeted by supporters including his cousin, Ronnie, who had been acquitted the day before.

Both loudly proclaimed that there were innocent people in prison and that the real murderer or murderers of Lynette White were still out there. The Cardiff Three were now serving life sentences for killing her.

Observers were shocked by the verdicts. According to some, Mr Justice Leonard himself was astonished, believing the five innocent. Now, Lynette White's murder had been an exceptionally atrocious crime, but when the judge came to pass sentence on the three convicted men, the usual language that judges employ in such circumstances was absent.

He described none of them as evil monsters and made no recommended minimum sentence for them to serve. Under the circumstances this was highly unusual. He merely sentenced them to life imprisonment. He could do nothing less. After one hundred and ninety-seven days the retrial ended in these bizarre verdicts. That jury had become the latest part of the criminal justice system to fail the defendants. This was an abysmal day for British justice.

The Fightback Begins

These verdicts were deeply unsatisfactory. The families and friends of the Cardiff Three could not understand how three of them could be convicted while the other two were not. How, they wondered, could Vilday and Psaila be witnesses of truth against the Cardiff Three but liars against the Acties? It just did not make sense. But there is strong evidence to suggest that the evidence of Vilday and Psaila had little or nothing to do with the verdicts as neither Vilday, Psaila, nor any of the witnesses against either of the Actie cousins had ever said that they were present but did nothing to Lynette. The only evidence to justify such a conclusion was the confession of Steve Miller. The jury had been told several times that Miller's confession could not be used as evidence against any of the other defendants, yet they had clearly relied on it in their deliberations on Ronnie Actie. This was after Miller had been convicted. They had ignored the law.

British justice had miscarried appallingly. Quite simply, it should never have been allowed to reach the stage where it resulted in wrongful convictions. They had seen the evidence proclaim the innocence of the defendants, yet three of them were behind bars. They too could not understand how three could be convicted while two were acquitted. And they could not understand how such a ridiculous case had been allowed to get that far. But that was of little comfort to the Cardiff Three and their families and friends. Now they had to make sense of it all. They were angry, but they did not know what they could do about it.

Two probation officers put them on the right track. The media were contacted and the Cardiff Three Action Committee was formed. It would later evolve into the Cardiff Three Campaign. It was spearheaded by the families of Yusef Abdullahi and Tony Paris, but it campaigned for Miller as well. The campaign's leading lights would be Yusef's brother Malik, Malik's wife Alex, Tony's brother Lloyd and his sister Rosie. There would be others too numerous to mention by name who would play important roles within the campaign.

And ringing in their ears was Yusef Abdullahi's chilling warning that the real killer would strike again very soon. In the early hours of December 22nd 1990, Geraldine Palk, a young shipping clerk, was raped and brutally murdered near her home in the Fairwater district of Cardiff. There were obvious similarities between the murders of Lynette and Geraldine, not least of which was that both were the victims of multiple stabbings. But there were differences. Palk was not a prostitute. She had been raped; Lynette had not been. Palk had been bludgeoned as well; Lynette had not been.

Despite the differences in the crimes, the similarities were enough for talk to start that the murders might have been committed by the same person. David

Rose, the Home Affairs Correspondent of the *Observer*, and Heenan Bhatti would soon be asking if there was a 'Cardiff Ripper' on the loose. Abdullahi was certainly convinced that both murders were the work of the same deranged mind.

But comparison was difficult. There was good quality DNA profiles obtained from semen in the Palk case using single-locus probes, whereas the DNA evidence in the Lynette White case was of woeful quality and had used the far less sensitive multi-locus probes. And conversely, it is difficult to obtain blood grouping results from semen, so there is no blood grouping evidence in the Geraldine Palk case, whereas there is very useful blood grouping evidence in the Lynette White case. Scientific comparison is therefore very difficult, but advances in forensic science would later mean that there could be a possibility to compare them.

It was now February 1991. The media were about to discover that the case of the Cardiff Three left more than a little to be desired. Heenan Bhatti and David Rose were the first journalists to question the convictions of the Cardiff Three in the national press. The *Observer* had beaten its rivals to the punch. Several journalists now began to show an interest. I was one of them.

March 1991 was to be a significant month. The campaign stepped up its activities. It attracted the interest of Duncan Campbell of the *Guardian* and television researchers were sniffing around. Channel Four broadcast the first documentary on the case, *Butetown : The Bridge And The Boys* in its *Black Bag* slot. It was a useful start. But there was no real campaign for Miller - yet. And now, four months after the retrial had ended, defence lawyers received the statements of twenty-two potential alibi witnesses, which Elfer had exercised his right not to disclose during the retrial.

Belated Disclosure

Now these statements were handed over to the defence. Those of Michael Taylor, his brother John, Johnny Crook, Taryn Ali and Janet McHue were no longer relevant as they referred to the movements of the Acties who had been acquitted. Had they been disclosed earlier, they would probably not have been called anyway.

But there were several witnesses who had seen Tony Paris at various times throughout the murder night. Taken as a whole it amounted to a complete alibi. But some of the claims were vague. And others contradicted each other. Others were of bad character. They may not have been called even if the statements had been disclosed in time for the trial or retrial.

Elias had known of all of these witnesses. Whilst he did not know precisely what they had said in all of their statements to police, he had the gist of them. In fact, he had referred to them in his closing address to the jury, telling them that Elfer must have accepted that these witnesses were telling the truth because he did not call them to refute their statements. There was no further mileage for Paris in these witnesses in legal terms.

But they contained information which backed up Paris' defence. Several of these witnesses referred to seeing Paris at different times throughout the murder night collecting glasses. They referred to the clothes that he wore, to the after hours drinking at the Casablanca and to his demeanour; Paris had been his usual cheerful self on the murder night.

This was evidence which might have been useful to the jury, but they had not heard it. Part of the reason for that was Elias' wish not to risk calling them blind. Some of them would not have been called in any case, but had the system allowed him to see these statements before the trial, the jury may well have received a fuller picture of Paris' alibi than they actually did.

At the very least, the claims of these witnesses indicated that it was extremely unlikely, if not impossible, that Paris could have been guilty. And Miller's case was even worse. His defence had been cautious. Roger Frisby had concluded that Miller's was not an alibi case. Some of these witnesses had contradicted the picture he painted of himself. Had these statements been disclosed earlier they would have established that there was no point in calling Eugene Savage at all. And Debbie Pennington and Yasmin Abdullahi did not take things much further.

But David Orton and Derek Ferron were another matter. Orton's initial accounts had amounted to a complete alibi. He had subsequently backtracked to include two missing periods. One of them had been covered by Ferron. And Ferron had seen Miller still in the Casablanca at the beginning of the other. And languishing in the unused material were the claims of Debbie Actie and Robyn Reed which covered the period Ferron and Orton could not. Suffice to say, there was what amounted to a complete alibi for the most likely time of the murder for Miller, which the jury did not hear.

While part of the reason for that may have been the non-disclosure of these statements, the rest was available to Miller's defence and was either missed by them or they considered it and decided not to use it for other reasons. That is either a sad indictment on the quality of the preparation and presentation of Miller's case by his lawyers or it is evidence that Frisby was perhaps too cautious in circumstances where Miller would probably have benefited from a more aggressive defence.

And then there was the vexed issue of Yusef Abdullahi's alibi. It had been the strongest of the alibis presented to the court. Abdullahi had wanted to call Brynley Samuel, believing that Samuel could provide vital support for his alibi. But Abdullahi had acquiesced with legal advice not to call Brynley Samuel blind. Now Samuel's statements had been disclosed. Abdullahi had apoplexy.

Brynley Samuel had made statements supporting Abdullahi's claims. Samuel arrived at the *Coral Sea* with Abdullahi and Peter McCarthy at about 7.00 p.m. on February 13th 1988, but he worked on a different part of the ship to Abdullahi. About midnight he went for a tea break and saw Abdullahi and McCarthy there. They were there for about half an hour. They went to work on different parts again. After about twenty minutes he and one of the Merseysiders that he was working with, realised that the metal was too heavy for them and went for help. Samuel's claims about this were remarkably similar to those of John Hulse.

Samuel's colleague went to the mess room and returned with Peter McCarthy and Yusef Abdullahi. They worked together for about forty minutes. According to Samuel's timings this would have been at about 1.30 a.m., about the time that Lawrence Mann had exchanged terse words with Abdullahi. Samuel, Abdullahi and McCarthy returned to the mess room. Samuel left the mess room for an hour. He was certain that Abdullahi had been there at 6.00 a.m., as he saw him rolling some oxyacetylene bottles on the quay.

Samuel subsequently backtracked on what amounted to a complete alibi for the most likely time of the murder. He said that he definitely had not seen Abdullahi between 10.00 p.m. and 4.00 a.m. on the night of the murder. But he felt that at about 4.00 a.m. Abdullahi and Peter McCarthy had assisted him in lifting some heavy metal.

The nature of the work and what followed was broadly similar to Samuel's previous story, but the times had changed. He claimed that he had a general conversation in the mess room with Abdullahi and McCarthy about football and women. He said that he didn't notice any change in Abdullahi's clothing or demeanour from when he had first seen Abdullahi before 10.00 p.m. and after 4.00 a.m.

First of all, there is a striking similarity between Samuel's claims about the work that was done on the night of the murder and those of Abdullahi, John Hulse and Peter McCarthy in particular. And if Samuel's early account was true, it made it difficult if not impossible for Abdullahi to have got to the flat in time to commit the murder.

Had Samuel's statements been disclosed to the defence there can be no doubt that they would have called him to give evidence on Abdullahi's behalf. But Roger Backhouse was keen to avoid any unexpected problems. It was too dangerous to call Samuel blind as by the time of the arrests Samuel could not remember what had happened.

On any view, Samuel was a witness the jury should have heard from. His claims were important. Abdullahi's defence had been bluffed into not calling a witness who could and should have been an important witness in this trial. Where is the justice in that?

Elfer had utilised disclosure rules to prevent Abdullahi's defence receiving Samuel's statements. Without the statements Abdullahi's defence could not have known how useful Samuel could have been to them. Had Samuel given evidence Abdullahi's alibi would have been even stronger. The jury were entitled to know that there was a witness whose evidence could all but prove Abdullahi innocent. The non-disclosure of Samuel's statements was clearly the most important of the batch which had now been belatedly disclosed.

The procedural rules of the adversarial system allow the Crown and CPS to withhold alibi statements. Barristers tend not to call witnesses blind. As such, they can be bluffed into not calling witnesses when they would have called them if they had known exactly what they had said to police.

But the belated disclosure of these statements was eclipsed by even more important news for justice campaigners which emerged this month. The convictions of the Birmingham Six for the 1974 Birmingham pub bombings had just been quashed. Kenneth Baker, the Home Secretary, ordered a Royal Commission to look at ways of improving the criminal justice system. Viscount Runciman would be its chairman. It would report in 1993 and would express its concern over the case of the Cardiff Three. But despite these concerns not one of its numerous recommendations would help to prevent a repetition of the sad case of the Cardiff Three.

Bad Representation

By now the Cardiff Three had already begun the appeals procedure. Within fourteen days of their conviction their lawyers had drafted grounds of appeal and applied for leave to appeal. Their applications were being considered by Mr Justice Hutchison. On May 5th 1991 he gave leave to appeal to Yusef Abdullahi and Tony Paris. But Miller was refused leave to appeal. He renewed his application as was his right.

Now, the grounds that Miller's barrister had drafted were decidedly hopeful to put it mildly. This was hardly surprising. Although Miller's junior barrister, Phillip Meredith, had tried hard on his behalf, Miller's case had been appallingly mishandled by his defence from start to finish. Geraint Richards had failed to protect Miller's interests adequately during the interviews with police. The confession was demonstrable nonsense, but it had not been challenged as effectively as it could and should have been. What amounted to a complete alibi for the most likely time of the murder had been gathering dust in the unused material. In fact, no alibi evidence had been presented on Miller's behalf.

This could have given the impression that Miller had no alibi to speak of. The claims of David Orton, Gerry Richer, Derek Ferron, Debbie Actie and Robyn Reed amounted to a complete alibi. Orton and Ferron were not called due to restrictions on disclosure of alibi material. And while Gerry Richer has told several people about Miller's clothes, she had not mentioned them in her statements to police.

Consequently, Frisby's decision not to call these witnesses can be justified. But Debbie Actie and Robyn Reed were a different matter. In June 1988 Debbie Actie had told police that she had seen Miller playing pool in the Casablanca at about 2.00 a.m. In July her claims were corroborated by Robyn Reed who thought that Miller had been wearing black trousers and had been carrying some drinks at about the same time as Actie had seen him. And Robyn's sister, Stephanie, had told police that the three of them had shared a taxi on the murder night which dropped her off in James Street at about 1.30 a.m. The other two had told her that they were going on to the Casablanca.

The claims of Actie and Robyn Reed amounted to a complete alibi for Miller for the most likely time of the murder, although Reed was mistaken about Miller's trousers as the evidence strongly suggests that he wore stonewashed jeans not black trousers. However, the significance of these witnesses was either completely missed by Miller's defence or these statements were seen by Miller's defence who then decided not to rely on them. If that is the case they were perhaps too cautious as the evidence of both these women could have assisted Miller considerably.

Debbie Actie would eventually give me an interview. Actie would say that she was sure that she made the journey with Stephanie and Robyn Reed on the night of the murder because they talked about it in the aftermath of Lynette's murder. They heard about the murder the day after it happened and remembered that they passed James Street about 1.35 in the morning. It was about the time of the murder. They thought that they might have seen something important. It would later emerge that they had, but it wasn't what they thought was important at the time. They were asked if they saw anything suspicious in James Street, but they were unable to assist.

After they had left the Transport Club, dropped Stephanie off in James Street and arrived at the queue outside the Casablanca at about 1.37, they spent another ten minutes arguing with the men on the door to get in.

Once inside they went to the bar for a drink. This took about five minutes. By Actie's account it was about 2.00. They started to mingle. They entered the pool room and saw Steve Miller playing pool. There were a lot of people in the room. The time was then about 2.15. She was adamant that there was no way that Miller could have passed her without her noticing from the time that she arrived at the Casablanca. She also pointed out that there was a queuing system to play pool there. She thought that he would have had to have been in the club for about three quarters of an hour before he got on the table.

She saw him playing pool at about 2.10-2.15. This meant that he would have been in the Casablanca from about 1.30. This coincided with one of Orton's missing periods. It is also significant that Derek Ferron placed him in the Casablanca at 1.30. She would insist that Miller could not have murdered Lynette between the time that she arrived at the Casablanca and when she saw him playing pool. She would say, "Miller could not have committed that crime between those times because I saw him there. There's no way that he could have passed me without me seeing him." I would ask her if she was sure and she would reply, "I'm positive, absolutely positive!"

This would have been devastating to the Crown's case against Miller. The jury must have thought that he had no alibi to speak of. They were misinformed. Orton was with him for most of the night of the murder. He gave two periods when Miller was out of his sight. The first had been accounted for by Miller showing up in the North Star about half past twelve. Debbie Actie's claims fill in the second gap. If she was telling the truth about Miller, and she has no reason to protect him, her claims give him a complete alibi at the most likely time of the murder.

Her claims suggest that if Miller was guilty he had to clean himself and the flat of all forensic evidence tying him to Lynette and the scene of the crime without betraying any attempt to do so or interfering with the rest of the forensic evidence and then calmly play pool in the nearby Casablanca without betraying any change in demeanour within fifteen minutes of the most likely time of the murder. To suggest that Miller, who had the IQ of a child, was capable of doing that is simply ridiculous. Debbie Actie offers convincing reasons for believing that Steve Miller was entirely innocent of any involvement in Lynette's murder.

Had she been called it is likely that Elfer would have cross-examined her long and hard, because an alibi for Miller was more than just a minor inconvenience. There was one line of attack Elfer would have discovered. Debbie Actie and John Actie were cousins, but they hated each other.

At the time of the arrests, John Actie was facing serious assault charges brought against him by Debbie's sister, Suzanne. Those charges were dropped. It still angers Debbie, so much so that she would still insist that John Actie wasn't in the Casablanca that night. The evidence strongly suggests that he was.

However, there is no reason at all to doubt her truthfulness in relation to Steve Miller, a man she hardly knew and had no reason to lie for. Consequently, there can be little doubt that she saw Miller that night at the times that she said and that her claims amount to a complete alibi for him at the most likely time of the murder. In other words, if the jury had had access to her testimony, the Crown's case would have been in serious difficulties.

Not surprisingly, Miller's barristers did not criticise the way they had handled his defence in their application for leave to appeal. And with Mr Justice Hutchison's decision not to grant Miller leave to appeal, legal aid was terminated. And Miller was advised that if he persisted in applying for leave to appeal he could lose the time that he had served on remand in terms of the time he would have to serve in prison. This was scandalous advice. Whilst it was technically possible that this could happen, the barrister had neglected to inform Miller that it only happened rarely.

As was usual for Miller, he acquiesced with the advice of his lawyer and agreed to abandon his renewed application for leave to appeal. Fortunately for him this information would never reach the Court of Appeal. By now Miller had arrived in Wormwood Scrubs Prison, an innocent man in prison without the ability to prove his innocence.

Miller was beginning to get disgruntled. He knew that he had not murdered Lynette. He had put his trust in his lawyers and he now felt that they had let him down. Now they were telling him that there was nothing more they could do for him. He would just have to serve his time unless he could find new lawyers to fight his case.

It is yet another flaw of the adversarial system that it assumes that everyone performs to the best of their ability in court. The performance of Miller's lawyers offers graphic proof that Miller did not receive the best of Roger Frisby's advocacy, especially in terms of his submissions on oppression. Frisby had argued during the trial within a trial that DCs Greenwood and Seaford had been trying to get to the truth. He did not impugn their good faith. Nevertheless, he argued that the officers had caused Miller's breakdown and that interview seven contained shameful bullying. Unfortunately, only the first sixteen minutes of that tape had been played to the judge when he made his ruling on oppression. Had the tape been played in full worse examples of bullying would have been heard and Mr Justice Leonard may have ruled differently and Miller's confession would not have come to dominate the whole case. Having taken the decision to argue that Miller had been bullied into confessing it is baffling that Frisby chose not to play the worst examples to the judge. Had he done so his submissions on oppression may well have been successful and Miller's confession would have been ruled inadmissible. That in turn would probably have resulted in Miller being acquitted. But Miller was left to carry the can for the failings of his legal team and the failings of a system that holds a man with the intelligence of a child as being as capable of running his defence as a lawyer of the ability of Michael Mansfield QC.

Miller now gave me his authority to find new lawyers for him. I appraised the renowned solicitor, Gareth Peirce, of his case. She had been involved in the successful appeals of both the Guildford Four and the Birmingham Six among many others. But Peirce did not want to commit herself to Miller just yet. Before she would take his case Peirce had to convince herself that she could prepare a meaningful appeal for him. She would later decide that she could and would be good to her word. She would instruct Michael Mansfield QC and Nicholas Blake, who would soon become a QC in his own right, to prepare Miller's case for appeal. Their reputations had gone before them. Any defendant fortunate enough to secure their services can rest assured that he or she will be represented most ably.

But she knew that there were specific problems. It was a case that ought to have been won at trial. There was evidence available that would have seriously undermined Elfer's case against him, but it was not used. The Court of Appeal had proved itself extremely reluctant to intervene over cases in which one of the grounds of appeal had been the quality of representation. Appellants who wanted to introduce evidence which had been available at trial but which was not used had great difficulty using such evidence on appeal. Before such evidence could be presented to the Court of Appeal it had to be shown that the reason it was not produced at trial was due to flagrantly incompetent advocacy.

Both Winston Silcott[1] and Satpal Ram insist that they acted in self defence, but were advised not to use that defence and rely on other defences. They claim that they acquiesced with that advice. But in their appeals neither were able to advance the defences that they had originally intended to use. In one form or another both

[1] For further details refer to the recently published *A Chronology of Injustice: The Case for Winston Silcott's Conviction to be Overturned* compiled by Legal Action for Women.

Ram and Silcott argued that they had been let down by their original lawyers, although Ram's appeal barrister, Patrick O'Connor, was careful not to try to argue that Ram had acted in self defence in order to avoid accusing Douglas Draycott QC of flagrantly incompetent advocacy. O'Connor, who would later become a QC, confined himself to criticising Draycott's failure to provide interpreters for Bengali speaking waiters, one of whom could not be understood properly without one because of the Court of Appeal's reluctance to intervene in such cases. Although it had not been argued the Court of Appeal, headed by the Lord Chief Justice, Lord Lane, exonerated Draycott of any suggestion that the quality of his advocacy was anything less than his usual high standards. Ram's appeal was dismissed as interpreters could have been provided for the waiters if Draycott believed them necessary.[1] Suffice to say, Miller faced great difficulties as the evidence of oppression, namely the whole of the tape of his seventh interview, among others, had been available at both trial and retrial as had the statements of Debbie Actie and Robyn Reed.

There was no question that Miller would have a mountain to climb. The onus would be on him to persuade the Court of Appeal to hear evidence which was available at the time of the two trials or was adduceable then. If he could not get over that hurdle he would undoubtedly lose his appeal unless there was new evidence which could persuade the judges to quash the convictions. It was Miller's greatest good fortune that his fate would soon be in the hands of Gareth Peirce and Michael Mansfield.

Campaign

Journalists now began to express an interest in Miller. Both Radio Four and the World Service devoted programmes to his case. And the campaign was busy too. Gerry Conlon of the Guildford Four publicly championed the innocence of the Cardiff Three. Malik Abdullahi and Lloyd Paris travelled all over the country to raise awareness of the case.

The campaign would organise two demonstrations in Cardiff, a vigil outside Wormwood Scrubs Prison and they would participate in numerous meetings. Wherever there was a platform on offer they would be there. They would secure high profile support from several luminaries including the controversial black American activist, Rev Al Sharpton, who would lead a march in Cardiff to highlight the injustice of the case. And the pressure group *Liberty* would take up the case in their campaign on uncorroborated confessions. And they assisted journalists by helping to secure access to the murder flat and to some of the witnesses. They could not have done more for the Cardiff Three.

The new year coincided with a flurry of media attention in the case. Rachel

---

[1] In 1995 Ram's case was referred to the Court of Appeal. His appeal on the grounds of the quality of representation by Douglas Draycott QC at his trial was dismissed by the Court of Appeal, led by Lord Justice Beldam, in a very controversial judgement which campaigners insisted was designed to keep the floodgates to such appeals closed.

Borrill of the *Independent* was now leading the pack. And television researchers were once again sniffing around for a story. On January 7th 1992 BBC Wales' *Week In Week Out* slot broadcast a documentary on the case. They questioned the convictions of all three convicted men. And Dr Tony Black, a psychologist with over thirty years experience, said that it would be expected that in savage killings involving multiple killers one or more of the killers would be likely to have thrown up. There was no sign of vomit in Flat One, 7 James Street when Lynette was murdered.

And in February, the BBC's flagship documentary series, *Panorama*, broadcast a programme on the case called *Unsafe Convictions*. This was the height of media interest in the case. The programme destroyed the credibility of the convictions. Miller's confession was analysed by Dr Eric Shepherd, who would later compile a report on the confession for Miller's appeal. Dr Shepherd strongly criticised the interrogation techniques that had been used on Miller. He showed that Miller's confession was demonstrable nonsense.

And Ronnie Williams decided that the time had come to retract. After being absolutely certain that he had seen Abdullahi in the North Star on the murder night, he now accepted that he could have been mistaken after all. He insisted that what he had said before had happened, but he was no longer sure when it had happened. For good measure Williams also retracted to Jennifer Nadel of ITN's *News At Ten*. *Panorama*'s documentary brought the case of the Cardiff Three to a wider audience. But the decision to use Jackie Harris, who had been somewhat economic with the truth herself, to call Vilday a liar was a classic case of the pot calling the kettle black.

The case of the Cardiff Three was now very high profile indeed. To the best of my knowledge it is the only miscarriage of justice case which has had three different documentaries broadcast about it before an appeal had taken place. And now Gareth Peirce was ready to take Miller's case.

Then the Ged Corley case ended with him accepting £235,000 compensation for his wrongful conviction. He had not given evidence at either trial of the Cardiff Five for legal reasons. There were no more legal reasons stopping him from assisting Paris. Corley would soon make a statement about Massey.

Retractions

It was now September 1992. Jackie Harris made a full retraction to me of the evidence she had given under oath at the trials of the Cardiff Five. She would soon swear out an affidavit to Abdullahi's lawyers and was now prepared to give evidence to the Court of Appeal that she had been deceived by the police into believing Abdullahi guilty and claimed to have been the victim of alleged police malpractice. It should, however, be pointed out that Harris cannot prove that her allegations of police malpractice are true as there is no requirement to tape conversations with witnesses. It will also be remembered that Harris had, by any account, been somewhat economic with the truth and that the police had not as yet had any opportunity to comment on her allegations.

Nevertheless, there was the matter of her meetings with Vilday. Harris gave her most detailed account of them to date. There had been four meetings. DI Joy Lott compiled a note of these meetings for the attention of DCS Williams in September 1989. She told Williams that both had been warned not to talk about the case. Harris now said that the point of these meetings was to get Vilday to clear up her doubts and that there was at least one occasion when DI Lott had to deal with another matter which gave Harris the chance to press Vilday for details despite DI Lott's warning. Harris was now prepared to give chapter and verse on her treatment by the police and the meetings with Vilday.

And she was not alone. It was now December 6th 1992. The appeals of the Cardiff Three was due to begin the following morning. Abdullahi's lawyers had been busy. They had interviewed several witnesses about the evidence they had given or the statements that they had made. Jane Sandrone had retracted her evidence and was now alleging police malpractice. Noreen Amiel also swore out an affidavit accusing the police of malpractice. And *Coral Sea* witnesses, John Hulse, Ian Moore, Sidney Arthur Harrop, Lawrence Mann and Peter McCarthy all swore out affidavits accusing the police of malpractice when obtaining their statements.

However, in fairness to the police, it ought to be pointed out that the police had as yet had no opportunity to comment on these allegations of malpractice. Brynley Samuel had also made an affidavit to Abdullahi's lawyers, but he made no accusation of malpractice. Roger Backhouse QC was set to make strong submissions on Abdullahi's behalf that he had been the victim of a dirty tricks campaign by the police based on the testimony that these witnesses would give in the appeal court. These submissions would be supported by some undisclosed documents which Abdullahi's lawyers had discovered in the police's incident room in Rumney. It would soon be up to the Court of Appeal, headed by the new Lord Chief Justice, Lord Taylor, to resolve these issues and more.

Part 3

THE WHITEWASH

"A judicial blunder has been committed; and in order to hide it, it has become necessary to commit a new offence every day against sound sense and equity.

From the condemnation of an innocent man flows the acquittal of a guilty man. Today they bid you to condemn me in my turn, because seeing my country on such a terrible track, I have cried out in my anguish. Condemn me then; but it will be just another blunder whose burden you will bear in history. And my condemnation, instead of restoring the peace which you desire, which we all desire, will only sew new seeds of disorder.

The cauldron of discontent, I tell you, is full to the brim; I do not make it so to overflow..."

Emile Zola (From J'accuse {1898})

CHAPTER 10

The Appeals

Four Days That Almost Shook The Criminal Justice System

The appeals began on December 7th 1992, four years after the arrests of the Cardiff Three, and, in the case of Yusef Abdullahi and Steve Miller, to the very day. They were heard by the Lord Chief Justice, Lord Taylor, Mr Justice Laws and Mr Justice Popplewell. Some hoped that the prosecution would see that it was fighting a hopeless cause and not oppose the appeals, but David Elfer was in no mood to concede defeat.

Elfer began by complaining that Abdullahi's perfected grounds of appeal had only been served on him that very morning. He wanted Abdullahi's appeal to be severed from that of Miller and Paris and delayed until April 1993. But Lord Taylor was unimpressed. The Court of Appeal was already concerned about the delay in getting the case before it. Lord Taylor asked Elfer if he was ready to deal with Miller and Paris' appeals. Elfer replied that he was, but renewed his application for severance of Abdullahi's appeal. Taylor remained unmoved, telling Elfer that they intended to begin the appeals in the afternoon with Miller's case and then added a very interesting aside. "Anyway," he said, "it might not get that far."

Mansfield In Action

Michael Mansfield QC began by highlighting the unreliability of the Crown's case against Miller. He pointed out that police relied uncritically on the evidence of Vilday and Psaila even though undisputed evidence from Professor Bernard Knight contradicted their claims. Mansfield also pointed out that Miller's confession was also contradicted by Professor Knight's evidence. He submitted that this was undisputed evidence that Miller's confession was itself wrong.

Mansfield complained that South Wales Police betrayed a presumption of guilt, that they relied on highly discredited witnesses and deceived and bullied a highly vulnerable Miller into giving them the confession they desired and that Miller was repeatedly told that police had smashed his alibi even though this was not true. Mansfield pointed out that Miller had given police an account of his movements in his early statements, that this account had in fact been accepted by police at the time and it had been supported at various times by Vilday and by others who had seen him on the murder night. And he had been seen by two women within minutes of the most likely time of the murder.

Mansfield continued to set the scene well. He pointed out that while police had a clear picture of Miller's movements in the week of the murder, Vilday constantly changed her story. Mansfield argued that Vilday's constant changing of her account had to be seen in the context of the police's standard line: "We have witnesses, why should they lie?" Mansfield argued that Vilday was a thoroughly discredited witness, but the police needed Miller to accept Vilday's account. He submitted that although they had a clear picture of Miller's movements which had been backed up by others, they told him the opposite.

Mansfield moved on to the blood evidence. He stressed that blood was deposited on Lynette's jeans which did not belong to the victim. It was a very rare blood group which did not belong to any of the defendants either. Mansfield referred to the Y-chromosome discovered in the sample and concluded that it had to have come from a man. He also referred to analysis showing that it was very unlikely to have been contaminated. Mansfield submitted that it indicated the presence of an unidentified man. Mansfield argued that this meant that South Wales Police were aware that they were looking for a male suspect with a very rare blood group and that none of the Cardiff Five possessed that group, or even a group that resembled it in any way. And then Mansfield delivered a bombshell that stunned the families and friends of the Cardiff Three in the packed public gallery.

He revealed that when Gill's only explanation for the Y-chromosome being detected in the blood on Lynette's jeans was that a man who possessed those blood factors was in the room, South Wales Police were aware of a suspect, whom Mansfield referred to as Mr X, who possessed those appropriate blood factors. He pointed out that X had been interviewed by police before Miller was arrested. X had then provided a blood sample. It matched all the factors on the jeans sample, but lacked the extra protein factor that was found on the sock.

Mansfield suggested that if the jury and the judge had known that the blood grouping information indicated that only one person had been present, or that a number of sources including X had been present, the case against the Cardiff Five would never have got off the ground. Mansfield pointed out that the significance of X was entirely unknown at the trial and retrial of the Cardiff Five. X had hardly been mentioned at all. Mansfield submitted that Mr X provided a far more plausible explanation for the rare blood group found in the flat than the one the Crown chose to advance.

Mansfield told the court that before the arrests of the Cardiff Five, Mr X had come in voluntarily for questioning. He made a statement on September 14th 1988 and a further one on December 15th. The defence had known about both statements at trial, but they had no knowledge of X's importance as a suspect from them. Two officers had interviewed X before the arrests, one of whom was DC Graham Toogood, who had replaced DC Evans on two of the hotly disputed interviews with Steve Miller. The other, DC Paul Fish, had interviewed Yusef Abdullahi.

Mansfield pointed out that Mr X knew two people (Atkins and Grommek) connected with 7 James Street and had been seen in the company of Atkins by police officers who were conducting surveillance of him in November 1988. Mansfield complained that while the defence at trial knew of the existence of X, they had no idea how important he was, or about any of the material now referred to.

Of Professor Canter's psychological profile of the likely killer, Mansfield said that Canter's report was of course speculative, yet the police clearly regarded it as very important. A police report had been sent to Detective Superintendent Ken Davies, dated October 25th 1988. It mentioned Canter's report and that X had the same rare blood group as the assailant in the Lynette White Inquiry. Mansfield dealt with X's possible motive. He argued that X had an antipathy towards women because he had been attacked by a woman, which left him scarred. That attack nearly severed his wrists. Mansfield pointed out that the injuries that X received in that attack bore a strong resemblance to injuries inflicted on Lynette, especially the facial injuries.

Mansfield then pointed out that X had been eliminated because of the blood on the wallpaper, but not by the blood on Lynette's jeans. Elfer perked up and announced that X had been eliminated on the basis of DNA. Mansfield responded by asking Elfer why the defendants weren't excluded for the same reason. Elfer had no reply.

Mansfield pulled the strands of his argument together. He said, "If X had been subjected to what Miller was subjected to, it may well be that we would not be here today." Mansfield developed his arguments on X. He complained that Detective Superintendent Davies had made a statement on October 3rd 1989 which was not disclosed to the defence. It set out the scope of the police's inquiry.

Mansfield pointed out that it mentioned a meeting with Canter, but made no forthright mention of what was happening regarding X. This material was not in Davies' second statement, which was disclosed. His second statement listed people who had been eliminated because of the blood on the wallpaper. It included X, but did not mention what his blood group was. Davies had this statement with him in the witness box when he gave evidence at the retrial. In it, X was not named as the prime suspect. Mansfield explained that the X material was very important because he had been eliminated on November 9th. The very next day Violet Perriam had made her first statement.

Mansfield submitted that Perriam's statement marked a significant turning point in the inquiry, away from X and towards the men who ended up in the dock. Mansfield pointed out that despite Perriam's statement being used against the defendants, she had positively stated that Miller was not one of the four black men that she saw outside 7 James Street on the night of the murder.

Mansfield pointed out that John Actie had been acquitted despite her certainty that she saw him. He argued that Perriam's statement led to Psaila's crucial interviews on November 17th and the further statement that she made on November 22nd, which indirectly led to Atkins and Grommek changing their accounts; and that on December 6th Vilday had changed her account from knowing nothing of interest to admitting that she was in the room when Lynette died. Mansfield highlighted the various changes in the key witnesses' accounts.

He established that each of them in turn were totally unreliable. He submitted that it meant that the police could not have thought that they had a solid basis for arresting Miller. Their only basis was Vilday, who had lied through her teeth.

The groundwork had been completed and it was time to move on to Miller's interviews, which would be the main substance of his appeal. Mansfield had established the context that Miller's interviews would be judged by. Now he moved on to deal with the interviews themselves. Mansfield claimed that the initial interviews set the scene for what followed and argued that there were three stages to the interviews. First of all, the police officers had to get Miller to admit that he was in the flat. Then they had to get him to say that he saw something and, finally, they had to get him to admit that he had done something.

Mansfield argued that the police provided Miller with information that they wanted him to know and planted their scenario in his mind by suggesting that he was on drugs to explain why he couldn't remember. His standard reply was, "Most probably." This had been interpreted as a reply of yes. The drugs scenario had put Miller in the flat. Mansfield strongly questioned this method. Then the police moved on to the second phase of their task, getting Miller to admit that he had seen something happen.

Mansfield told the appeal judges that the process of getting him into the murder room was oppressive. He argued that the police kept claiming that they had witnesses and that their witnesses didn't lie and that they (the police) knew the truth. Mansfield complained that the police ignored Miller's denials of presence at the scene of the crime, denials which he had made ***three hundred and three times***, although he accepted that the police were not and should not be obliged to accept a suspect's denials immediately. He protested that the police kept on rejecting Miller's explanations and told him that they had destroyed his alibi when they clearly had not. Mansfield complained that there came a point when even a suspect of Miller's limited intelligence would understand that he was going nowhere until he gave his interrogators what they wanted to hear.

Mansfield argued that Miller had been emotionally manipulated. He had been reduced to tears several times and was clearly distressed. Mansfield complained that Miller was frequently told that he was stuck there and that there was no way out. The period of Miller's custody was extended twice and he was often told that there were only a couple more points to go through.

Mansfield argued that this indicated that he would stay there until he agreed with what they wanted him to say. He also pointed out that Miller was told that the only chance of getting out of it before the other defendants implicated him was to implicate them first. He also claimed that the mention of a life sentence was a threat designed to weaken Miller's confidence in his denials.

Mansfield argued that the themes that he had set out constituted oppression and that Miller's admissions should not have been admitted in evidence because of it. Mansfield conceded that the officers were entitled to ask questions, perhaps a number of times, but they were not entitled to state their position as if there was no doubt.

The cornerstone of Mansfield's argument was tape seven of the Miller interviews. And Elfer told the appeal judges that tape seven had only been played up to page seventeen of the transcript. This would later prove to be very significant as the alleged bullying did not begin until page twenty. He did not know it, but Elfer had just made his task even harder.

Tape seven was then played in full. The atmosphere in the public gallery reflected the realisation that another significant moment in the appeal had been reached. Everyone in the court was visibly shocked by what they heard on this tape. Mansfield now reminded the court that in the first trial, Geraint Richards had given evidence that when he heard tape seven played back, he realised that he should have intervened. Mansfield argued that Miller was pressurised by the police to confess and the passive role played by Richards led to the concessions that they got out of Miller.

Mansfield went through the rest of the interviews, illustrating numerous flaws in them. He highlighted the methods that the police had used to extract a confession from Miller. He backed up his points with examples from the tapes and submitted that they clearly demonstrated that Miller's interviews were thoroughly unreliable.

Mansfield argued that Miller had obviously been distressed and had tried to backtrack on his admissions in tape twelve until he was threatened with a life sentence. Mansfield pointed out that Paris was introduced into Vilday's account only after first Psaila and then Miller had mentioned him. Mansfield argued that having got Miller into the murder room, the police had to fit Vilday into Miller's account. He argued that DC Murray had left Miller in no doubt that he would have to stay there until they got it right, which meant until he agreed with their favoured scenario.

The third day was now almost over, but Elfer still had not given up. At the trial and retrial Elfer used two of Miller's interviews to show that Miller held his own and volunteered information not suggested to him by the police. The tapes were played. Elfer argued that these tapes showed that Miller had volunteered information without prompting from the police in those interviews. Elfer submitted that this combined with the fact that Miller had not agreed with everything that the interviewing officers had put to him showed that Miller was not suggestible. However, Mansfield countered by arguing that none of the details that Miller had provided off his own back was supported by indisputable evidence. Mansfield submitted that the tapes that Elfer had asked the judges to hear showed that Miller had just been making up details to keep his interrogators happy because he did not want to have to face DCs Greenwood and Seaford again.

Now Mansfield asked for leave to call two further witnesses, Dr Eric Shepherd and Dr Olive Tunstall. Mansfield clearly felt that their testimony was important, but Lord Taylor said that he was unsure whether further evidence would assist them. Observers felt that this indicated Lord Taylor had already made up his mind and wanted to keep the appeals as short as possible.

A Buzz In The Air

The appeals had been listed for at least two weeks. It was now the fourth day. It would also be the last. Mansfield continued to develop his points which illustrated the unreliability of Miller's confession and the methods that had been used on Miller to obtain the admissions.

Lord Taylor had heard enough. Now he asked Elfer if it was possible to argue that tape seven was not oppressive. Elfer had no answer to this, but asserted that Miller had said that he was happy with it at the time, so he couldn't turn round and say that he had been oppressed afterwards. Lord Taylor insisted that it was not appropriate to conduct an interview when the interviewee was so obviously upset.

Now Elfer was reduced to claiming that Miller was crying because of remorse at what he had done to Lynette. This made no impression at all. "If your minds are made up," said the Crown's QC, "I will not waste your time trying to persuade you to the contrary. That must be the end of that." Miller had all but climbed the mountain. The atmosphere was electric. His confession had just gone out of the window. Surely Elfer would continue by saying that he would not seek to maintain Miller's conviction.

The Court of Appeal had given him every opportunity to concede defeat gracefully, but Elfer failed to pick up on this. The judges asked whether the case against Miller would be safe and satisfactory if Miller's confession was ruled inadmissible because of oppression. Elfer argued that it could rely on Tessa Sidoric and Debbie Taylor. The judges looked perplexed and informed Elfer that they did not consider the supporting material to be anywhere near strong enough to be the basis of a safe and satisfactory conviction.

Observers of the appeal were delighted. It was now obvious that Miller's long nightmare was coming to an end; but this was still not the end of the matter. Backhouse immediately asked the appeal judges to consider the possible prejudice that Miller's interviews had done to Abdullahi and Elias argued the same for Paris.

They adopted Mansfield's arguments on the unreliability of Vilday and Psaila and insisted that only Miller's interviews could account for the bizarre verdicts. This fact was supported by the clear inference that the jury must have had Miller's interviews in their minds when they were considering Ronnie Actie's case, which had been after Miller was convicted. It was beginning to look like it wasn't just Miller who would be freed that afternoon.

Elfer began by telling the Court that there was an independent case against Paris, exemplified by the evidence of Ian Massey. At this point Mr Justice Laws made a telling interjection: *"You mean the perjurer and armed robber,"* said the judge.

Elfer was silenced for a moment, then claimed that although Massey was a self confessed perjurer, the jury had heard him give evidence and could judge his credibility for themselves. That said, he moved on to Abdullahi. He insisted that there was an independent case against him, so it did not follow that Miller's confession was crucial.

The Court of Appeal was completely unimpressed with these arguments. And finally, at 2.50 p.m., Elfer conceded defeat with these words: "There is a case against these two, but if Miller's confession is excluded, it would be an unsatisfactory outcome if the other two are left in prison."

The public gallery cheered and applauded. The four-year long nightmare of the Cardiff Three was over at last. A large part of the credit for this belongs to Mansfield's impressive performance during the appeals. Justice had been done – to a certain extent, that is. The judgement was now eagerly awaited.

The Judgement

It was now December 16th. The Court of Appeal were ready to give their reasons for quashing the convictions of the Cardiff Three. Now Lord Taylor read out the Court of Appeal's judgement. Lord Taylor first referred to the prejudicial effect of Miller's interviews on Abdullahi and Paris. He pointed out that submissions had been made to Mr Justice Leonard to sever the trials because of the prejudicial effect of the Miller interviews on Abdullahi and Paris. Lord Taylor said, "In our opinion, the learned judge's exercise of his discretion against severance cannot be faulted."

The Court of Appeal concluded that although they had been properly directed not to, the jury must have relied on Miller's interviews in considering the cases of Abdullahi and Paris. They found that this, coupled with the finding that, because of the oppressive tactics, the interviews were not admissible against any of the defendants, made the verdicts unsafe and unsatisfactory. Lord Taylor felt that it would be fruitful to examine their cases as well. He began with Paris' case and outlined the unsatisfactory state of the evidence against Paris. Then he went on to deal with Massey. He acknowledged that Massey was a self confessed perjurer and armed robber and went through Massey's evidence.

Lord Taylor felt that it was difficult to fault the admission of Massey's evidence. He also insisted that an appeal based on the exercise of Leonard's discretion over Massey could not have resulted in a successful appeal.

Lord Taylor said, "In this Court's view, there is no sustainable criticism of the way in which the learned judge summed up...in relation to Massey's evidence." Lord Taylor went further, saying, "This Court detects no other good ground of appeal arising from the way the learned judge dealt with Massey's evidence once it had been let in."

In other words, as far as the Court of Appeal was concerned, the only merit in Paris' appeal was the prejudicial effect of Miller's interviews on Paris' case, but that alone was sufficient for the conviction to have to be quashed.

Turning to Abdullahi, the judgement outlined the case against him and his alibi. The Court of Appeal felt that the prosecution's case, as with the others, was by no means compelling. It pointed out that his original grounds related to severance and, after this was refused, that Miller's interviews prejudiced the case against him. At a very late stage, further grounds alleging pressure on witnesses and non-disclosure were submitted, but were not developed because Elfer had conceded defeat.

The Court Of Appeal's Conclusions

Lord Taylor addressed the issue of the apparent failure of PACE to prevent evidence that had been obtained as a result of impropriety and oppression from being admitted in evidence. He said, "In our judgement, the circumstances of this case do not indicate flaws in those provisions. They do indicate a combination of human errors."

Lord Taylor maintained that their method of interviewing Miller was wholly contrary to the spirit of PACE. And he criticised Geraint Richards as having done little more than sit in on the interviews. He quoted guidelines for solicitors on when they should intervene and stressed the responsibility of the solicitor to do so responsibly and courageously. He pointed out that if he or she failed to do that, her/his presence could constitute a disservice.

The Court of Appeal concluded that the officers took the view that unless the solicitor intervened their conduct was beyond reproach. Lord Taylor told them that if they thought this, they were wholly wrong. He said, "It is most regrettable that the worst example of police excesses (tape seven) was not played to the learned judge before he ruled on admissibility."

Lord Taylor then credited the record of timings and the tape recording of the interviews required under the provisions of PACE with allowing the Court of Appeal the chance to review the case.

A Judgement Too Far

It had been expected that the Court of Appeal would confine itself to Miller's case and the prejudicial effect that his admissions had had upon the cases of Abdullahi and Paris. This, after all, was all the evidence that they had heard. But they had seen fit to comment on the merits of Abdullahi and Paris' appeals without even hearing the arguments. This was patently unfair to all concerned including the judges themselves as if they had heard the evidence they might have reached different conclusions.

The Court of Appeal would not fault Mr Justice Leonard's exercise of his discretion over the issue of severing the trials. And they would not criticise the way that he exercised his discretion over admitting Massey's evidence either.

These were the substantive points of Tony Paris' appeal.

Gerard Elias QC had made a submission at the retrial to have Massey's evidence excluded in totality because of Massey's proven unreliability regarding Ged Corley's case. Mr Justice Leonard had rejected this submission as he believed that Massey's credibility was a matter for the jury to decide.

Elias' submission was that it was unfair for the defence to have to deal with Massey's evidence because it might have been obtained through inducements both known and unknown from early 1988. The second point was that it was unfair for the defence because the evidence against Corley was false and may have been the result of a conspiracy which Massey was involved in.

Elias had argued that the suspension of police officers involved in the Corley case made it very difficult to present the jury with the whole picture as it could have prejudiced possible court proceedings against people involved in the Corley case. Thus, Elias felt that Paris' defence was hamstrung due to proceedings in the Corley Affair. The desire not to prejudice possible court proceedings regarding the Corley Affair made it impossible for Paris' defence to present the whole picture of Massey's involvement in that case. Mr Justice Leonard rejected these submissions, believing that the jury would get a flavour of the Corley conspiracy and he directed the jury that they should exercise great care when assessing Massey's evidence.

Paris' defence felt that this was not sufficient. They believed that the judge ought to have advised the jury to exercise great caution rather than great care. The Court of Appeal felt that there was no distinction between the two and they could find no fault in the way Leonard had admitted Massey's evidence. However, it is extremely difficult to argue that the full extent of Massey's involvement in the Corley Affair was irrelevant to the question of his motives for giving evidence against Paris and his reliability as a whole, yet it seems that this was exactly what the Court of Appeal was saying. After all, a flavour of the Corley conspiracy was not the same as the full picture of Massey's involvement in that case. It could be argued that Paris had to prepare and present his defence with one hand tied behind his back, especially as Massey was the sole corroboration of the case against Paris.

The next point concerned severance. Mr Justice Leonard had exercised his discretion not to sever the trial of Miller from that of his co-defendants to avoid the inconvenience and expense of witnesses having to give evidence at two separate trials. Miller's confession was not admissible against anybody, yet it had demonstrably been the basis of the bizarre verdicts. Leonard had quite rightly given the jury clear directions that they were not entitled to use Miller's confession against the others. They had ignored him. This offers conclusive proof that the decision not to sever the trials had been disastrous for the interests of justice. Had he severed the trials Abdullahi and Paris' cases could not have been prejudiced by Miller's confession.

As with the Bridgewater case, this case shows that juries will cut through the niceties of the law to deliver what they consider to be just verdicts regardless of the judge's directions. It is naive to expect juries to do otherwise. That being so the only way to prevent Miller's confession overshadowing all the other evidence was to sever his case from the others. It is to be hoped that appeal judges will be more inclined to listen sympathetically to such arguments in the future.

And Abdullahi's case would have highlighted other issues which cried out to be resolved. Very serious accusations had been made against the police by several witnesses. The Court of Appeal was in the best position to resolve these issues. While the convictions were untenable as soon as Elfer conceded defeat over Miller's confession and the prejudicial effect it had upon the cases of Abdullahi and Paris the appeal judges could have granted bail and heard the rest of the appeal. Their decision not to hear the appeals of Abdullahi and Paris had the effect that very serious issues remain unresolved. If the allegations contained in the affidavits of these witnesses are true, they detail a shocking tale of police malpractice, but if they are false then these witnesses have maligned entirely innocent police officers, both of which are thoroughly reprehensible. It should also be pointed out that the Court of Appeal's decision not to hear this evidence deprived the police of the chance to defend themselves from these allegations. In short, this was unfair to both the appellants and the police. It is a compelling argument for appeals to be heard in full.

Although it would be churlish in the extreme not to acknowledge that this judgement set new standards on how interviewees were to be treated in a police station and criticised the performance of the solicitor in Miller's interviews there were criticisms that arose from the way Miller's case was dealt with. The Court of Appeal had accepted that bad legal representation was worse than no representation and Lord Taylor had concluded that it was most regrettable that the worst examples of police excesses had not been played to the judge when he ruled on the admissibility of Miller's interviews.

This raised an important point: why had Leonard not heard it? The reason was Roger Frisby's decision not to play the whole of that interview to back up his submission that Miller had been the victim of cumulative bullying. Although Miller had agreed to the tactics adopted by Frisby he was not capable of assuming responsibility for the conduct of his defence. Frisby's submission that Miller's confession had been obtained through oppression would have been far more effective if the whole of that tape had been played. The responsibility for the content and presentation of that submission must rest with Miller's defence lawyers at the second trial. The Court of Appeal had criticised that unfortunate decision, but made no recommendation to prevent a recurrence. Had they done so another failing of the criminal justice system would have been addressed and safeguards may have been introduced to prevent a repetition, especially regarding clients of Miller's vulnerabilities who should not be held legally accountable for the conduct of his defence as he was incapable of taking such responsibility, albeit through no fault of his own.

It should also be pointed out that Lord Taylor failed to criticise the CPS for its failure to enforce its Code of Conduct for Crown Prosecutors regarding its duty to ensure that any admissions were not obtained through oppression. Had the CPS applied its own principles properly, the issue of Frisby's failings would never have arisen. The Court of Appeal also failed to remind the CPS that it has a duty to ensure that only cases which are appropriate for trial get that far.

Nevertheless, this judgement was no technicality, but the Cardiff Three felt cheated of the complete exoneration that they had expected. There was still a whispering campaign against them, but they were not the only ones who felt cheated by the outcome of the appeal.

The Police Feel Cheated

South Wales Police felt that they had done absolutely nothing wrong and insisted that the Cardiff Three had been let out on a technicality.

The Chief Constable of South Wales Police, Robert Lawrence, sprang to the defence of his officers. He said that his force fully accepted that the admissibility of evidence was a matter for the judiciary to decide. Lawrence said, "The decision itself was not based upon the concealment or falsification of evidence or indeed upon the admission of any new evidence but on a question of oppression and its interpretation under Section 76 of the Police And Criminal Evidence Act which stipulates that any admission or confession which is held to have been obtained by oppressive means and therefore unfairly, cannot be used in evidence, even if true."

Had the appeals been allowed to proceed, Lawrence may have had more difficulty defending his officers. It should also be stressed that Mansfield proved conclusively that Miller had been lied to shamelessly in order to facilitate the confession that South Wales Police needed from him. Abdullahi had been lied to during his interviews. DI Graham Mouncher had admitted under oath at the retrial that during an interview with Abdullahi he told him that Ronnie Actie had implicated him when he knew that Actie had said nothing of the sort to try to put Abdullahi off his guard. And other witnesses had been ready to give evidence that they had been deceived by the officers who interviewed them, were pressurised by these officers and things had appeared in their statements which had not been said by them. The truth or otherwise of these allegations has never been determined. This is not a satisfactory state of affairs for anybody.

The police were making the decision seem like a technicality. Lawrence added that he did not support the use of oppression, but claimed that there were problems with the interpretation of the discretion to exclude such evidence. He felt that the police needed to know precisely when a rigorous interview would be considered oppressive.

He pointed out that two judges at two different trials had considered the interviews to be admissible, despite defence submissions to the contrary. These decisions had however been based on the inexcusable attitude of Mr Justice

McNeill and the failure to present important evidence to Mr Justice Leonard before he was asked to rule on the admissibility of Miller's interviews.

The appeal judges had heard the most detailed submissions on Miller's interviews. Their's was the most complete examination of the issues raised by Miller's interviews. Nowhere in his numerous comments on the aftermath of the appeals, did Lawrence, or South Wales Police, acknowledge this and what it meant. Clearly, the Court of Appeal was in the best position to decide on the admissibility of Miller's interviews.

Lawrence recognised one of the serious issues that seems to have escaped media comment. He said, "This case also raised questions as to the effectiveness of safeguards built into the trial process, including the fact that tape recorded evidence is not, as a matter of routine, listened to in full by all parties to the proceedings." He was quite right.

He also welcomed the decision of the Court of Appeal to refer tape seven to the Royal Commission, DPP and the Chief Inspector of Constabulary. He said, "...it is to be hoped that as a result the safeguards and guidelines concerning tape recorded evidence will be reviewed to ensure that the interests of justice are properly served." Again, there can be no complaint about this other than the fact that the Court of Appeal's decision in Miller's case had already done this.

Lawrence also scotched any suggestion that the case was racist by pointing out that black witnesses had helped South Wales Police in the course of the inquiry, implying that they would not have done so if they considered the police to be racist.

Then Lawrence asserted that his officers had always kept an open mind to the possibility that there were unidentified persons present during the murder of Lynette White. Yet he gave no grounds to support this assertion.

Lawrence defended South Wales Police's decision not to re-open the investigation. He advised those calling for a complete re-investigation of the case to remember that the police had serious problems of meeting the demand with the resources at their disposal. South Wales Police have very serious financial problems and there are other murder inquiries that have been all but dropped, but Lawrence fails to address the crucial issue of why his force got it so wrong in the first place.

Lawrence had more to add. He quoted Mr Justice Leonard saying, "Mr Frisby QC, for Miller, in the course of his *careful and full* submissions, accepted the *skill* of the interrogation which was carried out and added that he does *not* impugn the *good faith* of the officers who were conducting the interviews." [my emphasis] Far from exonerating the conduct of the police, all this does is expose the limitations of Frisby's advocacy compared to that of Mansfield.

Lawrence also felt that the public were entitled to an explanation as to how evidence could be admissible and lead to convictions, while two years later the same evidence was deemed to be inadmissible. He pointed out that it was the interpretation of Miller's interviews rather than the tapes themselves that had changed. He insisted that those who work in the criminal justice system are entitled to greater certainty over the admissibility of such evidence.

He seems to have forgotten that the Court of Appeal had given him that. It concluded that the way his officers interviewed Miller was unacceptable. It is up to South Wales Police and others to learn the lessons of what happened to Steve Miller and prevent it happening again. However, in fairness to the police, it ought to be pointed out that shortly after the convictions of the Cardiff Three were quashed, South Wales Police adopted a far more ethical approach to interviewing suspects than the ones used in the Lynette White Inquiry. This, at least, is a step in the right direction and the force deserves to be commended for it.

The gist of Robert Lawrence's comments on the case of the Cardiff Three leaves little room for doubt that he believed that his officers had convicted the right men and that the Court of Appeal had freed them on a technicality. However, any impartial review of the evidence would quickly reveal that the case of the Cardiff Three is among the worst travesties of justice in British legal history.

CHAPTER 11

Dirty Tricks, Whispering Grasses and Extreme Vulnerability

Supreme Injustice

The Cardiff Three had learned that the appeals process was not a retrial. The Court of Appeal was only concerned with whether the convictions were safe and satisfactory. The appeal judges had concluded that they were not after hearing Mansfield's arguments about Miller's confession. As far as the criminal justice system was concerned that was enough. But this left the case and the search for the full truth about this extraordinary case in limbo.

In the lead-up to the appeals of the Cardiff Three, Yusef Abdullahi's lawyers had obtained affidavits from Jane Sandrone, Noreen Amiel, Jackie Harris, Ian Moore, Sidney Harrop, John Hulse, Peter McCarthy, Lawrence Mann and Brynley Samuel. With the exception of Samuel the others made serious allegations of police malpractice. In general these allegations consisted of being deceived about the strength of the case against the defendants, pressure being put on them and things appearing in their statements which they claimed they did not say.

The allegations that they made were serious and deserved a full hearing in the Court of Appeal. Due to the collapse of the case against the Cardiff Three they were not heard. For legal reasons their affidavits cannot be quoted without having to prove that not only did the witnesses say what is contained in these affidavits, but that what they said was true in circumstances where it would come down to the word of these witnesses against that of the officers they accused even though these affidavits are legal documents. Had they been read out in open court or the witnesses repeated their allegations in evidence their claims could be reported without these restrictions.

Thus, the decision of the Court of Appeal not to hear these witnesses has deprived the public of access to the truth or lack of it of their allegations. This is a very unsatisfactory state of affairs. If these witnesses have told the truth certain officers are guilty of serious malpractice in dealing with them; if not they have unjustly maligned the reputations of honest police officers, both of which are equally reprehensible.

This is a matter of public importance which deserved a hearing. A fully independent public inquiry may well offer the last realistic chance to resolve the issues raised in these affidavits. But there is another matter of great importance that arises from them. Had they given their evidence before the Court of Appeal they would probably have been cross-examined vigorously by David Elfer QC about their veracity, especially those witnesses who had given evidence which flatly contradicted what they were now saying. It should also be pointed out that the police officers who dealt with these witnesses did not get the chance to give their side of the story. Had the Court of Appeal heard all this evidence they would probably have required the judgement of Solomon to resolve it without causing offence to the police or offering a fertile breeding ground for conspiracy theorists who believe that judges are hand in glove with the police.

But it need not have been like this. All it requires to resolve such issues without accusations of partiality is to afford to witnesses the same safeguards that are available to suspects, namely taping all interviews or better still, all contact between police officers and witnesses should be videotaped. This would provide corroboration for genuine claims of police malpractice and it would protect honest officers by exposing spurious accusations of malpractice. Consequently, it is in everybody's interests to adopt such procedures. Had the Court of Appeal heard the evidence of these witnesses and that of the officers concerned whatever their conclusions were on who was telling the truth they may well have decided that such safeguards are desirable.

There was also the question of disclosure obligations. This was a somewhat grey area as disclosure obligations changed after the Cardiff Three were convicted as the case of Judith Ward had placed a greater burden on the Crown in May 1992. This enabled defence lawyers to secure access to the police's Incident Room in Rumney. Among the material that defence lawyers discovered was Jane Sandrone's house-to-house enquiry form which had been obtained from her before she made her statement of April 15th 1988. In this she said she had not heard that conversation in the Dowlais but only heard of it from Amiel, who never went so far as to say that Abdullahi had confessed. But this account was vastly different from her statement and the evidence that she gave at both trials. Clearly, this house-to-house enquiry form affected the credibility of this witness and ought to have been disclosed to the defence. Had it been disclosed it would have been the basis of a vigorous cross-examination of Sandrone. Suffice to say, the jury were not in a position to fully assess the credibility of this witness regardless of her subsequent retraction. But there was further material which they did not hear which may have affected their evaluation of the credibility of other witnesses such as Ronnie Williams.

Whispering Grass

Police pressure and intimidation of witnesses was not the only argument that Abdullahi's defence would have used on appeal. They had discovered significant evidence which undermined the credibility of Ronnie Williams, who was the only witness from the *Coral Sea* who not only insisted that Abdullahi was not on the ship at the relevant time, but also put him in Cardiff on the night of the murder. The fact that bar Peter Brooks not one of several witnesses traced to the North Star had supported Williams' claims that he had seen Abdullahi there on the murder night and the fact that he had originally claimed to have been with Lawrence Mann rather than Peter Brooks that night established that there were clearly good reasons for doubting Williams' reliability at both trial and retrial. And there were even more uncovered by Abdullahi's defence amongst the undisclosed material they discovered in the Rumney Incident Room's files shortly before the appeals.

This evidence makes it clear that Williams was more than an occasional source of information. As early as March 1988 he had been providing the police with specific information for the Lynette White Inquiry. This was when he had told Page that his inquiries had revealed that Lynette went to the Casablanca to confront Miller about his relationship with another woman. A ludicrous and clearly false story followed concerning Lynette being stabbed at the Casablanca and then being taken back to James Street.

Williams provided the police with even more information during the inquiry. The undisclosed material shows that his claims were unreliable. Had this information been available at the outset, the irresistible inference would have been that Williams was clearly a police informer despite his claims to the contrary and that he was in the habit of supplying them with unreliable information. But Abdullahi's defence had been deprived of this evidence which was vital to his cause.

Had they been given the chance, Abdullahi's defence would have been able to present a strong case to the Court of Appeal. It would have established that not only had there never been any credible evidence against him, but also that the police ought to have been fully aware of this from an early stage in the inquiry yet proceeded to construct a case around him rather than let the evidence lead them to the murderer or murderers of Lynette White. Unfortunately, none of this evidence got the airing it deserved in the Lord Chief Justice's court. But this was not the only material which failed to get a hearing on appeal.

Ian Massey And The Villains' Charter

Before the appeals Paris' lawyers had also been busy. They had information showing that Ian Massey was even more unreliable than even they had suspected. Shortly before the arrests of the Cardiff Five, whilst in Cardiff Prison, Massey appeared to have been hunting around for a deal. He intimated that he had knowledge in a case of murder at Milford Haven, and this 'knowledge' was passed on to Dyfed-Powys Police. But they concluded that there was nothing concrete in Massey's information.

Had Paris' defence known that Massey had intimated knowledge in yet another high profile inquiry and that his information was not deemed worthy of further investigation, they would have put this before the jury. Given Massey's form, his claims regarding the Milford Haven murders could have been seen as the last straw regarding his credibility.

DI Mouncher had always insisted that the first he knew of Massey's identity was in August 1989. But now material which had not been disclosed revealed that Detective Superintendent Ken Davies had undoubtedly been aware of Massey's identity months before as he had written to colleagues in Greater Manchester Police about Massey. Tony Paris' defence lawyers discovered this letter in the files of the Police Complaints Authority on the Ged Corley case. There are three possible interpretations of this. Either South Wales Police had decided that they were going to use him before they would admit to knowing about him, or they kept him on the back burner until they felt that they had no option but to use him, or there had been a breakdown in communications between DI Mouncher and Detective Superintendent Davies.

Davies gave evidence at the trial and retrial of the Cardiff Five that disclosure obligations had been met by the police. However, Davies' own statement dated October 3rd 1989 was not disclosed to the defence.

Paris' defence also intended to argue that Mr Justice Leonard should not have admitted Massey's evidence as it was unfair to Paris and that once it had been admitted Leonard's warning to the jury that they should use great care when assessing Massey's evidence did not go far enough. They believed that he should have instructed them to use great caution rather than care. The Court of Appeal saw no distinction between advising the jury to use great care or great caution and more significantly they agreed with Mr Justice Leonard's decision that admitting Massey's evidence had not been unfair to Paris.

But Paris' defence strongly disagreed. They pointed out that since the first trial, new evidence had emerged showing that Ged Corley had been framed. They had been supplied with documents relating to the Corley Affair by West Yorkshire Police, who were then investigating Corley's case for the Police Complaints Authority. A lawyer for West Yorkshire Police accepted that no public interest immunity applied to documents which had already been disclosed to Paris' defence.

Paris' defence pointed out that it had been very difficult to fully probe Massey's involvement in the Corley Affair because at the time he was due to be interviewed by West Yorkshire Police. It was not known then if others involved in the Corley case would incriminate Massey. It was not possible to adduce evidence regarding Massey's possession of guns and that his sole reason in giving a statement against Corley was to get his sentence reduced on appeal.

Paris' defence clearly felt that they could not probe Massey's involvement in the Corley Affair properly. The issue of whether Massey had given the statement against Corley in expectation of a reduction in his sentence was extremely important as it would have established that Massey had given false information for his own ends. This was what Paris claimed Massey had done to him. His lawyers claimed that it was not possible to call any of the officers who had been suspended over the Corley Affair due to the possibility of proceedings relating to it. But the Court of Appeal insisted that an appeal on such grounds could never succeed.

Severance

Paris' defence had also intended to show that his chances of a fair trial had been hopelessly prejudiced by Mr Justice Leonard exercising his discretion not to sever Miller's trial from that of his co-defendants. The failure to sever the case of Steve Miller from the others had serious implications for the criminal justice system of England and Wales. At the heart of the issue was whether the trial of Miller's co-accused could be fair given the fact that the jury would hear Miller's confession.

The Court of Appeal accepted that both Yusef Abdullahi and Tony Paris had been convicted because the jury relied on Miller's confession even though the law did not permit them to do so. In practice, only severing Miller's trial from that of his co-accused could have prevented them from doing so. Mr Justice Leonard had declined to do so because of the extra cost and the inconvenience to witnesses of having to give their evidence at two trials. Although he had given the jury clear directions that they were not entitled to use Miller's confession against any of his co-defendants, Leonard's decision was open to criticism, but the Court of Appeal rejected the merit of Paris' lawyers' argument on severance without even hearing it. Had the appeal judges heard it they may have concluded that greater safeguards are needed to protect co-defendants from having their cases prejudiced by the confession of a co-accused than the direction of judges which can be ignored as it was in this case.

The Ethics Of The Miller Interviews

The convictions of Paris and Abdullahi had demonstrated the truth of the contention that no jury who heard Miller's confession could put it out of their mind.

The Court of Appeal strongly criticised the excesses of South Wales Police's interviewing methods on Miller and it slammed the inadequacy of Miller's representation in those interviews. It deserves to be commended for this. However, its decision not to allow Michael Mansfield to call expert testimony to support his arguments can be legitimately criticised. Mansfield clearly felt that both experts - Dr Eric Shepherd and Dr Olive Tunstall - had important contributions to give which would have helped us to understand Miller's vulnerabilities far better and have assisted the criminal justice system to identify vulnerable suspects much earlier and help to form effective guidelines to prevent other defendants from the suffering that Steve Miller endured. Sadly, a golden opportunity to take the debate forward on protection for the psychologically vulnerable and improve our understanding of a crucial area of the law was needlessly lost.

The Good Shepherd

Dr Eric Shepherd is a former career intelligence officer with a plethora of academic qualifications. His independence is beyond question. At the time of the appeal of the Cardiff Three, Shepherd was the Consultant Psychologist to the City of London Police.

Since 1981 he has been commissioned by several police forces to devise training programmes for officers. He established Investigative Science Associates in May 1992. ISA specialises in investigative interviewing. It analyses written or spoken text and the conduct and content of interviews. It also makes psychological assessments of individuals regarding suggestibility, compliance and social and intellectual functioning. Consequently, Miller's was an ideal case for him to examine. He termed his approach to interviewing 'ethical interviewing' and had some very pertinent contributions to make on the raging debate on the Miller interviews.

One of Dr Shepherd's most telling points was his comparison of the methods of unethical interviewers whose perceptions are self confirming with those of the Dominican monk, Tomas de Torquemada, who was appointed the first Inquisitor-General of the Holy Order of the Inquisition, known generally as the Spanish Inquisition, in 1483. Torquemada was aware that there were very few individuals who would not submit to authority.

Where - as with Miller - the police's standard technique is to use strong arm tactics to weaken the suspect's resolve and then use the nice approach, Torquemada saw the dangers of this leading to the wrong conclusions. Torquemada felt that frequent interrogation should not be employed except on the most stubborn interviewees because frequent questions result in variable answers. Torquemada believed that virtually anyone could be surprised into a contradiction. In other words, frequent questioning does not help to establish the truth. As Dr Shepherd put it:

> If resistance is taken to be guilt and sustained resistance is taken to require sustained stress-inducing interviewing, then the innocent who deny and protest and the guilty who deny and protest become indistinguishable. Unlike today's unethical interviewers Torquemada was aware of this.

Shepherd argues that stress-inducing interviewing involving frequent questioning, as used against Steve Miller, disorients and confuses interviewees into doubting their own recollections. Contradictions caused by confusion induced by repeated questioning are taken as indicators of guilt expressing itself rather than confusion and the interviewer fires more questions in the hope of widening the breach in the interviewee's defences. The police are not and should not be bound to accept an interviewee's denials immediately without question, but the use of frequent interviewing to secure contradictions constitutes oppression as far as the law is concerned.

Dr Shepherd analysed Miller's interviews. He believed that Miller had been oppressed and described the process leading up to the admissions and the methods which police used to secure those prized admissions from Miller.

Of Steve Miller, Shepherd said:

> Neither intellectual disadvantage nor level of disposition to suggestible questioning would remove from an individual such as Miller a firm belief in something which he had actually experienced. He would, however, be severely challenged to cope with assertions, questions and questioning behaviour which pressured him to accept a persistently, proffered line of logic. Any form of pressure, particularly cumulative pressure, would add to his difficulty in coping. In simple terms he would be devoting so much effort to keep up with, if not on top of, the intellectual demands of rapid fire conversation that he could be inexorably boxed in.
>
> Oppressive behaviour and inducements would weaken his resolve to deny, protest, and fight back particularly against a solid and sustained presentation of an impossible situation not the least being that denials taken as proof evident of guilt, and sustained denial as cumulative confirmation of guilt. No one can cope with this as the degrading history of unethical interviewing testifies.

Describing the pressure that Miller was under, Shepherd says:

> So it is that the run of interviews up to and including the seventeenth has Miller denying, then faltering and conceding yet still denying, then conceding and accepting yet still denying, then accepting and providing material under the sustained propositioning and prompting and only denying when the craziness of the lie-equals-truth process reasserts itself through respite and rest, and then ultimately to provide a flow of nonsense which does not accord with forensic fact but satisfies his questioners' *distorted* conceptions of fact and his guilt. On the journey he, and his questioners, become more than a little frustrated and confused by the emergent account and its inconsistencies.
>
> Miller, however, already reduced by the officers' oppression, inducement and perverse management of information could *not* cope with the enormity of the situation. His breakdown is as audible as it is disconcerting. His plight is unimaginable since he has had to turn the world on its head to provide the officers with a confession which was elicited by the logic of lie-equals-truth only to be

> told he was lying all along.
>
> Over the next two interviews the officers embark on the *most disgraceful* shaping of Miller to get him to verbalise the key facts of Psaila's presence and the women cutting Lynette White as a means to enforce her silence. ***He never once mentions Psaila's presence voluntarily***, he forgets this important detail which has to be reconstituted. [my emphasis]

Dr Shepherd's conclusions are worthy of note:

> The protracted process of unethical pressure, oppression, inducement, prompting and the application of inappropriate questioning and behaviour enabled the officers to coerce Miller to provide a first confession. Subsequently when the status of their initial invalid knowledge base was altered by more invalid material they embarked upon the same process, successfully in their eyes since he was in no fit psychological state mentally and emotionally to cope...
>
> The officers in their handling of information prior to interviewing Miller and in their subsequent interviewing of Miller failed him, their profession and our system of justice...
>
> Their unethical conduct, predicated upon a moral and professional indifference, amounted to an abuse of power such that in the pursuit of their ends, a confession, they exercised no respect for the integrity of Miller as a person and no respect for the integrity of the truth.

Had Dr Shepherd been allowed to give this evidence it would have opened up the whole question of ethical interviewing and the pursuit of the truth. Lord Taylor's criticisms of South Wales Police were broadly similar to many of Shepherd's points, but he left it at merely saying that he never wanted to hear an interview like interview seven ever again. The issue of exactly what constitutes oppression is still decided at the discretion of the trial judge. Consequently, we get wildly differing opinions on the same evidence.

It would be unfair not to point out that police forces as a whole have begun to adopt ethical interviewing following Home Office guidelines. They were gradually introduced from 1993. After the convictions of the Cardiff Three were quashed, South Wales Police themselves adopted a more ethical approach to interviewing. In theory it means that nobody will suffer the type of interviewing that Miller was subjected to ever again, but this approach does not carry the same weight as PACE.

Palpably Vulnerable

But Dr Shepherd was not the only expert witness whose opinions could have helped us to understand the full extent of Steve Miller's vulnerabilities. Dr Olive Tunstall was commissioned by Miller's defence to produce a psychological assessment of Miller for the appeal. Dr Tunstall has compiled several reports for use in legal cases on the psychological vulnerability of suspects, most notably in the case of Engin Raghip of the Tottenham Three. She has several academic qualifications and is a psychologist of considerable expertise.

Dr Tunstall studied transcripts of Miller's interviews with South Wales Police, Mr Justice Leonard's ruling on the admissibility of those interviews, Dr Gisli Gudjonsson's report on Miller and the draft grounds of appeal. She looked at Miller's school reports, interviewed members of his family, his former teachers, and the principal psychologist, probation officer and his teacher in the educational department of Wormwood Scrubs Prison. She also interviewed Miller himself. Accordingly, she was able to make a telling contribution to understanding Steve Miller and putting his vulnerabilities in context.

As early as 1976 Miller's school records show that his mental age was lower than his actual years. An assessment taken when he was nearly ten years old records his mental age as that of a seven year-old. His IQ was between 65 and 75 at that time. It justified him being placed in a special needs school for the educationally subnormal.

When Miller left school, aged sixteen, his reading age was equivalent to that of a child aged eight. Dr Gudjonsson subsequently confirmed that Miller had a verbal IQ of 74 and a performance IQ of 78. Gudjonsson reported that Miller's reading age was eight years and four months, and that Miller was abnormally suggestible.

In 1991 Miller was assessed by the psychologist in Wormwood Scrubs. The results confirmed those of the previous tests. Miller's IQ was recorded as less than 75 and he was deemed to be in the nation's lowest 5%.

Dr Tunstall reviewed Miller's educational and occupational record. She noted that he was brought up in a broken home and had been aware of problems between his parents before they divorced. His family had broken up when he was nine years old. By then he had been identified as having special needs. So Miller's vulnerabilities were clearly apparent during his formative years.

On leaving school Miller attended some courses to try to learn a variety of trades without really finding one suited to him.

Tunstall assessed Miller's level of social functioning. The results proved that Miller was an extremely vulnerable young man. His communication skills were equivalent to those of a five year-old; his daily living skills were equivalent to those of a twelve year-old; and his socialisation skills were equivalent to those of a nine year-old.

On this point Tunstall emphasised that Miller's abnormally low communication skills were particularly important in the context of his ability, or lack of it, to cope with the interviews with South Wales Police.

Tunstall noted that Miller's teachers and other professionals believed he had no self confidence, was unsure of himself and was prone to anxiety. She said, "As a defence to cover this, Stephen tries to project an image of confidence and adopts a rapid form of speech; his capacity to think cannot keep pace with the speed at which he talks and he resorts to the constant repetition of the same simple phrases and the use of clichés."

However understandable this defence may be, it can result in the untrained eye assuming that he is not as vulnerable as he actually is. This is important in the context of his interviews with South Wales Police. Even more importantly, it could have caused Miller's solicitor, Geraint Richards, to assume that his client was coping with the interviews far better than he actually was, thereby explaining Richards' repeated failure to intervene.

Tunstall noted that Miller had a limited concentration span and poor short term memory and because of this he could not keep up with the thread of a lengthy or complex conversation. She wrote, "He has difficulty organising information in his head in a logical way and cannot sustain an argument because by the time he has tried to structure what he wants to say he has forgotten the content."

Consequently, he would have had immense difficulty just keeping up with what was being said in the interviews, let alone answering their questions. Dr Tunstall also wrote, "At a superficial level Stephen may create an impression of verbal competence; closer analysis reveals his limited understanding of ideas and his lack of knowledge which he attempts to hide by a repetitious flow of hackneyed phrases."

Miller had found a mechanism for covering up his vulnerability. This should not be confused with believing that he wasn't vulnerable. David Elfer, like several barristers before him, imposed a standard of suggestibility that was impossible to meet. He submitted that to be considered suggestible the person had to agree with absolutely everything that was put to her/him. And Elfer argued that Miller held his own during interviews, including the crucial tape seven. But Dr Tunstall knew better.

And she pointed out that behaviour can be influenced by several considerations, such as age, ability, personality and circumstances in which the behaviour occurs. This includes the physical and social environment. In other words, the simple fact that a person does not agree with everything that is said to them *does not* mean that they are not suggestible. She wrote:

> To say that a subject is abnormally suggestible is to say that in any given circumstances he is significantly more likely than other people to yield to suggestion. That does not mean that he will always and under all circumstances yield to any suggestion.

And she continued:

> In the circumstances of the police interviews Stephen had denied having had any involvement in the murder of Lynette White but was being pressed by the police officers to admit to complicity in her murder. Stephen would have been likely to have clear knowledge of whether or not he had been involved in any way in the murder and it was a matter of the greatest importance to him. Despite his abnormal suggestibility, Stephen would be expected to resist pressure to admit to such a serious charge, if as he claims, he is innocent; it is not reasonable, in these extreme circumstances, to assume that because Stephen resisted many of the suggestions put to him by his interviewers he is therefore not suggestible.
>
> Nevertheless, Stephen's abnormal suggestibility would have made him significantly more likely than other people to succumb to suggestive questioning and to the pressures placed upon him in the interviews to admit to having been involved in Lynette's murder. In fact Stephen did eventually make self-incriminating admissions, whereas his four co-defendants made no such admissions.

This means that Miller's resistance does not mean that he was not suggestible. It meant that his responses in *all* of the interviews had been *entirely* consistent with suggestibility. His vulnerability meant that he was more likely to succumb to suggestions and it explains why his co-accused did not confess despite enduring similarly gruelling interrogations. His inability to cope with the demands that were placed on him by the police meant that despite his resistance, he would eventually say what they wanted him to say.

Elfer's standard of suggestibility was wrong. Expert opinion was convinced that Steve Miller was a very vulnerable young man. Elfer's submissions about Miller were such that nobody could ever be considered suggestible unless they never rejected anything that was put to them even if they knew for certain that it was not true. This is an absurd standard. Elfer maintained that Miller was not suggestible as he did not agree with everything - a view endorsed by Mr Justice Leonard during the trial - and despite the bad behaviour by police in tape seven Miller held his own, so he could not claim to be suggestible.

Had Dr Tunstall been allowed to give her evidence Elfer would have found the ground cut from beneath his feet. Each of his criteria for proving Miller was not suggestible was wrong. His submissions on suggestibility did not prove that Miller had hoodwinked everyone into believing him vulnerable when he wasn't; it suggested that he was unaware of the depth of Miller's vulnerabilities. This was valuable evidence which the Court of Appeal ought to have heard if only to improve the judges' understanding of vulnerabilities suffered by people like Miller.

But even this was not all that Tunstall had to say. She pointed out that Miller would have had great difficulty coping with the demands of a trial, especially as his case required two trials which lasted almost a year in total. She wrote:

> In the interests of justice defendants are given the right to hear the evidence that is given at trial and to testify in their own defence. To exercise these rights a defendant needs to be able to comprehend and record or remember what is said in evidence and to be able to express himself adequately when giving his own evidence. Although most defendants are supported in court by their lawyers those lawyers depend upon their client's instructions and cannot give their client's testimony for them.

Miller had rights, but he was incapable of using them as he didn't understand them and his lawyers failed to help him as much as they could have. Before the first trial began, Dr Gudjonsson had assessed Miller and it was patently obvious that Miller would not be able to cope with the demands of a trial unless his special needs were properly catered for and, even then, there would still be great difficulties to overcome.

Miller's vulnerabilities were exacerbated during the trial process. He had significant enough difficulties in coping, but to expect him to be able to retain information under these circumstances was expecting more of him than he could achieve given his considerable disabilities. The extraordinary length of the trial process made this even worse.

Tunstall also noted that his having to listen to protracted accounts of the brutal murder of the woman he loved in the trials and in the interviews with South Wales Police would have been deeply traumatising for him, especially due to the nature of the murder. Tunstall had no doubt that Miller was a very vulnerable person. Her conclusions are worthy of note:

> Stephen's psychological vulnerabilities would cause him to require appropriate support in the circumstances of a police interview and this need would be even greater in the case of interviews as protracted and arduous as those which were conducted with Stephen between 7th and 11th December 1988. Although Stephen had the benefit of a solicitor's presence during 17 of these 19 interviews it is my opinion that the solicitor *did not comprehend* either the *existence* or the *extent* of his client's disabilities and would therefore not have recognised the level of support which his client required. [my emphasis]

Dr Tunstall's opinions establish the extent of Miller's vulnerabilities and place them in a much needed context. But her conclusions also point to failings in Miller's defence team. Miller had special needs which ought to have been recognised and acted upon far earlier. Were it not for Miller's greatest good fortune in eventually securing the services of Gareth Peirce, Michael Mansfield QC and Nicholas Blake, the full extent of his vulnerabilities may never have been known about or put in the specific context of his gross inability to cope with the circumstances that overwhelmed him.

It ought to be pointed out that Miller's original defence team had in fact ensured that Mr Justice Leonard was aware of Miller's academic record. Consequently, Leonard can be criticised for failing to recognise the full extent of Miller's vulnerabilities.

In cases where people like Miller are not competent to be held responsible for the conduct of their defence, one solution to the problem might be for the lawyers to be held legally responsible for the conduct of the entire defence. And then, if it were to be subsequently shown that the performance of the lawyers was below the quality that the defendant was entitled to expect, this would constitute strong grounds of appeal, mandating a retrial at the very least.

Had the Court of Appeal been prepared to listen to Olive Tunstall's evidence it might well have felt it necessary to issue further guidelines on the treatment of vulnerable suspects aimed at securing greater efficiency in identifying the needs of vulnerable people like Miller before the damage is done, especially when the evidence was there from a very early stage in Miller's life. The Court of Appeal deprived itself of the opportunity to do this and with it a perfect opportunity to learn an important lesson was lost.

In the case of the Cardiff Three, there had been nothing to prevent the Court of Appeal from hearing all three appeals in full. Had it chosen to do this, there would have been none of the subsequent accusations that their Lordships' judgement was little more than an extremely perceptive damage limitation exercise. But the methods used by police to convict the Cardiff Three was only part of the story. New evidence would emerge which would offer the last realistic chance to unmask the real killer of Lynette White.

CHAPTER 12

The Heart of the Matter

Forensic Science In Action

The alleged pressure on witnesses, non-disclosure, ethical status of interviews with suspects, the fairness of allowing Massey to give evidence without being able to probe his motivation fully and the exercise of Mr Justice Leonard's discretion not to sever Miller's trial from that of his co-defendants were not the only serious issues not to be resolved during the appeals of the Cardiff Three. There was also the question of the use of forensic science.

There was no credible forensic evidence tying any of the Cardiff Five to the victim or to the murder room. Police clearly regarded the discovery of the rare blood group with the male chromosome in it as significant. Until they discovered that Angela Psaila possessed this rare blood group they had been looking for one man. However, Dr Peter Gill's sex determination test was undoubtedly consistent with a large amount of female blood mixing with a small quantity of male blood or vice versa, either of which would give the impression of male blood.

None of the Cardiff Five possessed blood groups that remotely resembled the blood that had been deposited in the flat. Several others had been eliminated on that basis. In his statements dated February 3rd and March 14th 1989 Dr John Whiteside listed the blood groups of the Cardiff Five, Learnne Vilday, Lynette White and Angela Psaila. Whiteside said that the blood on the jeans could have come from a mixture of Psaila's blood with that of Abdullahi, but it could not have come from any of the others. The cocktail theory was the closest that the Crown came to providing forensic evidence against any of the accused.

But there were serious flaws with this evidence. In the first place it depended on a vast quantity of Psaila's blood mixing in intimately with a small amount of Abdullahi's blood from a split second contact. Yet none of Psaila's accounts at the time of the murder refer to her having any kind of facial injury - bear in mind that she had given a statement to police soon after Lynette's body was discovered and no injury had been reported by the officer who took the statement - and it was strange that all five areas of the jeans that were tested indicated the presence of the male chromosome from a split second contact. But there is an even more serious problem with this explanation for the blood deposited on Lynette's jeans: it could not implicate Abdullahi and Psaila to the exclusion of everybody else. While it certainly applied to them, it applied to everybody else who had compatible blood groups. This applies to approximately twelve million people in Britain.

And then there is the evidence that Dr Whiteside gave at the first trial to consider. Whiteside had told that jury that if a large amount of female blood had mixed in with a small quantity of male material, ***any*** man could have been responsible for the presence of the Y-chromosome in the blood on the jeans. That widens the search to about thirty million men in Britain. In addition to this, there are approximately three thousand women who possess the male chromosome to be brought into the equation. And there are also about eight thousand women who possess the same blood group as Psaila to be considered as the cocktail theory applied to any of them just as much as it did to Psaila. This means that not only could the cocktail theory not conclusively tie any of the defendants to the murder room, but it could not exclude about half the population.

But this should have been academic as there is the evidence that Psaila gave at the retrial to throw into the pot. According to her testimony the only injury that she suffered that night was a cut on the inside of her lip which did not bleed much in any case. If, despite her previous history of lying, these claims are taken at face value, it would blow any cocktail theory involving her out of the water as a small quantity of her blood in the mixture would mean that the blood factors of the person who deposited the Y-chromosome in the mixture would have been detected. That in turn would have eliminated all of the defendants as Abdullahi's Gc result, which differed from the result obtained from the jeans, would have been detected. Suffice to say, if Psaila's injury did not bleed sufficiently to obscure the blood group of the donor of the male chromosome, the cocktail theory was in ruins unless the man's blood group just happened to be the same as Psaila's, which was somewhat unlikely to put it mildly.

In short, if Dr Whiteside was right to describe Psaila's blood group as "one hell of a coincidence," then this was the mother of all coincidences. But this was not quite the last word on the cocktail theory. It should be remembered that Dr Gill's sex determination test was extremely sensitive to the Y-chromosome, but could not determine the proportion of X and Y-chromosomes present in any mixture of male and female blood. Although Dr Gill had stated in evidence at the retrial that he would have expected the results to have been uniform if the source of the blood on the jeans was one man and some results were weaker than others, the fact that the test cannot determine the exact proportion of male and female material in any mixture means that if the mixture consisted of enough of the blood of a man who possessed that rare blood group to obscure a small enough quantity of female material, then any woman's blood could have been in the mixture.

It should also be pointed out that it was entirely possible that the killer's blood could have been deposited on or beside varying quantities of Lynette's blood. Some degree of mixing of the blood on the jeans between an injured killer and a mutilated victim is not only possible, or even probable, it offers a convincing explanation for the varying strengths of Dr Gill's results. And, as we shall see, there was some evidence indicating that the killer's blood probably had mixed with that of Lynette on one of the stains on the jeans and that this information was known to Dr Whiteside, but not by the defence until the appeal. All of this suggests that not only could the cocktail theory not conclusively tie any of the Cardiff Five to the murder room and the victim to the exclusion of all others, it seems that it cannot comprehensively exclude anyone. As such the cocktail theory is utterly worthless.

And it should be remembered that the possibility which applied to about eight thousand men that an unidentified man had deposited the blood in the flat on his own had never been conclusively eliminated. All of this raises the question of the fairness of adducing evidence which not only could not conclusively prove guilt, but appears to have been unable to exclude anybody on the face of the earth.

But there was further evidence which the jury did not hear which could have drastically affected the value of the forensic evidence presented in this case. Neither the defence nor the jury knew that police had considered at least two men who possessed either a strikingly similar or effectively identical blood group to the one deposited in the murder room. Suffice to say, if Dr Whiteside's cocktail theory applied to Psaila and any of the defendants, it also applied to both Mr X and Mr Y. But the blood groups of both X and Y had not been disclosed to Abdullahi's lawyers who were therefore unable to put this possibility to the jury. Both of their blood groups were known before the Cardiff Five were arrested, but both had been eliminated on DNA. Undoubtedly, the police believed that DNA had eliminated both of them. They may therefore have believed that there was no burden on them to disclose this information.

This was unfortunate. It would have been fairer if they had disclosed the full extent of their knowledge of both these men so the defence could investigate them for themselves if they thought it necessary. Had they done so the jury would have been able to consider the forensic issues from a position of knowledge of all the relevant facts and their verdict might well have been different. Mr X had been a prime suspect and Y's blood group was important. But DNA had eliminated them and DNA was foolproof wasn't it?

Getting to Grips With DNA

The discovery of the means of extracting part of the DNA chain was undoubtedly a significant breakthrough in the fight against crime. The dispute is simply over exactly how significant it is. The DNA chain consists of about three billion bits of DNA. If the testing procedure was based on examination of all three billion bits of DNA, the possibility of an accidental match would be very slight. However, the great breakthrough of DNA profiling is based on examination of only four bits of the DNA chain. And doubts have been expressed in the scientific community about the possibility of an accidental match.

The other important point concerns variation. Because any scientific analysis or measurement will produce some variation even between samples from an identical source, allowance has to be made for some acceptable range of deviation in assessing whether there is a match.[1] Consequently, the scope for wrongful matches to be declared exists as different experts allow different ranges of acceptable variations. In fact, Home Office guidelines allow a margin for error of plus or minus 2.8%. The fact that such a wide range of error is allowed for suggests that DNA may not be as foolproof as had been previously thought, especially in borderline cases.

DNA profiling is undoubtedly a valuable tool, but procedural, handling and statistical errors have occurred. In fact, Channel Four's 1994 documentary programme *Incredible Evidence*[2] revealed several causes for concern. The programme highlighted a case which secured a conviction by majority verdict in Scotland based on DNA profiling. This case was particularly worrying as there was substantial evidence that contradicted the DNA evidence, including the victim, a family friend of the suspect, insisting that he was not her assailant.

And the DNA tests themselves appear to have been flawed. After initial tests failed to yield any results the crime samples were then sent to Cellmark along with a blood sample from the suspect for comparison purposes. Cellmark only called a match on one of the crime samples. But Cellmark's procedures left something to be desired. *Incredible Evidence* demonstrated that there were procedural errors over the control checks. That particular error would have resulted in this evidence being inadmissible in the USA. But Cellmark had made an even more serious mistake. They ran the suspect's DNA in the neighbouring track to the comparison sample. By running his sample in the neighbouring track, there was a risk of spillage from the crime sample, thereby giving a false result. Cellmark's updated procedures acknowledge that there should be a gap between the tracks that the suspect's DNA and that of the crime sample are run in and that a control sample should also be run.

In 1988 an American lawyer named Pat Sullivan faced the difficulty of challenging DNA evidence which was being used for the first time in the USA. *Incredible Evidence* highlighted Sullivan's startling discoveries about Cellmark's procedures. Sullivan had discovered that Cellmark had wrongly called a match in a proficiency test organised by the California Crime Laboratory. In fact, this was the second time that they had taken the test. Cellmark denied the existence of the earlier test until a court order forced it into the public domain. Cellmark had wrongly called matches in that test as well. They explained the earlier test by saying that the results could not be interpreted. They improved their procedures as a result of that failed test. Every part of the testing procedure has to be witnessed now. That was designed to reduce the possibility of human error in the procedures. Cellmark took another proficiency test with the improved procedures in place, but they still wrongly called a match. They claimed that this error was

[1] The measuring of results is now done by computers rather than manually.
[2] This is the *Equinox* programme referred to by Michael Mansfield QC in his foreword to this book.

due to cross-contamination. Consequently, the scope for error has been established.

And the BBC's 1994 *Public Eye* documentary, *DNA: Do Not Accept*, showed that no account is taken of related characteristics such as blue eyes and blond hair.

There is, moreover, cause for concern over the statistical reliability of DNA profiling. Each genetic characteristic detected in a DNA profile is given a statistical interpretation such as one in one thousand. Then they are multiplied up to give the possibility of an accidental match. But these figures are just estimates. In order to present an accurate statistical interpretation of the possibility of a random match, every single person on the face of the earth would need to be sampled. These results would then need to be categorised according to characteristics such as racial origin and gender. Only then would we know the actual ratio of that genetic characteristic to the population. In other words, every single statistic that DNA profiling is based on is nothing more than an estimate which is multiplied up several times.

It is also based on an assumption that the four bits of DNA extracted for profiling provide a unique DNA profile - but with no compelling proof to support this assumption. This produces the scope for gross errors in the statistical validity of DNA profiling. Even the man who made the crucial breakthrough in developing the DNA testing system of multi-locus probe (MLP) DNA profiling, Professor Sir Alec Jeffreys, believes that there will be accidental matches between people who are unrelated.

If just one accidental match could be found that was not caused by procedural or handling error, then the assumption that DNA profiling can identify the donor of the DNA and exclude all others bar an identical twin would be proved false.

Incredible Evidence revealed that a sample of just seventy people had produced a random match from people who could not have been related and it was not due to error. It should be pointed out that this random match was produced in a twelve-band DNA profile. Advocates of DNA profiling had claimed that the possibility of a random match in a twelve-band profile was 1:95 million. But a sample of just seventy people produced a random match from two people who were not related. In other words, ***the true interpretation of the statistical possibility of a random match was not 1:95 million; it was 1:35.***

Incredible Evidence also showed that the FBI had compiled a DNA database. Eventually, Sullivan forced the disclosure of the database. He discovered that some of the results were missing. He later found that the complete database had found matches between unrelated people. The FBI tried to cover it up and even disclosed the sanitised database to two scientists at Yale University, who conducted a research project looking for matching samples in the FBI and other databases. They found none and published their work in a prestigious scientific journal, arguing that because there were no matches on the FBI database the validity of DNA typing had been proved. Sullivan's research showed that there had been matches which had been purged from the sanitised database. Twenty-two of the matches could be explained as duplicates made in error, but three of them defied explanation.

The myth of DNA profiling had been exploded. But it is important not to throw the baby out with the bathwater. DNA may not be unique as a means of identifying individuals, but it might be able to provide a greater degree of certainty than any other test available bar fingerprinting.

Nevertheless, it is extremely worrying that the Home Secretary, Michael Howard, has decided that a DNA database should be established and the police should have the power to forcibly take samples for DNA testing from anyone arrested for a recordable offence. It means that the scope for appalling miscarriages of justice exist. The perception that juries have of DNA evidence could easily result in one.

At the very least, juries need to be given a health warning over DNA evidence. When judges sum up in the future, they should warn juries about the reservations in DNA evidence as well as highlighting its benefits. Only then can a jury assess the proper weight that should be given to the DNA evidence. But if DNA cannot uniquely identify criminals the one thing it can be relied on to do is eliminate people - until now.

A Catalogue Of Errors

David Elfer QC had told the appeal judges that X was eliminated on DNA. Interestingly, Elfer did not say that X had been eliminated on fingerprints. This is surprising as police had taken a policy decision in February 1988 that fingerprinting evidence should take priority over forensic evidence. That decision led to the crucial samples being treated with the chemical Ninhydrin to bring out the latent fingerprints. Among the samples to be treated in this fashion was a wallpaper sample SS12. It would later prove to be the most important sample in the whole inquiry.

SS12 was one of several samples discovered by DS Stephen Steele, the police's fingerprint expert in the Lynette White Inquiry. Fingerprinting work was completed by September. SS12 was one of the wallpaper samples which were stored for three days in a locked property cupboard at Police Headquarters in Bridgend prior to being taken to Birmingham for DNA testing. And storing these samples in a cupboard rather than refrigerating them was ludicrous even though DNA profiling was in its infancy at the time.

The delay in subjecting these samples to DNA analysis and the treatment of them with Ninhydrin caused severe problems with obtaining DNA profiles and contributed to the high level of degradation in these samples. In the light of this information, it is clear that fingerprinting evidence offered a far greater degree of certainty than DNA evidence could in this inquiry. Consequently, it is baffling that police have never referred to Mr X, or other suspects for that matter, being eliminated on fingerprints.

Meanwhile, in October 1988, Dr Whiteside contacted the Incident Room to inform them that X's blood group was strikingly similar to that of Lynette's murderer. Whiteside recommended that a DNA test be conducted, but he made no statement referring to X's blood group. X's blood sample was forwarded to Dr Nicholas Prance, the inquiry's DNA expert, for that test to be carried out. It arrived on October 19th 1988. On November 9th Prance made a statement saying that X's DNA profile was different from the limited profiles obtained from the wallpaper samples SS2 and SS12. So police eliminated X from the inquiry as they had done with Mr Y just one month before. And in terms of the information they had at their disposal at the time they were quite right to do so.

Prance made statements in reference to his work in September, October and November 1988; and in April, November and December 1989. Bloodstaining was observed on the wallpaper and on Lynette's jeans. On September 27th 1988 he noted that attempts to prepare DNA profiles from the jeans had been unsuccessful. Prance thought that the failure to obtain profiles was presumably due to insufficient DNA, or that the DNA had degraded. Prance used MLP DNA profiling, then widely used, rather than the far more sensitive single-locus probes (SLP) which were available then and later came into favour at their expense.

On December 3rd 1988 Dr Paul Debenham reported that further attempts had been made to obtain a DNA profile. He stated that it had not been possible to detect any genetic characters in either of the samples from the jeans, despite his use of the three most sensitive probes. This ruled out Lynette's jeans as a source of any DNA evidence in the Lynette White Inquiry, or rather it did until the far more sensitive DNA test of Short Tandem Repeats (STR) was developed.[1] There was no attempt to subject Lynette's right sock to either a DNA test or a sex determination test as almost all of the sample was used up in conventional blood grouping tests. So, the DNA evidence in the Lynette White case related solely to the wallpaper samples.

Prance felt that DNA profiling could determine with a high degree of certainty whether a bloodstain originated from a particular individual, or whether that individual could be excluded as the source. But he added a significant proviso: "The strength of association *or exclusion* may not be as great if only a small amount of material is available." [my emphasis]

Then he went on to point out that attempts to prepare DNA profiles from two sections of wallpaper SS6 and RH26 had been unsuccessful because there was insufficient DNA, or it had degraded. On October 18th Prance pointed out that attempts to prepare profiles from two other sections of wallpaper had not failed totally. In fact, limited profiles were obtained from SS2 and SS12. Prance felt that

[1] The most significant benefit of STR typing is that it can work from very small bloodstains. This is because of the discovery of the means of amplifying DNA through the Polymerase Chain Reaction (PCR). Using different coloured dyes several PCRs can be conducted at the same time. This is known as multiplexing and is the method of PCR testing favoured by British forensic laboratories at the moment. There can be no doubt that multiplexing is a well validated technique which is sufficient in the vast majority of cases. However, in borderline cases, multiplexing can be found wanting. STR typing would later come to be of great importance in the Lynette White Inquiry.

they were different from each other and that one of them originated from Lynette White. These were the samples against which all the eliminations were obtained.

In his previous statement, Prance had suggested that eliminations may not be as accurate if only a small amount of material was available. It would not invalidate all of the eliminations that were achieved in the Lynette White Inquiry. All it proves is that the reliability of the eliminations would have been greater if there had been more DNA present in the wallpaper samples.

On April 25th 1989 Prance got to grips with the central issue, the samples from the wallpaper, SS2 and SS12. He felt unable to exclude Lynette as the source of these bloodstains. Yet, if he couldn't rule Lynette out, then surely DNA testing was useless in this case. He also said, "Due to the limited nature of the profile obtained from the blood on the section of the wallpaper SS12, the degree of discrimination obtained from a comparison of this profile with others was *not* of the level normally associated with DNA profiling." [my emphasis] So, Prance seemed to be saying that SS12 was worthless in terms of tying Lynette's murderer to his crime.

Prance concluded that he could reach no positive conclusions about SS2 and again repeated that he couldn't rule out Lynette. He was also unable to rule Lynette and Rashid Omar out as possible sources for SS12. But he pointed out that bloodstaining from wallpaper and skirting board close to SS12 did not originate from White and Omar. If these stains and SS12 had the same donor which Dr Whiteside claimed was reasonable to assume, then SS12 did not originate from White or Omar. But as we shall see this may not have been a reasonable assumption to make after all.

On December 14th 1989 Prance made a further statement. He pointed out that the DNA profile obtained from SS12 was incomplete and only contained a small amount of information compared to a complete profile, which made comparison difficult. He also suggested that the results of the DNA profiling of SS12 may have been interfered with by chemical treatment for fingerprinting. He admitted that he had no evidence to either prove or disprove this, but it has since emerged that Ninhydrin can indeed affect DNA. Prance stated firmly that the DNA on SS12 was highly degraded. Degradation can affect MLP DNA profiles as well.

Prance could not exclude the possibility that the blood on SS2 and SS12 originated from Lynette. If this was true, then it means that neither SS2, nor SS12 could have tied her killer to his crime. If Lynette was the source, then it was obvious that the murderer's profile would be different from them. In other words, the whole of the DNA evidence was utterly useless.

But Ronnie Actie's solicitor at the first trial, Stuart Hutton, commissioned a report from an independent forensic scientist, John Hayward, who reported on the forensic evidence, including the DNA evidence. He examined the DNA profiles obtained from SS2 and SS12. They consisted of four weak bands. Hayward was satisfied that SS2 came from Lynette.

However, he felt that only three bands out of the four were in place with

Lynette's DNA profile when compared with SS12. Those three bands were significantly weaker than those detected in the improved DNA profile taken from Lynette White herself, but the lack of intensity of the bands could be explained by the high level of degradation of the DNA in the sample.

But the one band that was in a position that did not correspond with any of the bands in Lynette's profile was far more significant. On this basis Hayward ruled Lynette out as the source of the blood on SS12. This suggested that all of the DNA eliminations on the basis of SS12, were safe and satisfactory after all.

According to Hayward, even though the bands in the DNA profile were fuzzy and practically useless, this one band which was slightly out of place was enough to justify South Wales Police's elimination of Lynette. But this neglects to consider the possibility that treatment of SS12 with Ninhydrin combined with heavy degradation had shifted that band out of position. This possibility was considered in the course of the investigation after it was advanced by Prance for the Crown. But Hayward appears not to have considered it.

Since the Cardiff Three were convicted, it has emerged that Ninhydrin causes chemical changes in DNA. This means that it can move bands out of position in a DNA profile. This alone affects the safety of *all* of the eliminations on the basis of DNA. It should also be pointed out that degradation can cause bands to shift out of position in DNA profiles, especially when multi-locus probes are used. Even in terms of scientific knowledge available in 1988 the mismanagement over storage of the key samples in a property cupboard rather than at low temperatures was staggering. And there were other possibilities which could have significantly affected the reliability of the results obtained from SS12 which never saw the light of day in Swansea Crown Court.

First, it was assumed that the blood on SS12 came from only one person and it wasn't from Lynette, so it must have come from the murderer. This assumption was fatally flawed. Disclosure obligations had changed since the trial of the Cardiff Five. By the time that the appeals were due to be heard John Hayward had been instructed by Miller's defence to report on forensic issues arising out of the discovery of Mr X as a prominent suspect. Hayward examined Dr Whiteside's results and saw the laboratory workbook. These results indicated that it was likely that there had been a mixture of the killer's blood with that of Lynette on stain four of the jeans.[1]

Neither the defence nor the jury were aware of this during the trial or retrial of the Cardiff Five. While a mix between one of the killers and a witness was highly improbable, a mix between an injured killer and a mutilated victim was altogether more plausible. Suffice to say, there was evidence that Lynette's blood was likely to have mixed with that of her killer. And if it had happened on the jeans

[1] The Hp result on stain four of the jeans had originally been recorded in the Laboratory's workbook as Hp 2-1. Further work by Dr Whiteside revealed that it was likely to have been a mixture of Hp 2 and Hp 2-1. Certainly, both Whiteside and Hayward believed that two Hp results were obtained even though the results were confusing.

might it not have happened on SS12 as well? Unfortunately, conventional blood grouping tests which could have resolved this issue were not attempted on SS12 until over a year after Lynette's murder and no results could be obtained. Thus, the possibility remains that the blood on SS12 may have been a mixture of Lynette's blood with that of her killer.

It means that Prance did not have access to information which could have drastically affected every DNA elimination achieved by comparison with SS12. To put it simply, the weakness of the bands obtained indicated a very high level of degradation. Had the samples been tested earlier more bands would have been detected. If the blood on SS12 was a mixture of Lynette's and her killer's, then it was unsafe to eliminate any suspect whose DNA profile included that band which was out of place with Lynette's profile.

Moreover, MLP DNA profiling has been known to produce spurious (artefactual) bands. There is evidence that DNA profiles obtained from blood or saliva taken from the same person have produced banding differences. Theoretically, DNA profiles taken from the same person should appear identical, or as close to it as makes no difference. Banding differences could give the impression of the profiles coming from two entirely different people. Thus, MLP profiles have been known to produce bands which have nothing to do with the actual DNA being tested. Therefore, the possibility that the one band that was out of place with Lynette's profile was a spurious band which should not have been produced has not been eliminated.

All this means that the importance of SS12 is minimal. Its only use is to eliminate suspects whose profile does not include a band in the relevant place and, possibly, not even that. The police turned to DNA because it was assumed that it offered a high degree of certainty that a match would not be a coincidence. But DNA was useless in this inquiry. A four band profile offers no less than a one in two hundred possibility of a random match. This narrowed the field down to about three hundred thousand people out of the population of Britain. And so, it was not much use. However, in this case, it could actually be reduced to a one band profile. The possibility of a match with a single band was about one in five. In other words, about twelve million people in Britain fitted the bill. DNA was therefore of no use in terms of tracking down Lynette's murderer and was not much better at eliminating suspects.

To sum up: we now know that degradation causes chemical changes in DNA and could move a band out of position. The crucial sample SS12 was heavily degraded. We now know that chemical treatment for fingerprinting using Ninhydrin causes chemical changes in DNA which could move a band out of position. SS12 had been treated with Ninhydrin. We now know that MLP DNA profiling cannot detect a mixture of two people's blood and that there was evidence that Lynette's blood had probably mixed with that of her killer on another crucial sample from which no DNA profile was obtained. Finally, we now know that MLP DNA profiles are capable of producing spurious bands which have nothing to do with the actual DNA under test, so the possibility remains that the one band that is out of place with Lynette's DNA profile was a 'rogue' band.

There are, therefore, four grounds of concern over the safety of the elimination of Lynette White as the source of the blood upon which all of the DNA eliminations were obtained. This in turn renders the DNA eliminations of all suspects in the inquiry unsafe and unsatisfactory as they may have been achieved from blood which originated from the victim herself. However, if Dr Whiteside was right to assume that SS12 had the same donor as RH27 and JAW27 all of the DNA eliminations could be relied on despite the reservations.

The belief that the blood on SS12 came from somebody other than Lynette was based on an assumption of Dr Whiteside's that it had the same donor as RH27 and JAW27 which had been proved by conventional blood grouping tests not to have been deposited on that wall by Lynette. In his statements of February 3rd and March 14th 1989 Whiteside said, "It is reasonable to suppose that all of the blood on the wall came from the same person although only two stains have been grouped by conventional means." Earlier in his statements he had said that he took JAW27 to be representative of the blood on the wall. However, Whiteside should have provided proof. At first, he saw no need to do so. But then he seems to have thought better of it.

After Dr Gill's sex determination test had failed to resolve the issue of the sex of the person who shed the blood on SS12, the sample was returned to Whiteside in February 1989. It was only then that he attempted to conduct conventional blood grouping tests on this crucial sample, but it was too late. Consequently, neither DNA nor blood grouping tests could rule Lynette out as the source of the blood on SS12, yet this was the sample upon which all of the DNA eliminations were obtained.

It is now clear that they were all eliminated on the basis of the assumption that one drip of blood of all the blood in that flat did not come from Lynette White, or a mixture of her blood and her killer's without conclusive proof.

In his statements of February 3rd and March 14th 1989 Dr Whiteside reported the blood grouping results of the bottom of Lynette's jeans as being AB; PGM 1+1-; EAP B/CB; Gc 2-1s; AK 1. It will be noted that there was no haptoglobin (Hp) result. In both statements, Whiteside specifically said, "*No* Hp group could be obtained." [my emphasis] Well, this was clear enough, or rather, it ought to have been.

The discovery of Mr X and his importance in the Lynette White Inquiry changed all this. John Hayward examined the results obtained from the jeans for Miller's defence at the appeal. Whiteside completely changed his position for the appeal. From reporting no haptoglobin result on the jeans at all, he decided that it was likely that there was a mixture of Hp 2 and Hp 2-1 results. As Lynette's haptoglobin was recorded as Hp 2-1, the Hp 2 result presumably belonged to her murderer which would have mirrored the result obtained from the sock.

Whiteside's change of opinion was extraordinary and he never gave an explanation for such an incredible change of mind, although to be fair to him he never got the chance to clarify his position at the appeal because the Crown conceded defeat before these issues could be resolved, but Hayward supported his conclusion that it was likely that there was a mixture of haptoglobin results on the bottom of Lynette's jeans. On any view, there was haptoglobin present on the jeans, yet Whiteside had reported no haptoglobin result in his statements. Consequently, until he spoke to Hayward the defence had no idea that haptoglobin had been detected on the jeans even though the results were confusing. Clearly, Whiteside had given two mutually exclusive results concerning the haptoglobin results.

In addition to that, it will be remembered that Whiteside felt that it was reasonable to assume that JAW27 was representative of all the blood on that wall which included SS12. Yet there was evidence that *one* bloodstain on the jeans probably came from *two* different sources. If that was true how could it be reasonable to assume that all the bloodstains on that wall came from the same donor?

After Dr Whiteside had conducted further work on stain four of the jeans he would have known that one stain on the jeans probably had two separate donors. Unfortunately, he did not clarify the issue of whether this knowledge affected his assumptions regarding SS12, although to be fair to him, he may not have thought that this information was so important that it ought to be disclosed. In fact, if he had disclosed the information regarding stain four of the jeans it is unlikely that the defence would have seen any relevance in this without having access to the blood groups of Mr X and Mr Y as DNA had eliminated their clients as the source of SS12 and once again they did not and would not have seen any need to attack it without access to the blood groups of X and Y. Suffice to say, the better practice would have been for both the Crown and the defence to be made fully aware of all the scientific information that forensic scientists had unearthed so the jury could be given the full picture and could reach their verdicts from a position of knowledge; nothing less will suffice.

Meanwhile, Mr X's haptoglobin was recorded as being Hp 2-1. In all other respects his blood group was the same as the blood on the jeans. Normally, blood grouping tests are corroborated by a second test. A corroboration test on X's haptoglobin factor was attempted, but no result was obtained. Consequently, the possibility of a handling error could not be ruled out, even though such an error was unlikely.

It ought to be pointed out that Whiteside thought that he had previously brought X to the attention of South Wales Police. He believed that X's blood group must have been recorded in the files at the Home Office Forensic Science Laboratory in Chepstow where he worked. At Hayward's request he checked the records. He found no record for X in 1987 or 1986 and revised his opinion. He decided that it was probably South Wales Police who brought X to his attention. Had he only checked the records for 1985, he would have found X's records from the attack on X by Margaret Liptovari. If a haptoglobin result had been obtained in the earlier test, then X's Hp result could have been corroborated. But it should be pointed out that the difference between the results Hp 2 and Hp 2-1 was such that you would not expect a handling error. However, with all the problems that have plagued this ill-starred inquiry, corroboration of X's haptoglobin result would be desirable and not impossible even at this late stage as police could simply check the files at Chepstow on the earlier case.

Secondly, it is highly surprising that Home Office Forensic Science laboratories appear not to have checked their own records to see if they had ever dealt with a person with the rare blood group that they were looking for. Had that been done when they realised that the murderer possessed a very rare blood group, X would have emerged as the prime suspect as early as March 1988.

However, Hayward explained that if the haptoglobin mixed, then it was strange that the AK factors didn't. Lynette's AK factor was recorded as AK 2-1, whereas the killer's was AK 1. While it might have been strange that they did not mix, it was not impossible. In fact, this has been known to have happened before. Perhaps the blood on the right sock could resolve the issue. Like the jeans, it differed in only one respect, that of the haptoglobin. This was reported as Hp 2. Hayward reported that he examined the photographs, but no recognisable result could be obtained from it. He pointed out that analysis of photographs is not the best way to verify results as it was possible that a result was obtained during the actual test that was not adequately reproduced on the photograph. This means that the Hp result on the sock cannot be confirmed or refuted, which brings us back to the jeans.

If Whiteside had conducted the further work on stain four of the jeans before he made his statements he did not report his findings indicating a likely mix in them, nor did he make a further statement about it after the work was completed. It was not until his conversation with John Hayward that the defence became aware of this. And there was no corroboration that X's haptoglobin was the Hp 2-1 that it was reported as, even though corroboration was almost certainly available at the time. Suffice to say, there was substantial uncertainty over the only blood factor of X's blood group that was reportedly different from that found in the flat. Consequently, X could not be safely eliminated on the basis of this alleged difference until and unless his Hp 2-1 result is corroborated even though the likelihood of making such a handling error was remote.

However, even if X was entitled to be eliminated on the basis of the haptoglobin results, there was still Mr Y whose blood group was effectively a perfect match to the blood on the sock. In fact, there were at least three others in addition to X and Y who were eliminated by DNA and not on blood grouping tests.

Mr Y's blood group was recorded as AB; Le a-b+; PGM 1+1-; EAP B/CB; Hp 2;

Gc 2-1s; AK 1. He had all six blood factors that were found on Lynette's sock. So, he possessed all five that were reported as being on her jeans and if the mixture on the jeans is taken into account he possessed all six factors that were deposited on the jeans by the killer. On any view, Y was a person whose blood group meant that he had to be investigated.

The Home Office Forensic Science Laboratory at Chepstow was where the overwhelming majority of the blood grouping tests were carried out. Dr Whiteside was the expert in charge of this side of the inquiry. He personally conveyed Mr Y's blood sample to Dr Prance for DNA testing on August 5th 1988. This strongly suggests that his blood sample must have been grouped before then and that Dr Whiteside had taken a personal interest in Mr Y.

On July 29th 1988 DC Allan Barker took a statement from Mr Y who was twenty-four years old at the time of the murder. There was nothing remotely incriminating in the statement. Y claimed that he had never ever seen Lynette White. He insisted that he had never been with prostitutes in the Cardiff area and had never been to 7 James Street.

Nevertheless, the discovery of his blood group would have confirmed beyond any doubt that Mr Y was a person who had to be looked into thoroughly at the very least.

In fact, police belatedly confirmed that they had compiled a dossier on Y, but the defence missed his importance for the appeal, so that dossier was not discovered by defence lawyers and has never been presented to a court. Had the defence realised that his blood group was every bit as important as that of X, if not more so, they would undoubtedly have investigated him themselves and the truth about his possible involvement in the murder of Lynette White could have been established beyond reasonable doubt.

However, the curse of DNA struck again. On October 18th Y was one of the men quite rightly eliminated by Dr Prance as the source of SS2 and SS12. In this case, however, it was potentially more worrying than any of the other eliminations for reasons which will become apparent below. His blood group was extremely rare. While there was some argument over the haptoglobin factor in X's case, the only difference in Y's case was a factor called Lewis (Le). This was no ordinary factor, as blood experts like Dr Whiteside would have known. The importance of Lewis is that it would only be detected in semen, saliva, or in a sample of liquid blood. The blood on the jeans and the sock had had more than nineteen hours to dry before the body was even discovered.

In other words, no matter how sensitive the tests for Lewis were on the blood in the flat, it ***would not and could not*** have been detected unless the relevant bloodstains had failed to dry. Consequently, the only difference between Mr Y's blood group and the one that was detected on the sock was a factor that could not have been detected on it. The implications of this for the Lynette White Inquiry are very serious. It means that South Wales Police actually considered a man whose blood group was effectively a ***perfect match*** to the blood in the flat and that they were aware of this information long before the Cardiff Five were arrested.

However, it ought to be pointed out that police would later confirm that Mr Y was not in the same league as X in terms of form and that he was never viewed as a serious suspect, or even as a suspect at all. He had been brought to their attention by the Chepstow laboratory because of his blood group. But this should not be confused with a presumption of guilt. There are approximately sixteen thousand people in Britain who possess the same blood group as the murderer. Possessing that blood group *does not* and *cannot* prove guilt.

Police were never able to link him to the scene of the crime or any of the crucial witnesses in this inquiry, or to Lynette herself. Although it would appear that there was absolutely no evidence capable of tying him to Lynette's murder, he could not be eliminated on blood grouping evidence, and his elimination on DNA cannot be relied on.

And if the results exonerate X and Y, there were yet more suspects worthy of further investigation who had occurred to police, but who were once again prematurely eliminated on DNA. Mr Y was not alone in being eliminated on DNA on October 18th 1988. There were three others whom I shall refer to as B, C and D.

B gave hair and saliva samples for blood grouping and DNA tests. His saliva sample was grouped as AB. No other blood factors were reported. On the strength of this result he cannot be excluded on blood grouping tests as the blood deposited in the flat contained the AB factor. B made a statement on July 22nd 1988 which was listed in the unused material. It is not known how seriously police were interested in him.

C is more mysterious. He gave hair and mouth samples. These appear to have been reserved for DNA testing alone as the list of blood groups of suspects submitted to the Chepstow laboratory before the arrest of the Cardiff Five makes no mention of his blood group. If he made a statement to police either it was not disclosed to the defence or it was in the unused material and the defence saw no importance in it.

But D is the most interesting of them. He made a statement to police on August 1st 1988, admitting that he used prostitutes, but the summary of its contents lacked detail. He gave a blood sample on the same day to DC Taylor of West Mercia Police. Taylor wasted no time at all in conveying that sample to Dr Prance. His sample appears not to have been subjected to blood grouping tests. This is surprising as, regardless of DNA, the blood group of the killer was a significant clue and grouping tests had eliminated several people. It is baffling that no grouping tests were conducted on this man unless tests were conducted at the Birmingham laboratory, but the results of such tests, if they did take place, were not among those disclosed to the defence and were not recorded in a list of blood grouping results of people submitted to the Chepstow laboratory up to December 1st 1988.

On any view, D was important. He lived outside of South Wales Police's jurisdiction, but had come to their attention. It appears that South Wales Police asked their colleagues in West Mercia to collect the sample and deliver it as a matter of urgency. He appears to have been one of the first suspects to be DNA tested. The fact that police appear to have wanted him to be tested as a priority suggests that he was an important suspect.

Suffice to say, B, C and D were not eliminated on blood grouping tests. Nor can their eliminations on DNA be relied on. It is likely that police would have compiled dossiers on them as well. As with Y, the contents of such dossiers remain behind closed doors, although this is not surprising as police would have been quite rightly satisfied with their eliminations on DNA in terms of the knowledge that was available to them at the time of their eliminations as the source of the blood on SS2 and more importantly SS12.

So it is not known if the investigation into these three men unearthed compelling evidence of innocence or whether the curse of DNA struck again. But there is indisputable evidence that every elimination on DNA cannot be relied on. This means that everybody eliminated on DNA should be looked into again unless there are other reasons for eliminating them. The point that they were eliminated should provide a good starting point for further inquiries. Either these people should be conclusively tied to the murder of Lynette White or they should be eliminated on an entirely safe and satisfactory basis.

But it should not have come to this. Although there can be no doubt that in October 1988 police were quite right to eliminate Mr Y on DNA, just as nearly a month later they were equally right to eliminate Mr X for the same reason, these eliminations were not as reliable as police then believed them to be.

In April 1989 Dr Prance revealed that he could not exclude Lynette as a possible source for the blood on SS12. This meant that none of the DNA eliminations could be relied on. Either police did not fully realise the significance of Dr Prance's opinion, or they understood it only too well, but applied this knowledge selectively. Undoubtedly, this information meant that the Cardiff Five could not be eliminated as the source of the blood on SS12 on the basis of DNA, but this applied to everybody else who had been eliminated by DNA as well, including X, Y, B, C and D, but neither the police nor the Crown saw fit to apply this information to any of the other suspects who had been eliminated by DNA.

CHAPTER 13

Re-Opened

Vacuous Responses

I was now convinced that the DNA eliminations were wholly unreliable. But what could be done about it? It was now February 1995. DNA profiling had been in its infancy when X, Y and others were prematurely eliminated. It had now matured. The mistakes that had been made in the Lynette White Inquiry would not now be repeated. And it was possible to put the Lynette White Inquiry back on the right track.

I had the great good fortune to make the acquaintance of a forensic scientist named Mark Webster of Forensic Science Consultancy in February 1995. At my request he considered the scientific evidence in the Lynette White Inquiry. He informed me that even now, seven years after Lynette's murder, it was still possible to obtain useful information from DNA profiling.

On April 26th 1995 I contacted Alun Michael, JP, MP, the Shadow Minister for Home Affairs, in whose constituency this appalling murder took place. I told him that the Home Office ought to re-open the Lynette White Inquiry and ensure that the more sophisticated DNA tests be conducted under Home Office supervision.

But before that was done the Home Office should order an external police force to seize the evidence to make sure that vital evidence was not destroyed by South Wales Police either by accident or design. I was aware that during the appeal of the Darvell brothers it had emerged that police had destroyed both the photograph and negative of a bloodstained handprint which belonged to the real murderer of Sandra Phillips and did not belong to either Paul or Wayne Darvell. This was incomprehensible at best and did not foster confidence in that police force.

The murder of Sandra Phillips had been investigated by the very same force which investigated the murder of Lynette White. Consequently, I felt that there was a real risk that vital paperwork may be destroyed. I had also seen re-investigations of other cases either reduced to going through the motions or becoming attempts to reconvict the original defendants.

I also appraised Michael of the results of my investigation into the quality of the forensic evidence in the Lynette White Inquiry. Mark Webster had promised to send a report on the forensic evidence in the Lynette White Inquiry as soon as he could. On May 8th 1995 his report was completed. It backed up my concerns about the mishandling and misinterpretation of the forensic evidence and indicated that further DNA testing was still possible even now. His report could not be ignored.

It was now clear that advances in forensic science raised many exciting possibilities. Scientists had discovered the benefits of the Polymerase Chain Reaction (PCR). Each person's DNA consists of two strands which are intertwined. These strands are inherited from each parent. PCR enabled these strands to be separated and amplified, a process which occurs naturally in the creation of babies.

PCR is probably the greatest advance in DNA testing systems. It enables DNA tests to be conducted from small samples. However, there are drawbacks. As with dust which can rise as well as fall, so can PCR generated DNA. This creates the possibility of cross-contamination if the testing area is not thoroughly cleaned before new tests are undertaken. But careful procedures can reduce the possibility of such contamination.

Another problem with PCR is that if too many cycles are attempted artefacts will be generated as well as DNA which will cause problems with interpreting the results. However, laboratories are required to optimise their procedures for each system to achieve the best results for that particular system. Consequently, although different laboratories may use different methods of extracting the original DNA, purifying it, methods of amplification (singleplexing or multiplexing), number of cycles, consistency and length of electrophoretic gels and methods of detection, as long as the conditions are properly optimised for each system, the method of amplification will be the most significant consideration, as will be seen below. However, differences in the protocols used by different laboratories may impact slightly on the likelihood of obtaining results.

In order to amplify DNA through PCR there must be original DNA to work with. PCR cannot be conducted from nylon membranes. This means that if the samples still exist and there is still original DNA on them, it would be possible even now to conduct the most sophisticated tests now available.

There are several tests that would be worth conducting even at this late stage. SLP DNA profiling could be attempted. STR typing, the state of the art test, could also be tried. And the samples could be subjected to the more sophisticated sex determination test known as the amelogenin test. This test reveals the proportion of male to female blood in mixtures and could resolve the issue of the cocktail theory once and for all. Clearly, PCR based testing offered several possibilities of obtaining useful results.

Alun Michael was now convinced that my concerns should be investigated. He was particularly interested in the fact that even now it was possible to obtain new forensic evidence which could identify the real killer. There was not and could not be any reason to refuse to re-open the Lynette White Inquiry. A respected forensic scientist and the Shadow Minister for Home Affairs shared my concerns and agreed that they should be investigated.

On May 24th Alun Michael wrote to the Home Secretary, Michael Howard, enclosing my letter to him, Mark Webster's expert report and a guide to DNA. He asked Howard to seize the evidence, order fresh inquiries by an external police force and conduct the more sophisticated DNA tests that we had requested.[1] He believed that the Home Office were in the best position to resolve the issues.

On June 22nd the Home Office Minister, David MacLean, replied to Alun Michael. It was not the reply we had expected. MacLean noted my willingness to help but had concluded that this was not a matter where it was appropriate for Michael Howard to intervene. MacLean went on to say that the investigation of crime is an operational matter for the Chief Constable of the force where the offence was committed and that the execution of their duties by police officers is also a matter for the Chief Constable of that force.

MacLean then said that it was up to the Chief Constable of South Wales Police to decide what further inquiries should be undertaken and by whom. He suggested that I should bring my concerns to the direct attention of the Chief Constable so he could decide what to do.

On August 31st Alun Michael replied to David MacLean's letter. Michael suggested that MacLean had not understood the action that was sought. He pointed out that there were specific concerns in relation to this case and its history. Michael asked MacLean to personally review the case that he had made out in his letter to Michael Howard and offered to meet with MacLean to discuss it before he made a final decision.

In MacLean's absence another Home Office Minister, Ann Widdecombe, replied to Michael's letter on September 18th. It was much the same as MacLean's letter. Widdecombe assured Michael that careful consideration had been given to the issues raised in my submission and that they had fully understood the action wanted. Widdecombe went on to say, "...we remain of the opinion that the *only appropriate* course of action for Mr Sekar is to bring his concerns about the investigation to the direct attention of the Chief Constable." [my emphasis]

This compounded the original error. It is difficult to imagine a more inappropriate course of action than the one suggested by MacLean and re-iterated by Widdecombe. At the very least, the Home Office should have used its discretion to ensure that an external police force carried out the new investigation. But there is no duty obliging the Home Office to do so. It has been done before in several cases including ones investigated by South Wales Police such as the case of the Darvell brothers. Royal Commissions have been ordered following miscarriage cases or there have been judicial inquiries such as the May Inquiry into the Guildford Four and Maguire Seven cases. Consequently, the Home Office have the power to do what was requested. But Widdecombe was having none of it. She even offered to forward the papers to the Chief Constable of South Wales Police.

---

[1] The forensic concerns which Alun Michael submitted to Michael Howard are published in Appendix 1.

On September 22nd Alun Michael replied to Widdecombe's letter. He pointed out that they were still missing the point as the Home Office had responsibility for the scientific services which was crucial to the investigation of this case. Michael insisted that the course set out in his original letter to Michael Howard was the correct approach. That said, he asked them to send the papers on to the Chief Constable, but asked that the outcome of his investigation be forwarded to both Howard and himself.

On October 2nd I agreed to let them send the papers on because if I refused it meant that my submission would be effectively stymied by the Home Office unless they could be forced into adopting the approach that Michael had suggested. But that was a time consuming exercise with no guarantee of success.

I sent Widdecombe a revised version of my original letter to Alun Michael to try to clarify some of the issues that had been raised. However, despite re-iterating my willingness to co-operate with any investigation into this extraordinary case I remain convinced that this was completely the wrong way to investigate all the concerns that had been raised. Recent research shows that the public have little confidence in the police investigating themselves. They have even less confidence in the same force investigating itself.

Re-opened

I contacted Lynette's natural mother, Peggy Pesticcio, and appraised her of my concerns. She took an active interest in my findings and adopted them. And she got her own MP, Rhodri Morgan, involved. On October 4th he wrote to both Michael Howard and to Assistant Chief Constable (ACC) Bob Evans outlining Mrs Pesticcio's concerns. He was particularly interested in getting the police to agree to conduct the more sophisticated DNA tests. Now both Alun Michael and Rhodri Morgan were taking an active interest.

On October 11th the papers were forwarded to South Wales Police. ACC Evans wrote to Alun Michael on October 17th to tell him that he would conduct a preliminary review of the points that I had made and when he was clear on the forensic issues that I had raised he would be in touch again. The Lynette White Inquiry had all but been re-opened. And it would later emerge that October 25th was a very significant date for the Lynette White Inquiry as Dr Gill and six colleagues at the Birmingham laboratory had written an article for a renowned scientific journal, the *International Journal of Legal Medicine*, which would prove to have very important ramifications on the scientific techniques which were now available.

October gave way to November. DCS Phil Jones replied to Rhodri Morgan's letter to Bob Evans on November 6th. Jones assured Morgan that they were now taking the issue forward. Jones said that all samples tested under old procedures relating to serious undetected crimes would be considered for more advanced testing and that included the samples obtained in the Lynette White Inquiry. Jones added that he was seeking advice from the Forensic Science Service (FSS) about this and would arrange for senior detectives to meet me to examine my findings.

On November 15th DI Reginald Hearse and DS Dave Knight met me in London. I outlined my concerns for them. I accepted that in terms of the scientific knowledge available to them in 1988 they were within their rights to eliminate X and Y on DNA, but stressed that before the trials those eliminations had been called into question and should have been investigated then.

That said, I went through the various DNA testing systems that were available to them. I began by explaining that PCR based DNA testing gave them the best hope of obtaining useful forensic evidence. If PCR succeeded they would be able to conduct STR typing, SLP DNA profiling and the amelogenin test which is the more sophisticated sex determination test. This test, part of seven sophisticated DNA based tests used on the Home Office's National DNA database also known as Second Generation Multiplex (SGM), was developed by Dr Peter Gill, together with Pavel Ivanov, Armando Mannucci and Kevin Sullivan. It is now possible to tell exactly how much male material there is in a mixture of male and female blood. Consequently, the more advanced sex determination test combined with adequate DNA profiling would be able to determine one way or another if the cocktail theory had happened or not. That meant that Psaila's blood could either be positively included or excluded once and for all.

If these tests yielded useful results they could be compared with DNA profiles obtained from Lynette White or anyone of interest. If a match was obtained to anyone bar Lynette, then this would provide useful evidence against that person or persons. But if no match was obtained then the results could be put on to the Home Office's DNA database where a match might be found now or in the future.

But if PCR did not work even though, despite difficulties caused by heavy degradation and treatment with Ninhydrin, there is no reason why it should fail, they could still obtain useful results by testing the nylon membranes using single-locus probes. Although this had been tried and had failed on the jeans in December 1988, it is possible that such testing could work even now and therefore useful results could be obtained and compared with the DNA profiles of the people the police were interested in - indeed, they could be compared with the DNA profiles of anybody who has been tested using single-locus probes provided such results still exist.

That said, I pointed out that if no useful forensic results were obtained by any of the new tests, the Lynette White Inquiry should still be actively re-opened as the original causes for concern over the DNA eliminations would not have been disproved. This means that the DNA evidence in this case should be thrown out in total and that the eliminations of all suspects on DNA was no longer reliable. The authorities had to deal with that information.

They promised to look into what I had said and assured me that they would seek advice from the FSS to take my causes for concern forward.

Things then went quiet for a couple of months. On January 12th 1996 Rhodri Morgan wrote to DCS Jones asking him what guidance had been received from the FSS and what the results of their discussion with me were. Most importantly of all he asked if the more sophisticated DNA tests were going to be used on the samples in the Lynette White Inquiry.

However, on January 15th the *Independent* reported that the Lynette White Inquiry had been re-opened and it was understood that more sophisticated DNA tests would be conducted. It was now public knowledge that the inquiry had been re-opened. Police would also realise that this inquiry would be subject to media interest.[1]

DCS Jones replied quickly to Morgan's latest letter. On January 19th he confirmed that officers had met me and that they had received advice from the FSS. That said, he assured Morgan that he intended to keep Mrs Pesticcio fully informed of developments and would arrange to meet her to discuss all the points that I had raised after the testing had been completed. And on January 22nd a revised version of the article written by Dr Gill and his colleagues was received by the prestigious *International Journal of Legal Medicine*.

Judicial Review

Once the Home Office had refused to act upon my submission things had gone as far as they could in my name. The only way to get the Home Secretary to follow the path suggested by Alun Michael and myself was to judicially review the Home Office's abdication of its responsibilities. Judicial review would be difficult, if not impossible, in my name as in legal terms I had no interest in the case. But they could not suggest that Mrs Pesticcio had no interest in it.

Shortly after receiving Mrs Widdecombe's disappointing letter I appraised Mrs Pesticcio of the facts that I had uncovered during my investigation of this case. I convinced her that what had been discovered needed to be investigated further, but in order to get the causes for concern properly investigated she would have to adopt the submission. She did so. That made Mrs Widdecombe's decision of September 18th 1995 judicially reviewable.

On October 27th Mrs Pesticcio made a statement outlining her concerns and requesting legal aid to begin the process of judicially reviewing the Home Office's refusal of the original submission. Her statement detailed the reasons why the current investigation by South Wales Police was inappropriate. It was sent to the South Wales Area Legal Aid Office. But on November 20th legal aid was refused on the grounds that Mrs Pesticcio had not shown that the Home Secretary's refusal had been unlawful, irrational, or procedurally improper.

Mrs Pesticcio was not content to leave it at that. She exercised her right to appeal against the refusal of legal aid which was heard on January 4th 1996 by an appeal panel consisting of three solicitors and a barrister. I attended the appeal and spoke on her behalf.

I clarified Mrs Pesticcio's position to the appeal panel that she wanted to judicially review Mrs Widdecombe's decision rather than that of David MacLean.

---

[1] The report in the *Independent* and a later one in *Wales On Sunday* can be seen in Appendix 2.

This was because she did not want to rush into judicial review. It was a last resort that she was adopting only because of the importance of this case and the fact that this approach was the last chance to get the Lynette White Inquiry back on an even keel. It was too important to just sit back and hope that things turned out okay.

I suggested that the Home Secretary's refusal was irrational as the current investigating force was the same force who got the original inquiry wrong in the first place. They had a vested interest in exonerating themselves. I pointed out that if evidence of police incompetence or malpractice was unearthed during the new inquiry it might be suppressed in order to hide police embarrassment. The appeal panel asked if that was likely to happen given the fact that the Chief Constable of South Wales Police was now involved in the new investigation. They were told that with all due respect it was doubtful that any officer who had decided to destroy or suppress evidence was likely to tell her/his superior officers that he or she was doing that or planned to do it.

That said, the appeal panel wanted to know if we would accept a discredited force such as the West Midlands conducting the new investigation. I replied that I would as they had no reason to act dubiously in this investigation canteen culture notwithstanding. If I had said no, they would then have been able to say that every police force had its share of complaints, so there was nothing to be gained by bringing in an external force.

In an ideal world the causes for concern that have been identified should be investigated by a public inquiry without police conducting the actual investigation as numerous others have identified a culture of policing which includes covering up alleged wrongdoing by fellow officers. But this is not an ideal world.

Justice should not only be done it should be seen to be done. For the investigation into the original submission to be seen to be fair it had to be seen to be impartial. It is therefore as much in South Wales Police's interests as it is in Mrs Pesticcio's for the new investigation to be seen to be impartial and fair to all concerned.

We left the appeal confident that we had won the argument and that legal aid would soon be forthcoming. We were not to be disappointed. But time was running out as judicial reviews must have the grounds lodged with the High Court within three months. Even allowing for the time lost awaiting a date for the appeal there was not much time left.

This is iniquitous as complex cases like this could either fail because of the time constraints or they can be inadequately prepared due to lack of understanding of the specific scientific issues and fail due to a perceived lack of evidential merit when having to work against the clock. But judges tend to be inflexible on time constraints despite the specific problems associated with this particular case.

But worse still, there is no duty obliging the Home Secretary to follow the path outlined by Alun Michael and myself. He has the discretionary powers, but cannot be forced to use them. Effectively, it means that the Home Secretary cannot be compelled by law to follow the path outlined by Alun Michael even if that is in practice the only realistic way to proceed which is fair to everyone concerned.

A Pleasant Surprise

On May 24th 1996 a meeting took place between Peggy Pesticcio, her solicitor David Evans, DCS Phil Jones, ACC Paul Wood and myself. Wood wanted to establish if a complaint was being made against any of his officers. Evans told him that we were not making a complaint at this time.

DCS Jones stated that the Cardiff Five were innocent and that Mr X's haptoglobin result had been corroborated as Hp 2-1 by an incident three years earlier. This was important as it establishes Mr X's innocence to all intents and purposes. Suffice to say, the only way that X could remain in the frame is by applying Dr Whiteside's implausible cocktail theory to him. But X's innocence does not affect the fact that the better practice would have been to supply the Cardiff Five's defence lawyers with complete disclosure of police interest in him as a suspect.

Jones then pointed out that Mr Y was not a villain and that their original investigation into him and a subsequent one necessitated by the submission had not produced any evidence linking him to the flat, victim or witnesses. He insisted that Y was never a suspect let alone a prime suspect. Jones established that Y had nothing in his personality to indicate that he was capable, let alone responsible, of murdering Lynette.

He claimed that Y had been brought to their attention by the Chepstow laboratory because of his blood group. He was simply a person to be traced, interviewed and eliminated. This suggests that it is unlikely that Y was involved in the murder of Lynette White.

I should point out that I had never accused either X or Y or anyone else of murdering Lynette. It had always been my case that the DNA eliminations of all suspects were unreliable and that evidence which could have compromised the integrity of the original investigation had not been considered by any court. Consequently, anyone eliminated on DNA alone should be looked at again and either be tied conclusively to Lynette's murder or be safely eliminated - nothing less will suffice.

This still leaves B, C and D as worthy of further investigation. They were also eliminated on DNA, but there is no record of eliminations by blood grouping. It may be that they can be eliminated by other means, like good alibis. As with X and Y, I simply question the validity of their eliminations on DNA.

The police assured us that they badly wanted to solve Lynette's murder. But they recognised that they needed new evidence to clear it up. They stressed that somebody must know who did it, but after eight years it was unlikely that anyone would come forward now. The police are seeking evidence that could lead to a conviction. This leaves advances in scientific technology as their best hope of solving it. They had sent the wallpaper sample SS12 to the Aldermaston laboratory for testing. Unfortunately, the attempt to obtain DNA evidence using STR typing failed, possibly due to degradation and chemical treatment for fingerprinting.

I raised the issue of saving DNA for future testing as advances in DNA technology suggest that some time in the future a DNA testing system will be developed that will be able to obtain a complete profile even from heavily degraded samples like the ones that exist in this case. ACC Wood was not averse to my suggestion of saving five nanograms of DNA from each sample provided there was enough DNA. However, he stressed that they did not want to suspend testing; they wanted to test the samples now and if that meant that there would not be enough for further testing so be it.

I suggested that they consider testing abroad as there have been considerable advances in DNA testing systems elsewhere in Europe. But they were adamant that Aldermaston was a centre of excellence. That said, they assured us that the inquiry would remain open and that they would do everything in their power to bring it to a successful conclusion.

They then turned to the criticisms of police contained in my letter to Alun Michael. Jones was clearly offended by the suggestion that they might destroy paperwork. However, that has to be seen in the context that it was written in.

It came in the light of my discovering evidence which questioned the integrity of the original investigation. Vital paperwork had been destroyed in other cases such as the contemporaneous notes of police interviews with Bob Maynard and Reg Dudley which contained hotly disputed admissions which convicted them of the murders of Billy Mosely and Micky Cornwall despite serious discrepancies in the case against them, although such papers should not have been destroyed. In fairness to the Metropolitan Police, they have acknowledged that these contemporaneous notes should not have been destroyed, but insisted that there was no sinister forces at work. And in the case of the Darvell brothers vital evidence - a photograph and negative of a bloodstained palmprint - had been destroyed. The Darvell brothers were freed by the Court of Appeal a few months before the appeal of the Cardiff Three. Suffice to say, at that point in time there was no reason to trust them to get it right second time round and I was concerned that any investigation of the whole case by South Wales Police would lack impartiality and may become nothing more than an attempt to exonerate their colleagues and reconvict the Cardiff Five. But having listened to ACC Wood and DCS Jones I am convinced that they have no intention of trying to reconvict the Cardiff Five.

Not Quite The Final Word

In the light of the stance taken by ACC Wood and DCS Jones, Mrs Pesticcio instructed her solicitor to stop judicial review proceedings. It was not in her interests to pursue it any further at this time. Police were clearly trying to solve the murder of her daughter and their investigation was not going to follow the pattern of the first discredited investigation. Her main concern was finding the person who killed Lynette not the methods that were used to build a case against the Cardiff Five. Once it became clear that the new investigation was not going to repeat the mistakes of the original inquiry there was nothing for her to gain by continuing her action against the police.

Meanwhile, the re-opened Lynette White Inquiry will continue to hunt for her killer. And even though there is the disappointment of not obtaining any result from the attempt to STR type SS12, it should be borne in mind that advances in forensic science mean that this need not be the final word.

ACC Wood was quite right in pointing out that the Aldermaston laboratory was a centre of excellence as far as DNA techniques are concerned. But there is a proviso and an important one at that. In Britain the FSS Laboratory in Aldermaston, which would later be closed down for financial reasons, is one of the most advanced in DNA techniques, but that leaves the rest of the world. Advances in DNA testing have been achieved in the USA and in Europe.

Scientists based at Aldermaston favour multiplexing. This consists of conducting several PCRs at the same time. The multiplexing methods used at Aldermaston are among the best in the world. In the overwhelming majority of cases multiplexing will yield useful results. But there are borderline cases, ones where DNA is in short supply or degraded. Naturally, it is essential to make the best use of the available DNA especially when there is not much to start with.

Take the case of Jack Unterweger, Austria's first serial killer, for example. Unterweger committed as many as eleven murders of young women, mainly prostitutes, in three different countries. In ten of these cases he had successfully removed all traces of his victims from his cars. But in the case of Blanka Bočková he had not been quite so careful. Police found one hair root, which contained a small amount of DNA, nine billionths of a gram, in the seat of a car that had been plundered for parts after Unterweger had driven it while in what was then Czechoslovakia.

It was sent to a renowned Forensic Science Institute in Berne and subjected to PCR based tests. The results of those tests indicated that Bočková could not be excluded and offered a high degree of certainty that the hair had indeed belonged her. It was the only forensic evidence that was ever discovered against Unterweger, who was convicted of nine of the eleven murders that he was charged with, including the September 24th 1990 murder of Blanka Bočková. Unterweger was sentenced to life imprisonment without possibility of parole. But within ten hours of being sentenced in July 1994 he hanged himself in prison.

The importance of the Unterweger case to this book is the performance of the Swiss laboratory. This was a case where there was only a limited amount of DNA. There was no scope for errors of any kind. They performed a variety of PCR based tests and produced important results. Without this evidence the case against Unterweger would have been considerably weaker and entirely circumstantial. It could easily have resulted in a particularly vicious serial killer remaining at large. The Swiss laboratory did a first rate job with the limited DNA that they had to work with.

And there are other laboratories where remarkable results are being obtained. Professor Bernd Brinkmann, Direktor des Instituts für Rechtsmedizin der Universität Münster in Germany is among the world's leading experts in the field. And he has tested samples in British cases as well as given evidence in British courts.

Professor Brinkmann has managed to obtain useful results from less material and from samples of such poor quality that British laboratories were unable to obtain any results. His technique involves a greater degree of amplification of DNA by PCR, thereby allowing him to obtain results from smaller bloodstains. His method is more sensitive than the multiplexing methods used at Aldermaston. He favours singleplexing. This consists of conducting the PCRs individually rather than several simultaneously. This enables him to generate more DNA than is obtained by conventional multiplexing. The only significant disadvantage of singleplexing compared to multiplexing is that it is more time consuming. But the advantage of it is that singleplexing has been known to succeed where multiplexing has failed.

Brinkmann's techniques are undoubtedly more sensitive than those used by the FSS and they are well suited to the needs of the Lynette White Inquiry where there is a limited amount of DNA of dubious quality which failed to yield useful results when SS12 was recently tested at the FSS Laboratory in Aldermaston.

On August 12th 1996 Professor Brinkmann confirmed that singleplexing can still be efficient in borderline cases where multiplexing had failed. The Lynette White Inquiry is one case where the original samples are of borderline quality at best. Brinkmann wrote that the chemical treatment of the samples with Ninhydrin and the age of the bloodstains will not substantially affect the results. He also wrote, "I'm ***absolutely optimistic in a case like this*** that a result ***will*** be obtainable." [my emphasis]

In the vast majority of cases, testing at Aldermaston would be sufficient. But we already know that this is a borderline case. The Aldermaston laboratory has already failed to obtain a result from SS12. Consequently, unless this sample is sent to Professor Brinkmann no evidence at all can be obtained from it. Therefore there can be no justification for failing to send it to Germany. And if Professor Brinkmann's techniques succeed in obtaining a DNA profile from it, that would prove that singleplexing is undoubtedly more sensitive than multiplexing. And it would raise the question of why there is no British forensic science laboratory that can conduct singleplexing to the level of amplification of DNA achieved by Professor Brinkmann. Surely, the more sensitive tests should be readily available if only to deal with borderline cases like this one more rapidly. That must be in everybody's interests.

And it should also be pointed out that recent advances in DNA testing systems suggest that further progress is likely to be made. For example, the Human Genome Project aims to examine the whole of the DNA chain. It is expected that on current progress scientists may be in a position to do so by the year 2005. If and when this is achieved it is likely that a DNA testing system based on the entire chain will not be that long in coming. And as PCR based testing shows, DNA tests can be conducted from as little as one nanogram of DNA so future advances in PCR may be able to work from even less DNA some time soon.

Consequently, it is possible that some time in the future a DNA testing system will be developed that will definitely obtain useful results even from heavily degraded samples like the ones in this case. Indeed, STR typing has been known to work on a fourteen year old sample that was stored at room temperature. And even if no match can be declared the results should be put on the Home Office's new National DNA Database. Then police can wait for the killer to identify himself sooner or later.

Professor Brinkmann's techniques offer yet more reason for optimism that useful DNA evidence can be obtained that will unmask Lynette's real killer at long last. In fact, they offer the last realistic chance of obtaining useful forensic evidence now and because they use less source DNA than multiplexing they offer a better chance of saving valuable DNA pending further advances in testing systems. The case for using singleplexing rather than multiplexing in this case is overwhelming.

At our previous meeting in May 1996 DCS Jones promised both Mrs Pesticcio and myself that they would arrange a meeting for both of us with the forensic scientists. However, just prior to the meeting Mrs Pesticcio claims that police told her that she would have to come alone as the room that they had booked in the Chepstow laboratory was too small for me to come as well.

On September 4th police met Mrs Pesticcio to appraise her of progress in their investigations. She was told that further testing at Aldermaston had also been unsuccessful. However, she wanted the samples to be tested in Germany. She was assured that Aldermaston was a centre of excellence in DNA techniques, but if she wanted Brinkmann's techniques to be used then police would ensure that they would send any sample which failed to yield a result at Aldermaston to Professor Brinkmann.

Mrs Pesticcio claims that she was told that there would be difficulties interpreting any results Professor Brinkmann obtained and that he could not give evidence in British courts. If she really was told this it is baffling for reasons which will become apparent below as such claims are demonstrably false.

Since 1989 there have been a series of exercises aimed at standardising protocols and DNA testing systems throughout Europe. The FSS have been regularly represented in these exercises and Professor Brinkmann's laboratory have also participated in them as have several other European forensic science laboratories. These exercises were conducted under the auspices of the European DNA Profiling group (EDNAP) which has now been incorporated into the International Society for Forensic Haemogenetics.[1]

The results of these exercises were that simple loci (target areas within the DNA chain) were suitable for adoption as common loci throughout Europe. These exercises resulted in certain loci being adopted at a European level as core systems routinely used in forensic casework. All but the last of three EDNAP exercises on STRs up to 1996 took place before I had contacted Professor Brinkmann regarding the Lynette White Inquiry. The EDNAP exercises are not the only standardisation efforts which have taken place. There have been national standardisation initiatives as well.

The importance of the EDNAP and other exercises, which are very well known in the forensic science community, to this book is that they clearly show that despite differences between the protocols of participating laboratories there is no reason to believe that the relevant samples could not have been tested in Professor Brinkmann's laboratory, especially the simple loci TH01 and VWA. And it ought to be mentioned that the FSS have developed a quadruplex system which utilises four loci which were the subject of EDNAP exercises and either adopted as common loci or deemed to be suitable candidates for standardisation before I contacted Professor Brinkmann. This means that there was no logical reason for refusing to utilise his kind offer of assistance in August 1996 and that valuable DNA need not have been wasted attempting multiplexing in circumstances where it was unlikely to yield useful results.

Suffice to say, had they taken advantage of Brinkmann's techniques when he offered and he obtained useful results, such results would not have posed problems with interpretation and could easily have been compared with DNA profiles contained in the Home Office's National DNA database as Brinkmann's laboratory tested samples at five of the seven loci used by the National DNA Database. It should also be re-iterated that it had been agreed at European level that although not every laboratory had to use identical systems, there were a number of core systems that every laboratory should use to facilitate international co-operation. And if the Professor was required to give evidence at some future trial, he is both fluent in English and has given evidence in British trials before.

Consequently, there appears to be no logical reason for any delay in testing these samples in Germany, let alone insisting on completing the current round of multiplexing before contemplating singleplexing. The cost of their decision not to utilise the Professor's techniques would be to waste eight months, resources and invaluable DNA for no apparent reason. The memory of Lynette White and society in general are entitled to know why this was allowed to happen, especially as there is only a limited supply of poor quality DNA to work with.

---

[1] Reports of the various EDNAP STR exercises have been published in *Forensic Science International* (FSI) Volumes 53, 65, 71, 78 and 86. It is also worth reading the article titled *Forensic DNA analysis in Europe: current situation and standardization efforts,* which is published in FSI Vol. 86 (1997).

Singleplexing Versus Multiplexing

Police had assured Mrs Pesticcio that no stone would be left unturned in the hunt to find Lynette's murderer. All of the crucial blood samples which did not originate from Lynette and SS12 were earmarked for testing by multiplexing and the amelogenin test. Unfortunately, none of these tests have yielded results on any of the samples tested to date. Clearly, the likelihood of obtaining useful results by multiplexing are at best unlikely.

The case for singleplexing is already compelling. In fact, given the previous history of these samples, namely that they were heavily degraded and had been treated with Ninhydrin, this case was a prime candidate for singleplexing from the start. Multiplexing may be more cost effective than singleplexing, but it has been known to fail to yield useful results before. And in those cases where this happens, multiplexing proves to be a false economy as if results are to be obtained then singleplexing has to be attempted, thereby incurring the expense of both methods of amplification. The Lynette White Inquiry was one such case where multiplexing was likely to fail and after each sample was tested and yielded no useful result the likelihood of obtaining results using this technique became less and less likely. In short, common sense tells us that there was no good reason for not beginning singleplexing after the first batch of samples had failed to produce results using multiplexing.

But this is not all, forensic scientists have been aware that singleplexing is more sensitive than multiplexing since about 1994. And it was worth remembering that as early as October 1995 Dr Gill et al had submitted an article called *A new method of STR interpretation using inferential logic - development of a criminal intelligence database* for the internationally renowned scientific journal, the *International Journal of Legal Medicine*. A revised version of this article was published in the August 1996 issue of that journal.

The relevance of that article to this book is the portion which says, *"The main purpose of using multiplexes is to speed the process of analysis. Inevitably, there may be some loss of efficiency of amplification since the conditions used are a compromise.* This has no significant implications for the database, since the operator has large quantities of undegraded DNA available for analysis. Furthermore, the DNA is never a mixture. *In casework, where the sample is less predictable, singleplexes may sometimes be used to identify difficult (e.g. degraded) samples* (i.e. singleplexing and multiplexing *are not mutually exclusive* techniques)." [my emphasis]

Remember that this article was published in the same month that Professor Brinkmann, who is involved with the *International Journal of Legal Medicine*, said that he was absolutely optimistic that a result could be obtained in a case like the Lynette White Inquiry. This article suggests that there can be little doubt that singleplexing is more sensitive than multiplexing. And it suggests that multiplexing is used more on the grounds of convenience than on the specific requirements of the samples requiring testing. The article clearly suggested that singleplexing may be used in identifying difficult or degraded samples. We know that the samples in the Lynette White Inquiry were a prime candidate for singleplexing from the start due to heavy degradation. As this information was undoubtedly known within the forensic science community it begs the question of exactly what advice the police were given in the first place? It should also be remembered that Rhodri Morgan had asked DCS Jones for this information, but had received no detailed answer in January 1996. However, as the likelihood of obtaining useful results cannot be predicted in advance, there was no harm in trying multiplexing first if only to see if it would work.

But by May 1996 it was known that multiplexing had failed on the first batch of samples tested, possibly due to degradation and treatment with Ninhydrin. Given the fact that Gill et al's article had been submitted to the *International Journal of Legal Medicine* as early as October 1995, this shows that the benefits of singleplexing were clearly known about before the Lynette White Inquiry had even been actively re-opened. This raises the question of exactly what advice the police were given over the most beneficial form of DNA amplification to attempt? It should therefore have come as no great surprise that multiplexing failed given the fact that the efficiency of DNA amplification involved is not as great as that achieved by singleplexing. And once the first batch had failed to yield useful results, it begs the question of whether further advice was sought from the FSS about which form of amplification would be most effective and if not, why not?

I forwarded Professor Brinkmann's response to the police in September 1996. And Mrs Pesticcio had also made it clear that she wanted the samples to be tested in Germany using Professor Brinkmann's techniques that same month. Although we did not know it then, a prominent expert on DNA involved in this very case agreed that singleplexing was more sensitive than multiplexing, especially in identifying difficult or degraded samples just one month earlier.

This means that by September 1996 South Wales Police were undoubtedly aware of the benefits of singleplexing as compared to multiplexing. Professor Brinkmann also suggested that if further information on his techniques was desired both Dr Gill and the CPS were aware of his methods and could be a useful source of information. In the light of the opinions expressed by Gill et al just one month earlier it begs the question of why singleplexing was not begun on all of the samples which had failed to yield results immediately?

However, no answer was forthcoming. The new year came and still no word. On January 26th 1997 *Wales On Sunday* entered the fray. It reported both my concerns and those of Mrs Pesticcio that nearly five months after police had been informed about Professor Brinkmann's techniques no news had been forthcoming. Mrs Pesticcio re-iterated her desire to have the samples tested in Germany. And *Wales On Sunday* quoted DCS Jones saying, "The work is incomplete, but when finalised, if it remains inconclusive, we will look to other sources which we believe may have the ability to contribute to the case."

To borrow DCS Jones' words, the testing on *all* samples *tested by multiplexing has been* inconclusive, so why have they not looked to other sources such as

Professor Brinkmann as there can be no doubt that without further testing these samples will not be of evidential value?

In February further information came to light. I was made aware of Gill et al's article conceding that singleplexing was more sensitive than multiplexing and a case came to trial which illustrated this point in practice. Edwin Hopkins was convicted of the brutal murder of teenager Naomi Smith. One of the samples which was DNA tested failed to yield a result by multiplexing. But DNA testing techniques in Britain had advanced to the point that singleplexing could be conducted in British laboratories. The sample which had failed to deliver a result with multiplexing was subjected to singleplexing and a result was obtained which further strengthened the case against Hopkins.

Nevertheless, it should be remembered that although the ability to conduct singleplexing now exists in Britain the level of amplification of DNA that British laboratories achieve is not as much as that of Professor Brinkmann and he has more experience of singleplexing as well.

Suffice to say, the delay in subjecting JAW12, JAW14, JAW27, RH26, RH27, SS5, SS6 and SS12 as well as SS11 and SS13, which were adjacent to SS12, to Professor Brinkmann's techniques at loci which are compatible with those used for the National DNA database is absolutely incomprehensible at best. Such testing would cost somewhere in the region of £1000 per sample plus expenses. The total cost of testing all relevant blood samples in this inquiry would therefore cost about £10,000. Although this may seem a lot of money it ought to be remembered that the authorities were prepared to waste at least £6m bringing an absolutely appalling case to trial.

In this context, £10,000 is a small price to pay. But if the police cannot or will not pay for Professor Brinkmann to test these samples, they should take advantage of the kind offer of Lee Jasper, Director of the 1990 Trust, who pledged £1000 for SS12 to be tested in Germany on September 3rd 1996 when the 1990 Trust heard of the benefits of singleplexing at Professor Brinkmann's laboratory. Consequently, it is absolutely baffling that nearly a year after further testing proved inconclusive on SS12 no further tests have been conducted on it. Suffice to say, the case for singleplexing to be conducted by Professor Brinkmann is absolutely overwhelming. And the police's failure to utilise the possibilities that Brinkmann's techniques offered them suggests that their assurance to Mrs Pesticcio that they would leave no stone unturned in the hunt for her daughter's killer has proved hollow.

Unturned Stones

In April 1997 police informed Mrs Pesticcio that the inevitable had finally happened, namely the attempt to amplify the DNA by multiplexing had failed on all samples that were tested. Unfortunately, none of the other DNA based tests that were attempted yielded any useful results. The entire DNA on the right sock was used up. And much of the precious DNA on other samples has been used as well. The police decided to attempt singleplexing in Britain rather than utilise the techniques of Professor Brinkmann. As all methods of DNA amplification will use up some DNA in the attempt there is clearly a concern that the precious DNA will be used up in such an attempt. Providing they guarantee that some of the DNA will be preserved on all relevant samples where DNA still exists there is no problem with singleplexing in Britain other than the fact that it will delay turning to Professor Brinkmann even more.

It is now more important than ever that Brinkmann gets the chance to use his techniques. We already know that there is a limited supply of DNA and that it is of poor quality. Suffice to say, impressive as Brinkmann's techniques undoubtedly are, he cannot achieve any results unless he has original DNA to work with. It therefore stands to reason that the finite supply of DNA is utilised in the most efficient manner. If the supply of DNA is used up in this second round of testing that will be the end of the matter; it will mean that no DNA evidence can be obtained and it will require a miracle to find the real killer of Lynette White. The memory of Lynette White deserves better.

The police also stressed that the use of the fingerprinting chemical Ninhydrin has caused difficulties with the DNA tests that have been attempted. This makes their reluctance to take advantage of Professor Brinkmann's offer of assistance even more baffling. It will be remembered that he believed that neither the age of the samples nor the fact that they had been treated with Ninhydrin would pose any problems and was absolutely optimistic that a result could be obtained in a case like this. Representations have been made to the police to ensure that the original DNA will not be used up before the samples can be sent to Brinkmann.

At this point Mrs Pesticcio's new solicitor, Sadiq Khan, wrote to the police reiterating Mrs Pesticcio's desire to have the samples tested in Germany. The police responded that they were conducting additional tests and that if no result was obtained they would consider further options which included contacting Professor Brinkmann.

On June 12th 1997, after a further exchange of letters, ACC Wood wrote, "Can I make it clear that this investigation continues to be taken forward by this Force and it will be a matter for senior officers here, after consultation with experts in the relevant field, to decide on the manner in which forensic examinations are to take place. This will include how any DNA test is to be carried out, who will carry out the examination process and whether *it is in the best interests of this investigation for all or some of the DNA which remains to be used up.*" [my emphasis]

Presumably, this means to trust the advice of the experts who recommended multiplexing in circumstances where singleplexing was clearly the more appropriate choice. And trust the judgement of the people who wasted invaluable DNA and several months attempting multiplexing. This case is too important to trust to luck. And as for the claim that they should be allowed to decide whether to use up all or some of the DNA it can only be stated that advances in forensic testing systems continue to be made on an ongoing basis, but in order to utilise these significant developments there must be original DNA to work with. In these circumstances the police must not use up all the remaining DNA or these novel developments will not be of any use in this inquiry. The remaining DNA must be utilised to the maximum efficiency.

For example, in 1995 the Human Genome Database at Johns Hopkins University in Baltimore, USA contained over seven thousand STR loci, more than two thousand of which are of the variety which are easiest to interpret the results of. New STR loci are discovered regularly and it is likely that more sensitive sets of loci than those currently available will be discovered and developed and will eventually be in routine use in forensic casework. This will substantially improve the power of identification that is currently available. However, the discovery of these more sensitive loci will only be of use in the hunt for Lynette's killer if there is sufficient DNA to test. It is therefore absolutely essential that the most efficient techniques are utilised and that no further DNA is wasted as it was attempting multiplexing in circumstances where singleplexing would obviously have been far more appropriate.

Consequently, it is absolutely essential that South Wales Police agree to abide by Sadiq Khan's request that at least five nanograms from each sample will be saved as these advances are meaningless if there is no DNA to work with. That should not be at the discretion of the police; it should be guaranteed if we are to benefit to the maximum potential of advances in forensic science, yet ACC Wood also wrote, "While appreciating the concern of your client (Mrs Pesticcio), it is clearly not practical, nor is it in the best interests of efficiency, for the decision making process to be shared outside of those charged with the investigation of this murder."

This is exactly why the Home Office should have assumed responsibility for the testing. The police insist on their right to decide what to do. This insistence has resulted in the waste of precious DNA, delay in utilising the well validated techniques of Professor Brinkmann and now the claim that they should have the right to use some or all of the DNA on the current round of testing. Should they be given the right to use up all the DNA the inevitable effect will be to ensure that any future advances in DNA testing systems cannot be utilised as there will be no original DNA left to amplify. And should that happen the last realistic chance to unmask Lynette's true murderer will be lost for ever. It seems preposterous that the police will not agree to save DNA pending Professor Brinkmann's techniques and further advances in forensic science.

It is also worth remembering that the recent May Inquiry into the wrongful convictions of the Maguire Seven and Guildford Four criticised forensic scientists for not ensuring that sufficient original material was stored for further testing. Consequently, it would appear that little has been learned from the errors made in those cases if the opinions of the police in the re-opened Lynette White inquiry are anything to go by. However, it should be pointed out that if the current round of testing succeeds there will be no problem with singleplexing in Britain, but if it fails there will be no way to take this case forward unless there is original DNA to work with.

In this context, it is essential that at least some original DNA is stored. After all, some European jurisdictions insist on testing being conducted by two independent laboratories. This is advisable wherever practical as independently verified results are more likely to be believed by everybody. It should be borne in mind that questions have been asked as to the independence of FSS scientists in the light of cases such as that of Judith Ward and the Maguire Seven, among others. Without impugning the integrity of any FSS scientist it is clearly desirable that an independent laboratory such as that of Professor Brinkmann conducts such testing as nobody could question his independence should a case ever come to trial. Consequently, police must agree to ensure that sufficient DNA will be preserved for further testing at Professor Brinkmann's laboratory if such tests are deemed worthwhile by him and for further more advanced testing if and when such tests become available. Nothing less will suffice.

At the very least, the police could have had the courtesy to keep Mrs Pesticcio fully informed as they had promised her on more than one occasion and why shouldn't they have the decency to explain to her exactly what they are doing and why? Then perhaps, her concerns would be satisfied.

On July 3rd ACC Wood wrote to Sadiq Khan, claiming that the force's position was clearly outlined to Mrs Pesticcio at their meeting with her on September 4th 1996 when she was told that she would be appraised of new findings in the case, but there haven't been any. Wood also stated that DI Reginald Hearse, who has recently retired, had contacted her by phone many times if only to convey an unchanged position. Wood then stated that fresh tests had been conducted on a sock Lynette was wearing, her jeans and blood from a section of skirting board and sections of wallpaper from the murder scene, but that the tests had not been completed yet. He also verified that any DNA recovered from the stains available to the FSS would be frozen and retained in that condition, but before that the samples are stored at room temperature in the laboratory. Wood concluded by inviting Khan to a meeting they and representatives of the FSS intend to have with Mrs Pesticcio soon, an invitation Khan accepted on July 10th, although the meeting has yet to be arranged.[1]

But even if the police use up all of the DNA from the relevant blood samples that need not necessarily be the end of the story. It will be remembered that semen, saliva and hairs were found at the scene of the crime. The aspermic semen was believed to be of limited importance as it could have been deposited up to six hours before Lynette's murder. However, it ought to be borne in mind that it could

[1] The aftermath of the submission to the Home Office can be seen in Appendix 2.

have been deposited far later. And even if the semen was deposited earlier, this need not necessarily exonerate the donor.

The second photofit was of a man who had been taken to 7 James Street with Lynette by the taxi driver, Glyn Sterling. In all probability this man was a punter. At the very least, it is possible that this man was the donor of the aspermic semen. If that is true, it establishes that he was a punter who could be linked to Lynette, knew of 7 James Street, what Lynette used it for and may well have had strong feelings of sexual inadequacy. His contact with Lynette may well have left him feeling even more emasculated than before. It could have provided him with a motive to try to defend his masculinity at Lynette's expense.

But even if this man was not Lynette's murderer, it is clear that the donor of the aspermic semen had contact with Lynette within hours of her death. He is a man who needs to be traced if only to eliminate him. Even now, it is possible that forensic science could help to unmask him. If the semen sample has been adequately stored it is possible through PCR based STR typing to obtain a DNA profile which could help to identify him. The aspermic nature of the semen could pose problems, but it is at least possible that a DNA profile could be obtained. However, if the police decide to attempt this, it is essential, due to the very limited quality of such DNA, that they attempt singleplexing at the most sensitive STR loci currently in routine use in forensic casework.

And if this fails there is no need for despondency. Forensic analysis of hairs has made advances in leaps and bounds. Back in 1988 the method of analysing hairs was morphological (under a microscope). This was far from ideal. But with the advent of PCR and STR new opportunities emerged. Previously, STR typing of hair depended on having hair roots containing an adequate quantity of DNA. Attempts to STR type hair shafts were promising but problematic as most loci required re-amplification which can cause artefacts to be generated. That in turn causes severe problems interpreting results.

However, further advances have been made which resulted in the discovery of another test known as mitochondrial DNA sequencing. This is the state of the art method of forensic analysis of hair and applies to both hair roots and shafts. It was recently announced that Kent Police had obtained DNA evidence using the technique in the high profile inquiry into the murders of Lin Russell and her six year-old daughter Megan and the attempted murder of ten year-old Josie Russell on July 9th 1996. The main drawback with it is the cost, but a compromise system known as mitochondrial DNA minisequencing is also available. If the hair samples still exist one of them should be tested by minisequencing and if no result is obtained then they should move on to full sequencing and do so with the other hairs as well, as the DNA is likely to be in similar, if not identical, condition in these hairs.

If results are obtained it should be remembered that all this will prove is that the donor(s) of the hairs had been in the murder flat, but not necessarily during the murder, although that would depend on precisely where the hairs were in the room. However, if the position of the hairs was not significant, identification of the donor(s) could still be useful if they had denied ever having been in 7 James Street as this would establish that they had lied.

The Lynette White Inquiry has been re-opened for over twenty months, yet there has been no mention of testing the aspermic semen or hairs with any of the advanced systems now available. South Wales Police assured Mrs Pesticcio that no stone would be left unturned in the hunt for Lynette's killer, so why have these stones been left unturned? We deserve an answer.

And these are not the only advances in forensic science worthy of mention. In June 1997 Australian scientists announced that they had succeeded in obtaining a DNA profile from fingerprints, although the fingerprint had to be taken from something that the donor was in regular contact with such as a pen. It will be some time before the technique is in routine forensic use, but, at the very least, it is likely that fingerprint specific extraction methods and other protocols will be developed which will result in greater sensitivity of testing systems for DNA obtained from fingerprints.

The likelihood is that eventually obtaining DNA from fingerprints will be routinely used in criminal investigations. Depending on the pace of such advances and the condition of the original fingerprints it is possible that this technique or a subsequent improvement on it can be utilised on the eleven sets of unidentified fingerprints found at the scene of the crime.

Nevertheless, I would remind readers that DNA evidence alone, should not be uncorroborated in any future case. Together with other evidence it can be a vital component in this case, but DNA is not infallible whatever the public perception is. The dangers of a mismatch contributing to a miscarriage of justice cannot be underestimated. But advances in DNA testing systems are not the only interesting developments in the search for the killer of Lynette White. It will be remembered that there were eleven sets of unidentified fingerprints in the murder flat as well as several other sets of prints which did not have the required number of ridge characteristics. Previously, fingerprints had to be compared by manual indexes. Technological advances offer exciting new possibilities.

For example, Kent Police use a system called PRINTRAK. This system can analyse two and a half million prints in a couple of minutes and will give a range of likely matches which can then be investigated by fingerprint experts. The fingerprints of approximately five million criminals are on record. It is no longer the incredibly time consuming task to compare the unidentified sets of fingerprints in the Lynette White Inquiry with all fingerprints on record in Britain that it once was as long as the quality of the marks are up to acceptable standards. In this context, it is worth noting that the police's fingerprint expert, DS Steele, described these marks as being of good quality in his evidence at the first trial of the Cardiff Five.

But it should be pointed out that there is no centralised database of all recorded fingerprints of criminals in Britain as different police forces prefer different computer systems. This means that checking every fingerprint on record requires checking each database individually. As long as the fingerprint characteristics are of sufficient quality it should be possible to do this. Although this is a more time consuming exercise than it would be if there was a centralised database using one system, it is still a great improvement on the extremely time consuming days when each fingerprint on record had to be checked individually.

Consequently, if the murderer of Lynette White's fingerprints are on record it may be possible to unmask him now. However, it should be pointed out that it is possible that even if all of the eleven fingerprints are accounted for, they may not belong to the murderer, although it should be remembered that the person who deposited the partial handprint almost certainly saw the murderer or committed it himself. At present there is no database for palmprints.

South Wales Police have been given a second chance to identify the real killer of Lynette White. Yet more than twenty months after the Lynette White Inquiry was re-opened they are still no nearer to unmasking the real killer than they were when my submission forced the authorities to re-open the case. Whilst accepting that the mistakes of the first ill-fated inquiry will not be repeated and that it is undoubtedly in the public interest to unmask the real killer of Lynette White without further delay, it is also necessary to learn from the mistakes of the original inquiry. Suffice to say, a fully independent public inquiry is the only way that the full truth of what happened in this extraordinary case can be established and the lessons learned in time to prevent it from happening again. The interests of justice and the memory of Lynette White deserve nothing less.

First they came for the Jews
And I did not speak out
Because I was not a Jew.

Then they came for the communists
And I did not speak out
Because I was not a communist.

Then they came for the trade unionists
And I did not speak out
Because I was not a trade unionist.

Then they came for me
And there was no-one left
To speak out for me.

Pastor Martin Niemöller
(Victim of the Nazis.)

Conclusion

On Valentine's Day 1988 South Wales Police began the ill-fated Lynette White Inquiry. They had high hopes that they would solve this terrible murder and that their inquiry would be held up as an exhaustive and extremely thorough one. But this was an inquiry which went badly off the rails. It resulted in an easily preventable travesty of justice. In fact, this was one of the worst miscarriages of justice in British history, This was an inquiry which relied on tried and tested methods of detection: methods which had contributed to other notorious wrongful convictions.

The purpose of this book is not to initiate a witch-hunt of South Wales Police - many of whom are now retired anyway - it is to learn the lessons that this extraordinary case can teach us in order to prevent it from happening again and to put the Lynette White Inquiry back on the right track if that is at all possible.

This was a case in which the criminal justice system failed miserably to ensure that justice was dispensed to all concerned without fear nor favour. South Wales Police had a presumption of guilt which was totally unjustifiable, especially in the light of their investigations into other suspects like Mr X. The quality of the evidence which they gathered against the five men who stood trial for Lynette's murder was woeful. There were so many contradictions that level headed police officers should have quickly seen that the Cardiff Five should never have been arrested, let alone prosecuted.

It also illustrates the dangers of relying on discredited methods. Police bullied a highly vulnerable suspect into making a ludicrous confession which was contradicted by indisputable evidence. Dubious confessions have been shown to lead to wrongful convictions several times, so much so that as a result of the collapse of the case against the three youngsters convicted of being involved in the murder of Maxwell Confait in the 1970s, legislation was introduced to protect the vulnerable. But PACE failed to prevent police securing the prized confession from Steve Miller, the one piece of evidence which dominated the case.

Even now police believe that they were entitled to question Miller in the way that they did even though the evidence of Miller's vulnerability had been available long before Lynette's murder. But police were apparently unaware of Miller's special needs. Why? Research into his background and educational history would have revealed his vulnerability before police interviewed him. Had they investigated this before arresting him they would have been able to interview him in an appropriate fashion.

Surely it is time that such vulnerabilities were identified before a suspect is interviewed. Anything less condemns the whole system to have to react to the discovery of such vulnerabilities after the damage has been done, which will inevitably mean that it will happen again. The point is not to leave it to the criminal justice system to rectify the situation after the interviews are over, it is to prevent it happening at all. PACE allows vulnerable suspects to be interviewed in the presence of an appropriate adult, but this depends on advance knowledge of the suspect's vulnerabilities. And these appropriate adults are not trained lawyers who would know if the police had overstepped the mark and could protect the interviewee's legal rights.

Indeed, Miller's case shows that not all solicitors are fully aware of the level of support and special needs for protection that suggestible people, especially those of borderline intelligence, require. This is particularly important in rigorous confrontational interviews. It is therefore essential for police to have to research the educational history of the suspect before he or she is interviewed and for solicitors to fearlessly defend the interests of such clients, as people like Miller are not capable of doing it for themselves.

And bereavement affects people differently. It even affects suggestibility. This is why Miller did not confess when he was questioned in February 1988. Dr Gudjonsson's colleague, Dr James MacKeith, had compiled a report on Miller which showed that Miller's feelings were not unnatural and nor was he faking suggestibility. Dr MacKeith pointed out that in February 1988 not only had Miller been denied the right to mourn Lynette's death, but he was subjected to a torrent of abuse about their relationship and treated like the police's chief suspect. The angry state this produced would have made him far less suggestible than later in the year and probably helped to prevent any confession that the police may have been hoping for by their provocative tactics during those immediate post crime interviews. But Dr MacKeith did not give evidence.[1] And the jury heard nothing of Miller's grief for Lynette nor of his exhaustive efforts to find her killer. But Miller's low IQ and high suggestibility and the lack of police understanding of the full extent of his vulnerabilities were only part of the problem.

There is also the question of the oppression that Miller endured. Police were not entitled to question him in the manner that they did. And once they had, the confession should have been ruled inadmissible immediately. Either the provisions of PACE were not adhered to by both the police and the criminal justice system or PACE itself does not provide sufficient safeguards. No less an authority than the former Lord Chief Justice, the late Lord Taylor, himself pointed out that even a person of average intelligence would have had difficulty coping with the bullying that was inflicted on Miller during those interviews.

This is an important point because it means that oppression would normally lead to a confession, but the confession may not be true. Interviewing that is geared towards establishing the truth does not require oppression of any sort. And consequently, the results of such interviewing will be more reliable. Confrontational interviewing seeks to establish a breach in the suspect's defences. And once that breach has been established

[1] Dr MacKeith is one of the commissioners of the recently established CCRC.

the interviewer seeks to widen the breach to the point of persuading the interviewee to adopt the interrogator's chosen scenario.

More often than not interviewing begins from the premise that the interviewee is guilty and must be persuaded to agree with the interviewer's perceptions. This presumption of guilt means that a denial of guilt is taken as proof of guilt and an admission of guilt is taken at face value. That makes it inevitable that the guilty who protest their innocence and the truly innocent who deny and protest become indistinguishable in the eyes of the police. Such a raison d'être of interviewing makes it difficult if not impossible to establish the truth which ought to be the one and only aim of interviewing. Anything less will result in yet more miscarriages of justice, meaning that the guilty go free.

The system would benefit from adopting the conclusions of Dr Eric Shepherd regarding ethical interviewing. While police have adopted a more ethical style of interviewing, it lacks legislative authority. The confrontational manner of interviewing must end. This is not to force police to investigate crimes with one hand tied behind their backs, it is to ensure that interviewing is designed to obtain the truth rather than a confession which may not be true and to ensure that the evidence that they gather will be of a higher standard. A false confession is worse than useless. Not only can it convict the innocent, but by doing so it protects the guilty. Interviewing a suspect must not be geared to obtaining a confession; it should have only one purpose - establishing the truth.

But interviews are only part of a wider problem. The methods of detection employed by police are just as important. Witnesses complained of being deceived by police of the extent of the evidence against the defendants. Several of Abdullahi's witnesses claimed in their affidavits to his lawyers that they were told that he had confessed. If their claims are true this is worrying because it would mean that any incriminating evidence obtained from these witnesses may have been obtained on a false basis as not only had Abdullahi not confessed then, he consistently protested his innocence.

There were also complaints of pressure being put on witnesses to get the evidence that they wanted. And there were complaints that police put words into witnesses' mouths. Such investigative techniques, if they were used, betray a closed mind and more often than not will produce unreliable evidence. Witnesses have to be treated in an open and honest fashion without having words put into their mouths. This may make it harder to obtain evidence, but the evidence gathered will be the more reliable for it.

However, it ought to be re-iterated that these allegations were never tested in court, so the officers never got the chance to refute their claims and David Elfer QC did not get the opportunity to cross-examine these witnesses long and hard about their veracity. But this merely highlights the deeply unsatisfactory nature of leaving such serious allegations as these in limbo in circumstances where they ought to have been considered by the Court of Appeal. It also raises the issue of the need to tape record or videotape all contact between witnesses and the police. Such a safeguard would provide corroboration of genuine claims of malpractice and it would protect honest officers from spurious accusations of malpractice. Consequently, it is in everybody's interests to introduce such safeguards without further delay.

But this is not all that needs to be addressed. The criminal justice system has resisted all attempts to rid it of the plague of supergrasses. There have been numerous victims of unscrupulous prison informers who claim that remand prisoners who have refused to confess during interviews with police were suddenly overcome by an irresistible need to confess to perfect strangers who almost invariably are the dregs of the prison population. Almost invariably these informers give evidence in expectation of some form of reward, usually early release. And these alleged confessions are never corroborated, or subject to any safeguard whatsoever.

Ian Massey was just one in a long line of such unreliable witnesses. More level headed police officers would quickly have seen that Massey was not a reliable witness. And the same is true of the rest of the criminal justice system. Massey had claimed that Paris' leather jacket was heavily bloodstained: it wasn't. Then he claimed that Paris had expressed delight that "forensics had messed up." This was not true either. At the time that Massey claimed to have had that alleged conversation with Paris it was proved that Paris had not had access to the results of forensic analysis. This proved that Massey had lied about Paris about crucial issues.

On this evidence alone Massey was totally unreliable and the criminal justice system was gravely at fault for washing its hands of responsibility for using him. Although Mr Justice Leonard advised the jury to exercise great care when they considered Massey's evidence, this cannot absolve the system of responsibility for allowing such an unreliable witness as Massey to give evidence in the first place, given the fact that he had demonstrably perjured himself about Paris. Suffice to say, the criminal justice system should not have left the admissibility of his evidence to the judge and jury; it should have concluded that Massey was at best a grossly unreliable witness and ensured that the system did not rely on him to convict Paris. But Massey was essential to the Crown's case. He was the sole corroboration of Vilday and Psaila. Without his testimony the Crown's case against Paris was virtually non-existent. It is a national disgrace that a witness of such appalling quality as Ian Massey was allowed to use and abuse the criminal justice system in the way that he did. And the system must take responsibility for it and take measures to prevent it from happening again.

The use of prison informers is the most unreliable form of evidence that can be obtained. Take the case of the Bridgewater Four for example. Two highly unreliable prison informers were used in that case against Jimmy Robinson and Michael Hickey. Brian Sinton originally claimed that Hickey confessed to him in the showers. Sinton later retracted, admitting that he had lied in return for inducements. And Mervyn "Tex" Ritter's evidence that Robinson had confessed to him was highly implausible to put it mildly. At the 1988-89 appeal, the longest in British legal history, the Court of Appeal threw out Sinton's evidence against Hickey, but their description of Ritter as a witness of truth was absolutely incomprehensible and even Ritter was surprised that they believed him. And there are numerous other victims of unscrupulous prison informers still languishing in British jails because the criminal justice system refuses to dispense with such utterly unreliable evidence. It is high time that such evidence is ruled inadmissible as a matter of course, or it should be made clear that prison informers will get no inducement or reward whatsoever, except protection if that is necessary. But such reform would almost certainly lead to the number of prison informers drying up, or rather, it would mean that only honest informers would come forward. And if that is the result of such reform it can't happen soon enough.

There is also the way that police exploited the one area where the defence had to disclose their evidence, namely their alibis. Police used the alibi notices, especially that of Abdullahi, as nothing more than a guide to what they had to discredit. The affidavits of certain witnesses relating to Abdullahi's alibi, namely John Hulse, Sidney Harrop, Ian Moore, Peter McCarthy and Lawrence Mann, claim that police officers used dubious methods on them while investigating Abdullahi's alibi, which included deceiving witnesses, pressurising them and putting words into their mouths. If true this suggests that there was no impartial investigation into the truth or lack of it of Abdullahi's alibi. While it should be stressed that police did not get the chance to refute these allegations and Elfer did not get the chance to cross-examine these witnesses about their allegations of police malpractice, it is worth bearing in mind that Michael Howard has introduced legislation obliging the defence to disclose their case to the prosecution while diminishing the obligations of the Crown to disclose information to the defence.

The investigation of Abdullahi's alibi shows that defence disclosure is used to attack the alibi, not to test its veracity. That is unacceptable, but it will not change until there is a fundamental change in the way police conduct their investigations from an adversarial approach to an inquisitorial one. Until and unless police adopt such an approach the defence should not be obliged to disclose its case in advance. And ludicrously, the police are to be trusted to disclose information which could assist the defence. Several cases including that of the Cardiff Three and Judith Ward, among many others, graphically illustrate the point that police cannot be expected to undermine their own case. Unless there are compelling reasons to withhold information, such as national security, there should be no discretion not to disclose information to the defence. And the defence should also have the right to decide for themselves what is relevant to their case.

But the possible abuse of defence disclosure obligations regarding Abdullahi's alibi was only part of the story regarding disclosure which was a somewhat grey area at the time, as there was material which affected the credibility of crucial prosecution witnesses such as Sergeant David Hathaway's summary of his conversation with Vilday regarding her drunken outburst, DI Lott's memo regarding Harris' meetings with Vilday, Jane Sandrone's house-to-house enquiry form which contradicted her statement and the full extent of Ronnie Williams' activities as a police informer. Neither the defence nor the jury were aware of the full extent of information available to police which clearly affected the reliability of these witnesses and ought to have been disclosed in the interests of fairness to all concerned. Juries must be trusted to have access to all the relevant information that the police have at their disposal. Anything less is not compatible with justice being seen to be done.

And then there is the greyer area of Mr X and Mr Y. Although both had been eliminated before the Cardiff Five were arrested, the cocktail theory applied to them just as much as it did to Abdullahi and the reasons for doubting the DNA eliminations of the Cardiff Five applied to everybody who had been eliminated on DNA not just the Cardiff Five. Although there may have been no specific obligation to disclose the blood groups of people eliminated by police, it would have been fairer to all concerned if the defence had been informed of the blood groups of X and Y because, at the very least, they were potentially important with reference to the cocktail theory. Without knowing these blood groups it was impossible to challenge the cocktail theory as effectively as it could and should have been challenged. And the jury were unaware of information which could have affected the weight that they put on the cocktail theory. The failure to reveal this to the defence meant that the jury were deprived of evidence they had a right to hear. In fact, Abdullahi feels that he was deprived of his supposedly inalienable right to a fair trial because of it.

Although there have been significant advances in disclosure obligations following the case of Judith Ward which allow defence lawyers access to police incident rooms, there is still the scope for important information to be hidden or destroyed. After all, the material relating to X and Y and others was gathered before the arrests of the Cardiff Five. As the CPS are dependent on the police for its information and will not be brought into play until an arrest has been made, it would be simplicity itself to disappear or destroy such material before either the CPS or defence lawyers could see it.

The only way that such temptations could be seen to be avoided would be to establish an independent authority to supervise police investigations from an early stage. For example, in France as soon as it is established that a crime has been committed an examining magistrate (juge d'instruction) is called in to supervise the investigation. The magistrate has powers to order forensic tests to be conducted, instruct pathologists, and anyone detained by the police will be interviewed by the magistrate in an environment which is not intimidating to the interviewee as he or she will be treated as a witness until the magistrate believes that there is sufficient evidence to justify viewing the interviewee as a suspect. Adopting such a system could help to resolve all of the above mentioned issues.

Of course, this system, like any other, depends on the integrity of the examining magistrate. Although there may be problems with such a procedure and it should not be transplanted from France to England and Wales without considering the specific requirements of the system to the needs of the English and Welsh system, it is surely time to research the feasibility of such a system with a view to adopting the safeguards that it provides sooner rather than later, especially as such a system not only protects the rights of defendants, it protects the police from spurious accusations of malpractice.

It is also important to note that police are subject to intense pressure to get results, especially in appalling crimes like the murder of Lynette White. This was a case where the police could not be seen to fail to make arrests. The public expected results and that created pressure to cut corners in their investigations. But it is ironic that South Wales Police conducted two distinct Lynette White Inquiries; one highly secretive, but which was a model of modern inquisitorial techniques; the other highly publicised, but which followed old fashioned investigative techniques and resulted in thoroughly unjustifiable arrests. Had police followed the approach they used in their investigations of Mr X and Mr Y in their investigation of the Cardiff Five there would have been no need for this book. In short, whatever pressure police were under to solve such a terrible crime there was no justification for arresting the Cardiff Five on evidence of such a woeful quality. Quite simply, it should never have happened.

But the failings of the police in this inquiry ought to have been academic. The police may have become emotionally involved to the point that they wanted to believe the Cardiff Five were guilty so much that they convinced themselves that they had arrested the right men in spite of the plethora of evidence pointing to the opposite conclusion. The CPS have no such excuse. Its function is to cast an independent eye over the evidence gathered by the police. Its duty was to prevent such an appalling case from ever coming to trial. Unfortunately, it failed to observe its own criteria on the sufficiency of evidence to justify the decision to prosecute. There can be no excuse for such failings. And this case will taint its claims of complete independence from the police for some time to come.

However, in fairness to the CPS, it was almost certainly deprived of crucial evidence before deciding to prosecute. It is inconceivable that it would have prosecuted the Cardiff Five if it had been aware of police interest in X and Y as suspects. But in August 1994 the CPS wrote, "All existing guidelines on disclosure were complied with in the Cardiff Three case - the defence were provided with full disclosure." Yet crucial information like Jane Sandrone's house-to-house enquiry form which clearly affected her credibility as a Crown witness was not disclosed in time for the trial or retrial of the Cardiff Five. Either the CPS knew of this inconsistent account and chose not to disclose it to the defence or it too was unaware of it at that time.

The CPS refused to confirm or deny if it was aware of the full extent of police knowledge of both X and Y. Secrecy for its own sake offers a fertile breeding ground for conspiracy theories where there may not be one. It is time that it was open with such information. After all, revealing whether it knew of the importance of X and Y was hardly likely to bring the system crashing down.

This raises the issue of the dependency of the CPS on the police for information. It proceeds on the basis that it has been given everything that it needs to know. The issue of whether the CPS allowed an appalling prosecution to take place in ignorance of the importance of the X and Y material or whether it was fully aware of it and decided to keep the defence in the dark about this potentially explosive material remains to be resolved. But regardless of this material there was enough evidence for it to see that this was a case that should never have been allowed anywhere near a court.

On any view, the CPS failed the test of the Cardiff Five miserably. And if it can get it so spectacularly wrong can it be trusted not to make the same mistakes again? Perhaps the time has come to replace the CPS with a genuinely independent prosecuting authority with powers similar to those enjoyed by a juge d'instruction in France. And this is no villains' charter. To those who say such a system would mean that guilty people will be able to evade prosecution, I would point out that the one and only certain way of making sure that the guilty escape sanction is to convict the innocent.

But the CPS was not alone in failing to stop this abysmal prosecution. Two magistrates committed the Cardiff Five for trial despite the appalling quality of the evidence that they heard. To be fair to them, their hands were tied to some extent by the Galbraith judgement which prevented them from usurping the function of the jury. But *Regina v Galbraith* notwithstanding they had the powers not to commit the case for trial and should not have committed it.

However, in fairness to the criminal justice system, it has recognised the need to untie the hands of magistrates to such an extent that in the recent case of Francis Marnell the magistrate was prepared to acquit him by refusing to commit him for trial over the murder of Jean Bradley when it became clear that he had a good alibi. If magistrates are prepared to exercise these powers dispassionately it would suggest that a case like that of the Cardiff Five would not come to trial now, although it ought to be pointed out that cases like that of the sisters Michelle and Lisa Taylor and the 1997 case of the Merthyr Tydfil Three (Donna Clarke, Annette Hewins and Denise Sullivan), among others, show that not only are appalling cases still getting past the CPS and committal hearings, but are resulting in scandalous convictions despite the paucity of credible evidence.

Unfortunately, the CPS compounded its initial error by failing to review its case against the Cardiff Five in the light of the awful performances given by their star witnesses during the old style committal hearings. But it ought to be pointed out that defendants have lost the right to opt for committal hearings where witnesses have to give live evidence before they are committed for trial. This is yet another of Michael Howard's numerous follies as it has removed an important mechanism for preventing ludicrous cases from wasting time and expense clogging up the courts. Such penny pinching is a false economy and has no place in a competent and efficient criminal justice system.

Far from reviewing the evidence and concluding that this was not an appropriate case to bring to trial, the CPS brought in David Elfer QC to lead the prosecution. His submissions regarding Miller's confession and the way that it was obtained graphically illustrates the need for lawyers to undergo some training on the vulnerability of people like Steve Miller. Given the performance of Mr Justice McNeill, the same is true of judges as well. But it ought to be pointed out that the judiciary has woken up to these issues, as was shown by Mr Justice Mitchell over the confession of George Heron to the murder of seven year old Nikki Allen. In November 1993 Mitchell refused to allow the jury to hear it on the grounds of oppression as a result of the Court of Appeal's decision in the appeal of the Cardiff Three. Heron was subsequently acquitted by the jury.

And after the death of Mr Justice McNeill the CPS added insult to injury by failing to review the evidence again. But there was an added consideration. Through nobody's fault the entire case was already in the public domain. The decision to hold the second trial in the same court as the first was scandalous as any jury may well have been contaminated by press coverage of the first trial. A simple reform mandating new trials to take place outside the catchment area of the local press in the aborted trial could easily prevent even the appearance of unfairness in all but the most notorious of cases.

The retrial raised other issues. After getting a judge (Mr Justice McNeill) who did not seem to know what oppression was under PACE, a change of barrister completed the miserable performance of the criminal justice system. Roger Frisby may not have been the right choice of QC to defend Miller. He did not argue that Miller had been bullied as effectively as he could and should have done. By not playing the whole of Miller's seventh interview to the judge to back up his points on oppressive interviewing Frisby made a serious mistake which could have had even more serious consequences if the Court of Appeal had refused to hear Mansfield's arguments as the evidence of oppression was available at the retrial. Suffice to say, this was far from Frisby's finest hour.

Even though Mr Justice Leonard could still have ruled the confession inadmissible due to bullying, it was unfortunate that he did not hear the worst examples of bullying in an interview the Court of Appeal described as a "travesty." Had Frisby's submissions been as effective as they should have been it is possible, even likely, that Mr Justice Leonard would have heard enough to conclude that the confession ought not to be admitted in evidence.

That in turn would have prevented the jury from relying on it to convict Abdullahi and Paris. And Leonard's decision not to sever Miller's trial from that of the others, notwithstanding his warning to the jury not to use Miller's confession against any of his co-defendants, made a miscarriage of justice inevitable. And the case of the Cardiff Five is not an isolated example. Take the case of the Bridgewater Four for example. In 1979 Jimmy Robinson and the cousins Vincent and Michael Hickey were convicted of the September 1978 murder of teenage newspaperboy, Carl Bridgewater, and Pat Molloy was convicted of manslaughter. There was no forensic evidence against them and fingerprinting evidence that could have exonerated them was not disclosed to them at the time. The case against them relied on prison informers, dubious witnesses and most crucially of all, the confession of Pat Molloy.

On legal advice, Molloy did not challenge it and his co-accused were also deprived of the opportunity to challenge it because Molloy acquiesced with legal advice not to give evidence. Molloy's decision not to contest his confession must have had the effect of reinforcing it in the eyes of the jury. After all, if Molloy was innocent why didn't he retract it and protest his innocence?

Unbeknown to the jury, Molloy had retracted as soon as he was allowed access to a solicitor. He claimed that he had been assaulted by the late DC John Perkins, one of the most corrupt officers in the now disgraced West Midlands Serious Crimes Squad, and that he had been shown a statement purportedly made by Vincent Hickey which incriminated him. Molloy claimed that police brutality, combined with a desire to get even with Vincent Hickey, induced him to confess, implicating his co-accused in the process. Unknown to Molloy, Hickey had not made a written statement implicating him.

The jury knew none of this as Molloy acquiesced with legal advice not to run this defence as juries tended not to believe such tales of police malpractice in those days. And so, the jury believed that it was properly obtained and true. Time would eventually prove that it was neither. The jury were entitled to use it against Molloy, but the law does not permit them to use it against his co-accused. But once they had seen it, it was unrealistic to expect them to put it from their minds when dealing with Molloy's co-defendants.

After the four were convicted Molloy tirelessly set about trying to set the record straight even offering to take the truth drug. He died in Gartree Prison in 1981 still protesting his innocence.

But the issue of his confession refused to die with Pat Molloy. It was the basis of a submission to refer the case back to the Court of Appeal in the early 1990s. First of all, expert evidence cast doubt on the police's insistence that it had been dictated to them by Molloy. Then, expert evidence cast doubt on the police's version of how the confession was obtained. And finally, the integrity of the investigation was destroyed in February 1997 when an electrostatic depression analysis (ESDA) test proved that contrary to police claims, Molloy had been shown a statement purportedly made by Vincent Hickey. This clearly demonstrated that the confession had been obtained improperly and was therefore thoroughly unreliable. Molloy's conviction was quashed posthumously and his co-defendants were immediately freed on bail pending the inevitable quashing of their convictions. It was eighteen years too late.

Like Yusef Abdullahi and Tony Paris, Jimmy Robinson and Vincent and Michael Hickey were convicted by the confession of a co-defendant which wasn't even admissible against them. Only severing Molloy and Miller's trials from that of their co-accused could have prevented this. Judges should have no discretion on severance. In cases where a co-accused has confessed severance should be automatic. The interests of justice demand nothing less. Had that been in place at the time of the retrial the wrongful convictions of Yusef Abdullahi and Tony Paris could have been prevented.

And then there was the most difficult area to tackle, that of the jury. The Cardiff Five were tried by a jury who did not observe the law. Clearly, they used Miller's confession against his co-accused despite the law not allowing it. The reaction of the jury to Miller's confession shows that juries will cut through the niceties of the law to deliver verdicts they believe to be just. Quite simply, they could not put Miller's confession out of their minds once they had heard it.

Nor was this jury alone in doing this. In the case of the Bridgewater Four the jury had been told that they could not use Pat Molloy's confession as proof of the guilt of his co-defendants. Several years later, Tim O'Malley, the foreman of that jury, revealed that Molloy's confession was the basis of their verdicts even though they were not entitled to use it. O'Malley insists that anyone who had seen that confession could not put it out of their mind. The evidence is clear: juries will ignore the law in order to bring in verdicts they believe to be just regardless of the niceties of the law just as they did in both the case of the Bridgewater Four and also that of the Cardiff Five.

A knee jerk reaction to this will not suffice. It is essential that juries remain an integral part of the criminal justice system. But the consequences of perverse verdicts like these have to be dealt with far sooner. Despite O'Malley's admission in the Bridgewater case, it took over eighteen years for justice to be done.

In the USA trial judges have the right to set aside verdicts if he or she believes that the evidence did not justify the verdict. This occurred in the now notorious case of the Scottsboro Boys in the 1930s - one of the worst travesties of justice in American history. More recently, it was the procedure that the English au pair, Louise Woodward, asked her trial judge, Hiller Zobel, to use to overturn her conviction for the murder of baby Matthew Eappen. Zobel was not prepared to go as far Judge Jim Horton did in the case of the Scottsboro Boys, but he did substitute Woodward's murder conviction with one of manslaughter and imposed a sentence of time served, which resulted in Woodward being freed after two hundred and seventy-nine days in jail.

There is no similar facility available to British judges and those who fall victim to ludicrous or even unlawful verdicts must wait and hope for the Court of Appeal to set the record straight. Despite the verdict being demonstrably unlawful in the cases of Abdullahi and Paris, the Cardiff Three had to wait over two years for their appeals to be heard. Quite simply, such an appalling delay is totally unacceptable. At the very least, where a verdict can be shown to be unlawful, as it could in this case, there should be a speedy sitting of the Court of Appeal which should set aside the verdicts and order a retrial.

But this is not the only area concerning juries that can be addressed. The right to pre-emptory challenge must be restored without restriction and in cases where race is an issue juries must contain at least four jurors of the same race as the defendant. To those who say that this would interfere with random selection of juries I would answer that it need not. All that would need to happen is to have two jury pools, one to select the four members from the defendants race and the other to select the other eight. All twelve jurors could be randomly selected from within their respective pools. But for all its faults, the jury which convicted the Cardiff Three was cheated by the failure to present all the relevant material to them.

And then there was the appeal process itself. The Court of Appeal belatedly restored the Cardiff Three to their families and friends. But the way that it was done robbed them of the complete exoneration that they were entitled to receive. The Court of Appeal quite rightly quashed the convictions on Miller's confession and the prejudicial effect that it had on his co-appellants. But that was all that it was prepared to hear. There were other grounds of appeal which deserved an airing. Had the rest of the evidence been heard the whispering campaign against them would have been silenced at source. Appellants ought to be entitled to have their appeals heard in full. Anything less can work an unfairness as occurred to Abdullahi and Paris especially.

All things considered the case of the Cardiff Five was one of the most appalling miscarriages of justice in living memory. It was an easily preventable travesty of justice and one which illustrates the numerous flaws in the criminal justice system. This was a case which laid British justice bare for all to see. Rarely has so much gone wrong in the one case, although the flaws in the criminal justice system which have been exposed in this book are responsible for the miscarrying of justice in other cases. Had the appeals of the Cardiff Three been heard in full the judgement would have been cited in other cases on several issues for many years to come. And the Court of Appeal would not have been able to ride out the crisis in British justice caused by the quashing of the convictions of the Guildford Four in 1989. It would have been inconceivable for the appeal court to have delivered questionable judgements as happened in the cases of Michael Davis, Raphael Rowe and Randolph Johnson (the M25 Three), Gary Mills and Tony Poole and Satpal Ram, among others. But even now it is not too late; the lessons of the case of the Cardiff Five can still be learned, but there must be the will to do so. The criminal justice system must learn that it is responsible for delivering justice to all concerned without fear nor favour. Nothing less is good enough.

So freeing the Cardiff Three is not enough. There must be guarantees that this will never happen again. But without a fully independent public inquiry into the whole case and how it was allowed to happen, how can we learn all the lessons that this extraordinary case can teach us about the workings of the criminal justice system? Yet even this is not all that this case has to offer.

Our criminal justice system is based on the adversarial model. Under such systems barristers tend to jockey for position. And systems such as the French which use a more inquisitorial approach are also prone to spectacular failures. The case of Moroccan gardener, Omar Raddad, is a case in point. As with the Lynette White Inquiry the whole system presumed Raddad guilty and the very safeguards which are so lauded by admirers of the French system failed to function as they should have done.

The French system is no panacea for the ills of our system. Similarly, the Scottish system has its admirers. Some look enviously at the corroboration requirement that is so lauded elsewhere. But the case of Thomas Campbell and Joseph Steele (the Glasgow Two) shows that such trust is misplaced.[1] In practice, the corroboration requirement has all the hallmarks of a paper safeguard which does not work. In fact, it is worse than our system as it has the appearance of effective safeguards which have been watered down to such an extent that they hardly exist in practice. A corroboration requirement for confessions, or even the whole case, is only as strong as the definition of corroboration. A low definition of what is capable of amounting to corroboration can and will result in miscarriages of justice.

Had the Cardiff Five had the misfortune to be tried in Scotland there is no reason to believe that they would have fared any better. In fact, given the hostility to miscarriages of justice in that country's criminal justice system, there is every reason to believe that

---

[1] In December 1996 the Glasgow Two were freed on bail pending their appeal. Their appeal was controversially dismissed in February 1998 by the Scottish Court of Appeal, comprising of senior judges Lord Sutherland, Lord McCluskey and Lord Cullen, who refused to hear the evidence of the thrice convicted perverter of the course of justice, William Love, the chief prosecution witness, who had retracted his previous evidence alleging police malpractice, even though this evidence meant the complete collapse of the case against them. The Glasgow Two plan a further appeal. It should also be noted that had their case occurred in England or Wales their convictions would have been unsustainable as Love's evidence would have been heard on appeal and would almost certainly have had to be taken out of the case against the Glasgow Two: the author.

not only would the Cardiff Three still have been convicted, but that they would still be in prison as much of the evidence which emerged for the appeal would not and could not have emerged in Scotland due to the constraints imposed on defence lawyers there. Suffice to say, the Scottish system offers few useful safeguards for us to adopt.

Adversarial systems are prone to miscarry as they do not seek to establish the truth. Lawyers only seek to establish what they want the jury to hear. Tactical considerations frequently result in juries not hearing pertinent evidence. There is little that can be done about this as the interests of those prosecuting and defendants are obviously separate. Any system has to have an adversarial phase to it. In fact, trials cannot be anything but adversarial. But our adversarial system would benefit from having a far more inquisitorial approach to it during the earlier stages.

The investigation of crime needs to be entirely inquisitorial. The review of evidence gathered needs to be far more inquisitorial. Committal hearings by definition have to have an adversarial bent to them, but there is room for an inquisitorial phase to it.

Magistrates should also have an investigative department and have the powers to initiate their own inquiries to search for the truth. Their inquisitorial function would serve the public interest in searching for the truth. Their investigations would then be forwarded to the trial judge who can invite submissions from both the Crown and defence on the admissibility of the evidence unearthed by the magistrates' investigation. The judge would then have the power to call witnesses he or she believes would assist the jury.

On any view, the fundamental raison d'être of any criminal justice system must be to ensure that the jury is supplied with all the evidence it needs to establish the truth about crimes without exception. Unless our system seeks to base itself on such principles and addresses all the issues that have been raised by the sad case of the Cardiff Five it is inevitable that the innocent will continue to suffer wrongful imprisonment while the guilty savour their ill-gotten freedom.

There was a presumption of guilt over the forensic evidence as well. Forensic science is undoubtedly capable of providing compelling evidence of guilt. It is also capable of providing proof of innocence. It must be interpreted and acted upon honestly whether the results are inconvenient or not. The lack of forensic evidence against the defendants in this case proved their innocence. Common sense tells us that the extent of the forensic evidence in that flat meant that if any or all of the Cardiff Five were guilty of the murder of Lynette White there would have been forensic evidence tying them to the crime. There was none. That alone meant that they were entitled to be eliminated.

But this did not happen. Each of the Cardiff Five freely gave samples of their blood for elimination purposes. The results of those tests meant that they should have been eliminated on the grounds of blood grouping. That did not happen. None of their fingerprints were found in the murder flat. A handprint almost certainly placed in the room at the time of the murder did not belong to any of them. That also indicates that the Cardiff Five were entitled to be eliminated on the grounds of fingerprints. And then there were the hairs, semen and saliva which did not prove that the Cardiff Five had been in the murder room. They were entitled to be eliminated on that as well. But even that was not all.

DNA was the forensic technique which has the most public faith in it. Although it cannot uniquely identify a criminal it has always been able to eliminate suspects safely until now. Several suspects had been eliminated by DNA, but even though the Cardiff Five were entitled to the same courtesy it was denied to them. Police had no right to interpret DNA results selectively. They were certainly entitled to cast doubt on the eliminations if their information was credible. And in this case it was. They were therefore entitled to question the DNA eliminations of the Cardiff Five. But the information that they relied on to discredit their eliminations applied to everyone eliminated by DNA as well.

The selective interpretation of such information is not acceptable. It meant that everybody eliminated on DNA ought to have been re-investigated as soon as the information became known. But police had already arrested and charged the Cardiff Five and they had been committed for trial. It was too late to turn the clock back without massive public embarrassment. This is yet another reason for requiring independent supervision of police investigations. An independent body could have interpreted and acted on this information accordingly.

It should also be pointed out that police handling of crucial samples prior to DNA testing left a lot to be desired and may have contributed to valuable evidence being lost to the inquiry at that time. If police officers are to collect forensic evidence they must receive adequate training on how to do it in such a way that guarantees the integrity of the crime scene and crime samples.

But one of the most important lessons that the Lynette White Inquiry can teach us concerns the management and interpretation of scientific evidence. Rather than say that there was no forensic evidence capable of tying any of the Cardiff Five to the murder of Lynette White, Dr John Whiteside advanced a hypothesis which was unlikely.

Conventional blood grouping tests had established the blood groups of Mr X and Mr Y before the arrests of the Cardiff Five. And the eliminations of these people and others on DNA was not as safe as it had been thought to be at the time. But until Dr Whiteside advanced the cocktail theory there was no forensic evidence capable of tying any of the defendants to the murder room or to Lynette. However, after Dr Whiteside mentioned this possibility in relation to Abdullahi and Psaila new information emerged which destroyed the credibility of the DNA eliminations of Mr X and Mr Y as well as those of the Cardiff Five. In this context the blood groups of X and Y became important once again. It meant that Dr Whiteside's cocktail theory applied to them just as much as it did to Abdullahi.

In fact, in his evidence at the first trial, Whiteside accepted that if the mixture contained a large quantity of female blood and a small amount of male material, then *any* man could have donated the Y-chromosome. This means that no man could be eliminated by the cocktail theory. And not only did it apply to Psaila, but to all women who possessed that rare blood group. Consequently, it could not even prove that Psaila's blood had definitely been found in the murder room. And there was evidence to suggest that Psaila was not injured at all, although Psaila suggested that she was cut on the inside of her mouth which did not bleed much. However, the cocktail theory depended on enough of her blood being present in the mixture to obscure the blood groups of the man.

And as the sex determination test cannot determine the exact proportions of X and Y-chromosomes in any mixture at that time, it is possible that a man who possessed that blood group deposited a large amount of his blood which mixed in intimately with a small amount of female blood. If that happened then no woman could be eliminated either. This means that the cocktail theory could not exclude anybody at all. And the possibility that the blood in the flat had been shed by one man was never conclusively eliminated. Abdullahi's defence were unaware of this information which could have enabled them to mount a vigorous challenge to the cocktail theory.

It should be pointed out that defence forensic scientists can now inspect FSS results, but this depends on knowing who and what to investigate. The confusion over X and Y and others could happen again if vital information about their blood groups was not disclosed as a matter of right. The confusion over the blood grouping evidence suggests an urgent need for an independent Defence Forensic Science Service to be established and properly resourced without delay. They should have the right to be present at the testing of all forensic samples by FSS scientists on pain of any evidence obtained in their absence being inadmissible. That would oblige the FSS to comply with these requirements and it would ensure that useful results cannot be withheld from the defence.

This is essential as the jury, for all its faults regarding their dependence on the Miller confession, was not aware of the full truth regarding the forensic evidence in this case. I do not say all this to initiate a witch-hunt of forensic science or scientists. The one and only function of forensic science should be to establish the truth. It should not be to provide possible but unlikely explanations for results which are inconvenient to either the prosecution or defence. Although there may have been no burden of disclosure concerning the blood groups of X and Y, the better practice would have been to disclose it. The jury would then have been in a better position to consider the weight that they should give to the cocktail theory as a possible explanation for the rare blood group with the male chromosome in it that was deposited in the murder room. Such an approach will help to prevent miscarriages of justice. And it should be remembered that convicting the innocent is certain to ensure that brutal criminals like the real murderer of Lynette White remain in our midst, perhaps to kill again.

But the problems with forensic science and interpretation of forensic results is only part of the problem. There is no adequate system to investigate the serious causes for concern outlined in this book. The police investigating themselves is not good enough. The Home Office's abdication of its responsibilities show that it cannot be trusted, especially with a Home Secretary whose greatest concern seems to be political posturing for the benefit of the Tory faithful rather than providing an efficient and just criminal justice system, although the recent change in government offers fresh hope for an impartial investigation of the forensic issues as Alun Michael is now the Minister of State for the Home Office, second in authority for home affairs only to the Home Secretary, Jack Straw.

The criminal justice system delivered partial justice to the Cardiff Three by freeing them. And then it washed its hands of the whole mess. There was no apology to the Cardiff Three for their ordeal. There was no support for them in terms of the trauma of their wrongful imprisonment. They were just left to get on with their lives as if nothing had happened. Compare this to the treatment that the Beirut hostages received on their release from wrongful imprisonment at the hands of Hezbollah. They received counselling and were helped to cope with the post traumatic stress disorder that they suffered. The victims of British justice are entitled to the same consideration.

There was no re-opening of the Lynette White Inquiry even though there was evidence justifying such action. The system had to be dragged kicking and screaming all the way. And it has taken nearly eighteen months from the re-opening of the inquiry to find out that no useful results could be obtained from multiplexing in circumstances where this was a prime candidate for singleplexing from the beginning. Although the facility to singleplex now exists in Britain the level of amplification achieved here is apparently not of the level achieved by Professor Brinkmann in Germany. And it should be remembered that within the forensic science community it was known that singleplexing was more sensitive before my submission had even been sent to the police. Consequently, the use of multiplexing, especially after the initial batch of samples had failed to yield results was incomprehensible as it used up valuable DNA in circumstances where there was a limited supply of poor quality DNA without the best possible prospect of obtaining useful results.

However, it should also be pointed out that STR typing is such a sensitive test that storing the crucial wallpaper samples in the cupboard rather than at low temperatures would not pose any extra difficulties. The use of Ninhydrin on them poses far more problems, although it is possible that some of the DNA below the top of the bloodstain may not be affected by it. There is therefore no reason for despondency as further testing may yet yield useful results which could tie Lynette's murderer to his crime. And Professor Brinkmann's techniques offer even more reason for optimism. As testing at the Aldermaston laboratory failed to yield results through multiplexing, singleplexing, especially Professor Brinkmann's techniques offer the only immediate prospect of obtaining any forensic evidence from the crucial samples and this opportunity must be seized. If his techniques are employed on the other samples as well it would increase the likelihood of original DNA being available for further testing in the future if and when even more sensitive tests become available.

South Wales Police assured Mrs Pesticcio that the new investigation would leave no stone unturned in the hunt for Lynette's killer. At her meeting with police in September 1996 she was assured that every sample which failed to yield useful results at Aldermaston would then be sent to Professor Brinkmann. Clearly, police are taking their promise to Mrs Pesticcio very seriously. They deserve to be commended for this. But their reluctance to utilise the more sensitive techniques used by Professor Brinkmann in circumstances where they clearly offer the best prospects of obtaining useful results must go to their debit. Their decision to attempt singleplexing in Britain will have no significant implications as long as the police ensure that enough DNA will be saved for Professor Brinkmann to work with. However, police recently suggested that they would use up some or all of the DNA if they thought it necessary. It should also be remembered that the decision to use the inappropriate technique of multiplexing has used up valuable DNA that could have been put to better use thereby increasing the prospects of saving DNA pending future advances in DNA testing systems. Such opportunities have been needlessly lost. The blame for that rests with South Wales Police and the forensic scientists advising them.

Meanwhile, the police confirmed that the Lynette White Inquiry remains open, but that they require new evidence to advance the inquiry. That appears to be a very narrow interpretation of the results. The failure to obtain useful results means that all suspects eliminated by MLP DNA profiling alone must be investigated again starting from when they were eliminated. That is *new* information. It may not be sufficient to result in a conviction or convictions, but it would provide a useful starting point for further inquiries which may lead to credible evidence that could be presented to a jury.

And if Professor Brinkmann's techniques also prove to be unfruitful the samples should be stored adequately pending further advances in DNA testing systems as further STR loci are being discovered regularly. At the very least, it is possible that further developments in DNA analysis will continue to be discovered and that some time in the future a DNA testing system will be developed that will succeed in obtaining useful results from seemingly useless samples like those obtained in the Lynette White Inquiry. It would appear that time is on the side of justice as long as some of the original DNA is saved pending further improvements in the efficiency of DNA amplification.

It should also be remembered that hairs found at the crime scene could be tested by mitochondrial DNA sequencing which was recently used in the high profile inquiry into the murder of Lin and Megan Russell and the vicious attack on Lin's other daughter Josie. Police could also attempt to STR type the aspermic semen, yet despite their much vaunted promise to Mrs Pesticcio that no stones would remain unturned, these stones remain conspicuously unturned. Why? We deserve an answer.

And advances in DNA testing systems are not the only interesting developments in the fight against crime. It is no longer the excessively time consuming task that it once was to compare sets of unidentified fingerprints to the fingerprints of all criminals whose fingerprints are on record in Britain. Computer systems have been devised that can search records and provide a range of likely candidates which can then be analysed in detail by fingerprint experts. If, as seems likely, the murderer of Lynette White has committed other crimes which mean that his fingerprints are on record then it is possible that one of the computer systems currently on line could assist the police to focus attention on him within the range of likely candidates that the system identifies. And as advances in various technologies continue to be made unsolved crimes like the murder of Lynette White may not appear to be as difficult to solve as they once were.

Nevertheless, the fact that this inquiry seemed to depend on my zeal to see that justice was done to all concerned is a terrible indictment of our criminal justice system. There should have been an adequate mechanism to spot and halt appalling cases like this one built into any criminal justice system. Had I listened to those who declared this story dead and buried once the Cardiff Three were freed the evidence which eventually forced the system to re-open the Lynette White Inquiry may never have emerged. It is precisely that blinkered approach which prevents the lessons of miscarriage cases from being learned and allows the system to paper over the cracks, thereby making it inevitable that there will be other Cardiff Threes.

It does not therefore feel like a great triumph that justice seems to depend on investigative journalism in an environment where there are fewer and fewer outlets for those wishing to expose institutional failings.

But it should also be pointed out that South Wales Police have clearly learned some lessons from the original case. I had expected the new investigation to be little more than them going through the motions or that it would be an attempt to justify the original case. But I have to admit that ACC Wood and DCS Jones are not trying to reconvict the Cardiff Five. They accepted that they were innocent and wanted to move on. Their attitude was refreshing and I wish them well in their search for Lynette's real murderer. But their attitude to Brinkmann's techniques and the overwhelming need to save DNA pending further advances in DNA testing systems may prove to have dire consequences. And their personal honesty notwithstanding, they are the wrong people to investigate what went wrong in the original inquiry for reasons which have been made clear earlier in this book. The Lynette White Inquiry has been actively re-opened. But there needs to be another inquiry independent of South Wales Police into what went wrong in the original inquiry and how and why the criminal justice system performed so appallingly in this case. Had the Home Office not abdicated its responsibilities there would not have been a need for this second inquiry.

Unfortunately, there is no efficient and impartial investigative body to consider the findings outlined in this book. But this case is too important to leave like this. The original investigation was severely flawed and it needs an impartial public inquiry to discover exactly what went wrong and how it can be prevented from ever happening again. Even now, nearly five years after the scandalous convictions of the Cardiff Three were quashed, these concerns still need to be addressed. There must be a fully independent public inquiry into the whole of this appalling case. Anything less will be a complete betrayal of the interests of justice and the memory of Lynette White.

Author's Note

THE FINAL INSULT

The long awaited meeting between Mrs Pesticcio, her solicitor Sadiq Khan, ACC Paul Wood, DCS Jones and representatives of the FSS was scheduled to take place on October 6th 1997. Prior to this meeting Mrs Pesticcio had been expressing mounting dissatisfaction with the way that the re-opened Lynette White Inquiry had been conducted. Also present were Chief Inspector Woodward and Frank Pesticcio. Mrs Pesticcio was told that none of the wallpaper samples had yielded any results with either the amelogenin test or STR typing and that there was nothing left on the skirting board sample to test. Two bloodstains were discovered on the sock. Mrs Pesticcio was informed that they were subjected to analysis by the aforementioned testing systems and it was found that the one which yielded a result, the only sample which had yielded a result in the re-opened Lynette White Inquiry to date, had been deposited by Lynette herself.

That left the jeans. Only two bloodstains remained, but nothing had been done on them yet. Mrs Pesticcio said that she wanted Professor Brinkmann to conduct the tests on the remaining samples, but the police refused to do this and told her that Dr Gill would assess them and would decide which tests were the most useful to do. The police told her that tests would be conducted by the FSS as Peter Gill is at the cutting edge of new technology.

The police then said that Dr Gill and Professor Brinkmann had spoken about the case at length and that Dr Gill was conducting a review of the case and would speak to Brinkmann during it. ACC Wood said that he had total confidence in the FSS and Peter Gill. Mrs Pesticcio was told that the analysis would be carried out by the FSS and that the results would be passed on to anyone they wanted it to be given to.

In answer to Mrs Pesticcio's request that DNA should be stored for future use, they said that they would do whatever Dr Gill advised them to do. They then said that Dr Gill probably would not agree to the samples being sent to Germany. They refused to give an undertaking to save DNA for future analysis and re-iterated that they would do whatever Gill advised them to do, so if that meant that there wouldn't be any DNA, then that was hard luck.

Mrs Pesticcio was then told that they could not use Professor Brinkmann because he does not have the same quality standards that the FSS have and they could not vouch for his reliability. They claimed that his evidence may not stand up in court and that Brinkmann was prepared to push the tests to the limit, whereas the FSS won't go that far because the results can't then be verified. Professor Brinkmann is an expert on DNA techniques of international renown who has worked with the FSS several times without complaint and has given evidence in British courts before. It will also be remembered that both FSS laboratories and that of Brinkmann have co-operated in EDNAP exercises and Dr Gill and six colleagues in the Birmingham laboratory published an article with ramifications on this case in the prestigious *International Journal of Legal Medicine*, a publication that Brinkmann is deeply involved with.

It should also be pointed out that Brinkmann has ensured that his laboratory is optimised for each testing system. This fact is well known to the FSS. Consequently, it should be re-iterated that Brinkmann's techniques are extremely well validated and that he is an eminent forensic scientist of high international repute throughout the forensic science community. Consequently, the criticisms of his methods voiced at the meeting are without foundation to put it mildly. After this unwarranted attack on Brinkmann's methods and, by implication, his scientific integrity, the police said that they would allow Brinkmann to attend the testing and would co-operate with him, but they would not pay for him to attend.

Mrs Pesticcio re-iterated her desire for DNA to be saved pending further advances in DNA testing systems, but was told that it was for South Wales Police to decide whether all the DNA would be used up or not. This flies in the face of common sense. The police had accused Brinkmann of pushing his tests to the limit, yet they refuse to give a commitment that they will not ignore the benefits of future advances in DNA testing systems to conduct tests now which will not be of the standard or quality of tests which will be in routine use in forensic casework in the future. Tests will be developed at more sensitive STR loci. Already DNA has been obtained from fingerprints and from a single cell. Who knows what further wonders will be available in years to come? But without original DNA to work with none of them will be of any use in this inquiry. In this context, can there be a more absurd example of pushing tests to the limit than the stubborn and frankly ridiculous refusal to give an unequivocal guarantee that some DNA will be stored pending the inevitable advances that will be discovered in DNA testing systems in the future?

Mrs Pesticcio also raised the question of testing other samples which could provide relevant information. For example, Professor David Canter believed that the killer had rolled Lynette over in her leather jacket and suggested as long ago as May 1988 that forensic analysis could resolve that. It is still unclear nearly ten years later whether the police acted on this advice then. However, she was told that nothing relevant, including fingerprints, was found on the jacket, but they would let her know about the jacket in due course.

Mrs Pesticcio inquired about the hairs which were discovered at the scene of the crime. The police said that they had checked if Lynette went to grab somebody's hair, but had discovered no clutched hairs. The police refused to conduct mitochondrial DNA sequencing as they regard the amelogenin test and STR typing as the way forward. That may well be true for blood, saliva, semen and even hair roots, but not for testing hair shafts. In the absence of clutched hairs, the hairs found at the scene of the crime could still indicate presence in the flat, which would be significant if the person or persons who had shed hair had denied ever going there. In this context, it is worth pointing out that none of the hairs found at the scene of the crime have been subjected to any kind of DNA test.

And identifying the donor of the aspermic semen could also prove useful. But the police refused to conduct these tests. They re-iterated that it was for them to decide what was relevant and what wasn't. They not only refused to conduct these tests themselves, but refused to allow Mrs Pesticcio access to those samples so she could get them tested herself. According to the police the only relevant samples were JAW 12, JAW14, JAW27, SS2, SS5, SS6, SS11, SS12, SS13, RH26 and RH27. So much for their promise to leave no stone unturned.

They assured Mrs Pesticcio that they had done everything possible with the unidentified fingerprints, which, it will be remembered, included a partial palmprint almost certainly deposited during the murder, but accepted that they had not consulted Interpol or any other foreign agency. This is particularly important as it will be remembered that two ships left Cardiff docks on the murder night for what was then West Germany and the far east. They promised to check their investigations regarding these two ships and forward the results to Mrs Pesticcio.

The police promised to keep Mrs Pesticcio appraised of further developments in writing. ACC Wood stressed that there were three options open to them, to let the FSS do the tests using current validated techniques, to wait for further advances or to get Brinkmann or some other eminent scientist to use invalidated techniques. Khan told them that they would prefer to wait for scientific advances and not use up all the DNA, but the police re-iterated that it was not for Khan or Mrs Pesticcio to make those decisions; that was the privilege of the police.

A number of issues arise from the attitude of the police. Firstly, they have adopted an intransigent approach. While they may not see the relevance of testing some samples, that does not mean that such tests would be irrelevant for reasons which have been identified earlier in this book. Secondly, their refusal to consult international agencies regarding the unidentified fingerprints is frankly baffling. After all, given the fact that two ships left Cardiff on the night of the murder, why should it be assumed that Lynette's murderer did not flee on one of them? And even if the murderer did not use that escape route there are other means of going abroad. Suffice to say, there is no evidence that the real killer of Lynette White has not fled our jurisdiction. Consequently, common sense demands that any unidentified fingerprints in this case should be checked against all those on record, especially through Interpol and any other renowned foreign agencies.

Thirdly, the stubborn refusal of the police to guarantee that some DNA *will* be stored pending further advances in DNA testing systems defies logic. Forensic science and DNA testing systems in particular have made advances in leaps and bounds since the tragic murder of Lynette White. 1997 alone has seen significant developments such as the discovery of DNA on fingerprints. Not only is

there no reason to believe that such important discoveries have peaked, but there is reason to believe that things we can only dream of now will not only be possible in the future, but the time will come when such techniques will be in routine use in forensic casework. In this context, it is absolutely ridiculous to continue testing with what is currently available at the expense of the chance to utilise these exciting new techniques if and when they become available even if that is what they are advised to do by their advisors in the FSS as a result of the review that is currently going on, although, in fairness to the FSS and Dr Gill in particular, it is right to point out that there is reason to believe that the police *will not* be given such inappropriate advice.

Nevertheless, this misses the point as South Wales Police *should not* have the right to use up all of the DNA and so deprive the inquiry of this chance to unmask Lynette's real killer under any circumstances whatsoever. Their position on this point as explained to Mrs Pesticcio and Sadiq Khan offers graphic proof of the need to take such decision making powers away from them once and for all. If they cannot or will not give an unequivocal commitment to preserve an adequate quantity of DNA when the needs of this case demand that DNA be saved pending further advances in forensic techniques, then the government must act. There must be a legally enforceable stipulation that the police must store at least five nanograms of DNA from every scene of crime sample containing bodily fluids or hair pending further advances. Under no circumstances should it be tolerated that all the original DNA is used up. Anything less than such a legally enforceable stipulation is a betrayal of the interests of justice which is manifestly unacceptable.

Mrs Pesticcio and Khan left the meeting with the distinct impression that their concerns, especially over the need to save DNA for future testing had been fobbed off at best, if not fallen entirely on deaf ears. This was very unfortunate as the police had access to information which could and almost certainly would have eased their concerns considerably. They had been informed that Dr Gill and Professor Brinkmann had discussed the case at length, but Mrs Pesticcio and Khan were given no idea of the content of the conversations of these two eminent scientists.

Had the police been fully open with them about the content of these conversations Mrs Pesticcio would have realised that the scientists were not insensitive to her concerns as both Gill and Brinkmann were keen to do everything possible to ensure that DNA remained for testing in the future. The police had stated that they would do whatever Dr Gill advised. Consequently, it seems likely that Gill *will* advise them to ensure that some DNA *is* saved pending further advances and that the police will follow his advice. If the police had made this position crystal clear at the meeting both Pesticcio and Khan would have realised that their concerns were being taken seriously after all. It would later emerge that there was much more of interest in the content of the discussions between the two eminent experts on DNA.

Nevertheless, it is worth remembering that in another case in South Wales Police's jurisdiction the approach to vital samples was found to be sadly wanting and has proved to have had dire consequences. In the recent case of the Merthyr Tydfil Three a crucial issue was whether the petrol used to set the fire which claimed the lives of Diane Jones and her two infant children was leaded or unleaded. The evidence suggested that it was unleaded and Annette Hewins had been seen on the security camera putting leaded petrol into her car. Unfortunately, the forensic scientist Andrew Sweeting, who was involved in the case of the Cardiff Five, used up the entire carpet samples from Diane Jones' home in his tests to try to determine whether the petrol used to set the fire was leaded or unleaded, thereby depriving the defence of the chance to conduct their own tests.

Sweeting's tests did not detect the presence of the lead component of petrol, although Sweeting suggested that it would not have been detected even if it had been present because of the size of the samples. There has also been some question about the validity of the tests that Sweeting conducted and the conclusions that he drew from them. This makes it even more unfortunate that the entire samples were used up in the tests as the defence had effectively been denied any input into what was an absolutely crucial issue in the case of the Merthyr Tydfil Three. Sweeting ought to have ensured that sufficient material was preserved to enable the defence to conduct their own tests, or if that was not possible due to the size of the samples requiring testing, there should have been a legally enforceable obligation to ensure that any testing of such samples is conducted in the presence of an accredited independent scientist of high repute.

This was not the only controversial issue relating to the scientific evidence in this case. Sweeting conducted further tests on samples from his laboratory coat which were consumed in the tests without resolving the issue. Sweeting concluded that the lead component of petrol would not have been detected even if it had been present and so he remained unsure if the petrol used in the fire was leaded or not, even though any evidence obtained from it ought to have been worthless as the fabric of the coat was completely different to the carpet. Such tests are therefore of questionable scientific value.

And it should be remembered that not only has Sweeting's approach to the crucial carpet samples deprived the defence of the right to conduct their own tests, but if and when a forensic test is developed that could unequivocally solve the riddle of the carpet, there is no crime scene sample that could be subjected to such a test. This is a completely unsatisfactory state of affairs and if South Wales Police refuse to adopt a policy of ***guaranteeing*** that scene of crime samples ***will not*** be tested to death, then the decision ***must*** be taken from them by the government enacting legislation which makes it legally binding on the police to ***ensure*** that vital source material ***is*** saved pending advances in forensic or chemical testing systems or if that is not possible due to the size of the samples then ***any*** testing ***must*** be conducted in the presence of an accredited independent scientist of high repute.

The situation in the re-opened Lynette White Inquiry has not reached the stage where there are no vital samples left to test yet and there is reason for optimism that it never will as Dr Gill is undoubtedly aware of the importance of saving DNA pending future advances in DNA testing systems. However, it ought to be pointed out that with the exception of two samples, all of the samples which originated from Lynette's killer have been used up in tests that have failed to yield any useful information. Consequently, the inquiry has been deprived of any of the benefits that such testing could provide if and when they become available. This is unfortunate at best. Furthermore, it offers graphic proof of the need to give an unequivocal commitment that this will not be allowed to happen to the remaining samples.

The next point concerns the police's attitude to Professor Brinkmann throughout the re-opened Lynette White Inquiry. It will be remembered that the police insisted on attempting to multiplex all the relevant samples, despite the inappropriate nature of such testing and the suitability of Brinkmann's techniques to the particular needs of the samples in this inquiry. And this error was now compounded by the police's claims about Brinkmann's techniques and his ability to give evidence in Britain which are totally without foundation. On November 3rd I wrote to the professor outlining the police's position as explained to Mrs Pesticcio and Sadiq Khan at the meeting of October 6th, asking him to comment on the claims that had been made about his techniques at that meeting.

At the outset it should be re-iterated that Brinkmann is a world renowned expert whose techniques are well validated and he has given evidence to British courts before. Both of these facts are well known to the FSS. On November 14th Brinkmann replied to my letter, mounting a vigorous defence of his methods. Brinkmann wrote, "The claim by the police 'that we do not have the same quality standards that the FSS have and that they could not vouch for your (Brinkmann's) reliability' is incorrect and is not based any factual evidence."

As Brinkmann points out, his laboratory has worked with the FSS several times and there has been no criticism of the quality of their work. And as for the claim that it may not stand up in court, Brinkmann points out that is also incorrect because a joint strategy had been agreed where any testing at his laboratory would have been conducted under the joint supervision of the FSS who would then be able to testify to the correctness and validity of the techniques used.

This raised an important point. What was the joint strategy that Brinkmann referred to? Professor Brinkmann informed me that Dr Gill had been given permission by South Wales Police to contact him. The aim was to formulate a joint approach for the next steps in the investigation. Professor Brinkmann wrote, "Dr Gill was very co-operative and neutral during our (verbal) discussion and the possibilities and various strategies for subsequent investigations were considered. We agreed to issue a joint statement on the most appropriate approach for further investigations in this case. Dr Gill formulated a document which I agreed to and it was proposed that this should be made available to the parties concerned."

Brinkmann then referred to two paragraphs of my letter to him of November 3rd which stated that Mrs Pesticcio was told by the police that the final decision on what to do would be taken by Dr Gill who probably would not agree to samples being sent to Brinkmann because it would be of limited benefit to senior officers and that the police would not ensure that they would save DNA pending further advances in DNA testing systems, but would do whatever Gill advised them to do even if that meant using up all of the DNA. Brinkmann stated that this would seem to indicate the opposite of what he had agreed with Gill in the joint statement.

Brinkmann also wrote, "In the light of what has preceded it may well be that no further investigations are possible but the discussions with Dr Gill seemed to indicate that everything would be done to ensure that some material remained for further testing."

It should also be pointed out that according to Brinkmann's colleague, Dr Stephen Rand, neither Gill nor Brinkmann were bothered about where the actual testing was conducted and both were keen that representatives of both the FSS and Brinkmann's laboratory should attend wherever the testing was actually carried out. This would seem to contradict the police's claims that Gill probably would not agree to the samples being sent to Brinkmann.

Thus, it seems that both Dr Gill and Professor Brinkmann were in fact in agreement on an approach that would have considerably eased Mrs Pesticcio's concerns. Consequently, it is baffling that the police chose not to inform her directly of the contents of the conversations between Brinkmann and Gill and ensure that she had a copy of the joint statement agreed by the two eminent scientists before the meeting took place. Had they done so, the meeting could have progressed in a different manner and Mrs Pesticcio would not have been left with the impression, rightly or wrongly, that the police never intended for her to find out about the joint statement. It is unfortunate that the police did not specifically disclose it to her as it creates the impression that they had something to hide whether that is true or not and it is hardly likely to restore her already dented confidence in their investigation.

Professor Brinkmann's letter clearly indicates that a joint statement was agreed and that Mrs Pesticcio should have received a copy of it. Not only has this never been disclosed to her, but she was unaware of its existence until Brinkmann referred to it. It seems to defy common sense for the police to go to the level of allowing Dr Gill to discuss the case with Brinkmann in depth and agree a joint statement on the best way forward for the investigation and then to launch an unwarranted attack on Brinkmann's extremely well validated methods which would have been inconceivable had the full extent of the co-operation between Dr Gill and Professor Brinkmann been known to both Khan and Pesticcio.

It should also be pointed out that in their recent meeting with South Wales Police and representatives of the FSS, nobody saw fit to inform either Khan or Pesticcio of this joint statement even though the subject of Professor Brinkmann was raised more than once. On December 11th Sadiq Khan wrote to ACC Wood pointing out that it had been proposed that Mrs Pesticcio ought to have received a copy of the joint statement. He expressed disappointment that the joint statement was not given to them at the meeting or subsequent to it.

Khan quoted Brinkmann's reply to me and asked for an urgent explanation as to the parameters of Gill's review and whether the FSS still intends to work in partnership with Professor Brinkmann. On December 16th Detective Superintendent D.W. Phillips replied to Khan's letter. Phillips informed Khan that DCS Jones had recently retired and that he would now be assisting ACC Wood. Phillips also informed Khan that he had brought his concerns to the attention of Dr John Bassett of the Chepstow laboratory and asked him for a response. He also promised to write as soon as possible in relation to Khan's concerns and give an up to date position regarding Dr Gill's review. Phillips' response was conspicuous by its absence of an explanation for the police's failure to disclose the joint statement agreed to by Dr Gill and Professor Brinkmann. And it will be noted that Phillips did not take this opportunity to disclose it. This is unfortunate as Khan clearly believed that the police ought to have disclosed the joint statement to them at the meeting or subsequently. This has still not happened. It is also significant that Khan wanted clarification on whether the FSS still intended to work with Professor Brinkmann. This suggests that Khan is sceptical as to whether there is any joint approach to speak of now.

Consequently, we are entitled to know why a joint statement was agreed and then effectively ignored, culminating in an astonishing and totally unwarranted attack on the methods and abilities of Professor Brinkmann, which, contrary to the opinion of ACC Wood, are extremely well validated. It is also worth noting that the failure to disclose this information has undermined Mrs Pesticcio's confidence in the conduct of the re-opened Lynette White Inquiry even more - possibly beyond repair. It could and should have been so different if only the police had seen fit to disclose that document in advance, rather than re-inforce her suspicions that they have something to hide. Had they done so there would have been no possibility of attributing a sinister motive to the failure to disclose this pertinent information and confidence in South Wales Police's current investigation may have been restored rather than damaged yet more. At the very least, it was unwise of them not to ensure that Mrs Pesticcio had access to this vitally important information as such decisions offer fertile ground for conspiracy theories whether one exists or not.

Nevertheless, it is also worth pointing out that if the police continue to refuse to give an unequivocal guarantee that DNA will be saved pending future advances in DNA and are advised to conduct tests now, they will do so and if those tests yield no useful results the last realistic chance to unmask the real killer of Lynette White will have been lost once and for all. There are only two samples capable of providing direct evidence against the real killer left, although there are other less important samples which could still be tested. The FSS have tested all the samples they believe to be relevant to date and failed to get any results with multiplexing even though the police were warned that this would happen in September 1996. In April 1997 the police conceded that this had happened. Of all the samples that they have tested via singleplexing, only one result has been obtained and that turned out to have been deposited by Lynette herself. This can hardly be said to be a glowing triumph of the approach favoured by the police.

The tragedy is that their intransigent approach towards Professor Brinkmann throughout the re-opened Lynette White Inquiry, notwithstanding them allowing Dr Gill to discuss the case with him, has robbed us of the possibility of knowing if Brinkmann's techniques might have proved more fruitful than the tests that the FSS have used in this inquiry. And their failure to be frank with all the relevant information at their disposal has further undermined Mrs Pesticcio's already shaken confidence in the re-opened Lynette White Inquiry, possibly beyond repair. In short, the conduct of the police in the re-opened Lynette White Inquiry from the moment my submission forced the investigation to be re-opened back in 1995 has left more than a little to be desired when it could and should have been so different. Small wonder Mrs Pesticcio re-iterated her position at her recent meeting with the police and FSS that she wanted an external police force to take over the investigation.

December 19th 1997

Joint Statement re. Murder of Lynette White[1]

P. Gill; B. Brinkmann.

1) On the initiative of South Wales Police force, Dr. P. Gill made contact with Professor Brinkmann (Munster) on 8th September with the aim to agree a strategy for the joint examination and DNA typing of stains relevant to the murder case of Lynette White.

2) We understand that there are body fluid stains (and/or) extracts from articles taken from the scene of the crime. In particular there are stains on wallpaper and stains on the jeans of the victim.

3) We understand that the victim, Lynette White, was killed by multiple stabbing, hence the majority of the blood staining would be expected to have come from her.

4) In addition it is not disputed that an individual "Psaila" was present at the time of the murder. It is understood that she participated in stabbing the victim. Further it is understood that she bled at the scene.[2]

5) Therefore the presence of blood which matches either the victim or Psaila presumably does not provide useful information in this case.

6) We understood that it is alleged that 'unknown' perpetrator(s) committed the murder. Further we understand that there are no suspects in this case which are available for comparison purposes.

7) If an analysis is carried out and a DNA profile is obtained which matches neither Lynette White nor Psaila, then the following possibilities must be considered.
   a) The DNA came from the perpetrator or co-perpetrators *or*
   b) The DNA came from an individual unconnected with the crime,
   ie there has been a transfer of DNA by some other means.

8) The absence of available suspects in this case is a clear disadvantage in making an interpretation in the event that DNA from an unknown source is discovered. We cannot give information about ***when*** a particular body fluid was deposited. But we can sometimes make inferences based upon the stain formation and analysis of droplet formation.

9) If DNA is discovered from an unknown source, it is not clear what the next steps would be if there are no available suspects for testing purposes. The implications of this will need careful consideration by all concerned with this case.

10) If it is decided that further testing would be useful, then we propose that this is carried out as a collaborative exercise between the FSS and Professor Brinkmann.

11) The first step to decide the strategy to be used must be to provide Professor Brinkmann with an opportunity to examine the case material. This can be carried out at an FSS laboratory. Once Professor Brinkmann has examined the material in conjunction with an FSS scientist we will propose a testing strategy. (In addition we will need to review results of previous testing, consider possibilities for testing stains and consider possibilities for testing 'new' stains).

A breakdown of costs for the first meeting can be provided.

---

[1] This is a handwritten version of the document written by Dr Gill on September 8th 1997. A typed version was sent to South Wales Police. The responsibility for publishing this version is mine: the author.
[2] It should be remembered that this information was supplied to Gill by the police. However, it should be noted that there is no indisputable and credible evidence that Psaila was present at the scene of the crime. The discovery of her blood group there does not prove that she was there as approximately sixteen thousand people in Britain possess that blood group and given her history of untruths in this inquiry her insistence that she was there cannot be taken

APPENDIX 1

The New Forensic Evidence[1]

(1) Alun Michael's letter to Michael Howard dated 24/05/95

(2) Mark Webster's report dated 08/05/97

(3) A guide to DNA

[1] For editorial reasons I have not included my letter to Alun Michael as the issues raised in it have been thoroughly rehearsed in the main text.

24 May 1995

Dear Michael,

I am sure you will recall the case of Lynette White, the woman who was murdered in the Docks area of Cardiff and whose murderer or murderers have not been brought to justice. There was considerable publicity when those accused of her death were tried and subsequently found not guilty by the Appeal Court.

I have been contacted by Satish Sekar, an investigative journalist specialising in crime and justice issues, who has taken a special interest in the application of scientific methods to the investigation of crime.

Mr Sekar has set out his findings and concerns in a letter which I attach to this letter. His concerns are supported by the first reaction of an expert whose response I also enclose for your information. As you will see, he believes that Mr Sekar is "on the right lines" with his inquiries and the concluding paragraph of his report states that it is "not a question of an investigation where it is too late to hope for a positive outcome."

I am sure that you will agree on the importance that his conclusions are fully investigated, particularly in view of the unsatisfactory nature of scientific investigations at the time and suggestions that there are two suspects who should be considered further in the light of the evidence. As DNA testing is at the heart of the issue, I also enclose a simple guide to DNA issues for your information.

In view of these claims, I would ask you to take immediate steps to secure the files and evidence at Chepstow and the files and evidence in the incident room at Rumney Police Station before giving full consideration to the need for a detailed investigation. This is of particular importance since answering the question "what exists?" will lead to conclusions regarding what tests can now be undertaken.

If Mr Sekar is correct in his analysis, it would appear that many or all of the decisions that were taken by the police at the time are understandable in the light of the scientific knowledge then available. However, Mr Sekar's analysis calls into question the failure to produce some of the scientific evidence - which was therefore not available to the Police or the Crown Prosecution Service - and suggests that different conclusions are likely if the scientific evidence is now re-examined in the light of methods and knowledge now available.

I shall be grateful if you will order a full inquiry, together with a detailed assessment of the scientific evidence, in the light of Mr Sekar's submission. This is a step which I understand, is within your powers and has been taken on a number of occasions in the past.

I have spoken to Mr Sekar again today and he has confirmed his willingness to make available all the material that he has been able to obtain in the course of his investigations to help with such an inquiry.

I look forward to hearing from you and hope you will be able to give a positive response.

Yours Sincerely

Alun Michael
Shadow Minister for Home Affairs

The Lynette White Murder

Report on aspects of blood evidence

8 May 1995

Mark Webster

Forensic Science Consultancy

Summary

1 This report is based on a limited amount of information provided by Mr Satish Sekar, and information derived from various scientific reports. My opinions are offered conditionally, sight of the original scientific tests and records of processing might present additional information which would alter my opinions.

2 Angela Psaila was accused of involvement in the murder of Lynette White, partially on the basis that "foreign" blood found at the scene and on the deceased's clothing was the same combination of groups as Ms Psaila's blood.

3 This "foreign" blood was tested and found to contain substances characteristic of male blood. An opinion was offered in court that this male reaction could have come from a tiny proportion of contaminating male blood, the majority of the blood staining originating from Ms Psaila. However, at least one other potential source of this blood was identified by the police: a man Mr Y, who was of the same blood groups as Ms Psaila.

4 Mr Y appears to have been eliminated from enquiries as a result of a mismatch being declared between his DNA profile and a very partial DNA profile obtained from blood staining found on wall paper at the scene - despite the fact that one of the Crown's scientists offered the opinion that the blood on the wall paper could have come from Lynette White herself, and may not have been the attacker's blood.

5 The judgement that the blood on the wall paper came from the attacker and not Ms White herself appears to have been made on the basis that this blood staining was adjacent to some of the "foreign" blood staining on the skirting board. Two stains which are adjacent need not necessarily have a common origin. More sensitive DNA tests, which could have resolved this issue, appear not to have been carried out. It might be possible to carry out such tests now.

1 Circumstances

1.1 On the 17th February 1995 Mr Satish Sekar sent to me various papers including scientific statements made by Home Office forensic scientists during the investigation of the murder of Lynette White. Mr Sekar has asked me to comment on specific aspects of this evidence.

1.2 I had some peripheral involvement in the investigation of this offence as I was working in the DNA profiling unit of the Birmingham Home Office Forensic Laboratory at that time. Dr Nicholas Prance was responsible for the DNA profiling in this case, but would routinely have shown me many or all the profiles he prepared, and I would have agreed on the comparisons made between profiles.

1.3 A number of blood stains were found at the scene of the murder and on the dead woman's clothing. The stains were tested using a variety of body fluid profiling techniques (blood grouping and DNA profiling) in an attempt to discover the sources of the blood staining. Mr Sekar has informed me that certain suspects were eliminated from police enquiries as a result of this testing.

2 Qualifications and experience

2.1 I hold a first class honours degree in Biology. I have worked as a forensic scientist since 1979. In the period up to 1991 I was employed by the Home Office Forensic Science Service. In 1992 I held the position of Scientific Support Manager of a provincial police force with responsibilities including the use of forensic science in police investigations and management of scenes of crime officers. In the last two years I have worked in private practice as a forensic scientist.

2.2 I have very extensive experience of scientific evidence types involved in the investigation of the murder of Lynette White. I have examined hundreds of cases involving DNA profiling and blood grouping. I have offered expert evidence about these matters on many occasions to the courts.

3 The statements provided

3.1 The copies of statements provided by Mr Sekar are not the original statements provided by the forensic scientists. It appears to be common practice for original signed statements submitted to the police to be re-typed. These re-typed statements form the committal bundle. This is often done when an incident is being investigated using the HOLMES system. All statements are entered into computer records, and it is these computer recorded statements which are then output as hard copy for disclosure to the defence team.

4 DNA tests

4.1 Samples of blood stained wall paper recovered from the scene of the murder were sent to the Birmingham Forensic Science Laboratory for DNA profiling. Two of the samples submitted yielded no profile. This is not unusual; blood can contain very little DNA, and even large fresh stains often fail to yield a profile using the techniques of DNA profiling which were available to the Home Office labs at that time.

4.2 Two of the wall paper samples yielded DNA profiles. The DNA profiling technique used on the samples is known as Multi-Locus Probe (MLP) profiling. This is the form of DNA profiling invented by Alec Jeffreys, and was the first form of DNA profiling introduced into operational forensic investigation in the UK.

---

[1] The HOLMES system was not used in this case: the author.

4.3 An MLP profile consists of a pattern of bands similar to the bar codes seen on food packaging. A "full" MLP profile, prepared from an adequate quantity of DNA in good condition, for instance from a very large fresh blood stain, would on average show approximately eleven bands - though full profiles which consist of anything from seven to seventeen bands have been observed. Where the amount of DNA available for analysis is limited, or the DNA has become degraded ("gone off") then the number of bands seen in the profile will be reduced. Such a partial profile is not as characteristic as a full profile, and might coincidentally match a fairly large proportion of the population, rather than a mere handful of individuals.

4.4 The Home Office laboratories adopted a policy that a profile consisting of less than four bands would not be used to incriminate, though of course adopting the principle of giving the benefit of the doubt to a defendant such a partial profile might be reported if it tended to eliminate an accused person.

4.5 In the early nineties MLP profiling was almost completely superseded by another form of DNA profiling called Single Locus Probe (SLP) profiling. In this type of DNA profiling the profile is built up step-by-step using a series of tests called single locus probes. The SLP technique has significant advantages over the earlier MLP technique. SLP profiling requires less blood to obtain results, and often a full profile can be obtained from partially degraded DNA when MLP profiling has failed to obtain useful results.

4.6 In addition it became apparent in the operational use of MLP profiling that the technique was subject to various technical problems which sometimes resulted in artefactual bands being generated. Often DNA derived from two different samples taken from the same person would show band differences when in fact they should in theory give identical banding patterns. Differences were observed in the banding patterns of one in five matched semen and blood samples. Sometimes even the same type of sample, for instance blood samples, derived from the same person yielded different banding patterns when analysed.

4.7 Despite these problems MLP profiling proved to be a valuable investigative tool; when samples matched this generally provided strong evidence that the two samples had originated from the same source. When samples had originated from different individuals one would generally expect to see very large differences in the profiles, and an elimination could be reported with a high degree of confidence. However when there were only slight differences then some judgement would have to be made as to whether the differences were of such a magnitude that the samples were likely to have originated from different sources.

5 The wall paper stains

5.1 I understand that a four banded profile was obtained from the sample of wall paper SS2. The bands present in this profile appeared to correspond in position to the strongest bands in a profile derived from an authentic control sample of Lynette White's blood. This is what would be expected if the blood on the wall paper was in fact Lynette White's and the DNA in the blood was limited in quantity or had become degraded. In my opinion it is reasonable to assume that this blood stain originated from the dead woman.

5.2 A second stain SS12 yielded a profile also consisting of four bands. Apparently this showed some similarity with the dead woman's profile but also showed significant differences. Dr Prance concluded that he could not eliminate this stain as having come from Lynette White. In my opinion, this was an appropriate interpretation; it would be wrong under these circumstances to assume that the blood had necessarily originated from an attacker.

5.3 The DNA profiling results were also inspected by Mr John Hayward, a forensic Scientist instructed by the defence team. Mr Hayward offered the firm opinion that the stain SS12 was not Lynette White's blood. He appears to have been unaware of the differences in DNA profiles which are often seen in samples taken from the same individual. In my opinion Dr Prance's interpretation, based on his extensive experience of DNA profiling, was the correct one.

5.4 Dr Prance pointed out that the differences seen in the profile derived from the blood stained wall paper, and Lynette White's blood could be accounted for by the degradation of the blood on the wall paper, and by chemical changes that might have been brought about in the DNA by treatment of the blood stained wall paper with a fingerprinting chemical called Ninhydrin. Ninhydrin does cause chemical changes in DNA, and in my opinion it is entirely possible that the chemical could have caused the differences seen in the profiles.

5.5 Dr Prance offered further opinions about the blood staining. He pointed out that a stain on the skirting board JAW27, adjacent to the wall paper stain SS12, and taken by Dr John Whiteside to be ***"representative of the blood on the wall"*** had been tested by Dr Whiteside and found to be of groups PGM 1+1-, AK 1. This is different from the blood of Lynette White who was of groups PGM 1+, AK 2-1. This blood could not have originated from her. Whether the blood on the wall paper SS12 came from the same source as the blood on the skirting board is a matter of speculation; I cannot agree with Dr Whiteside's opinion that it is reasonable to suppose that all the blood on the wall had the same origin.

5.6 Further attempts were made to characterise this blood staining. The blood stained wall paper was returned to the Chepstow Laboratory where attempts were made to carry out conventional blood grouping tests. These could have resolved the issue, and might have shown that the blood staining was different from

Lynette White's blood. In the event these tests were unsuccessful. Similarly attempts were made to determine the sex of the individual who shed the blood. These tests were unsuccessful.

6 The elimination of Mr X and Mr Y

6.1 It has been put to me that Mr X and Mr Y, both of whom had blood groups which match the blood groups obtained from the skirting board stain JAW27 were eliminated as suspects on the basis that their DNA profiles did not match the profiles obtained from the blood stained wall paper samples SS2 and SS12.

6.2 Dr Prance tested a blood sample from Mr X and reported that his profile was different from that obtained from the blood on the wall paper. However if the blood on the wall paper originated from Lynette White then this comparison is of no value whatsoever in eliminating Mr X from any involvement in the offence. However conventional blood grouping tests carried out on other blood staining did show a difference in comparison with Mr X's blood sample, and these staining could not have originated from him.

6.3 Another individual, Mr Y, was apparently also considered as a possible source of the blood left at the scene of the murder. This individual was also DNA profiled by Dr Prance and eliminated as the source of the blood on the wall paper. Again if the blood on the wall paper in fact originated from Lynette White, as Dr Prance thought it might have done, then this comparison is of no value in eliminating Mr Y's alleged involvement.

7 Conventional blood grouping tests

7.1 Conventional blood grouping tests generated extremely useful information during the course of the enquiry. "Foreign" blood, by which I mean blood which could not have originated from the deceased but which might have come from an attacker, was found at the scene and on the dead woman's clothing. The "foreign" blood on Lynette White's jeans and sock was of a rare combination of groups. The blood grouping on the sock was the most complete, there was sufficient blood staining present to obtain results in six different grouping tests. The blood on the jeans yielded results in five of these tests, but the results obtained indicate that blood stains on the two different garments could have originated from the same person. Likewise the limited blood grouping carried out on the stains taken from the skirting board JAW27 and the wall by the curtain RH27 indicate that this blood could have come from the same single source.

7.2 Angela Psaila's blood sample was tested and found to be of the same combination of groups. Therefore on the basis of these results alone she could be considered a source of this "foreign" blood found at the scene. Mr Y's blood grouping was also exactly coincidental with the groups of the "foreign" blood staining found on the dead woman's clothing.

7.3 Mr X's blood grouping was the same as the blood staining on the dead woman's clothing, in five out of six groups. However he differed in the Hp typing test; he was of Hp type 2-1 and the blood on the dead woman's clothing was of group Hp 2. Doubts were raised about the validity of these grouping tests which I do not intend to rehearse here. However if the results were valid, then Mr X can be eliminated as a source of the blood on the sock.

8 DNA Sex testing

8.1 Plainly, grouping tests demonstrated that the "foreign" blood present on the deceased's clothing could have originated from either Angela Psaila or Mr Y. In an attempt to resolve this issue the staining was sent to Dr Peter Gill of the Home Office Forensic Science Service's Central Research Establishment in Aldermaston. He carried out novel tests, not routinely employed in forensic casework, for the presence of DNA characteristic of male blood and obtained positive results. On the face of it, these results should have eliminated Angela Psaila as the source of the blood staining. However, later Dr Gill offered the opinion that the blood staining could be a mixture of male and female blood, and that only a small proportion of male blood would have to be present to give a positive reaction in the DNA test he used.

8.2 It is undoubtedly true that a mixture of male and female blood will give a reaction characteristic of male blood, and that a mixture could be mistaken for a single simple male blood stain using this type of DNA technology. It is also true that there was other evidence of a mixture of blood being present in one of the stains on the clothing. John Hayward noted that one of the stains on the jeans (no 4) showed some evidence of a mixture of blood being present, in that the Hp grouping result appeared to be a mixture of Hp 2-1 with Hp 2. John Hayward expressed surprise that the other grouping systems did not show evidence of a mixture. I do not consider this at all surprising. In carrying out blood grouping tests different portions of a stain would be removed for the different grouping tests. If a stain actually consists of areas of staining of two different people's blood which have come to lie alongside each other, some portions (and therefore individual tests) may show evidence of a mixture, but others may not.

8.3 John Hayward suggested that one explanation for this result was that a small proportion of the deceased's blood had become mixed with the "foreign" blood. In my opinion this is entirely reasonable.

8.4 Irrespective of these complications there was a "foreign" blood type present on the dead woman's clothing which gave a reaction characteristic of male blood. Despite the fact that the grouping results obtained matches Angela Psaila, the male reaction obtained would eliminate her as the source of the blood. Indeed, that is why the test would have been carried out - to distinguish Angela Psaila from Mr Y as the source of the blood. I am unaware of the circumstances which caused Dr Gill to advance the theory that the male reaction he obtained was caused by a minority component of male blood being present, and that in fact the majority of the blood had come from Angela Psaila. In my opinion had Dr Gill been aware that there was possibly another viable suspect of the same blood groups as Angela Psaila, who was a man, he might have taken the view that this suspect was an equally likely, if not more likely, source of the incriminating "foreign" blood staining.

9 Additional testing

9.1 SLP DNA profiling has the potential to obtain information from degraded stains which have not yielded useful results using MLP profiling. SLP tests can also unequivocally indicate the presence of a mixture of blood from more than one person in a stain. Indeed SLP profiling was attempted on the stains on the deceased's jeans, but unfortunately no result was obtained. At that time the Home Office Forensic Science Service did not have the facilities to carry out routine SLP testing, and consequently the samples were sent to Dr Paul Debenham at Cellmark Diagnostics for the tests to be carried out.

9.2 It is not clear to me why such additional testing was not attempted on the DNA extracted from the crucial stain on the wall paper SS12. If this stain was tested and found to be of the same SLP profile as Lynette White, then the elimination of Mr Y on the basis that his DNA profile did not match the profile of this blood would be shown to have no valid basis.

9.3 It would be possible to attempt this DNA profiling test even now, years after the initial investigation. Extracted DNA is immobilised on nylon hybridisation membranes. These membranes are retained at the forensic science laboratory for many years under extreme low temperatures. The membranes could be subjected to SLP profiling, though there is no guarantee that such tests would work.

DNA profiling: MLPs, SLPs, PCR - and introducing STRs!

STR analysis - a summary

STR analysis is a new form of DNA profiling in which DNA from tiny amounts of evidential material is "grown" in a process which mimics the natural growth of living creatures.

This DNA is rapidly analysed using automatic computer controlled machines developed as part of the human genome project.
An STR profile is a complex pattern of coloured bands which has the potential to offer near certainty of identification.

DNA

DNA stands for deoxyribose nucleic acid. This is a complex chemical which occurs in most human tissues and body fluids. DNA is like a chemical blueprint which determines how our bodies are built up. Each cell of the human body carries effectively identical DNA; so the DNA in a man's sperm will be identical to the DNA in his blood.

The DNA is a long linear "message" built up of sub-units called bases. In places this message stutters and the number of stutters seen in different people's DNA will vary: one person's DNA may read, "Mary hadhad a little lamb," another's may read, "Mary hadhadhadhad a little lamb." The difference between the two individuals is that one has two stutters of the word "had," the other has four stutters. Many different areas of the DNA message are stuttered in this way. Analysing a number of different "stutters" can show differences between different people's DNA, and can potentially identify the source of a body fluid sample with a great degree of certainty.

The first forms of DNA profiling developed work by cutting the stuttered areas of the DNA free from the mass of ordinary DNA. The stutters are then spread out according to size. This process is called "electrophoresis;" the samples of DNA are applied to a slab of gel and an electric current is passed through the gel. Small fragments of DNA consisting of short stutters are driven through the gel faster than large fragments. At the end of the process the DNA stutters have been sorted according to their size. The DNA fragments are then transferred on to a sheet of nylon membrane by a process known as "blotting."

Individual stuttered "words" can then be highlighted on the membrane in a series of tests called single-locus probes. Each probe reveals just one word; for instance one probe will reveal stutters of the word "had," another might reveal stutters of the word "Mary." The processes used generate dark bands on a photographic film. These bands are a physical representation of the position of the DNA fragments in the electrophoresis gel, the position of the bands is a measure of the size of the stuttered fragments.

The size of individual stutters in different samples can be compared. If the size of stutters of a particular word are the same then the bands revealed in the DNA profiles of those samples will appear in the same position in the DNA profiles. If the samples do not match, the stutters are of different sizes, then the bands will appear in different positions.

Each test or single-locus probe actually reveals two bands in each sample. This is because human beings have two sets of DNA; one from the mother and one from the father. Each of the two bands is inherited from one parent.

The type of DNA profiling described here is the type which is currently used most commonly in forensic science called Single-Locus Profiling (SLP) and differs from the type of DNA profiling, Multi-Locus Profiling (MLP) invented by Alec Jeffreys.

In MLP analysis many different stuttered words are analysed at the same time. This produces a complex profile which consists of many different bands. Single-locus probing produces just two or one bands with each test, and a more detailed (and characteristic) profile is built up in a series of stages using more than one single-locus probe test.

SLP analysis is currently used in preference to MLP analysis as it is generally thought to be more sensitive (will work with smaller samples) and is more likely to work with a sample which has become degraded ("gone off"). The simple profiles produced by single-locus profiling are easier to measure and analyse using computerised image analysis techniques.

STR analysis

In places smaller sections of the DNA message are stuttered. It is as if the individual letters of the words were stuttered, rather than whole words. So one person's DNA might read, "the ccccat sat on the mat," whereas another person's DNA might read, "the ccat sat on the mat." These short repeated sequences are called Short Tandem Repeats or STRs.

The Polymerase Chain Reaction

In fact DNA has a double structure. The message of the DNA is written twice in two strings which lie alongside each other like two halves of a zip fastener.

This double strand of DNA can be unzipped into two single strands. It is then possible to recreate two new double strands by copying the single strands.

Using our previous example, a section of double stranded DNA message reads:

.....the cccat sat on the mat.....
.....the cccat sat on the mat.....

Unzipping the double strand gives two single strands:
.....the cccat sat on the mat.....
and
.....the cccat sat on the mat.....

It's now possible to recreate two double strands by using the single strands as templates, reading off the existing single strands, adding letters to create two new strands of DNA identical to the original.

.....the cccat s.....
.....the cccat sat on the mat.....

and
.....the cccat sat.....
.....the cccat sat on the mat.....

This process occurs in living creatures. When a human egg is fertilised it starts to divide; one cell into two, two cells into four and so on. Eventually after nine months a human baby consisting of billions of cells results. Each time a cell divides to create two new cells the DNA also divides, and a copy of the original DNA strand is given to each of the new cells.

The process of PCR imitates this natural process in the test tube. Using repeated "cycles" of heating and cooling of a DNA sample in a chemical solution it's possible to make a single DNA molecule replicate itself. After thirty or so cycles there will be many million times more DNA than at the beginning of the process. This was the technique used to recreate dinosaur DNA from the small amounts of DNA extracted from the stomach contents of an ancient fossilized blood sucking insect trapped in amber in the film "Jurassic Park."

Large amounts of DNA are easier and quicker to analyse than small amounts. And multiplying DNA means that samples which would otherwise be too small, are suitable for analysis.

As the technology stands it is not possible to multiply all the DNA message. In fact it is rather difficult to accurately multiply a long section of the message. So forensic scientists are concentrating on small sections of the DNA message which can be accurately duplicated. It is not possible to accurately multiply up those sections of the DNA analysed by MLP and SLP analysis (whole stuttered words like "hadhad," but it is possible to multiply up the sections of the DNA containing STRs (short stutters like "cccc").

The Gene Scanner

There is a world-wide project to read the whole of the human DNA message called the Human Genome Project. At the current rate of development it is likely that the whole of the human DNA message will have been read by the year 2005. Machines have been developed to assist scientists in this project, and it has been possible to adapt one of these machines to assist in forensic analysis of DNA.

To carry out an STR analysis the scientist extracts DNA from the samples of interest, for instance small numbers of sperms in a tiny semen stain, or from the few mouth cells in a saliva sample taken from a suspect.

Selected STRs, stuttered letters in the DNA message, are then multiplied up by the process of PCR. The new strands of DNA created in the multiplication process are tagged with a coloured fluorescent chemical. Each different stutter is labelled with a different coloured chemical. So in a section of the DNA message numerous copies of the different stuttered letter sections will be generated:

.....the ccccat sat onnnnn the mat.....

PCR selects and multiplies up the stuttered sections:

cccc nnnnn
cccc nnnnn
cccc nnnnn
cccc nnnnn

The stutters of the letter "c" might be labelled with a blue coloured chemical, those of the letter "n" will be labelled with a different colour - perhaps yellow. Using different colours in this way allows the forensic scientist to analyse more than one stuttered section of the DNA message at once. Using the SLP technique all the DNA stutters were revealed as black bands, and it was not possible to analyse more than one stutter at a time because it would be possible to confuse one stuttered region with another.

Only a limited number of different coloured labels are available but even so it's possible to carry out four different STR tests together (as a "quadruplex") or even perhaps six different tests (a "hexaplex").

The gene scanner sorts the DNA fragments generated by the PCR process according to size in a modified process of electrophoresis. The fragments of DNA are driven through a short slab of gel, eventually falling of the end of the slab. As in any process of electrophoresis the smallest fragments travel fastest, and arrive at the end of the slab of gel before the largest fragments. As the fragments arrive at the end of the gel, and before they fall off, a laser beam illuminates the gel, and the presence of coloured DNA fragments is detected by a sensitive light detector.

A computer records the arrival of the coloured fragments at the edge of the gel and displays on a monitor a multi-coloured multi-banded DNA profile. STR profiles match when the position the similarly coloured bands in two profiles correspond.

The use of a quadruplex test is likely to offer moderately strong evidence, allowing the scientist to say that a profile is likely to occur in only one in thousands of the population. A hexaplex test could offer much stronger evidence, equivalent to the near certainty of identification offered by previous DNA profiling tests such as MLP and SLP analysis - combined with the incredible sensitivity offered by PCR.

APPENDIX 2

The Aftermath of the Forensic Submission[1]

(1) David MacLean's reply to Alun Michael's letter to Michael Howard dated 22/06/95
(2) Alun Michael's reply to David MacLean's letter dated 31/08/95
(3) Ann Widdecombe's reply to Alun Michael's letter on David MacLean's behalf dated 18/09/95
(4) Alun Michael's reply to Ann Widdecombe's letter dated 22/09/95
(5) My letter to Ann Widdecombe dated 02/10/95
(6) Rhodri Morgan MP's letter to Michael Howard dated 04/10/95
(7) Rhodri Morgan's letter to Bob Evans (Deputy Chief Constable of South Wales Police) dated 04/10/95
(8) David MacLean's reply to Alun Michael's last letter to Ann Widdecombe dated 17/10/95
(9) Bob Evans' letter to Alun Michael dated 17/10/95
(10) DCS Phil Jones' reply to Rhodri Morgan's letter to Bob Evans dated 06/11/95
(11) Rhodri Morgan's reply to DCS Jones' letter dated 12/01/96
(12) The article published in the *Independent* on January 15th 1996
(13) DCS Jones' reply to Rhodri Morgan's second letter dated 19/01/96
(14) Rhodri Morgan's letter to W.R. Lawrence (the Chief Constable) dated 02/04/96
(15) David Evans' second letter to W.R. Lawrence dated 11/04/96[2]
(16) Assistant Chief Constable Paul Wood's letter to David Evans dated 16/04/96
(17) My letter to Professor Brinkmann dated 09/07/96
(18) Professor Brinkmann's reply dated 12/08/96
(19) Lee Jasper's letter dated 03/09/96
(20) My letter to DI Hearse dated 10/09/96
(21) The article published in *Wales On Sunday* on January 26th 1997
(22) My letter to Alun Michael dated 14/02/97
(23) My letter to Rhodri Morgan dated 14/04/97
(24) Rhodri Morgan's letter to Anthony Burdon (the new Chief Constable) dated 17/04/97

---

[1] My meeting with DI Reginald Hearse and DS Dave Smith and the meeting between ACC Paul Woods, DCS Phil Jones, Peggy Pesticcio, David Evans and myself have been omitted for editorial reasons.
[2] David Evans' first letter to W.R. Lawrence dated 14/03/96 has had to be omitted for legal reasons.

(25) My letter to Professor Brinkmann dated 18/04/97
(26) Professor Brinkmann's reply dated 21/04/97
(27) Peggy Pesticcio's new solicitor, Sadiq Khan's letter to ACC Wood dated 06/05/97
(28) DCS Jones' reply to Rhodri Morgan dated 07/05/97
(29) ACC Wood's reply to Sadiq Khan dated 13/05/97
(30) Sadiq Khan's letter to ACC Wood dated 29/05/97
(31) ACC Wood's letter to Sadiq Khan dated 21/05/97
(32) Sadiq Khan's letter to ACC Wood dated 03/06/97
(33) ACC Wood's letter to Sadiq Khan dated 12/06/97
(34) Sadiq Khan's letter to ACC Wood dated 19/06/97
(35) ACC Wood's letter to Sadiq Khan dated 03/07/97
(36) Sadiq Khan's reply to ACC Wood dated 10/07/97

To Alun Michael Esq MP

22 June 1995

Thank you for your letter of 24 May to Michael Howard enclosing correspondence from Mr Satish Sekar, who has been researching a book about the murder of Lynette White in Cardiff in 1988.

I am grateful to you for letting me see the detailed findings of Mr Sekar's research into this case and I note his willingness to co-operate with an inquiry to re-examine the original murder investigation. I am afraid, though, that this is not a matter in which it would be appropriate for the Home Secretary to intervene.

The investigation of crime is an operational matter for the chief officer of the force where the offence is alleged to have occurred. The actions and decisions taken by police officers in the course of their duties are also a matter for the chief officer. It therefore falls to the Chief Constable of South Wales Constabulary to determine what further inquiries should be undertaken in this case and by whom they should be undertaken.

I can only suggest that Mr Sekar is advised to bring his findings to the attention of the Chief Constable direct, so that he may reach a proper judgement on whether any further action is required.

DAVID MACLEAN

31 August 1995

Dear David,

Thank you for your letter of 22 June regarding the Lynette White murder. I think you have misunderstood what Satish Sekar is requesting. I appreciate that you have a massive amount of correspondence to deal with but there are specific concerns in relation to this case and its history which is why I am approaching you.

Please will you review, personally, the case made out in my letter of 24 May, a copy of which I enclose for your ease of reference. I will be more than happy to meet with you to discuss this case before you make a final decision.

I shall be very grateful for an immediate response to my request. If you are prepared to meet me to discuss the matter, can your office please contact my assistant, Lorraine Barrett, to arrange a suitably convenient time.

I look forward to hearing from you.

Yours Sincerely,

Alun Michael

To Alun Michael Esq MP

18 September 1995

Thank you for your letter of 31 August to David MacLean about Mr Satish Sekar's investigation of the murder of Lynette White in Cardiff in 1988. I am replying in David's absence.

I am sorry that you were disappointed by David's reply to your letter of 24 May. I can assure you that careful consideration was given to the matters raised in Mr Sekar's papers and it was fully understood what action Mr Sekar had sought.

I am afraid, though, that we remain of the opinion that the only appropriate course of action for Mr Sekar is to bring his concerns about the investigation to the direct attention of the Chief Constable. I would be happy to forward any papers to the Chief Constable if you consider this would be helpful.

David will respond to your request for a meeting on his return.

ANN WIDDECOMBE

22 September 1995

Dear Ann,

Thank you for your letter of 18 September in reply to my letter to David MacLean of 31 August.

I still feel that the point is being missed in that the Home Office has responsibility for the scientific services which are crucial to the investigation of this case and that the course of action suggested in my original letter to Michael Howard on 24 May 1995 is the proper way to deal with the matter.

If you are adamant in rejecting that approach, I shall be grateful if you will forward the papers to the Chief Constable as proposed in your letter and ask that the outcome of his investigations be communicated to the Home Secretary and to myself.

Thank you for your consideration to this matter.

With best wishes,

Yours Sincerely,

Alun Michael

2nd October 1995
Dear Mrs Widdecombe,

I have just received a copy of your letter to Alun Michael. I am extremely disappointed by your response to say the least. I cannot see how you could have understood all of my complaints and concluded that the only appropriate course of action is to refer them to the Chief Constable of South Wales Constabulary. However, while I remain convinced that the Home Office are in the best position to resolve my causes for concern in the Lynette White Inquiry, especially the scientific ones, I have no objection to you forwarding my concerns to the Chief Constable of South Wales Police, although I am concerned that any investigation ordered by him may lack the objectivity and impartiality necessary to resolve the issues raised, especially as many of them raise criticisms of the very force who will be called on to investigate further.

Despite my reservations may I take this opportunity to affirm my willingness to assist in any inquiry, although I fear that justice cannot be seen to be done when my complaint has been referred to the very force complained against for investigation. I remain convinced that is not the appropriate form of investigation of my causes for concern. At the very least, I feel that an external police force should have been asked to investigate my concerns further. However, as I said, I will assist any inquiry into this extraordinary case. Would you kindly convey my willingness to assist in any inquiry to the Chief Constable and ask him if he would be willing to meet with me so I can appraise him personally of my concerns.

May I also request that you disregard my original letter to Alun Michael and send on the amended version that is enclosed with this letter to the Chief Constable of South Wales Constabulary. I have amended the letter in order to clarify certain issues which arose in it.

Thank you for your attention in this matter. Please send a copy of any reply to Alun Michael.

Yours Faithfully,

Satish Sekar
cc Alun Michael

---

4 October 1995

Re-opening of Lynette White Murder Investigation - Forensic Tests

Dear Michael

I am writing on behalf of Mrs P Pesticcio who has attended at my constituency surgery on the 30 September 1995 to ask for my assistance in having the above unsolved murder case re-opened, via a combination of the Forensic Science Service and the South Wales Police.

Following the exchange of correspondence between Alun Michael MP, my colleague and Labour's Shadow Home Affairs Minister, and David MacLean and Ann Widdecombe your ministers, earlier this year, the Home Office position as far as I understood it was that it did not have a role in stimulating the South Wales Police to do anything else to reactivate this case.

However, Lynette White's mother, my constituent, Mrs Pesticcio, has now put the request directly to me to get government pressure brought on the Forensic Science Service and the South Wales Police to have the case activated, since it is clearly not satisfactory to have a situation where there is no person convicted of this crime, nor is there an active investigation of it.

The position is made even more absurd by the availability of forensic evidence in the shape of blood samples, which have not been subjected to modern state of the art DNA forensic testing, which could very well provide either additional leads not so far explored by the South Wales Police, or a better basis for taking further police investigative action, even if the persons whose blood matches the samples found in the flat were questioned in the original investigation, but later discharged from the South Wales Police enquiries.

As you can imagine my constituent, the mother of the murdered girl, is in a state of total despair about the case, due to the complete inaction of the South Wales Police since the people convicted of the murder were released on appeal. It has also been brought to her attention forcibly recently, as you are aware, by the researches of Mr Satish Sekar, that there were two separate strands of blood available in the blood samples found in the flat, which do not belong to Lynette. For the purposes of convenience we can refer to those other strands of blood as belonging to Mr X and a Mr Y.[1]

The simplest thing, therefore, would be for these two strands of blood to be subjected to modern state

---

[1] This is mistaken. There were six bloodstains in the flat which did not originate from Lynette. These bloodstains, reported by Dr Whiteside, were consistent with the blood groups of Mr X and Mr Y. Although they may not have originated from either X or Y, they were never satisfactorily eliminated as the source of these bloodstains: the author.

of the art DNA analysis, to see whether the police could match them with any other people that they have already questioned in the original enquiry, or to any other suspects.

What this case needs obviously now is a kick start and it is a matter of indifference to myself, or my constituent, who actually does the kick starting. It has got to be re-commenced in some way or another. It cannot be left as an open case, with nobody doing anything about it. For that reason I am obviously copying this letter to the Deputy Chief Constable in the hope that he will see his way forward to re-commence the enquiry, in the same way that I am hoping you can do the same as the Minister responsible for the Forensic Science Service and I look forward to your sympathetic response to this appeal.

Yours

Rhodri Morgan

cc Alun Michael MP
Deputy Chief Constable Bob Evans, South Wales Police
Mrs P Pesticcio

---

4 October 1995

Lynette White Murder Enquiry - Mrs P Pesticcio

Dear Bob Evans

I am writing on behalf of my constituent of the above name who has approached me at my constituency surgery on the 30 September 1995 to request a re-opening of the Lynette White murder investigation, and in particular to request a full modern state of the art forensic science examination of the blood samples.

I enclose a copy of the letter I have sent to Michael Howard, the Home Secretary, along similar lines to those which were sent earlier this year by Alun Michael MP to Home Office Ministers. If you read that letter I think you will see that it is incumbent on the South Wales Police to "do something" about this case to ensure that no stone is left unturned, and in particular no blood sample is left without modern state of the art forensic examination, to see whether it would provide a useful line of enquiry which might lead to this unsolved murder case being taken several steps further, and possibly to a successful solution.

Yours

Rhodri Morgan

cc Rt Hon M Howard MP
Alun Michael MP
Mrs P Pesticcio

17 October 1995

Dear Alun,

Thank you for your letter of 22 September to Ann Widdecombe about Mr Satish Sekar's investigation of the Lynette White murder case.

Mr Şekar has also written to Ann enclosing a revised version of his report and reiterating his willingness to assist with any inquiry into the case.

I have arranged for the papers to be forwarded to the Chief Constable of South Wales. I am sure that the Chief Constable will consider carefully the issues raised and write to you in due course. If, when you have received the Chief Constable's reply, there is anything on which you want to come back to me, please do not hesitate to do so.

Yours

David MacLean

17th October 1995

Dear Mr Michael

<u>Lynette WHITE Murder Case</u>

Your correspondence to the Home Office including the letter to you from Mr Satish Sekar has been forwarded to me for attention.

I will conduct a preliminary review of the points made by Mr Sekar and when I am clear in my mind on the forensic issues will communicate with you again as it may be necessary for us to speak to Mr Sekar to clarify the exact points he is making.

In the meantime if I can be of any further assistance please do not hesitate to contact me.

Yours Sincerely

Bob Evans
Assistant Chief Constable
(Designated)

6th November 1995
To R. Morgan Esq., M.P.,

Dear Sir,

Lynette White Murder Enquiry

Thank you for your letter dated 4th October, 1995, relative to the above matter. I am now taking this issue forward.

Insofar as DNA Forensic Testing is concerned all relevant samples tested under old procedures and relating to undetected serious crime will be considered for further analysis using new techniques. Those samples obtained following the murder of Lynette White are amongst them and I am actively seeking guidance in this matter from the Forensic Science Service.

With regard to the research carried out by Mr Satish Sekar, I intend to arrange a meeting between him and Senior Detective Officers in this force for the purpose of examining his findings.

I will be in touch with Mrs Pesticcio this forthcoming week to inform her of my intentions.

Yours Faithfully

P. J. JONES
Detective Chief Superintendent

RHODRI MORGAN, MP for Cardiff West
12th January 1996

Dear DCS Jones

RE: LYNETTE WHITE MURDER ENQUIRY

I am writing further to my letter of 4th October 1995 to which you replied, very encouragingly, on the 6th November to ask about further progress.

In your letter of the 6th November, you mentioned you were 'actively seeking guidance' from the Forensic Science Service. What guidance have you received from the FSS? Are you now proceeding to use the new analytical techniques on the blood samples available vis a vis this undetected serious crime?

As regards the research of Satish Sekar, did the meeting you refer to between Mr Sekar and the senior detectives to examine his findings take place? If so, on what date and what was its outcome? Can you briefly summarise it for the benefit of myself and my constituent, Mrs Pesticcio.

Looking forward to your assistance on this matter.

Yours Sincerely

Article published in the *Independent* on January 15th 1996[1]

Prostitute's murder trial 'based on faulty tests'

by Heather Mills (Home Affairs Correspondent)

Police have re-opened the investigation into the murder of Lynette White, the prostitute hacked to death seven years ago on St Valentine's day, a case which led to one of Britain's most serious miscarriages of justice.

Three years after three men were cleared by the Court of Appeal of her murder, South Wales Police are investigating claims that at least two original suspects may have been wrongly eliminated from inquiries because of inadequate DNA and blood-group testing.

Yesterday South Wales Police said officers had met with forensic scientists to re-evaluate the scientific evidence in the case. Concerns had been raised by Alun Michael, Labour's home affairs spokesman, and Satish Sekar, who has been researching the case.

Ms White, 20, was killed in her "punters' room," above a betting shop in Butetown, Cardiff. She was stabbed more than 50 times, her left breast was almost severed and her throat was slit to the spine. Blood had been spattered everywhere.

Within days, South Wales Police had details of their prime suspect, a white man seen in blood-stained clothing in a distressed state outside her flat after the murder. A photofit was issued and Detective Chief Superintendent John Williams said in March 1988: "this man almost certainly had the blood of the deceased on him."

But 10 months later, five black men were charged with murder, largely on the evidence of two prostitute friends of Ms White's, one of whom had named a succession of different people in 18 statements to police. There was also a so-called confession by one of the five, Stephen Miller. He had a mental age of 11, and his "confession" was obtained only after 300 denials during five days of interviews.

After one of the longest murder trials in Britain, lasting 197 days, three of the five, Mr Miller, Tony Paris and Yusef Abdullahi, were convicted.

Supporters mounted a campaign and two years later the Court of Appeal cleared the three, after the judges ruled Mr Miller's "confession" had been obtained in a "travesty of an interview."

Mr Sekar has since discovered that the blood groups of two earlier suspects, both white, were almost identical to the rare grouping found in the dead woman's flat. Both were eliminated by DNA profiling which has since been called into question. It is understood the samples will be re-tested.

Mr Sekar, who has researched the case for a book, ***Fitted In***, said yesterday: "I am not accusing either of the two men. I am saying that their elimination from the inquiries can no longer be relied upon. It is tragic that it has taken six years for anyone to notice that the original DNA testing was unreliable." In a statement, South Wales Police said: "We are acutely aware of advances in forensic science."

The statement added that officers were evaluating "a number of crimes over the past year including the murder of Lynette White."

[1] This article appears by kind permission of Heather Mills.

Rhodri Morgan

19th January

Dear Sir

Lynette White Murder Enquiry

Thank you for your letter dated 12th January 1996 and your continued interest in this matter.

It is my intention to keep Mrs Pesticcio up to date with our current work and in that regard my officers have met and had conversations with her on a number of occasions between November and the present. In so far as your queries are concerned I will confirm that a senior officer met with Mr Sekar in London on 15th November, 1995.

Following that meeting Scientists at Chepstow met with the officers and they are still in the course of analysing certain items using technology which is now available to us. As soon as their work and that of the officers concerned has been completed, it is my intention to meet with Mrs Pesticcio and to discuss with her each of the issues identified by Mr Sekar as well as the way forward.

I would have no objection to you being present at that meeting provided of course Mrs Pesticcio is in agreement.

Yours Faithfully,

P. J. Jones
Detective Chief Superintendent

---

2 April 1996
Dear Mr Lawrence

Lynette White Murder Enquiry Re-opening

I am writing on behalf of my constituent Mrs Peggy Pesticcio the mother of Lynette White, who has approached me for my support concerning the progress being made on the re-opening of the enquiry into Lynette's murder.

The particular point that is being raised is whether it is fair for the forensic re-examination of the blood specimens to be undertaken at the Forensic Science Laboratory at Chepstow, in the light of the part played by Dr John Whiteside, who I understand is still a senior scientist at Chepstow, in the first trial.

What procedure would there be to ensure that none of the scientists carrying out further forensic work on the specimens would not be inhibited in any way by the possibility that their re-examination might result in the reputation of Dr Whiteside being adversely affected. I don't think any of us are in a position to say that it might come out that way, but it is merely the possibility of there being an outcome of that type that poses the question. Might it not therefore be better if the DNA testing, etc, was carried out at another forensic science laboratory?

There are also some technical factors in relation to the use of DQ Alpha testing in that this could 'use up' DNA without necessarily giving the same amount of sophisticated results that more effective more recently developed tests, which are still outside the competence of the Chepstow Laboratory, could give if carried out elsewhere.

I shall be grateful therefore if you could let me know your reactions to these suggestions. They are very much along the lines of the suggestions contained in the letter from David Evans of Hutton's who is acting in a professional legal capacity on behalf of Mrs Pesticcio.

Yours

Rhodri Morgan

cc Mrs P Pesticcio
David Evans

---

11 April 1996

Dear Sir

RE: LYNETTE WHITE MURDER ENQUIRY RE-OPENING

We refer to our letter to you of 14th March 1996 acknowledged by your letter of 18th March. We regret in spite of the urgency of the situation that we have not had a formal response as yet.

This being the case, we must call for your full response by Friday of this week failing which we believe we will have no alternative but to consider that no action is to be taken with respect to the issues raised and our client will consider her position on such basis. Any judicial review proceedings which may follow, if appropriate, will be issued without further notice.

Yours faithfully

David Evans

16th April 1996
Dear Mr Morgan

Lynette White Murder Enquiry

I refer to your previous correspondence and particularly your letters of 4th October 1995, 12th January 1996 and 2nd April 1996, and subsequent replies.

I am now able to inform you that in spite of a significant improvement in DNA techniques recent tests conducted on forensic samples relative to this investigation have proved unsuccessful and have not advanced our enquiries. These examinations were conducted at the Forensic Science Laboratory at Aldermaston - a centre of excellence in so far as DNA techniques are concerned. Other samples remain untested however and the feasibility of further analysis in respect of them is underway.

In so far as Mr. Satish SEKAR is concerned, he has discussed his feelings with two of my officers and every issue he has raised has been examined. Where further work has been necessary it has been commenced and this will be the subject of a further meeting I will be having with Mrs. PESTICCIO and, hopefully, her legal representative, in the near future.

Can I reassure you that the investigation remains open and that we will continue to act on any fresh evidence as it is received.

Yours Sincerely,

P. Wood
Assistant Chief Constable (operations)

09/07/96

Dear Professor Brinkmann,

I am writing to you as I have been advised to do so by a forensic scientist in Britain. I am currently writing and publishing a book on a notorious miscarriage of justice case in Britain. My research into the case has shown that not only were the Cardiff Three innocent, but that several suspects had been eliminated on DNA profiling rather dubiously. Suffice to say, my findings revealed that the victim had been prematurely eliminated as the source of the blood upon which all the DNA eliminations were obtained. Naturally, this means that all DNA eliminations are questionable to say the least.

Following this discovery I was fortunate enough to secure the help of Mark Webster of Forensic Science Consultancy. His report on the case forced the British authorities to take notice. The Lynette White Inquiry was re-opened as Webster's report established that it was still possible to obtain useful results if the original samples still existed and that the nylon membranes could be tested as well.

I had originally asked the Home Office to take responsibility for investigating what had gone wrong with the whole case and testing the samples using the most sophisticated techniques now available. But they insisted on referring the matter to the same police force who got it so horribly wrong in the first place. Because of what had happened before I could not trust the police to investigate their own competence, but they have proved willing to conduct new tests.

There are several items which even now could provide useful evidence, but the original samples were heavily degraded. In other words, the DNA is of poor quality and the source DNA is at a premium. It is therefore essential that the remaining DNA is subjected to the most effective tests which give the most sensitive results from the least material.

This was a particularly brutal murder and these tests offer the last realistic chance of unmasking the killer. I have been advised that your techniques offer the best possibility of this. Since my findings forced the inquiry open again the police have tested one sample at the Forensic Science Service Laboratory at Aldermaston. No result was obtained using STR typing (hexaplex) possibly due to Ninhydrin and degradation. I am concerned that further testing at Aldermaston will face the same problems. I believe that your techniques have succeeded where ones in Britain have failed. I would therefore greatly appreciate it if you could forward some information to me on your techniques, the cost of these tests and your availability to conduct these tests. If you are not available to conduct such tests I would appreciate it if you could recommend another laboratory where such testing can be conducted. If you require further information please do not hesitate to ask.

Yours Faithfully,

Satish Sekar

Prof. Dr. med. B. Brinkmann
Direktor des Instituts für Rechtsmedizin der Universität Münster
12/08/1996

Dear Mr Sekar,

Thank you for your letter of July 10 which unfortunately I can only answer today because I was on holiday in the meantime. Your letter raises several questions. We are of course familiar with the technology applied in the police laboratories in England. These are extremely efficient and well validated multiplexing methods. This means that one investigation leads to e.g. four or even six results. Our laboratory for instance is more specialised in singleplexing. The approaches have one major difference; multiplexing is less sensitive than singleplexing. Therefore in borderline cases multiplexing can fail while singleplexing is still efficient. From the description given by you one could feel that this is a borderline case.

We are also familiar with the British Legal System. We have been involved in several cases.

Singleplexing however leads to one result per amplification. Thus you have to perform six PCRs to obtain six results. It is therefore more labour intensive but this is the only disadvantage. - I must also say that our investigation in a case you mentioned was not advantageous for the defence.

I have no detailed information about your case but if blood stains are still available, there is still a good chance to obtain a valid DNA profile. The chemical treatment with Ninhydrin and the age of these stains will not substantially affect the results. I'm absolutely optimistic in a case like this, that a result will be obtainable.

The other problem is the problem with the British officials. I mean the prosecution and the police etc.. We have made the experience that if they want they can completely obstruct or at least considerably delay such investigations, but we would nevertheless be willing to assist. But the authorities interested should please avoid including us in a longlasting or never ending letter exchange with mainly legal arguments. This is extremely boring and ineffective and disadvantageous for our work because it costs time.

Dr Peter Gill from the Forensic Science Service in Birmingham and also the prosecution service know us quite well and they could be a good source of information about the technologies applied here and also about the quality of our work.

I therefore conclude that we are available to conduct additional tests. The costs depend very much on the number of specimens to be investigated and also on the time which is needed. The costs will be in the range of £1000. This does not include any costs for travel expenses or for witnessing such investigations in other laboratories. But this also includes the costs for a type written report.

Kind regards

Prof. Dr. med. B. Brinkmann

The 1990 Trust
3rd September 1996

To Whom It May Concern:

We have been made aware of the current status of DNA testing in the Lynette White Inquiry. We welcome the decision of South Wales Police to re-open the case and to conduct more sophisticated tests. We regret that the attempt to conduct STR typing on a sample SS12 failed. Mr Satish Sekar has explained to us that it is still possible to obtain results from that sample. We have seen the opinion of Professor B. Brinkmann, a world renowned expert in DNA testing. We note that he is "absolutely optimistic" that a result can be obtained from that sample notwithstanding the age of the sample and the fact that it had been treated with the fingerprinting chemical Ninhydrin.

Mr Sekar has explained to us that as the multiplexing testing failed to obtain a result at Aldermaston, there is no chance of obtaining any forensic evidence from SS12 in the foreseeable future unless Professor Brinkmann is allowed to test it. Given the appalling nature of the murder of Lynette White we believe as we are sure you do as well that no stone can be allowed to remain unturned in the hunt for her killer. We therefore believe that at the very least SS12 must be sent to him without further delay as this offers the last realistic chance of obtaining a result as he uses the more sensitive method of singleplexing.

We are acutely aware of the competing demands for financing that South Wales Police face as there are several other crimes that demand their attention. However, we believe that the case for using Professor Brinkmann's techniques outlined by Mr Sekar is overwhelming. Therefore, as a last resort, we are prepared to donate the sum of one thousand pounds towards the cost of testing that sample at Professor Brinkmann's laboratory in Germany. We hope that this will be of assistance in helping to unmask Lynette's murderer.

Yours Faithfully

Lee Jasper (Director)

10/09/96

Dear Mr Hearse,

Further to our telephone conversation I am sending you the response of Professor Brinkmann as promised. As you will see he is "absolutely optimistic" that he can obtain a result from SS12 notwithstanding its age and the fact that it was treated with the fingerprinting chemical Ninhydrin.

Following Mrs Pesticcio's recent meeting with police I understand that you wish to consider the possibility of using Professor Brinkmann's techniques. May I take this opportunity to clarify that I only wrote to Brinkmann after testing on SS12 had failed at Aldermaston as there might still be a chance of obtaining useful evidence. May I stress that in doing so I am in no way criticising forensic scientists at Aldermaston. I fully accept that Aldermaston is a centre of excellence on DNA. Generally multiplexing will obtain useful results from all but the most stubborn stains. Unfortunately, at least as far as SS12 is concerned, this seems to be one of those stubborn cases. I hope that this information is of some use to you. If I can be of further assistance please do not hesitate to ask.

Yours Sincerely,

Satish Sekar

Article published in *Wales On Sunday* on January 26th 1997[1]

Mother's plan to trap killer

by Martin Shipton

The mother of Lynette White, whose Valentine's Day murder nine years ago has never been solved, claims new forensic tests could confirm the identity of her daughter's killer.

Mrs Peggy Pesticcio believes she knows who the murderer is and is calling on South Wales Police to release blood samples to her so she can prove it.

Lynette, 20, worked as a prostitute in Cardiff's Butetown, where she was stabbed to death in 1988.

Two years later three men received life sentences after being found guilty of her murder. But in 1992 their convictions were quashed by the Court of Appeal.

Blood found at the scene of the crime and originally assumed to come from the killer is now thought possible to have been Lynette's.

That means other blood-stains in the murder flat could hold the key to identifying the killer claims Mrs Pesticcio.

Unfortunately, DNA tests on these blood samples have proved inconclusive.

But Satish Sekar, the author of a soon-to-be-published book on the case, has established that more sophisticated tests could be undertaken at the University of Munster, in Germany. The London based writer said: "The laboratory would be happy to carry out the tests, and last September Lynette's mother was told this would happen. But since then, nothing has been heard about the testing in

---

[1] This article appears by kind permission of Martin Shipton.

Germany."

Mrs Pesticcio, who lives in the South of England, said, "The police have not come up with anything new from tests at their Chepstow laboratory. It is time they sent the samples to Germany.

"I have come to my own conclusions about who the murderer is, based on earlier blood tests that were not sufficient for a prosecution.

"I believe two people were with Lynette when she was killed, although only one was responsible for her death.

"If South Wales Police are not prepared to do the tests, they should release the samples to me."

Chief Superintendent Phil Jones, head of South Wales CID, said forensic tests are still being carried out.

"The work is incomplete, but when it is finalised, if it remains inconclusive, we will look to other sources which we believe may have the ability to contribute to the case," he said.

14/02/97

Dear Alun,

Sorry for the delay in writing to you as promised. I have been awaiting further information which has only just arrived. During further research the following facts have come to light. As you know the Lynette White Inquiry was actively re-opened by South Wales Police following your intervention. The police took advice from the Forensic Science Service before deciding to attempt to obtain STR DNA profiles using the system known as multiplexing. To date many of the crucial samples have been tested using this method. Unfortunately no results have been obtained.

Following the failure on the first batch of samples tested I wrote to Professor B. Brinkmann, Direktor des Instituts für Rechtsmedizin der Universität Münster in Germany. A copy of his reply is enclosed. As you will see he is "absolutely optimistic" that a result could be obtained in a case like this using the method known as singleplexing. The difference between multiplexing and singleplexing is that multiplexing performs multiple PCRs at the same time where singleplexing performs them individually. Consequently, singleplexing allows for greater amplification of the DNA and is therefore more sensitive.

The point of all this is not to attack multiplexing. In the vast majority of cases where there is DNA of reasonable or sometimes even poor quality multiplexing will prove sensitive enough to obtain results. The problem occurs in the stubborn or borderline cases where multiplexing fails. In these cases which unfortunately the Lynette White Inquiry has proved to be singleplexing may prove useful. I point this out because it is obvious from the initial failure of multiplexing in this case, reinforced by further failures on all samples tested to date that the available DNA is of poor quality and that there is not much left.

As you may well be aware the facility to singleplex now exists in Britain. In the recent case of Edwin Hopkins, convicted of the brutal murder of teenager Naomi Smith, multiplexing failed to yield a DNA profile on one of the samples, but singleplexing succeeded. It therefore stands to reason that singleplexing must be more sensitive than multiplexing.

In addition to this, may I draw your attention to a recent article written among others by Dr Peter Gill whom you may recall was involved in the original case (a copy is enclosed for your attention, but only the highlighted portion is relevant). That article was published in January 1996 a full nine months before I passed on Professor Brinkmann's reply to the police. This suggests that the police were either aware of the benefits of singleplexing before I told them or at the very least perhaps they ought to have known it. Either way, by the time I forwarded Professor Brinkmann's response there can be no doubt that the Lynette White Inquiry was a borderline case which could and probably would have benefitted from singleplexing in Germany as Brinkmann's techniques involve greater amplification of DNA than British singleplexing let alone multiplexing.

It has now been nearly five months yet the police insist on completing the current round of multiplexing before considering whether singleplexing would be worthwhile. I believe that I have now established that the case for singleplexing in this case is absolutely overwhelming and that the best possibility of obtaining useful results would be for all relevant samples to be tested in Germany. I would therefore appreciate it if you could ask the following questions of Michael Howard.

1) What research has been conducted to compare Professor Brinkmann's techniques in singleplexing with those used in Britain?

2) Will he guarantee that multiplexing has not been utilised over singleplexing solely on the grounds of convenience and expense?

3) Is there any policy that singleplexing will be used as a matter of course in borderline cases?

4) Is it government policy that the most efficient DNA testing techniques will be used as a matter of course?

5) Does he feel it is appropriate for the police to effectively ignore the benefits of singleplexing in a case which is at best borderline as the quality of the available DNA leaves much to be desired as does the quantity of available DNA?

6) Will he use his influence to ensure that the most sophisticated DNA tests currently available are employed without further delay?

Thank you for your continued interest in this matter.

Yours Sincerely,

Satish Sekar

14/04/97

Dear Rhodri,[1]

I am writing to you to appraise you of the latest developments in the Lynette White Inquiry. On April 10th your constituent Peggy Pesticcio phoned me and told me that the police have finished their attempts to amplify DNA by multiplexing. As expected multiplexing has failed to amplify the DNA. However, police have attempted other DNA based tests such as the Second Generation Multiplex (SGM) which consists of the six STRs and the more sophisticated sex determination test which can

[1] A very similar letter was written to Alun Michael. This letter has been slightly amended for publication: the author.

identify the proportion of X and Y-chromosomes in any mixture of blood which is used on the Home Office's National DNA database. Even attempts to amplify DNA will use up valuable DNA.

I must remind you that we are dealing with a finite quantity of DNA which is of poor quality. Consequently, all the latest advances in DNA based testing can only be utilised if there is sufficient DNA to work with. I am therefore baffled that the police have used up DNA multiplexing samples where there was little reaslistic prospect of success as multiplexing had already been found wanting more than once on samples which had been treated in a similar manner. After the initial failure of multiplexing the remaining samples should have been earmarked for the more sensitive technique of singleplexing, particularly that of Professor Brinkmann immediately.

The blood on the sock has all been used up. To be fair there wasn't much to start with on that sample, but in some ways this illustrates my point that the most sensistive test currently available ought to have been used as that would have given us the best chance of obtaining useful results. It is now too late to obtain anything from that sock.

I am extremely concerned that time and effort was wasted by the police insisting on completing their attempts to multiplex in circumstances where it was fairly obvious that such attempts were likely to fail as the wallpaper samples had been treated in much the same manner. The more attempts that failed the less likely that multiplexing would succeed. It was still possible, but it was unlikely. You don't have to be Professor Alec Jeffreys to work that out.

Since the advent of singleplexing in Britain as shown in the case of Edwin Hopkins who was recently convicted of the murder of teenager Naomi Smith, the police have decided to attempt singleplexing. Although I am somewhat annoyed and concerned by the delay in trying singleplexing and concerned by their use of the DNA on other tests, I have to say that the information I have suggests that the level of DNA amplification achieved by Professor Brinkmann is greater than that achieved in Britain. It therefore stands to reason that the best prospect of obtaining DNA evidence in this case lies with Professor Brinkmann's laboratory. It will be remembered that in his response to me Professor Brinkmann said that he did not think that the treatment of the samples with the fingerprinting chemical Ninhydrin would pose any problems, whereas the police have told Mrs Pesticcio that it has been causing problems to them.

Consequently, the approach of the police flies in the face of common sense and logic. I can just about live with them trying singleplexing in Britain as long as they don't use up so much of the precious DNA that nothing is left for Professor Brinkmann. Suffice to say, good as Brinkmann's techniques undoubtedly are, not even he can achieve results if there is no DNA to work with. If the police are allowed to use up all the DNA that will be the end of the matter. It will then require a miracle to uncover the real murderer. Should that happen the actions of the police in refusing to use the best available methods of DNA amplification will have the consequence that the murderer of Lynette White will almost certainly never be found and the blame for that will rest entirely with the police as it was their approach to the scientific issues I raised with you many months ago that will have caused this to happen.

I cannot allow this to happen if there is anything that can be done to prevent it. I therefore ask you to contact the Home Office and South Wales Police and obtain an undertaking from them that enough DNA will be preserved to attempt to amplify DNA in Germany. Providing they do not use up too much DNA attempting to amplify it by singleplexing in Britain I can live with them doing that, but not if it means using too much precious DNA. Mrs Pesticcio is in full agreement with my concerns. I believe she will contact you very soon. We do not want the police to leave any stones unturned, but if they use up all the DNA before Professor Brinkmann gets the chance to use his techniques that will inevitably happen unless singleplexing succeeds here.

Mrs Pesticcio is taking legal advice to see if it is possible to persuade the police to adopt the suggested approach. Failing this she will examine her options. Suffice to say, we do not intend to wait until this becomes an academic question. I hesitate to bother you as I know that you are extremely busy with the election, but felt that this was so important that I had no choice. Thank you for your attention in this matter.

Yours Sincerely,

Satish Sekar

Rhodri Morgan
17 April 1997

Chief Constable A. Burdon

Dear Chief Constable

Lynette White Inquiry - Mrs Peggy Pesticcio (mother)

I am writing on behalf of the above resident of Cardiff West, who has approached me indirectly via Mr Satish Sekar to express her concern about the way in which South Wales Police have been using up the small amount of remaining DNA from the Lynette White murder forensic evidence, without using the laboratory of Professor Brinkmann in Germany, in terms of the most up to date singleplexing technology.

I understand nothing of the scientific side of the contents of Mr Sekar's letter to me of 14 April, but I should be grateful to have your reaction to it and whether there are aspects of it with which you would agree, and whether we can therefore avoid any dispute on this matter in relation to ensuring that not all of the different blood samples are 'exhausted' in such a manner that there is no way of passing any of it along for use in laboratories equipped with the latest singleplexing technology.

Yours

Copies Mrs P. Pesticcio
Alun Michael
Satish Sekar

18/04/97

Dear Professor Brinkmann,

I am writing to you as requested by your colleague Stephen Rand following our telephone conversation of yesterday. The current situation in the Lynette White Inquiry is that following your kind offer of assistance I forwarded it to the police, but they seem to have ignored it. As I feared multiplexing failed on every sample tested. Earlier this month they completed the current round of testing, but unfortunately it failed to yield results. In short, multiplexing has achieved nothing but wasting invaluable DNA in circumstances where there was only a limited supply of heavily degraded DNA which had been treated with the fingerprinting chemical Ninhydrin.

They claim that the whole of the DNA on the right sock has been used up. This is a pity as blood grouping tests for six different groups had yielded results, revealing that the killer had a very rare combination of blood groups. The blood on the victim's jeans was also a very rare combination of blood groups. All the blood stains which clearly did not come from Lynette were consistent with having been shed by one man. The jeans are black. The attempt to multiplex in somewhat inappropriate circumstances is causing some difficulties. The police have decided to attempt singleplexing.

I am aware that there is very little original DNA left. I am therefore concerned to ensure that the best possible use is made of it. Could you kindly tell me how many cycles you use in your amplification techniques and what differences if any there are between your methods and those used by the Forensic Science Service. Could you also tell me if your techniques are compatible with the following loci which are used in the Home Office's National DNA database (1) amelogenin, (2) HUMVWFA31/A, (3) HUMTH01, (4) D6S502, (5) D18S51, (6) D21S11 and (7) HUMFIBRA/FGA. I would also like to know if the black dye in the jeans would pose any problem for you in obtaining a result. Unfortunately, time is of the essence as I fear that the police will try to stall this and all the DNA will be used up. I am determined to prevent this happening if at all possible. I await your earliest reply.

Yours Sincerely,

Satish Sekar

Prof. Dr. med. B. Brinkmann
21.04.1997

Dear Mr. Sekar,

Thank you for your fax dated 18th April 1997, which arrived together with several communications relating to this case.

In my original letter from 12th August 1996 I outlined the essential differences between multiplexing and singleplexing for DNA investigations and also indicated that we could conduct additional tests if requested.

The situation in the Lynette White Inquiry which you briefly describe in your letter is unfortunate and it is also very difficult for me to make comments considering the small amount of information available. Perhaps I can attempt to answer your questions first and then make some comments which, however, maybe of limited use as I have very limited information on the case and no direct knowledge of the stains involved.

1. In our amplification techniques for singleplex systems we use 27 or 30 cycles depending on the system. Each system has been optimized to obtain maximum efficiency and to avoid artefacts. There may be slight differences in the protocols used by us and those used by the Forensic Science Service

for amplification of individual systems (singleplexing) but small variations will occur depending on the equipment used and the circumstances prevailing in the individual laboratory. It is also internationally accepted that these differences are not incompatible and that the optimal conditions used in a particular laboratory may not necessarily be the same as those used by another laboratory. It is only important that the system has been optimzed for use in that laboratory.

2. Of the systems in use in the National database the following loci are compatible: Amelogenin, HUMVWFA31/A, HUMTH01, D21S11 and HUMFIBRA/FGA. It has been agreed at a European level that not every laboratory must test identical systems but that a number of core systems should be used for international co-operation.

3. The black dye used on the jeans is a problem for every laboratory when attempting amplification using PCR techniques. This can to some extent be removed from the extracts by a variety of purification methods (e.g. centricon) and the Home Office Laboratory is well aware of this.

Additional comments:
1. The advantages of singleplexing over multiplexing, which I detailed in my original letter (12.8.1996) seem no longer to be relevant, if the laboratory in question has adequately optimized the systems for singleplexing.

2. Blood grouping results have already revealed "a very rare combination of blood groups" so that information on the blood type of the killer is already available. This could also be used to identify the donor of the blood stains on the clothing.

3. It seems reasonable to ask the question how was it possible to obtain blood grouping results but DNA using the PCR technique, a very sensitive method gives negative results?

4. If the blood stains were on articles of clothing (as outlined in your letter) why were they treated with Ninhyrdin?[1]

5. PCR is generally a very sensitive method so that is not necessarily true that all the blood stains would have been used up by the initial investigation. This of course depends on the size of the blood stains: I have no information on this.

I hope that this of some use to you. If you need more information, please contact me at the above address.

Yours Sincerely

Prof. Dr. med. B. Brinkmann

---

[1] The mistake here was mine. From my letter it could be inferred that I had suggested that Ninhydrin had been used on the items of clothing. This is not the case. Ninhydrin was used on all relevant samples apart from the jeans and the sock: the author.

6 May 1997
F.A.O. Paul Wood
Assistant Chief Constable of Operations

Dear Sirs,

RE: LYNETTE WHITE - MURDER ENQUIRY

We have been instructed by Mrs Peggy Pesticcio, mother of Lynette White, in relation to the conduct of further DNA testing which has been carried out on the blood samples obtained from the murder scene.

You will be aware that Mrs Pesticcio and the investigative journalist, Satish Sekar, have requested for a considerable time that the DNA samples should be amplified by singleplexing techniques carried out by Professor Brinkmann, Direktor des Instituts für Rechtsmedizin der Universität Münster, Germany. You will be aware of the numerous advantages of singleplexing over multiplexing and of the expertise of Professor Brinkmann.

Despite the various requests made, it was decided by South Wales Police that attempts should be made to amplify the DNA by multiplexing. We understand that multiplexing has failed to amplify the DNA, as predicted. Further, the police have also attempted other DNA based tests such as Second Generation Multiplex (SGM), which has meant that more of the DNA has been used up.

We understand from our client that police are now trying to amplify the DNA by singleplexing in laboratories in Britain. We think it sensible that if you are instructing experts in Britain to do singleplexing, then they should use the most sensitive loci currently available; D18S51, D21S11, and HUMFIBRA/FGA. If the first batch of the most sensitive loci fail to yield positive results in Britain, then we would ask you to provide an undertaking that you will not use up any more DNA and will send one of the other samples to Professor Brinkmann in Germany.

We are concerned that the South Wales Police Force have continually refused to follow expert advice obtained by our client which has resulted in a valuable quantity of DNA being used up and have failed to utilise the techniques of Professor Brinkmann.

We would ask you to inform us how much DNA still remains from the original murder scene and to provide an undertaking that when you instruct your forensic scientist, in Britain, to carry out the further singleplexing test that enough DNA will be preserved to attempt to amplify the DNA in Germany, using Professor Brinkmann's technique, should the testing in the British laboratories be unsuccessful.

We look forward to hearing from you by return.

Yours faithfully

Sadiq Khan

CHRISTIAN FISHER (Solicitors)

7th May 1997
To Mr Rhodri Morgan M.P.

Dear Sir

Lynette White Inquiry

Thank you for your letter dated 1st April, 1997, relative to the above named. You may be aware that the South Wales Police have undertaken a full review of the forensic evidence in this case in the light of new DNA technology which has become available. To date a number of items have been re-examined, unfortunately with no success thus far, but our intention is that each and every item will be subject to further scrutiny.

I am advised in this matter by leaders in the field from the Forensic Science Service, in whom I have total faith and who I know are aware of all techniques which are available both in and out of that Service. Have no doubt that if an examination is considered feasible which the Forensic Science Service are incapable of carrying out, then this Force will not hesitate to seek furtherance elsewhere.

Yours faithfully,

P.J. Jones
Detective Chief Superintendent

13th May 1997
(To Messrs. Christian Fisher, Solicitors)

Dear Sirs,

Lynette White - Murder Enquiry

I refer to your letter dated 6th May 1997, and your facsimile dated 12th May 1997, concerning the above.

As you will be aware, we have been liaising with the Forensic Science Service on this matter and the points you have raised will be discussed with them at the next regular meeting, which is to be held shortly, attended by our Head of CID.

I will then write to you in more detail.

Yours sincerely,

P. Wood
Assistant Chief Constable
(Operations)

29 May 1997
To P.J. Wood
Assistant Chief Constable (Operations)

Dear Sirs,

RE: LYNETTE WHITE - MURDER ENQUIRY

We acknowledge receipt of your letter dated 13th May 1997.

In your letter, you informed us that the points we had raised in our letters would be discussed at the "next regular meeting" you have with the Forensic Science Service which was due to be "held shortly."

We are concerned that we have still not received a substantive reply to our letter of 6th May 1997. In addition to the points raised in the above letter, we also ask you to let us know what condition the DNA that the FSS still have is in, how much there is and how it is being stored.

We would also be grateful if you would let us know whether there are any hair samples available from the murder enquiry scene.

We look forward to hearing from you shortly.

Yours faithfully,

CHRISTIAN FISHER

F.A.O. Christian Fisher
21st May 1997.[1]

Dear Sir,

Lynette White - Murder Enquiry

Thank you for your letter dated 6th May, 1997, relative to the above. At the outset, it may be useful if I advise you of the position of this Force in this matter. We have undertaken a review of all relevant exhibits recovered during the investigation into Lynette's murder, with a view to identifying whether, in the light of new technology, further DNA analysis is possible. This is a working practice which we have employed in relation to all undetected serious crime, in an attempt to make the best use of a science which is advancing very quickly.

This process has been taken forward by senior detectives and scientists from the Forensic Science Laboratory at Chepstow, who have, and will continue to advise in this matter. Their approach has included the use of sensitive tests, coupled with high discriminatory power - the rationale behind multiplexing. It has also included singleplexing techniques, using sensitive loci as identified in your letter. The tests which have been completed have failed thus far to identify DNA, but others are contemplated and will be put in hand.

---

[1] This letter was received by Sadiq Khan on May 30th a day after he wrote to ACC Wood.

Part of the remit of the forensic team is to seek best practice, both in and out of the Forensic Service and in the matter of Professor Brinkmann, as Mrs Pesticcio is aware, the service he provides will be examined by forensic scientists when the need arises and will be followed up by written recommendations to the senior investigating officer, as to whether it should be utilised. To achieve this I am aware that scientists from Chepstow intend to speak personally to the Professor.

Yours faithfully,

P Wood
Assistant Chief Constable (Ops)

---

3 June 1997
To P.J. Wood
Assistant Chief Constable (Operations)

Dear Sirs,

RE: LYNETTE WHITE - MURDER ENQUIRY

We are in receipt of your letter dated 21st May 1997 which we received on 30th May 1997.

In our letter of 6th May 1997 we asked you to inform us how much DNA still remains from the murder scene and to provide an undertaking that when you instruct your Forensic Scientist, to carry out any further singleplexing tests that enough DNA will be preserved to amplify the DNA in Germany, using Professor Brinkmann's technique, should the tests in the British laboratories be unsuccessful. This has not been addressed in your reply and we would be grateful if you would respond to this as soon as possible.

We would also be grateful if you would inform us of what tests have been completed so far by the Forensic Science Laboratory to identify the DNA analysis referred to in your letter of 21st May 1997. We also look forward to receiving a reply to paragraph three of our letter of 29th May 1997.

Yours faithfully,

CHRISTIAN FISHER

12th June, 1997.

F.A.O Christian Fisher

Dear Sir,

Lynette White - Murder Enquiry

I refer to your letter dated 3rd June, 1997.

In the first instance, can I make it clear that this investigation continues to be taken forward by this Force and it will be a matter for senior officers here, after consultation with experts in the relevant field, to decide on the manner in which forensic examinations are to take place. This will include how any DNA test is to be carried out, who will carry out the examination process and whether it is in the best interests of this investigation for all or some of the DNA which remains to be used up.

While appreciating the concern of your client, it is clearly not practical, nor is it in the best interests of efficiency, for the decision making process to be shared outside of those charged with the investigation of this murder.

As far as other issues in your letter are concerned, they will be addressed as soon as I have the relevant information.

Yours faithfully,

P Wood
Assistant Chief Constable (Ops)

---

19 June 1997[1]
To P.J. Wood
Assistant Chief Constable (Operations)

Dear Sirs,

RE: LYNETTE WHITE - MURDER ENQUIRY

We write further to our letter of 3rd June 1997.

We have now had a chance to consider fully your letter of 21st May 1997 (which you faxed again on 4th June 1997).

In your above-mentioned letter, you state that you have "undertaken a review of all the relevant exhibits recovered during the investigation into Lynette's murder, with a view to identifying whether, in the light of new technology, further DNA analysis is possible."

We would ask you to let us know what relevant exhibits have been recovered and to indicate whether this includes hair, saliva and semen from the scene.

Mrs. Pesticcio, mother of Lynette White, is considerably concerned that the police have not been keeping her in touch with developments into the investigation into her daughter's death, as had been previously promised in meetings in Cardiff and in Chepstow.

We would ask you to provide us with a letter setting out the steps that the South Wales Police Force has taken since the last meeting with Mrs. Pesticcio, so that we can forward this to her.

We look forward to hearing from you shortly.

Yours faithfully,

CHRISTIAN FISHER

---

[1] This letter was written before ACC Paul Wood's letter of 12th June 1997 was received by Sadiq Khan.

3rd July, 1997.
F.A.O. Christian Fisher

Dear Sir,

Lynette White - Murder Enquiry

I refer to your letter dated 19th June, 1997, received at this Headquarters on 23rd June, 1997. It makes no mention of a letter I sent to you on 12th June, 1997, which I presume you have now received. I trust you have found the contents useful.

Insofar as the supply of an exhibit list to you is concerned, at this moment in time I am not inclined to provide you with it and will be seeking advice from our Force Solicitor before taking any further action. In the matter of Mrs Peggy Pesticcio, she was seen by Detective Chief Superintendent P J Jones, Head of South Wales C.I.D., on 4th September, 1996, at the Home Office Forensic Science Laboratory in Chepstow, when the position at that time was clearly identified to her, as was the intention of the South Wales Police. She was told then that she would be appraised of any new findings in the case, but you will appreciate between then and now there have been none.

In spite of this however, Detective Inspector Reg Hearse who has recently retired from this Force was to make contact with her by telephone on a number of occasions between September, 1996 and May, 1997, albeit to convey to her an unchanged position.

I will now deal with the other issues identified in previous letters, which I was not able to answer at that time:-

(a) Fresh tests for DNA have been carried out thus far on a sock Lynette White was wearing at the time of her murder, a pair of her jeans, blood from a skirting board and sections of wallpaper from the murder scene. These tests have not yet been completed.

(b) Any DNA recovered from the stains available to the Forensic Science Service will be frozen and retained in that condition. Prior to such finding, samples are stored at room temperature at the Laboratory and that will continue to be the case.

I would now like to arrange a meeting with Mrs Pesticcio, at which the Home Office Forensic Science Laboratory will also be represented. You may, as her representative, feel that you would wish to be present and in this regard I invite your comment.

Yours faithfully,

P WOOD
Assistant Chief Constable
(Territorial Policing)

10th July 1997

ATTENTION: P. WOOD

ASSISTANT CHIEF CONSTABLE

Dear Sirs,

RE: LYNETTE WHITE - MURDER ENQUIRY

Thank you for your letter dated 3rd July 1997.

Subsequent to our letter of 19th June 1997 we also received your letter of 12th June 1997.

We have written to Mrs. Pesticcio, sending her a copy of your letter to ourselves.

We note the final paragraph of your letter relating to the proposed meeting with Mrs. Pesticcio, at which the Home Office Forensic Science Laboratory will also be represented. As Mrs. Pesticcio's solicitors, it is clearly desirable that we are also present at this meeting.

We look forward to hearing from you regarding this meeting, in the near future.

Yours faithfully,

CHRISTIAN FISHER

Epilogue

by John Alderson CBE, QPM[1]

In our system of justice the police are the agents of the prosecution. They are the first actors in the line of those whose coercive and judicial function affects the suspect, the accused, and the convicted offender.

Police officers' view of 'justice' is conditioned by their experience, which differs profoundly from that of lawyers, judges and administrators. Uniquely, police officers are often witness to the anguish and suffering of victims; they know the reputation, including the previous criminal convictions, of the accused; they labour, sometimes risking their safety, and even their lives, in the cause of criminal justice. Being human they sometimes suffer disillusion when the guilty go free, though in theory they should remain detached. They develop strong corporate loyalties which sometimes exact a high price in rectitude. For example, concern to support their colleagues and their own view of what justice is, can lead and has led to practices of falsely enlarging the evidence to fit the criminal accusation. Much of their work in the investigation of crime is carried out unobserved either by the public, or by their supervisors, and particularly by their most senior officers, whose remote position requires a peculiar strength of influence in order to prevail. Endowed, as they are, with a unique battery of powers over the rights and freedoms of people, they are vulnerable to corruption unless properly constituted, and imbued with adequate protection which flows from an ethical predisposition. They sometimes view the system of criminal justice with a jaundiced eye.

An example of dangers besetting the system of criminal justice in its police context, arises where the investigators become cynical, and in pursuit of what may seem to be justice, or a just end to their labours, resort to unjust means. This can represent a considerable temptation where crimes are horrific, the public alarmed, and where sections of the news media generate phobia. In such cases the whole system from investigators to the judiciary is placed under considerable stress. It is well understood that the road to where the end justifies the means,

---

[1]This is an abridged version of a piece written by Mr Alderson which appears in *Criminal Justice Under Stress* edited by Eric Stockdale and Silvia Casale. The epilogue appears by kind permission of Mr Alderson who retains the copyright. Mr Alderson, a former Chief Constable of Devon and Cornwall Police, is a qualified barrister, former Assistant Commissioner at New Scotland Yard and currently lectures on policing and the criminal justice system. He has been awarded a CBE and is a holder of the Queen's Police Medal.

leads ultimately to the justification of torture, or inhuman and degrading treatment.

The task of the police is to collect the evidence, to support the accusation that a criminal offence has been committed and that it was the accused who committed it. This is not the same as conducting an inquiry into the whole circumstances of the affair, for to do this in every case would far outstrip the resources and expertise of the police. It is at the stage of treating a person as a suspect that the investigator has to avoid allowing a suspicion to become a conviction that the perpetrator of the crime has been identified. Subsequent inquiries may point to another person altogether; meanwhile valuable time and evidence are lost.

Our adversarial system of criminal justice which characterises our mode of trial as a conflict out of which emerges proof of guilt beyond reasonable doubt or not, unsurprisingly also characterises the investigation. There is a subtle, but important, distinction between an objective inquiry into the truth of criminal behaviour, and the collection of evidence to establish guilt within the system and its rules. The testing of evidence for truth is the responsibility of the courts. The investigator feels that he has done his job when he has delivered what he believes to be a case for the prosecuting authorities to steer through the court to victory.

There are those who see the role of the prosecution, including the investigator, as encompassing a duty of making inquiries for the benefit of both sides. Of course such evidence to help the defence which they may stumble across should be produced for the prosecuting authorities to offer to the defence. They also have enlightened self-interest in checking any alibi, often to disprove it, should it be damaging to their accusations of 'guilt'. But to suggest that they embark on inquiries to assist the defence may be a theory, but it does not coincide with practice.

Whether or not the stress arising out of conflict between the police and other sections of our system of criminal justice is inevitable, and constructive, may be argued, but stress there undoubtedly is. Reformers should examine the situation carefully, not only for defects of organisation, but also for the stress which arises from these differing experiences and perspectives. The Royal Commission on Criminal Procedure's report of 1981 spoke of the intractability of many problems with which they had been faced, of how 'interests conflict'; and of the fact that 'even those safeguards provided may at times be inadequate.'

Police who have arrested a person suspected of serious crime regard themselves as acting in the best of public interests in seeking evidence pointing to the suspect's guilt to warrant formal charging with the crime. On the other hand, the detainee, whether guilty or innocent, has an interest in the exercise of legal rights. Society as a whole has an interest in procedures being exercised properly, efficiently and justly.

For most detainees, arrest, detention and incarceration can be traumatic.

Another problem which may arise from interrogation in police detention concerns people who are innocent of any crime, but nevertheless decide to confess their guilt. This may be due to pressure of interrogation techniques. Psychologists comment, "There are in theory many ways in which a suspect can be led, or lead himself, to the conclusion that a false confession is the most attractive option open to him," and "Some children are brought up in such a way that confession always seems to produce forgiveness," (Royal Commission on Criminal Procedure 1979) in which case a false confession may be one way of bringing an unpleasant situation (interrogation) to an end. It is for these and other reasons that the question of access to solicitors by detainees becomes very important and often contentious.

The introduction of a solicitor into the relationship between the interrogator and the detainee certainly complicates the matter. It makes the task of the police questioner more difficult and protracted. An adversary has been introduced, often marking the beginning of the contest as a battle of wits and tactics. The police officer knows that almost invariably the solicitor's advice to his client will be to say nothing. This declares to the police, 'You are making these allegations. It is for you to prove them, for it is no part of the duty of my client to help convict himself.' Nor is it feasible, from present resources, for a confession to be valid only if validated by the presence of a solicitor.

The question of the power to delay access to a solicitor is set out in S58 of PACE, but remains contentious; and it seems inevitable that it always will, for there is a genuine conflict of interest. Police may only delay (not deny) access, where it is believed, on reasonable grounds (by a senior officer), that exercise of the right to consult a solicitor :

(a) will lead to interference with or harm to evidence connected with a serious offence or interference with or physical injury to other persons; or

(b) will lead to the alerting of other persons suspected of having committed such an offence but not yet arrested for it; or

(c) will hinder the recovery of any property obtained as a result of such an offence.

There are a number of qualifications to this power which mark out the uneasy accommodation arrived at between the need to prevent and detect serious crime, and the importance of human rights. If a person decides to take advantage of his right of access to a solicitor (and the police *must* inform him of this right and record it), there still remains the question of the adequacy of solicitors to deliver it.

The power to put people before the court, without having to convince any other body to do so, was in itself a coercive device, particularly when combined with the notion of a prima facie case to answer. Significantly the CPS abandoned the concept of a prima facie case in favour of the test of 'a realistic prospect of conviction', thus immediately raising the level of proof and abandoning the more coercive and questionable standard employed by the police.

Police find the CPS' use of powers of discontinuance irksome and frustrating. Termination of proceedings before trial is regarded as a win for the crook. But the former DPP Sir Thomas Hetherington wrote, "Perhaps it is too much to hope that the day will soon arrive when the police regard it as their only function to investigate an offence once it has been committed." Active detectives are given to expressing the view that some in the CPS are no match for the 'forensic trickery' of their counterparts for the defence. It is generally admitted that the CPS was badly under-resourced, and hastily imposed, creating difficulties in attracting career-minded lawyers in some parts of the country, and this in turn leads to allegations of aggravating incompetence. Time, good management and a new sense of identity for the CPS will undoubtedly remove some of these current difficulties, but there is an in-built stress in these relationships which should not be underestimated, and which should be acknowledged and minimised.

Comments emanating from the lower operational police ranks suggest that cases which would have gone forward under the police prosecution system are not going forward under the CPS; too much 'plea bargaining' takes place, often due, it is alleged, to economic and managerial convenience, rather than in the public interest; it is said by some police officers that the CPS does not have sufficient regard for, or understand, local sensitivities and problems which police claim to understand.

Yet it is argued by the first DPP to be in charge of the CPS and others, and it seems rational, that if the CPS has the power to discontinue criminal process at any stage on evidential, public policy or other grounds, then the decision on whether to caution offenders should also be determined by it. The police discern just another proposal to diminish their role and status within the system of criminal justice. But the suggestion which generates most reaction is that the CPS should play a gradually increasing role in the investigation process itself.

The Royal Commission on Criminal Justice appointed by the then Home Secretary, Kenneth Baker, following outrageous practices and shortcomings of the entire system of criminal justice, revealed in such cases as the Guildford, Birmingham and Tottenham miscarriages of justice, had to consider :

(a) The conduct of police investigations and their supervision by senior officers, and in particular the degree of control that is exercised by those officers over the conduct of the investigation and the gathering and preparation of evidence.

(b) The role of the prosecutor in supervising the gathering of evidence and deciding whether to proceed with the case, and disclosure of material, including unused material to the defence.

There is clearly room for change in the business of gathering evidence in criminal cases.

There have been signs over recent years that the police institution has lost a great deal of its reputation for fairness and objectivity. Opinion polls, whilst showing some respect for the police, indicate a steady and continuous decline in public satisfaction. Police appear less sure of their place in the social order, and now the Police Federation, representing all the less senior operational ranks, has joined the call for the appointment of a Royal Commission on the police to set the service on a modern footing. There is much to commend this approach for political, as well as for operational reasons. Meanwhile the police, collectively, have articulated and promulgated their perceived professional common purpose and values. The police statement, among other things, declares its commitment to 'uphold the law fairly and firmly' and 'to pursue and bring to justice everybody who breaks the law' (which in one form or another means almost everybody who is active including the police themselves). If this statement is meant to be taken literally, that they are to pursue and bring to justice everybody who breaks the law, including themselves, it may well bring the whole system of criminal justice to a halt. If it is one of those statements of rhetorical purpose, with a touch of crusading zeal, and an avenging spirit, it may be well-meaning, but it sets an unrealistic social agenda. Apart from laws which remain on the statute book but are obsolete or obsolescent (for example some of the law on drug-related offences, such as smoking cannabis), there remains a whole catalogue of regulatory laws which are honoured in the breach - for example, obstruction of the highway by parked vehicles. Perhaps the statement does not mean each and every breach of the law, but only those laws which create serious offences. But again this presents a minefield of decision-making, choice and discretion.

Modern liberal democracies require much more of their police than a crusading zeal to fill the courts with offenders, however, important that may be at times. There is now a growing moral awareness which impinges on the subject of criminal justice, namely the value of freedom and related human rights which require protection and enhancement, but which the police statement does not adequately address. This may be because in Britain we do not have a Bill of Rights for the police to address, or by way of which to become 'rights conscious'. Reference to a set of human rights values would reflect the spirit of the times and bring the best of modern policing principles into a new dimension. The basic principles of police in a modern liberal democracy might be couched in the following terms :

(a) The protection of human rights and fundamental freedoms.
(b) The protection of the institutions of a liberal democratic (in the ordinary philosophical, not the political meaning) government, and of public order.

Under (a) above, the inviolability of the person and peaceful enjoyment of property would be guaranteed. Under (b), all those measures, including security services, required to safeguard the State and public order would be justified. At every step of the police function, including the system of criminal justice, the principles of justice as informed by the laws of human rights and fundamental freedoms, as enacted and enforced under the European Convention, would influence ethical behaviour. Police action to the contrary would be *ultra vires*. Police would thus be enabled to see themselves in a positive role as protectors of human values, rather than merely seeing themselves in the negative avenging role which they otherwise may do. This spirit might make its mark on the system of criminal justice whichever form an amended police participation might take.

So far as police participation in the investigative and prosecution functions is concerned, serious consideration might well be given to a system of recruitment of law graduates directly into the Criminal Investigation Department. As the role of the criminal investigator evolves, and becomes more demanding, the need for more highly qualified entrants will be necessary.

However one views the future for criminal justice and the system, it seems unlikely that it will reach its full potential in the absence of wider constitutional reform. The steady recourse to the European Commission on Human Rights has already shifted the 'fountain of justice' in human rights and fundamental freedoms to Strasbourg and the European Court. The police are, and will be, judged not only for what they do and why they say they do it, but by what they represent; what is behind them; what is the source of their legitimacy. Anything which weakens their moral and constitutional stance will diminish their role in criminal justice itself. A Bill of Rights would set an agenda, and a framework, within which the police could judge and be judged.[1]

[1] This epilogue has been included because I believe that its relevance to the issues raised in this book are only too apparent: the author.

Abbreviations

ACC: Assistant Chief Constable
AK: Adenylate Kinase (a blood factor)
CCRC: (The) Criminal Cases Review Commission
CID: Criminal Investigation Department
CPS: (The) Crown Prosecution Service
DC: Detective Constable
DCI: Detective Chief Inspector
DCS: Detective Chief Superintendent
DI: Detective Inspector
DNA: Deoxyribosenucleic Acid
DPP: (The) Director of Public Prosecutions
DS: Detective Sergeant
EAP: Erythrocyte Acid Phosphate (a blood factor)
EDNAP: (The) European DNA Profiling group
FSI: Forensic Science International
FSS: (The) Forensic Science Service
Gc: General (Scientific) component (a blood factor)
Hp: Haptoglobin (a blood factor)
HOLMES: (The) Home Office Large Major Enquiry System
IQ: Intelligence Quotient
JAW: Samples removed by Dr John Whiteside
JP: Justice of the Peace
Le: Lewis (a blood factor)
MLP: Multi-locus Probe (DNA profiling)
PACE: (The) Police And Criminal Evidence (Act 1984)
PCR: (The) Polymerase Chain Reaction
PGM: Phosphoglucomutase (a blood factor)
QC: Queen's Counsel
RH: Samples removed by DI Reginald Hearse
SGM: Second Generation Multiplex (Advanced system of seven DNA tests used on the Home Office's National DNA database)
SLP: Single-locus Probe (DNA profiling)
SS: Samples removed by DS Stephen Steele
STR: Short Tandem Repeats (Advanced form of DNA testing)
WCRO: (The) Western Criminal Records Office

The Key Players In The Lynette White Inquiry

Lynette White: Victim of the murder at Flat One, 7 James Street in the early hours of February 14th 1988.

The Cardiff Five (Tried for the murder of Lynette White)
Yusef Abdullahi: Convicted.
John Actie: Acquitted.
Ronnie Actie: Acquitted.
Steve Miller: Convicted.
Tony Paris: Convicted.

Alternative Suspect
Mr X: Very important suspect. Eliminated on the basis of dubious DNA evidence before the arrest of the Cardiff Five.

Others Investigated By Police
Malcom Morris: Early suspect eliminated on alibi and lack of forensic evidence.
Mr Y: Possessed the rare blood group that was found in the flat. Not a villain, but dubiously eliminated on DNA.
B: Dubiously eliminated on DNA.
C: No records of blood group, but dubiously eliminated on DNA.
D: Admitted using prostitutes. No records of his blood group, but dubiously eliminated on DNA.

The Prosecution Witnesses
Learnne Vilday: Prostitute and allegedly Lynette's best friend. Tenant of Flat One, 7 James Street. It was her concern that led to the discovery of Lynette's body. The crucial prosecution witness.
Angela Psaila: Fellow prostitute and friend of Vilday. Her evidence supported Vilday's. Alleged eyewitness whose blood group was the same as that belonging to the murderer.
Mark Grommek: Resident of Flat Two, 7 James Street. He was a vital witness against Abdullahi and Ronnie Actie.
Paul Atkins: Friend of Grommek who may have been with him on the night of the murder. Originally due to be a prosecution witness, but was eventually called as a Judge's Witness.
Jackie Harris: Yusef Abdullahi's then common-law wife. Very important witness against him.
Ronnie Williams: Harris' brother-in-law. A police informer and vital witness against Abdullahi. Worker on the *Coral Sea* who 'broke' Abdullahi's alibi.
Peter Brooks: A friend of Ronnie Williams who supported Williams' claims that Abdullahi was in the North Star club in Butetown on the murder night.
Violet Perriam: The witness whose claims led to the arrest of the Cardiff Five. Witness against John Actie.
Ian Massey: Supergrass and sole corroborative witness against Tony Paris.

The Prosecution's Experts
Dr Nicholas Prance: DNA expert.
Dr John Whiteside: The Chief Scientific Officer at the Home Office Laboratory in Chepstow. He was aware of the blood group of Mr X and devised the 'cocktail theory' of Abdullahi and Psaila's blood to explain traces of a very rare blood group with the male chromosome in it.
Dr Peter Gill: Discovered the male Y-chromosome in the blood on Lynette's jeans.
Professor Bernard Knight: The pathologist.

The Police
Detective Chief Superintendent John Williams: Head of South Wales CID. He was in charge of the Lynette White Inquiry and was aware of the importance of Mr X in the inquiry.
Detective Superintendent Ken Davies: Williams' deputy. He was aware of the importance of Mr X and also referred to Mr Y.
Detective Inspector Graham Mouncher: Interviewed Yusef Abdullahi and tried to break Abdullahi's alibi. He took the crucial statement from Massey, yet focused attention on Mr X.
Detective Constable Peter Greenwood: Interviewed Steve Miller. The main officer who bullied Miller. Also interviewed Tony Paris. Fully aware of the importance of Mr X.
Detective Constable John Seaford: Greenwood's partner. Also took statements from Violet Perriam.
Detective Constable Simon Evans: Interviewed Steve Miller. One of the officers who pretended to be Miller's protector.
Detective Constable John Murray: Evans' partner.
Detective Constable Graham Toogood: Replaced Evans in two of Miller's interviews. Also interviewed Tony Miller and took a statement from Mr X.
Detective Constable Paul Fish: Interviewed Yusef Abdullahi and took a statement from Mr X with DC Toogood.
Detective Inspector Richard Powell: Interviewed Steve Miller in February 1988. Arrested and interviewed John Actie. Also responsible for the hypnotising of Vilday.
Detective Inspector Thomas Page: Handler of police informer, Ronnie Williams. He drank at the Yachting Club, where Violet Perriam worked as a stewardess.
Detective Constable Mike Cullen: Corroborative police witness against Abdullahi. Also on the surveillance of Mr X.
Detective Inspector Joy Lott: Vilday's handler. Knew of Vilday's meetings with Harris. She kept DCS Williams informed of the meetings.
Detective Constable Geoff Thomas: First to focus police attention on Mr X in April 1988, along with eleven other suspects. No other apparent involvement in the case.
Sergeant William Bisgood: Accompanied Vilday to Flat One, 7 James Street on February 14th and, together with Police Constable Prosser, discovered Lynette's body. No other involvement in the case.
Detective Sergeant Stephen Steele: The police's fingerprint officer. He discovered several samples, including the most important wallpaper sample SS12. No other apparent involvement in the case.

Defence Witnesses
Brian Spriggs: Put a roof over Vilday's head after the murder and was a witness called by Ronnie Actie.
Johnny Crook: Originally due to be an alibi witness for Ronnie Actie. At the second trial he was called as a witness regarding Actie's car.
Michelle Actie: Ronnie's sister. Witness regarding his car and the clothes he wore on the night of the murder.
Helen Prance: Originally a prosecution witness. She turned hostile at the retrial and totally supported Paris.
Nicola Heysham: Friend of Vilday who received the tell-tale letter from Vilday.
Cheryl Rogan: Rebuttal witness for Abdullahi regarding Ronnie Williams and Peter Brooks' claims.
Peter McCarthy: Worker on the *Coral Sea* and alibi witness for Abdullahi.

John Hulse: Worker on the *Coral Sea* from Merseyside and alibi witness for Abdullahi. He did not know Abdullahi.
Lawrence Mann: Worker on the *Coral Sea* and main alibi witness. He contradicted his friend, Ronnie Williams, even though he disliked Abdullahi.

Expert Defence Witnesses
Dr Gisli Gudjonsson: Miller's expert on low IQ/suggestibility. He wasn't allowed to give evidence to the jury at the first trial.
John Hayward: Blood expert at both trials.
Dr Eric Shepherd: Expert on police interviewing techniques for the appeal, but not called.
Dr Olive Tunstall: Further expert on suggestibility for the appeal. Not called to give evidence.

Other Potentially Important Witnesses
Professor David Canter: Pioneer of psychological profiling in Britain. He compiled a report which fitted Mr X, but didn't give evidence at either trial or appeal.
Courtney Davies: Armed robber and rebuttal witness of Massey's claims at the first trial. Not called at the second trial.
John Eaton: Armed robber and rebuttal witness of Massey. Friend of John Actie. Not called at either trial.
David Orton: Friend of Steve Miller. Potential alibi witness for Miller who spent a lot of time in Miller's company in the days leading up to and beyond the murder. He was also aware of the issue of Miller's clothes as was his friend Geraldine Richer. Not called at either trial despite being available.
Debbie Actie: Potential alibi witness Miller didn't even know about. Never gave evidence in this case.
Robyn Reed: Potential alibi witness Miller didn't know of. She was with Debbie Actie. Also not called to give evidence.
Brynley Samuel: Worker on the *Coral Sea* and potentially important alibi witness for Abdullahi. Never given evidence about this case.
Ged Corley: Former Greater Manchester Police officer. He was framed by several armed robbers and supergrasses including Massey. Never gave evidence at either trial. Made a statement for Paris' defence for the appeal.
Melanie Mail: Her recollections led to the first photofit being compiled.
Glyn Sterling: Taxi driver who drove Lynette and a client to 7 James Street within hours of the murder. His recollections led to the second photofit being compiled.
Derek Ferron: Potential alibi witness for Miller. He had a very low opinion of Miller. Never gave evidence at either trial or appeal.
Kenneth Spurlock: The Chairman of the Bench who committed the Cardiff Five for trial. Presided over the committal hearing. He was a defence witness at the first trial regarding the events at the committal hearing. He was not required for the retrial.

Judges
Mr Justice McNeill: The judge at the first trial.
Mr Justice Leonard: The judge at the retrial.
Mr Justice (now Lord Justice) Hutchison: The judge who considered the applications for leave to appeal.
Lord Taylor: The Lord Chief Justice. He was the senior judge at the appeal. Retired for health reasons and subsequently died earlier this year.
Mr Justice Laws: One of the appeal judges.
Mr Justice Popplewell: One of the appeal judges.

Lawyers
David Elfer QC: Lead barrister for the prosecution.
Roderick Evans QC: Elfer's number two. He led for the prosecution at the committal hearing.

John Charles Rees: Junior barrister for John Actie at the first trial and his lead barrister at the retrial. Now a QC.
Stuart Hutton: Solicitor for John Actie at both trials and for Ronnie Actie at the first trial.
David Farrington: Lead barrister for Ronnie Actie at the retrial.
Roger Backhouse QC: Lead barrister for Yusef Abdullahi at both trials and the appeal.
Bernard de Maid: Solicitor for Abdullahi at both trials and the appeal.
Gerard Elias QC: Lead barrister for Tony Paris at both trials and the appeal.
Anthony Evans QC: Lead barrister for Steve Miller at the first trial.
Roger Frisby QC: Lead barrister for Steve Miller at the retrial.
Graham Dobson: Solicitor for Steve Miller at both trials.
Michael Mansfield QC: Lead barrister for Steve Miller at the appeal.
Gareth Peirce: Solicitor for Steve Miller at the appeal.

The New Evidence Which Emerged After The Cardiff Three Were Freed
Mark Webster: Forensic expert whose report on the blood evidence in the Lynette White Inquiry helped to re-open it.
Alun Michael, JP, MP: The Shadow Minister for Home Affairs (now Minister of State for the Home Office). The murder of Lynette White happened in his constituency. He supported my concerns over the safety of the DNA eliminations.
David MacLean, MP: Home Office Minister who considered the submissions (now an opposition backbench MP).
Ann Widdecombe, MP: Another Home Office Minister who considered the submissions further in David MacLean's absence (now also an opposition backbench MP).
Peggy Pesticcio: Lynette's natural mother. Following her adoption of my forensic findings South Wales Police pledged to leave no stone unturned in the hunt for Lynette's killer and keep her informed of further developments in the case.
Rhodri Morgan, MP: Mrs Pesticcio's MP who has taken up her case.
David Evans: Mrs Pesticcio's solicitor for her judicial review proceedings.
Sadiq Khan: Mrs Pesticcio's new solicitor who is protecting her interests in the re-opened inquiry.
Assistant Chief Constable (Operations) Paul Wood: Senior officer involved in the re-opened inquiry.
Detective Inspector Reginald Hearse: Scene of Crime Officer in the original inquiry. He worked on the re-opened inquiry, but retired earlier this year.
Detective Chief Superintendent Phil Jones: The Chief of South Wales Police's CID. He is in charge of the re-opened inquiry. He retired very recently and was succeeded by Detective Superintendent D. W. Phillips.
Professor Bernd Brinkmann: German expert on DNA who specialises in singleplexing, the most sensitive method of DNA amplification. He was "absolutely optimistic that a result could be obtained in a case like this" but the police refuse to utilise his techniques to date.

Chronology

1988

February 9th: Lynette White walks out on Steve Miller.

February 14th: She is brutally murdered at 1.45-1.50 a.m. Her body is discovered at 9.17 p.m.

February: Steve Miller is picked up for questioning and subsequently released without charge. Learnne Vilday makes the first of her numerous statements. Main photofit drawn up. The crucial blood samples are collected. Some were obtained in March as well.

April: Dr Peter Gill discovers the male chromosome in the blood on Lynette's jeans. Second photofit compiled. DC Thomas draws up list of twelve suspects which includes Mr X.

May: Vilday's drunken outburst accuses Yusef Abdullahi and Steve Miller of Lynette's murder after conversation with DI Richard Powell who had mentioned them. Professor Canter compiles psychological profile of the killer. A Management Meeting decides to view Abdullahi and Miller as possibly involved in the murder.

June: Statements taken from Ronnie Williams, DC Mike Cullen and Yusef Abdullahi. Vilday retracts accusations against Miller and Abdullahi. Vilday hypnotised at the request of police.

July: Statement taken from Mr Y.

August: Dr John Whiteside takes the blood sample of Mr Y to Dr Prance for DNA testing along with other important samples. Mr Y's blood group establishes him as a person who must be eliminated safely.

September: Very important wallpaper samples collected by police from fingerprint department and are stored in a locked property cupboard prior to being conveyed to Birmingham for DNA testing. Statement taken from Mr X.

October: Mr Y is eliminated on DNA. Police discover Mr X's blood group. Sample sent for DNA testing. Surveillance initiated on Mr X. Trawl nets Violet Perriam.

November: Mr X is eliminated on DNA on November 9th. November 10th and 16th Perriam makes important statements. November 17th Angela Psaila's resistance begins to crack. November 22nd statements obtained from Angela Psaila, Mark Grommek and Paul Atkins.

December: On December 6th Vilday, Psaila, Grommek and Atkins all make crucial statements. Vilday claims to have seen who killed Lynette. December 7th Steve Miller, Tony Miller, Ronnie Actie, Yusef Abdullahi, Rashid Omar and Martin Tucker are arrested. December 9th Tony Paris and John Actie are arrested. The Cardiff Five were charged on December 11th and the other three were released after further statements from key witnesses. December 12th Cardiff Five are remanded into Cardiff Prison. December 26th Vilday writes important letter to Nicola Heysham.

1989

February: Magistrates commit the Cardiff Five for trial despite numerous discrepancies in the evidence. Ian Massey loses his appeal against sentence.

April: Dr Nicholas Prance questions the DNA elimination of Lynette White from the crucial wallpaper sample SS12.

September: Ian Massey makes statement that Tony Paris confessed to him in prison.

October: First trial of the Cardiff Five begins in Swansea Crown Court.
November: Further DNA test excludes Yusef Abdullahi as source of blood at 7 James Street.

1990
February: The first trial ends with the death of Mr Justice McNeill just before he was due to sum up.
May: The second trial of the Cardiff Five before Mr Justice Leonard begins in Swansea Crown Court.
November: The longest murder trial in British legal history ends on November 22nd after Yusef Abdullahi, Steve Miller and Tony Paris are convicted, while John and Ronnie Actie are acquitted.
December: In the early hours of December 22nd Geraldine Palk, a young shipping clerk, is murdered. She had been stabbed eighty-three times and raped near her home in Fairwater, Cardiff. The murder of Geraldine Palk bore striking similarities with that of Lynette White. To date, there has been no arrest.

1991
February: The Cardiff Three Campaign holds its first public meeting to fight against the convictions. The *Observer* becomes the first national newspaper to question the convictions of the Cardiff Three.
March: Alibi statements from twenty-two witnesses are disclosed to the defence. Among them is Brynley Samuel, whose claims amount to a complete alibi for Yusef Abdullahi. Channel Four's *The Black Bag* becomes the first national television documentary to question the convictions.

1992
January: BBC Wales' *Week In Week Out* documentary questions the convictions of the Cardiff Three.
February: BBC's *Panorama* documentary *Unsafe Convictions* broadcasts new evidence. ITN's *News At Ten* broadcasts Ronnie Williams' retraction. Gareth Peirce takes over as Steve Miller's solicitor.
December: The appeal of the Cardiff Three begins on December 7th. On December 10th their convictions are quashed. The judgement is delivered on December 16th.

1993
January: Channel Four's *The Black Bag* broadcasts the last documentary on the case to date. It suggests that the police should re-open their inquiry and begin by investigating Mr X again.

1994
December: The *Western Mail* publishes its concerns over the DNA eliminations in the Lynette White Inquiry and its investigation into Mr X.

1995
April: I discover new evidence affecting the reliability of the DNA eliminations. I also discover the importance of Mr Y in the inquiry. I write to Alun Michael, JP, MP, the Shadow Minister for Home Affairs.
May: Mark Webster of Forensic Science Consultancy compiles an expert report on the blood evidence in the Lynette White Inquiry. His report backs up my concerns on the reliability of the DNA evidence. He recommends further DNA testing which could still tie the murderer of Lynette White to his crime. Alun Michael writes to the Home Secretary asking him to re-open the Lynette White Inquiry and conduct further DNA tests. My letter and Mark Webster's report are also sent to Michael Howard.
June: Home Office Minister David MacLean refuses to do what has been asked of him. He insists that the Chief Constable of South Wales Police is the appropriate person to decide if further investigations are necessary.
August: Alun Michael writes to David MacLean asking him to reconsider. He asserts that the Home Office is the appropriate authority to deal with the submissions, especially in the light of criticisms of South Wales Police.
September: Another Home Office Minister, Ann Widdecombe writes to Alun Michael on David

MacLean's behalf assuring him that my submissions were fully understood and that they remain convinced that the Chief Constable of South Wales Police is the only appropriate body to consider if further investigations are necessary. Alun Michael replies to her letter, asserting that he still believes that the Home Office are the appropriate body to deal with my submissions, but asking that the papers to be forwarded to the Chief Constable. He asks that both himself and the Home Secretary be kept informed of the results of any investigation by the Chief Constable of South Wales Police.
October: I write to Ann Widdecombe expressing concern that South Wales Police will be investigating themselves, but agreeing to co-operate with any inquiry. South Wales Police receive the submissions and begin investigating them. Rhodri Morgan MP writes to both the Home Secretary and the Deputy Chief Constable of South Wales Police on behalf of his constituent, Peggy Pesticcio. She begins the process to judicially review the Home Office's refusal of my submissions.
November: South Wales Police discuss my concerns with me in London. Mrs Pesticcio is refused legal aid to get a barrister's opinion on the merits of judicially reviewing the Home Office's refusal of my submission. She announces her intention to appeal against the refusal of legal aid.

1996
January: Peggy Pesticcio's appeal against the refusal of legal aid results in legal aid being granted. The *Independent* reports that South Wales Police have re-opened the inquiry on the basis of my concerns over the DNA eliminations. The police confirm that samples are being retested. The *International Journal of Legal Medicine* receives the revised version of Dr Gill et al's article.
April: Advances in forensic testing in Europe attract my attention. Police confirm that the attempt to STR type wallpaper sample SS12 at the FSS Laboratory in Aldermaston had failed.
May: Meeting with ACC Paul Wood and DCS Phil Jones results in confidence in their investigation being restored. Mrs Pesticcio drops judicial review proceedings and trusts Wood and Jones with the hunt for the murderer of her daughter.
August: Professor Bernd Brinkmann, Direktor des Instituts für Rechtsmedizin der Universität Münster in Germany, says that he is "absolutely optimistic" that he can get useful results using the more sensitive technique of singleplexing, notwithstanding the age of the samples and the fact that they were treated with Ninhydrin. The *International Journal of Legal Medicine* publishes the article by Dr Gill et al which accepts that singleplexing is more sensitive than multiplexing.
September: Police assure Mrs Pesticcio that they will do whatever they can to find Lynette's killer. Further testing at the FSS Laboratory in Aldermaston has been unsuccessful. Police agree to send all samples which fail to yield useful results to Professor Brinkmann in Germany. The 1990 Trust offer £1000 to pay for Professor Brinkmann to test a sample in Germany.

1997
January: Wales On Sunday publishes an article suggesting that the time has come to send the samples to Germany for more sensitive testing.
February: Edwin Hopkins is convicted of the brutal murder of teenager Naomi Smith in a case where singleplexing in Britain yielded a result where multiplexing had failed. I receive copy of Dr Gill et al's article confirming that information on the greater sensitivity of singleplexing was known before I forwarded Professor Brinkmann's response to the police. The three surviving men convicted of the murder of teenage newspaperboy, Carl Bridgewater, are freed after eighteen years of wrongful imprisonment. The conviction of the fourth, Pat Molloy, who died in prison is quashed.
April: The round of DNA testing using multiplexing fails to yield any results. Very little DNA remains. Police decide to singleplex in Britain.
May: The General Election sweeps the Conservatives from power after eighteen years with a Labour landslide. Alun Michael becomes Minister of State for the Home Office. Sadiq Khan writes to ACC Wood outlining the concerns of his client, Mrs Pesticcio, especially her desire to have the samples DNA tested at Professor Brinkmann's laboratory.
June: In a letter to Sadiq Khan, ACC Wood asserts that the decision on how any DNA test will be

carried out, who will do it and whether it is in the best interests of the investigation for some or all of the DNA to be used up will be made by the police after consultation with forensic scientists.
July: In a further letter from ACC Wood, Khan was informed how relevant samples were stored, but was told that at the moment they were not inclined to provide an exhibit list to him. However, Wood suggested arranging a meeting between them and Mrs Pesticcio, which Khan agreed to. This meeting subsequently took place on October 6th and the issues that emerged as a result of it are detailed in the Author's note.